# Survival and Change in the Third World

# Survival and Change in the Third World

Ben Crow, Mary Thorpe et al.

Polity Press

First published 1988 by Polity Press
in association with Basil Blackwell.

Editorial Office:
Polity Press, Dales Brewery, Gwydir Street,
Cambridge CB1 2LJ, UK

Basil Blackwell Ltd
108 Cowley Road, Oxford OX4, 1JF, UK



**British Library Cataloguing in Publication Data**
Survival and change in the Third World.
1. Developing countries——Economic conditions
I. Crow, Ben II. Thorpe, Mary
330.9172′4 HC59.7

ISBN 0-7456-0332-7
ISBN 0-7456-0166-9 Pbk

Typeset in 11 on 12 pt Sabon
by Photo-graphics, Honiton, Devon
Printed in Great Britain by Page Bros (Norwich) Ltd.

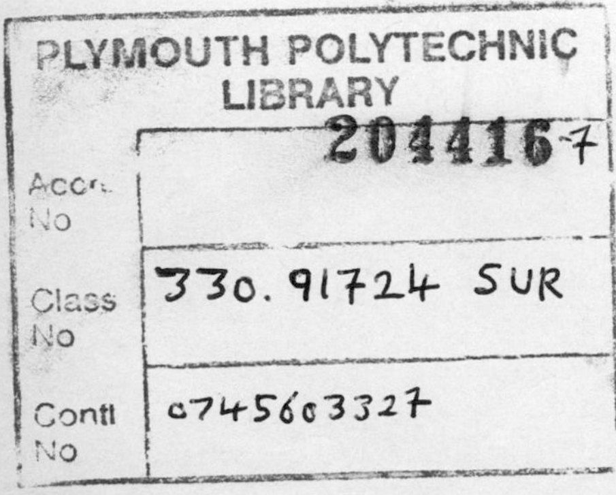

# Contents

# Notes on the Authors

**Henry Bernstein** studied history and sociology at Cambridge and London, and has taught in Tanzania and Turkey and at several British universities. He is currently Director of the External Programme at Wye College, University of London, and Senior Research Fellow in the Development Policy and Practice Research Group (DPP) which he co-founded when Lecturer in Third World Studies at The Open University. He has published widely on theories of development and underdevelopment, the political economy of peasantry, and African historiography, and is co-editor with T. J. Byres of the *Journal of Peasant Studies*. His current research interests focus on the agrarian question in Africa, in particular the political economy of food in Central and Southern Africa (a DPP project), and state–peasant relations in Tanzania.

**Terry Byres** is Senior Lecturer in Economics at the School of Oriental and African Studies, University of London. He is editor of the *Journal of Peasant Studies* and has written extensively on new technologies in South Asian agriculture.

**Ben Crow** is Lecturer in Third World Studies at the Open University. He has a first degree in civil engineering and a PhD in development studies. He has worked as an engineer in Kenya, Tanzania, Botswana and Yemen, as a development aid administrator in Bangladesh, and as a researcher in India, Bangladesh and Nepal. His current research includes work on food markets and food policy and on the potential for small scale technological innovation. He has previously worked on international water resource development. He is an author of the *Third World Atlas* Open University Press, 1983, and is currently Chair of the Open University Third World Studies course and co-Chair, with David Wield, of the Development Policy and Practice research group.

**Diane Elson** has a BA from the University of Oxford and is Lecturer in Economics, University of Manchester. She was previously employed as a tutor on the Open University Third World Studies course, and as a research officer at the Institute of Development Studies, University of Sussex. Her research interests are developing countries in the international economic system, and women and development. Relevant publications include: 'Imperialism', in S. Hall, D. Held and G. McLennan (eds) *The Idea of the*

*Modern State* Open University Press, 1984. D. Elson and R. Pearson (eds) *Women and Multi-Nationals in Western Europe* Macmillan, forthcoming. D. Elson (ed.) *Male Bias and the Development Process* Manchester University Press, forthcoming.

**Laurence Harris** is Professor of Economics at the Open University. He studied economics at the London School of Economics. His research interests are focused on monetary economics, political economy and development economics. He has recently done consultancy work for the Overseas Development Agency (ODA), United Nations Industrial Development Organization (UNIDO) and UN Habitat on the development of Palestinian banking, and UN Conference on Trade and Development (UNCTAD) on international finance. He worked in Mozambique in 1978 on agricultural credit and rural development. His publications include: L. Harris (with J. Coakley) *City of Capital* Basil Blackwell, 1983. L. Harris *Monetary Theory* McGraw Hill, 1981. L. Harris (with B. Fine) *Rereading Capital* Macmillan, 1979.

**John Humphrey** is Research Fellow at the Institute of Development Studies, Brighton, formerly he was Senior Lecturer in Sociology and Latin American Studies and Head of the Sociology Department at the University of Liverpool. Author of *Capitalist Control and Workers Struggle in the Brazilian Auto Industry*, Princeton University Press, 1982, and other articles on Brazilian industry. His current research interests are the sexual division of labour in Brazilian industry, and the impact of economic crisis on male and female industrial workers.

**Hazel Johnson** has degrees in Sociology and Social Administration in Developing Countries. She was Central America Programme Officer for War on Want until coming to the Open University in 1980. Her research interests focus on agricultural and food production. She spent three months researching rice production and distribution in Eastern Java, Indonesia, in 1985, and is at present on a two-year secondment to the Autonomous University of Honduras, as Lecturer in Agricultural Development and researching basic foods in Central America.

**Ed Rhodes** has a B.Sc. from the London School of Economics and worked as an extra-mural Lecturer before becoming Lecturer in Industrial Relations at the Open University. He has published books on industrial relations, on technology and skills, and on technology management.

**Mary Thorpe** is a lecturer in educational technology, in the Institute of Educational Technology at the Open University. She has a degree and postgraduate qualifications in English literature and education from the University of Cambridge. She worked for three years in the then University of Botswana, Lesotho and Swaziland and authored material for educational programmes on the National Development Plan. She has written on development strategies for the Open University Third World Studies course, and is currently a tutor and member of the course team. She has also carried out research into teaching and staff development in distance education, and has recently published 'Open Learning for Adults' (with D. Grugeon).

**David Wield** is Lecturer in the Technology Faculty in the Open University. He has qualifications in physics and metallurgy and previously taught and researched in the Technology Policy Unit in Aston University, the Institute of Development Studies at the University of Dar es Salaam, Tanzania and the Engineering Faculty and the Centre of African Studies in Eduardo Mondlane University, Mozambique. His research in development has focused on technology transfer and industrialization processes and policies, particularly with respect to East and Southern Africa.

# Preface and Acknowledgements

This book has emerged from a long, collective endeavour. It has its origins in the teaching materials produced for the British Open University's Third World Studies course. The ideas it contains reflect, in part, the ideas of the course team which produced that course. They have been developed first during the production of the course (1980–3) and brought into this final form during 1985–7, after the course had been running for some time. Because Open University courses are produced for a large student body, more consideration is generally given to their structure and content than can be given in most universities. The combination of a large course team and several years over which to prepare course materials results in courses that may be more integrated than elsewhere. In a multi-disciplinary area such as the one covered by this book, there are particular benefits to be achieved by this way of working.

Although each chapter has been the responsibility of one or two authors in particular, the content and style of the book as a whole has been significantly influenced by the practice of collective working established during the production of the Open University Third World Studies course. The first debt to be acknowledged is, therefore to the course team, and to Alan Thomas especially, who was largely responsible for initiating the course and was chair of the production course team.

Many further debts are, of course, acknowledged in the text and references of the book. But we would wish to identify the following for making particular contributions to the book: Gretchen Walcott (who typed many drafts); Maria Francis-Pitfield (who typed much of the original material); Iris Manzi (who typed drafts of chapter 16); and Nessie Tait and Karen Bateman (who assisted in the coordination of the book at various stages).

## Derivation

The chapters in this book have been developed, with more or less reformulation and addition, from the Open University *Third World Studies* course as follows.

Chapters 1 and 2 are from Block 2 *The making of the Third World*, Part D 'The colonial experience', by Margaret Kiloh and Henry Bernstein;

Block 2 *The making of the Third World*, Part C 'The establishment of colonial rule', by Margaret Kiloh with Alan Thomas. Chapters 3, 4 and 5 are from Block 1 *The 'Third World' and 'development'*, Part B 'Development', by Henry Bernstein. Chapter 6 is from Block 3 *Making a living: production and producers in the Third World*, Part C 'Third World economies: diversity and integration', by Henry Bernstein. Chapters 7 and 8 are from Block 3 *Making a living: production and producers in the Third World*, Part A 'Production on the land', by Hazel Johnson. Chapter 9 is from Case Study 5 *The Green Revolution in India*, by T. J. Byres, Ben Crow and Mae-wan Ho. Chapter 10 is from Block 3 *Making a living: production and producers in the Third World*, Part B 'Industrial Production: Factories and Workers', by David Wield. Chapter 11 is from Case Study 6 *Industrialization and energy in Brazil*, by John Humphrey and David Wield and Raul Ampuero. Chapter 12 is from Block 3 *Making a living: production and producers in the Third World*, Part B 'Industrial Production: Factories and Workers', by David Wield. Chapter 13 is from Block 4 *The international setting*, Part C 'Dominance and dependency', by Diane Elson. Chapter 14 is from Case Study 7 *Clothing the world: First World markets, Third World labour*, by Ed Rhodes, Noeleen Hayzer and David Wield. Chapter 15 is from Case Study 8 *Banking on the Fund – the IMF*, by Laurence Harris.

# Introduction

This book is about the ways in which people make a living in the Third World. It is, therefore, concerned with the livelihoods of the majority of the world's population. It provides an analytical framework for understanding production and producers in the Third World. In so doing it suggests concepts for understanding some of the great issues in the world today, issues such as the persistence of poverty, the periodic recurrence of famine, the crisis of international debt, and the consequences of the international restructuring of industry.

It is an ambitious book, firstly because it draws upon some 500 years of world history and almost all the world's continents for evidence and analysis. Secondly, it represents a distillation of a large undergraduate course developed at the British Open University.

Two factors have prompted the endeavour to make a university course on development more widely accessible, in book form. The first is a commitment to study and research on the important questions of world development. In many parts of the world, and notably in Britain, governments are responding to economic crisis by narrowing the fields considered proper for education and research, making them more 'vocational'. As a result development studies is under attack. We felt it particularly important therefore, to give wider currency to a perspective on the intellectual concerns of this area that demonstrates that they are neither exotic nor peripheral. On the contrary, the key issues at the heart of this book – forms of production, especially within capitalism, and the ways in which productive capacities can be increased within particular societies – are issues of universal significance. Those who study them are not engaging in a specialism remote from major issues of social theory, nor in the analysis of processes and mechanisms with only local significance. The economic and social processes analysed here are common to the experience of producers in the 'first world' as well as in the 'third world'. Examples from a number of chapters include these; the effects of capitalist forms of production on the different opportunities open to producers for making a living; the transfer of technologies of production internationally as well as between producers within countries; the development of an international division of labour which entails the geographical separation of different parts of a process of production unified via the operation of transnational corporations.

The second factor is related and arises from the fact that there is a lack of readily available material on development and Third World issues. The Open University course on which this book is based is now widely used in other institutions of further and higher education. However its size and complexity represent something of a barrier for the individual user with limited time and resources. The existence of a demand for an accessible book in this area has been impressed on us by the fact that now well over 3,000 students have registered for the Open University course, including a sizeable number of people not studying for an OU degree but whose work or experience in other ways motivates them to spend a considerable amount of time and money studying the Third World in greater depth. There are many others with a similar interest but unwilling or unable to commit themselves to the extensive study required by an OU course. This book is for them, as well as for the many students in Britain and elsewhere who need an accessible textbook alongside the other resources provided as part of their course work.

In signalling a concern with 'Third World' economies, we have not thereby espoused a particular set of assumptions about the nature of national inequalities in economic and political power, their causes and, by extension, the strategies through which they might best be addressed. It is not taken for granted here that the division of First, Second and Third World is always a useful and justifiable one, or that there exists a coherent theoretical analysis of the dominance and exploitation of one group of countries over others. Our focus is rather on production and producers, on the primary significance of the access of producers to the means of production, whatever the impact of other divisions such as nationality, gender, religion or culture.

We have been concerned not to promote a particular model for development or categorizations that homogenize highly differentiated countries and economies. We are concerned, however, with the effects of worldwide changes brought about by colonialism and the development of capitalism, primarily on producers and on countries less able to influence directly the forms these changes have taken and the nature of their effects.

The analytical approach adopted here to these (and other) issues embodies a commitment to analysis and deeper understanding prior to prescription. It has been our aim to elaborate, firstly, a historical and conceptual framework within which the analysis of development can be taken forward. The first two parts of the book for example, provide a critical review of the main analytical tools and theories, and many of the substantive issues that constitute a curricular grounding for later chapters.

Secondly, as suggested earlier, this analytical approach offers the reader conceptual tools that can be applied in the study of societies and themes other than those designated by the term 'Third World'. It counters any tendency there may be to marginalize issues as relevant 'merely' in a Third World context, or within a narrow specialism of development studies. It is directed more towards understanding underlying processes and mechanisms of uneven development, rather than simply emphasizing differences in their forms and effects which we may recognize directly from our own experience.

Thirdly, this analytical framework offers those who will continue to study in this area a means of coming to terms with the diversity of economic and social conditions they will encounter, whether through case studies, textbooks or direct personal research.

Juxtaposed to the analytic concerns of each chapter, are two areas of debate central to current development controversy, and particular chapters provide much relevant material for the explicit consideration of these debates, which is provided by the concluding chapter. The first of these debates is that of the rival contentions of 'the Old Orthodoxy' of economic growth versus those of the latter-day populists (whether Nyerere, Schumacher, Lipton or International Labour Office – ILO – consultants) as the focus of progressive and effective strategies for development (Kitching, 1982). The second is that of integration or withdrawal from the international economy for some if not all Third World economies – whether this might be a feasible strategy in some circumstances, or whether 'isolationist' tendencies are misguided and a recipe for greater, not lessened, dependence.

Although the authors do not share identical views, each of the chapters highlights some aspect of one or both of these themes. The coherence of the book derives also from its structure. The first two sections provide the conceptual groundwork on which the rest build, moving through agricultural and household production in part III, industrial production and manufacturing in part IV to aspects of production relations in the world economy, in part V.

Before introducing the themes of each of the chapters, we need also to comment on issues which could not be substantially covered. It was not intended of course, to provide an exhaustive study of the field and important areas of social structure and relations have been omitted or referred to only briefly, for example, institutional forms of education, health and government.

However, the book does include case-study material and analysis of struggles deriving from the differences between individuals and groups in their relation to the means of production and to the appropriation and distribution of the surplus product. Indeed, one of the innovatory features of this text is its attempt to go beyond a narrow economic analysis of production forms and to open up questions about their impact on people's working lives, on gender relations and on the distribution of power in society more widely.

The academic analysis of political relations has often been restricted to the analysis of the institutional forms of government. Chapter 12, in particular, proposes an alternative conception that includes all struggles, whether or not institutionalized, of individuals and groups attempting to increase their control over aspects of their social conditions. Such struggles as these within civil society, and even at the level of the individual or household, have implications for analyses of the state and its 'intervention' in development. The groundwork for such an analysis has, therefore, been laid and pointers to some of the key questions and issues are taken up again in the conclusion.

The book has five parts. Part I focuses on the implications of colonialism and the expansion of European capitalism for social organization and forms of production in the Third World, and for their incorporation into a growing world economy. Part II provides a conceptual framework, building up from analysis of particular concepts (productivity, the division of labour, appropriation, consumption and accumulation) to major theories of development (economic growth and production-oriented models, modernization, distribution-oriented models) and their relationship to capitalism, socialism and nationalism.

Chapter 6 in part II looks at diversity and integration *between* national economies as well as within them, and explores the effects of uneven and combined development in generating the variety of forms this takes. It is suggested that the different types and degrees of subsistence, semi-proletarianization and petty commodity production in Third World economies, are determined by the different forms of integration in capitalist economy, national and international. Capitalism both creates opportunities for, and limits the development of, generalized commodity production.

Parts III and IV divide respectively between agriculture and industry, a dichotomy which is itself part of the analysis in chapter 10, where the characteristics of an industrial production process are defined and the differences between small-scale and large-scale production, and between different production sectors, are discussed.

In part III, chapter 7 focuses on the effect of (different degrees of) commoditization on the technical relations of production in agriculture and on the capacities of different forms of agricultural production. Three production processes with very different levels of commoditization are analyzed: the economy of the Mundurucu society in the Amazonian forests of Brazil, small-scale maize production in India and plantation sugar production in Tanzania. Chapter 8 focuses on small-scale production on the land and on the economic and social dynamics of peasant production. It addresses the key question of why small-scale production persists and the conditions under which some households are able to accumulate and grow, while others are dispossessed and have to seek waged work.

Parts III and IV each incorporate a case study, within which empirical material on the technical and social relations of production are integrated in a (broadly) historical treatment of the topic – the Green Revolution in India (chapter 9) and industrialization in Brazil (chapter 11). Chapter 12 concludes part IV with analysis of the effects on productivity of industrial production processes, focusing especially on concepts of scale, linkages and skills. It ends with a wide-ranging consideration of the broader social changes associated with industrialization, and their impact on the lives of workers in very different forms of production.

The fifth and final part analyses the effect of the internationalization of capital and of production, especially since the Second World War. Chapter 13 provides a necessary overview of the extent to which Third World countries are integrated into the world economy. It examines opposing interpretations of this integration: that of neo-classical economics which sees it as mutually beneficial, and dependency theory, which sees integration as the result of First World imperialism and the means by which the Third World is underdeveloped. Both views exclude important dimensions. Neo-classical economics ignores the quality of the relations of exchange between the First World and Third World, which are often exploitative and oppressive. These relations of exchange, however, are not necessarily polarizing, and the dependency perspective fails to account for the fact that greater integration has led to a degree of independent industrialization in particular economies and to the appearance of Third World transnational corporations.

Chapter 14 explores the issue of relocation of industry in greater detail, especially the degree to which this is caused by low wages and labour costs in Third World countries. It concludes that relocation is only one option open to firms facing falling profits, and that labour costs generally, as a factor in relocation, varies in significance between different industries and for different firms at different times.

Chapter fifteen provides a historical framework within which the changes documented in chapters 14 and 15 can be interpreted. It outlines the role of the International Monetary Fund (IMF) in the regulation of the world market and the integration of individual countries within it. It focuses in particular on the way the IMF has changed from the intentions of some involved in its establishment – Keynes and White especially – who hoped that funds would be accessible to member nations without restrictive conditions attached. In contrast, the IMF has come to operate more like a conventional banking organization, in that its funds are available only on conditions which must be strictly adhered to. The effects of these conditions (such as devaluation, abolition of price controls, imposition of wage controls, reduction of trade barriers) has been to reduce the role of governments in trade and to strengthen that of firms, and of transnational corporations (TNCs) in particular.

The conclusion draws together earlier themes and issues in a wide-ranging discussion of the relationship between capitalism and development. It focuses especially on the contradictions and unevenness of capitalist development, within as well as between economies. It reminds us also that though there are dramatically different forms of production, highly diverse ways of making a living, they are almost all integrated, to lesser or greater extents, and in varying ways, into the capitalist world economy. It is also inevitable that we should return in conclusion to issues of definition – of what we mean by 'development', and 'capitalism' – where the assumptions we make condition how we might answer the key question of whether capitalism can develop Third World economies.

This question is an immensely challenging and provocative one, where we expect the reader may concur with some parts of our thinking and take issue with others. We see such debate as desirable and as a reflection, in a sense, of one of the contentions of the book itself, which is that development can never be either a simply technical or rational activity, devised by states and implemented 'on behalf of' their people. Development, however defined, involves struggles between people with different needs, interests and identities, whose goals therefore differ and may often be polarized. Some of the more obvious features of development strategies may be their use of planning procedures and the application of technical solutions to social problems. However it is not possible to understand either why particular strategies are undertaken, nor the effects they have, in isolation from those social and historical forces which shape them. By focusing on how people make a living, as the context for creation of these differing interests and goals for development, we have illuminated debates over development by bringing them back precisely to those social and historical forces to which they relate. In so doing, we have drawn upon the methods and concerns of a political economy approach in order to offer, if not an easy answer to the questions posed, then at least a practical contribution (because grounded in an analysis of production) to how they might be more adequately addressed and some provisional (if not uncontroversial) conclusions.

# PART I

# The Making of Third World Economies

CHAPTER ONE

# The Expansion of Europe

It seems ethnocentric to begin a discussion of the making of Third World economies with 'the expansion of Europe'. At the least, the meaning of this connection has to be specified with some care, which this chapter will try to do. The reason we start here, however, is because of the significance of the expansion of Europe in the creation of a world market and an international division of labour from the sixteenth to the twentieth centuries.

The commodities that sustained this global economy were, of course, produced by the labour of those inhabiting what we now call the Third World, whether as slaves, tribute labourers, indentured workers, peasants or proletarians, as well as by the labour of workers and farmers in Europe itself and in other parts of the world. But the conditions and uses of the labour of these millions of people were structured by the interests and conflicts of the ruling classes of Europe as it underwent its long transition from feudal to capitalist society, and its subsequent industrial revolutions.

One issue addressed here, therefore, concerns the relationship between the expansion of Europe and the development of capitalism. Within the sweeping heading of 'the expansion of Europe', and the processes it encompassed over the five centuries indicated – from plunder, pillage and slavery to 'legitimate trade' and investment – special attention will be given to *colonialism* or direct rule of non-European areas and peoples. The boundaries of those areas typically established the political territories we know as Third World countries today.

## Colonialism and Capitalism

Different views of capitalism are discussed in chapter 4. One thing on which they agree is that capitalism is a system of production of goods and services for market exchange (rather than consumption by the producers) in order to make a profit. It is useful here to elaborate this definition and give it some historical content.

The production of commodities (i.e. goods for exchange), the existence of markets for them, and the use of money as a medium of exchange, are not exclusive to capitalism. Some pre-colonial societies produced a surplus and had well-developed markets and trade networks, considerable specialization in the social division of labour, and classes of rich merchants and money-lenders, all, however, without having undergone a transition to capitalism.

In its simplest definition, capital is a sum of money invested to gain a profit, which it can do in various ways. For example, *merchant's capital* is invested in buying commodities from their producers and reselling them to consumers. The notion of the 'middleman' (sic) expresses precisely the merchant's role as the intermediary link between producers and consumers of commodities. While merchant's capital facilitates the circulation of commodities and the development of markets for them, it plays no direct role in production itself; the merchant's profit necessarily derives from *unequal exchange*, from selling commodities for more than he or she paid for them. Merchant's capital is one form of capital that existed widely before capitalism; another is *money-lending capital*, advanced to gain an interest which provides its means of profit. Many of the wars of medieval Europe were financed through loans from rich merchants and money-lenders to feudal monarchs and lords, who repaid them out of the plunder and tribute they gained.

These types of capital, then, existed in various pre-capitalist societies in association with different types of commodity production based on slavery or on feudal or other kinds of tribute-paying peasantry, without leading to capitalism as a distinctive mode of *production*. The word 'production' is stressed here because capitalism is distinguished by the emergence and central importance of *productive capital* – capital invested in production. Productive capital invests in means of production and labour power, which it then organizes in a production process, making new commodities and creating new value as the necessary step towards realizing a profit. Capital invested in the circulation of commodities (e.g. by wholesalers, chain stores) and in the provision of finance and credit (e.g. by banks) continues to play an important role in a capitalist society in which commodity production is generalized, but its functions are determined by the activities and needs of productive capital.

It is only productive capital which presupposes that labour power and the means of production are available as commodities. As most pre-capitalist societies were predominantly agrarian (hence the common synonym 'pre-industrial'), a crucial step in the transition to capitalism was that land should become a commodity, to be freely sold or rented without restriction by customary laws, the rights of monarchs, feudal lords, peasant communities, or whatever. In England such restrictions on the commercialization of land, imposed by the class relations of feudalism (one type of pre-capitalist society), were undermined far earlier than anywhere else in Europe. Historians have stressed the importance of the capitalist 'agricultural revolution' in England that preceded, and undoubtedly contributed to, the more celebrated industrial revolution (see chapter 4).

Productive capital invested in means of production can do nothing, however, without labour power to use those means of production. Just as land and other means of producton had become commodities, there had come into existence a class of people possessing no other commodity than their labour power. The related emergence of productive capital and a working class – basic conditions of capitalist production – are part of the process called 'primitive accumulation' that resulted from particular processes of change and disintegration in pre-capitalist societies. This meaning of 'accumulation' is broader than the usual notion of amassing wealth or capital, since it includes the historical formation of a class of people whose labour power is necessary to the production of wealth and capital.

The aspect of 'primitive' accumulation that was most important in the creation of labour power and the working class was the dispossession of the peasantry and of other kinds of small-scale producers such as artisans and craftsmen. Various legal and political devices were used to separate peasants from land that was increasingly commercialized, enclosed for purposes of capitalist production, and required far fewer hands to work it as technical innovations raised the productivity of agricultural labour. The dispossessed peasantry formed the historical core of the emerging industrial proletariat, together with rural and urban artisans whose economic viability as small commodity producers was undermined by the emergence of factories producing the same commodities in much greater quantities and much more cheaply.

Marx summed this up in saying that capitalism requires free workers: freed from access to any means of production with which to produce their subsistence, and consequently free to sell their labour power to others who own means of production. This was an ironic usage, of course, in that 'freed' means dispossessed: those who have lost their means of production, or have never had any, are compelled to sell the one thing they do possess, namely their labour power, in order to survive.

We can now summarize the historical context of the development of capitalism, and suggest its implications for considering the colonial experience and its variations in time and place.

1 North-western Europe, 'led' by Britain, underwent a transition from feudal to capitalist society over a long historical period, basically the sixteenth to the nineteenth centuries, when the industrial revolutions took off. This period of transition was one of continuous (albeit uneven) expansion of commodity production and exchange, facilitated by a range of social, political and cultural changes; it saw the formation of the two basic classes of capitalism: the capitalist or bourgeois class and the working class or proletariat.

2 The formation of the bourgeoisie (owners of productive capital) and of the working class (labour power) went hand in hand with the destruction of feudal society, a process that included the commercialization of landed property and of agricultural production on a capitalist basis, and the dispossession of the peasantry and many other small producers who became 'free' to sell their labour power.

3 The process of primitive accumulation was helped by the 'expansion of Europe' in the same period, as a result of which vast amounts of wealth

flowed in Europe from the plunder, conquest and colonization of many of the pre-capitalist societies of Latin America, Asia and Africa. In itself, this flow of wealth was not different in character from the riches amassed through other great imperial ventures in history, such as those of the Ottomans, the Mughals and the succession of Chinese dynasties. It would not have led to capitalism if it had not been able to feed into *changes in the conditions and relations of production already taking place in Europe.* For example, much of the treasure extracted from their colonies by Spain and Portugal went to buy commodities from north-western Europe where the transition to capitalist production in manufacturing as well as agriculture was taking place. The relatively slow transformation of feudal relations in Iberian society resulted in the declining wealth and power of Spain and Portugal compared with those countries that were pioneering capitalism.

4 The development of capitalism had a global dimension from the beginning, therefore, which was experienced by the pre-capitalist societies of the Third World through their incorporation in an emerging world market and an international division of labour, typically initiated during a period of European colonial rule. In this sense, capitalism came to these societies from the 'outside' rather than resulting from their internal dynamics.

5 These broad statements give some indication of the time-scales that are appropriate for examining such fundamental social changes, and of the very uneven character of capitalist development in different countries and areas of the world. On the first point, one is struck by the very long period – about three centuries – between the beginning of the breakdown of feudal society and the onset of the industrial revolution, which provided the emerging capitalist society of Britain with its distinctive type of production process – large-scale machine production. Once capitalist industrial production was firmly established and had begun to develop elsewhere in Europe, in the USA and in Japan, the striking feature by contrast was the 'acceleration of history', caused by the tendency of capitalism constantly to revolutionize technology and methods of production and to accumulate capital on an ever larger scale.

This conceptual and historical framework suggests both key themes in the relationship between capitalism and colonialism, and significant variations in the colonial experience arising from specific combinations of:

1 different stages in the emergence of capitalism, and its uneven development between colonizing powers and within the areas they colonized;
2 different types of colonial state and the interests they represented;
3 the diversity of the pre-colonial societies on which European domination was imposed.

With respect to the first point, for example, Spain and Portugal colonized

Latin America while they were still feudal societies, and did so at an early stage of the transition to capitalism in north-western Europe. At that time, the demands of the emerging international market focused on precious metals (gold and silver) and on tropical products for 'luxury' consumption by the wealthy classes of Europe (e.g. sugar, coffee, spices, precious woods and fabrics). But by the time Britain, France and Germany were competing for colonies in Africa in the last quarter of the nineteenth century, they were already industrialized or rapidly industrializing capitalist countries. The international market had changed with the industrial revolution to produce an enormous demand for raw materials for manufacturing – both minerals and agricultural products like cotton, jute, rubber, and sisal – and for mass consumption by new and large urban populations (e.g. tea, sugar, vegetable oils). It should also be remembered that periods of colonial rule in different areas of the Third World cut across those stages in the development of capitalism. For example, most of Latin America consisted of independent states, created from struggles against the Spanish and Portuguese crowns, *before* most of sub-Saharan Africa was incorporated into the colonial empires of European powers.

This connects with the second and third points, which entail consideration of the duration of colonial rule as well as when it was initially imposed. Most of Latin America, for example, experienced at least three centuries of colonialism, while in parts of Africa the period of colonial rule lasted less than the lifetime of some individuals. Again, for Latin America and the Caribbean, colonialism was a brutal first introduction to the emerging world economy of the sixteenth century, and existing ways of life were shattered. In many parts of West Africa, on the other hand, the development of an agrarian commodity economy involved in international trade – 'the major revolution in the lives of the peasants' (Crowder, 1968, p. 7) – had begun long before the beginning of the colonial era in the late nineteenth century, although it was certainly restructured and intensified under colonialism (Shenton, 1986).

The profound changes in the lives of millions of people brought about by colonialism and capitalism, and particularly in the conditions of their economic activity, are discussed in chapter 2 on colonial labour regimes. The rest of this chapter elaborates the elements of a periodization of the expansion of Europe sketched above, and then presents some ideas about the formation and contradictions of colonial states. Periodization of the 'stages' of European colonialism and their relation to the development of capitalism provides an analytical framework for the historical processes of the making of Third World economies, as indeed of First World economies. This is not the same as, nor a substitute for, the detailed investigation of the economic histories of Third World countries, of which many illuminating accounts have been written using this kind of framework.

### *The crisis of feudalism and the first stage of expansion*

It can be suggested, following the work of Michael Barratt Brown (1963), that the motivations, forms and cumulative intensity of the expansion of

Europe in the sixteenth century were closely linked to the crisis of feudalism there. One aspect of crisis in the old order was a transition from one kind of commodity economy, controlled and constrained by the power of landowning aristocracies, to another that was being initiated by increasingly independent groups of merchants based in the towns. They encouraged the development of urban production (crafts, simple manufacturing) and exploited the weakening control of feudal lords over the agrarian economy and its peasant producers.

Late feudalism was marked by dynastic wars for sovereignty within and between existing political territories, and the emergence from them of new states confronting the effects of the massive costs of continuous military expeditions, the disruption of the agrarian economy, and a series of peasant uprisings. The need of these states for further sources of revenue stimulated the search for, and seizure of, the wealth of other societies.

> The movement to the New World, the establishment of forts and trading posts along the coasts of Africa, the entry into the Indian Ocean and the China Seas, and the spread of the fur trade through the boreal forests of America and Asia all represent ways in which these goals were sought and fulfilled. New goods entered the circuits of exchange: tobacco, cacao, potatoes, tulips. African gold and American silver, as Braudel has said, enabled Europe to live beyond its means. (Wolf, 1982, p. 109)

The agents of this first wave of expansion were explorers, mercenaries and merchant adventurers. From their forts and trading posts, these gangster entrepreneurs collected from local societies the luxury goods valued by the wealthy classes of Europe, whether by plunder, trickery, or establishing commercial monopolies. Portuguese traders, among others, used their forts and especially their fleets for 'not merely protecting their own trade but also selling "protection services" to others, forcing Asian merchants to pay for the privilege of sailing the seas in peace' (Curtin, 1984, p. 137).

In the sixteenth century, systematic colonial rule was imposed only in the Caribbean and Latin America, where the aftermath as well as the immediate methods of conquest had devastating effects. The quest for treasure that had first spurred exploration of a western route to the Indies led to the opening of the great silver mines of Mexico and Peru. It is estimated that the 'silver mountain' of Potosi absorbed the forced labour of one-seventh of the male population of Peru in the second half of the century (see chapter 2). From 1503 to 1660, shipments from Spanish America to Castile tripled the amount of silver in Europe.

At the same time, to the extent that American silver sustained the feudal regime of Spain it did so at its expense over the longer term. The domestic economies and overseas trade of Spain and Portugal were to face increasing competition from England and Holland in particular – small countries on the periphery of Europe that were moving much more rapidly towards capitalism.

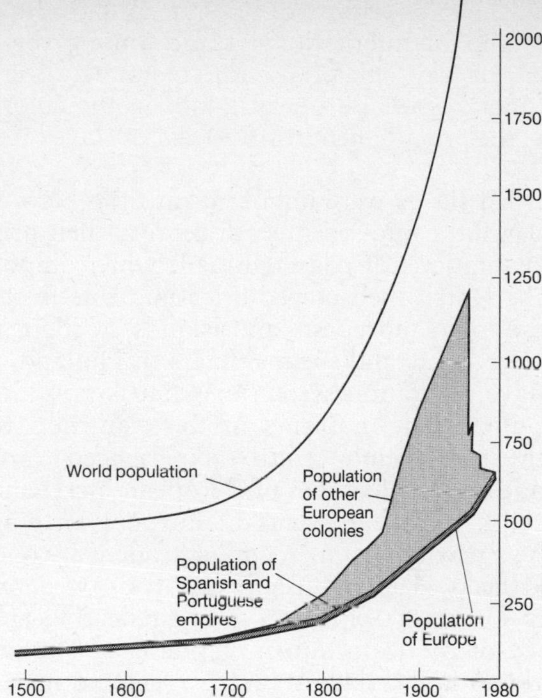


FIGURE 1 Population of European colonies, 1500–1980

## *Merchants, slaves and plantations*

In the course of the seventeenth century, a different kind of European expansion was added to the Spanish pursuit of treasure by plunder and excavation (mining) in the west, and to merchant-adventurer trade in luxury items from the east. Alongside these 'feudal' types of colonization and commerce (and ultimately displacing them), new forms of settlement and trade – exemplified by English interests in North America and English and Dutch activity in the Caribbean – linked more directly with the development of manufacturing and the transition to capitalism in Europe.

In the first two decades of the seventeenth century, Sir Edward Sandys succeeded in reforming the Virginia Company, previously the preserve of the Crown and the merchant elite of the City of London, to satisfy the needs of manufacturers and smaller independent merchants. On one hand, this was an important victory over royal and feudal-type monopolies and privileges in (and restrictions on) overseas trade. On the other hand,

> the result of Sandys' efforts was to establish the slave-owning plantation-culture of the south, but at the same time to ensure supplies of Virginia tobacco and cotton for British manufacturers. These were to become far more important than all the spices and silks of the east. The American colonies later became, in fact, the main markets outside England for the products of England's new manufactories. (Barratt Brown, 1963, p. 37)

In short, English colonization of North America and the Caribbean initiated a new kind of international trade linking the systematic large-scale production of raw materials for manufacturing in Europe, the development of markets for European goods in the colonies, and also, for several centuries, the procurement from Africa of slave labour for plantation production.

The first recorded slaves were imported into the New World from West Africa in 1518. Until the mid-seventeenth century their principal destination was the sugar plantations of coastal Brazil, which imported about 4,400 slaves a year. The Dutch then played a leading role in the spread of slave production to the mainland coasts and islands of the Caribbean, to meet the demand by merchants and sugar refiners in Holland, while the English developed the slave plantation system of what is now the southern USA.

Despite these important moments in the transition to capitalism, the latter half of the seventeenth century experienced a relative decline in international trade and the fortunes of European merchant companies. This was connected with turbulent events in Europe, including dynastic wars and, significantly, a new type of mercantilist trade war conducted principally at sea by armed fleets. The eighteenth century saw a revival and further intensification of European expansion, both reflecting and contributing to the resumed pace of the transition to capitalism. This was manifested in the growth of the Atlantic slave trade to meet the increased demand for tropical commodities. Figure 2 is based on the work of Curtin (1969); recent studies regard even this as an under-estimate.

Estimates of European profits made during the eighteenth century include £50 million from the French slave trade and £75 million from the English one, and between £200 million and £300 million from slave production (mainly sugar) in the British West Indies alone (Crow and Thomas, 1983).

It was merchants who financed and organized the slave trade and the shipment of tropical commodities and European goods, to their own benefit and that of the emerging industrialists of north-western Europe. During this period, adventurers and merchants also extended their exploration, pillage and pursuit of commercial advantage along the coasts of Africa and within Asia. These activities continued and developed the forms of European expansion that had begun in the sixteenth century, and were marked by armed conflict between Europeans (as well as between them and the people of the areas on which they sought to impose their domination), for example, between the Portuguese and the Dutch in the Spice Islands (now Indonesia, Malaysia, and the Philippines), and between the French and the English in India where the power of the Mughal emperors was in decline.

The Dutch wrested control of the Spice Islands from the Portuguese after a long struggle; the Dutch East Indies Company extracted remittances, dividends and spices to an estimated value of £60 million between 1650 and 1780 (i.e. prior to the establishment of systematic plantation production in Java). In India, Clive's victory in Bengal in 1757 put paid to French hopes and hastened the downfall of the Mughal order. While Clive's activities, in their purpose and their methods, had much in common with the original phase of European expansion, and were accompanied by

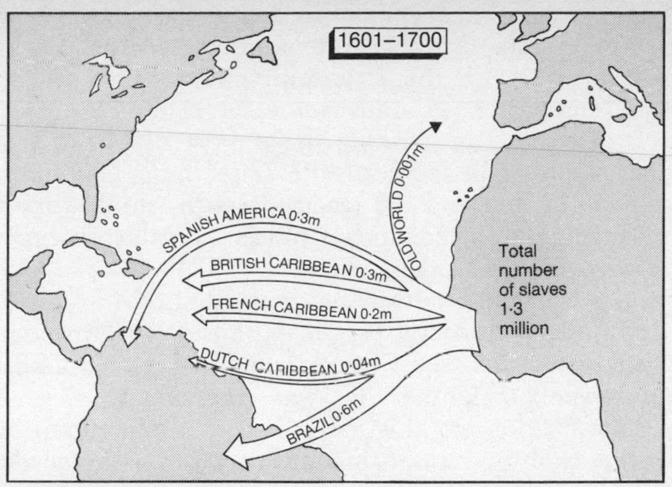
1601–1700
OLD WORLD 0·001m
SPANISH AMERICA 0·3m
BRITISH CARIBBEAN 0·3m
FRENCH CARIBBEAN 0·2m
DUTCH CARIBBEAN 0·04m
BRAZIL 0·6m
Total number of slaves 1·3 million

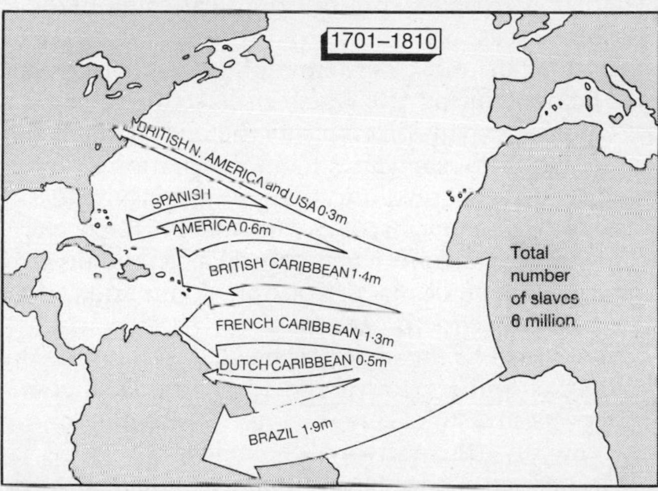
1701–1810
BRITISH N. AMERICA and USA 0·3m
SPANISH AMERICA 0·6m
BRITISH CARIBBEAN 1·4m
FRENCH CARIBBEAN 1·3m
DUTCH CARIBBEAN 0·5m
BRAZIL 1·9m
Total number of slaves 6 million

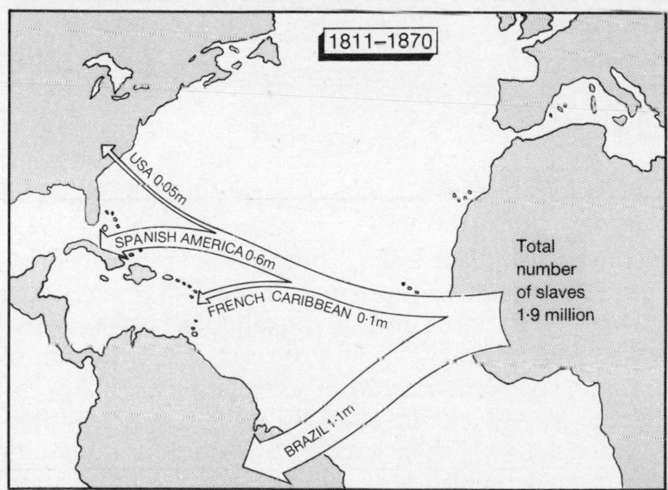
1811–1870
USA 0·05m
SPANISH AMERICA 0·6m
FRENCH CARIBBEAN 0·1m
BRAZIL 1·1m
Total number of slaves 1·9 million

FIGURE 2 The Atlantic Slave Trade, 1601–1870

massive plunder organized through the British East India Company, their effect was soon to establish the systematic integration of India and its mostly peasant producers in the developing international division of labour shaped by the emergence of industrial capitalism in Europe. As British manufacturers succeeded in banning the import of Indian textiles, which had been the major trade item of the East India Company, the latter promoted tea production and the tea trade with China, for which opium produced in Bengal (and forced on the Chinese) was the principal commodity exchanged to finance the trade.

This extremely schematic outline has suggested that in the course of the eighteenth and nineteenth centuries, the expansion of Europe intensified in ways connected with its accelerated transition to capitalism and the international division of labour that was emerging from it. At the same time, most colonization in this period was undertaken by merchant companies rather than by European states themselves (however much these states assisted their merchants through political, diplomatic, and military – above all naval – measures).

The consolidation of more systematic colonial rule including state formation (see below) during the nineteenth century, as well as the last great wave of colonial expansion towards the end of the century, involved a more direct role for European states in an international context structured by the effects of industrial revolution. Again, it is highly suggestive that the original 'feudal' colonialisms of Spain and Portugal were losing their American possessions at a time when capitalist colonialism was about to embark on its most significant period of domination, from the mid-nineteenth to the mid-twentieth centuries.

The types and volumes of raw maerials needed by a rapidly industrializing Europe, new market outlets for its factory-produced commodities, the character of overseas investment, new types of shipping and of communications more generally (the railway, the telegraph) together with their strategic implications, all made the capitalist colonialism of the nineteenth and twentieth centuries very different from its sixteenth-century antecedent in Latin America.

### *Colonialism and imperialism*

In India, the rule of the East India Company was replaced by that of the British state after the 'Mutiny' (uprising) of 1857–8. In subsequent decades, colonial rule was also imposed and/or consolidated by the British in Burma, Sarawak and the Malay States, and by the French in Indochina. The most rapid and dramatic wave of European expansion in this period, however, was 'the scramble for Africa'. In 1876, European powers ruled about one-tenth of Africa. By 1900, they had extended their domination to nine-tenths of the continent, which was thus the last great 'frontier' of colonial capitalism. Africa was carved up principally between Britain and France, with substantial areas also seized by Belgium, Germany and Portugal.

The causes of the partition of Africa in the late nineteenth century are fiercely debated by historians. Colonialism was a controversial issue among leading European capitalists and politicians of the time, not least in Britain where some preferred the 'imperialism of free trade' to that of direct political rule, with what they considered its unnecessary costs.

> Britain's industries were reared behind protective walls, nourished on imperial tribute and encouraged by the destruction of all competition from the east. But, once established they needed protection, plunder and protected markets no more ... the factory product could undersell the work of handicraftsmen in any country in the world. All the industrialists asked was the freedom to trade – to obtain food and raw materials wherever they were most cheaply produced and to open up the whole of the world as markets for their wares. (Barratt Brown, 1963, p. 52)

Even the advocates of such international free trade, however, had to recognize the strategic nature of their trade routes (and the sources of their raw materials) and, hence, the need to guard them. This meant, at the least, an effective network of naval bases, and often the political and military capacity to guarantee communications and the flow of commodities across great land masses.

The scramble for Africa occurred during the great depression of late nineteenth century Europe (1873–96), which was the first major manifestation of the cycles (boom followed by slump and crisis) of the new world economy of industrial capitalism. The connection between these two processes was made by Lenin in his pamphlet *Imperialism: The Highest Stage of Capitalism*, written in 1916 with two immediate and related objectives: explaining the causes of the First World War, and winning the workers of Europe away from mutual slaughter in the interests of 'their' ruling classes.

For Lenin, the great depression of the late nineteenth century marked a critical turning point in capitalism, from an earlier 'competitive' stage to what he termed 'monopoly capitalism'. This does not mean that competition ceased to exist, but rather that it took more extreme and dangerous forms (leading, in 1914, to war) which were generated by the massive concentration and centralization of capital (see chapter 6) among rival capitalist countries. At that time, the most potent conflict was between Britain and the new industrial power of Germany.

The conflicts intrinsic to monopoly capitalism were expressed not only through competition for overseas sources of raw materials and markets for European manufactured goods (both in ever increasing volumes), but also through competition for investment opportunities. The *export of capital* was fuelled by a tendency for rates of profit to decline in Europe, generating 'surplus' capital which sought more profitable outlets elsewhere, including colonial territories whose people and resources were available for (further) capitalist exploitation (some indications of the dramatic expansion of foreign investment in colonial territories are shown on Map 3).

The accuracy of Lenin's account for the historical period he considered has been contested (among others, by Barratt Brown, 1963). On the one hand, British capital exports accelerated rapidly in the later nineteenth century and early twentieth century, and from the 1880s about 40 per cent of British overseas investment was directed to railways, plantations, factories, government stocks and finance in the Empire. While Britain at this time best exemplified Lenin's thesis of capital export, it was Germany, on the other hand, that best exemplified the thesis of the concentration and centralization of capital in the form of giant industrial corporations closely linked with banks. Lenin termed this particular combination of industry and banking 'finance capital', which he saw as the distinctive and dominant form of capital in the period of imperialism or monopoly capitalism.

Lenin's analysis may be considered 'exaggerated' in that two of the principal characteristics of imperialism he identified – capital export and the formation of modern finance capital – were respectively exhibited by two countries with quite different paths of capitalist development – Britain and Germany – rather than being combined. However, the trends in the internationalization of capitalist production and finance that Lenin may have 'exaggerated' for his time have become much more powerful and evident since then, notably in the operation of transnational corporations and banks (see chapters 13 and 15). For this reason, Lenin's analysis of imperialism thus retains, and indeed has increased, much of its force towards the end of the twentieth century.

A second reason that Lenin's analysis retains its significance is that it highlighted a striking feature of capitalism in its imperialist phase, namely the gap between the continuously increasing *internationalization* of capitalist production and finance and the persisting political organization of capitalist societies through *national* states. Lenin and another leading Bolshevik, Bukharin and, indeed, other contemporary socialists, were very alert to the dangers of instability and war that this widening gap produces.

While Lenin was able to connect the great depression of late nineteenth-century Europe, the emergence of imperialism, and the last great wave of capitalist colonization in Africa, a third reason for the continuing relevance of his analysis is its insistence that imperialism, as 'the highest stage of capitalism', does not *necessarily* depend on colonies.

> Since we are speaking of colonial policy in the epoch of capitalist imperialism, it must be observed that finance capital and its foreign policy, which is the struggle of the great powers for the economic and political division of the world, give rise to a number of *transitional* forms of state dependence. Not only are there two main groups of countries, those owning colonies, and the colonies themselves, but also the diverse forms of dependent countries which, politically, are formally independent, but in fact are enmeshed in the net of financial and diplomatic dependence typical of this epoch. We have already referred to one form of dependence – the semi-colony. An example of another is provided by Argentina.
>
> ...It is not difficult to imagine what strong connections British finance capital (and its faithful 'friend', diplomacy) ... acquires with the Argentine bourgeoisie, with the circles that control the whole of that country's economic and political life.

> A somewhat different form of financial and diplomatic dependence, accompanied by political independence is presented by Portugal... Great Britain has protected Portugal and her colonies in order to fortify her own positions in the fight against her rivals, Spain and France. In return Great Britain has received commercial privileges, preferential conditions for importing goods and especially capital into Portugal and the Portuguese colonies, the right to use the ports and islands of Portugal, her telegraph cables, etc, etc. Relations of this kind have always existed between big and little states, but in the epoch of capitalist imperialism they become a general system, they form part of the sum total of 'divide the world' relations and become links in the chain of operations of world finance capital. (Lenin, 1974, pp. 263–4)

As the last sentence quoted here indicates, imperialism as the distinctive form of modern capitalism has a different and more precise meaning than imperialism in the colloquial usage of 'empire'. The latter tends to include the British Empire, for example, as simply one of a line of great empires in history. Lenin suggests both how the British Empire was different from those that preceded it, and that British imperialism could survive the end of its formal empire and decolonization (on the analogy of Argentina and Portugal). In this respect, too, it is worth noticing that the First World War, caused by the rivalry of industrial capitalist powers, also resulted in the final demise (after long decline) of the remaining pre-capitalist empires of Eurasia: those of the Hapsburgs (Austro-Hungary), the Romanovs (Russia), and the Ottomans (Turkey and its possessions).

In the decades following the Second World War, the capitalist colonial empires were dismantled. Decolonization occurred relatively quickly in the Caribbean, Asia and Africa, compared with the period during which European domination had been established over these areas. The end of empire was primarily the result of anti-colonial and anti-imperialist struggles pursued by the peoples of the Third World, but post-war decolonization was also supported by both the USSR and the USA, though for different reasons.

The USA was to prove the dominant international capitalist power after 1945, hence the dominant imperialist power in Lenin's sense. It had little in the way of formal colonies; the Philippines which had been taken over by the USA from Spain in 1898 (having been Spain's principal Asian colony for nearly four centuries) became politically independent in 1946. The expansion through which the economic power of US capitalism emerged had taken place mostly through its own internal 'frontier', at the expense of indigenous Americans, and of Mexico to the south. Before the First World War, however, US capitalism had actively expressed its imperialist character in the countries of Central America and the Caribbean (as well as in the Philippines). Following the decolonization of Asia and Africa, its economic, political and military activity extended to other areas and intensified, confirming the role of the USA as the leading power in an imperialism now without colonies.

## Colonial State Formation

The politics of colonialism, centred around the formation of colonial states, was inextricably bound up with the economics of the expansion of Europe, the development of capitalism, and the creation of a world market and international division of labour. While colonial states were central to establishing some of the conditions of generalized commodity production, including various labour regimes geared to export production (see chapter 2), this does not mean that the politics of colonialism (as any other politics) are simply reducible to economics, to the economic interests and projects of particular classes.

For one thing, political conflicts have a complex relationship to specific differences of interest that exist between and within dominant economic groups, whether divided on lines of national rivalry (as emphasized in Lenin's *Imperialism*) or by their particular economic base (e.g. metropolitan manufacturers, colonial settler farmers and planters, imperial traders, mining capital, banking capital). More fundamentally, the political systems of colonial rule, and the economic aims they were typically called on to promote, were resisted by those on whom they were imposed. Whether methods and means of resistance were more or less overt, more or less direct, more or less organized, the actions of the colonized inevitably frustrated, in a variety of ways, the blueprints of colonial 'good government' drawn up in the capitals of Europe and those of the colonies themselves.

It is impossible to convey much of the complexity of the politics of colonialism in the kind of overview presented here, which selectively emphasizes and illustrates some major common themes and variations in the history of colonial states. Nonetheless, it is worth repeating that the boundaries of the countries of the Third World that we know today are a legacy of how colonial territories were established and ruled. Together with the often extreme regional differentiation resulting from the uneven and combined development of capitalism (which has continued beyond the end of colonial empire – see chapter 6), these inherited boundaries make their own contribution to international and internal conflict.

### *Common themes and variations*

Major common themes in colonial state formation include the following.

1 Colonial territories were established as political entities typically through conquest; the actual or implied use of force. The domination over their subjects of colonial states once created, like that of all states, ultimately rested on their ability to mobilize and deploy military and other forms of coercive power. This could present problems in colonies where Europeans were generally a tiny proportion of the population, and with distant lines of communication to the imperial country.

2 Together with military and other coercive apparatuses, colonial states established structures and procedures of administration to carry out the daily tasks of government. As noted, the latter included important economic objectives and had important (if often unintended) economic effects. Colonial states were expected minimally to develop a revenue base to be self-supporting financially, and usually also to promote the provision of commodities, markets, investment opportunities, and profits for the traders, capitalists, and exchequer of the imperial power.

3 In order to establish and maintain political stability, administrative efficiency, and economic profitability, colonial states often tried to secure the consent to, and even active participation in, their subordination on the part of colonized peoples, or at least key groups among them. The project of legitimating colonial rule could employ both material means (limited opportunities for selected groups in relation to land, trade, Western education, jobs in the colonial administration, etc.) and ideological means, above all through conversion to Christianity and/or access to Western education (the latter again for a select few). The appeal of 'indirect rule' (see below) was the hope that it would both reduce the costs of administration and prove ideologically effective by incorporating within colonial states the authority of 'traditional' (i.e. pre-colonial) rulers. The success of the ideological project in the colonies was, at best, very limited and fragile. All the measures indicated were inevitably subject to the contradiction at the core of colonial rule, and experienced by those subjected to it, namely that of racial domination and resistance to it.

4 The example of 'indirect rule' points to another broader common theme of colonial rule. According to the specific circumstances of time and place, its viability depended to a greater or lesser extent on introducing potentially wide-ranging changes while attempting to control and contain their potentially disruptive effects. These changes could be political (administration, law, taxation) and cultural (religious conversion, education, new consumption needs, medical practices) as well as economic (labour tribute, commercialization of production, monetization of exchange). To try to achieve desired changes while maintaining social and political stability, colonial states operated selectively both 'traditional' forms of social organization and legitimation ('traditions' that were often invented by the colonizers), and those associated with European states and a (developing) capitalist economy. Again, their success was limited by the fundamental contradiction noted above, and also by the frequent ignorance of colonial rulers about indigenous societies and cultures which provided the colonized with a variety of means of hidden and open resistance (including the invention or reconstruction of their own 'traditions').

These common themes, problems, contradictions, and struggles in the politics of colonialism were, of course, manifested in ways as complex and varied as the long history of colonialism itself. The following were important sources of such variation.

1 The first, linked to the economics of European expansion and its periodization (above), concerns when colonial rule was established and by which European country. Both the stage in the (international) development of capitalism *and* the position of a given European country within that stage, were crucial determinants of the type of colonial state that was formed.

2 Also central in determining specific types of colonial state was the nature of the indigenous society or societies occupying a territory on which colonial rule was imposed. One broad difference between pre-colonial societies (noted in chapter 2) was whether they were subsistence or surplus-producing, the latter often with elaborate state systems of their own. A further dimension of complexity and variation thus follows recognition of the *interaction* of different types of colonizing countries in different periods, with different kinds of pre-colonial societies and political structures.

3 Also relevant in this context are what have been called the technologies of colonial conquest, including armaments and means of transport and communications, and their forms of military and political organization. Colonial powers drew on different technologies of conquest and rule in the various stages of European expansion. These technologies became increasingly powerful over time as Europe industrialized, so that the 'gap' between them and the military technology and organization of pre-colonial societies also tended to get bigger.

The extraordinary account of the conquest of Mexico by Bernal Diaz (1973), one of Cortes' officers, shows how similar in many respects the military methods and politics of the Aztecs and the Spanish were in the early sixteenth century. Both represented pre-capitalist cultures of a very hierarchical kind, of which state religion, the accumulation of treasure, and intense personal factionalism were all central features. Despite the impact of their horses and guns, the Spanish were only able to defeat the empire of Montezuma through alliances with other Mexican groups, and after protracted and bloody campaigning. By the 1890s and the expansion of the British into the eastern Cape (South Africa), the colonial confrontation had a very different character: 'Rhodes mowed down a mealie field with machine guns before the eyes of the paramount of eastern Pondoland and his councillors and explained that their fate would be similar if they did not submit' (quoted in Low, 1973).

4 A further source of variation of colonial states – and of the nature of colonial society more generally – was whether colonies had substantial European settler populations or not. Colonial settlers were important in North America, Spanish America and the Caribbean, and in Africa in Algeria, Kenya, Southern Rhodesia (now Zimbabwe), Angola, Mozambique, and South Africa, but were largely absent in West Africa and India. Where there were significant settler populations they sought to exercise control over the colonial state as an instrument of their own particular interests, often coming into conflict with the imperial power (not least when the

FIGURE 3 (a) Humiliation inflicted on the Incas: the execution of Atahualpa (H. Roger-Viollet, Paris)

latter presented itself as the guardian of the rights and interests of 'the natives'). The different fates of settlers in the Americas and Africa are instructive.

Both the USA and the countries of Latin America were established as independent countries through revolts and wars of independence against the colonial powers of Britain, Spain and Portugal, in the late eighteenth and nineteenth centuries. Two aspects of their experience deserve emphasis. Firstly, these anti-colonial movements achieved their success *before* the capitalist colonialism of a rapidly industrializing Europe had entered its major period of global domination. Secondly, while struggles for indepen-

FIGURE 3 (b) H. M. Stanley with the Maxim Automatic Machine Gun: the Emin Pasha Expedition, 1887 (Mary Evans Picture Library)

dence mobilized and combined the energies of different classes and groups in colonial society, they were led by landed aristocracies of settler descent whose project of an independent state excluded any reforms detrimental to their own position. The colonial aristocracies of both North and South America derived their wealth and power from a history of plunder, enslavement and oppression.

In the African colonies mentioned above, settler populations were established during the peak period of capitalist colonialism. Generally, their fate was sealed with decolonization and 'the end of empire' brought about on one hand by the struggles of the colonized peoples and, on the other hand, by changes in the global development of capitalism which no longer required direct colonial rule (see above). In most cases, political independence in the former settler colonies of Africa was accompanied by a mass departure of their resident European populations. South Africa is an exception both in its relatively longer history of European settlement, and in its survival to date as a white minority state reproduced through the systematic racial oppression that was virtually definitive of colonial rule. The term 'internal colonialism' is often used to characterize the social and political structure of South Africa, and sometimes to refer to the oppression of 'Third World' populations in the Americas, both indigenous Americans ('Indians') and blacks descended from African slaves.

Just as the politics of colonial rule and the nature of colonial states differed according to the presence or absence of significant settler groups, so did the politics of decolonization. In general, since 1945, it was politically easier for European countries to relinquish those colonies without substantial settler minorities. Independence with majority rule in former settler colonies was typically achieved only after periods of bitter armed struggle against the forces of the colonial power and/or settler society.

5 A general convention in classifying different institutions of colonial government is the distinction between 'direct' and 'indirect' rule. Direct rule refers to a model of centralized administration within the colony itself, and in its close links with the metropolitan or imperial state. An example is provided by the French colonies of Africa which were regarded in constitutional terms as merely overseas 'departments' of France. The model of direct rule was often combined with notions of the 'assimilation' or 'elevation' of a privileged elite of colonial subjects educated as Europeans, and hence qualified to participate in the administration of their own societies. A British equivalent of this view (which had its Belgian and Portuguese as well as French versions) was captured in Macaulay's view of the aim of educational reform in India in the 1830s: the creation of 'a class of persons Indian in blood and colour but English in tastes, in opinions, in morals and intellect' (quoted in Worsley, 1964, p. 52).

The philosophy of indirect rule had a somewhat different reading of the same underlying (and racist) notion of racial difference. Colonial administration that integrated the political offices of indigenous societies, at both their higher levels (Indian princes, northern Nigerian Emirs) and lower levels (sub-chiefs, village headman) was deemed to have several advantages, as noted above. It saved the expense of a larger bureaucracy staffed by Europeans (at much higher levels of payment) and – or so it was believed – local rule through their 'own' rajahs, chiefs, patriarchs, and 'native courts', would legitimate colonial rule to its subjects.

Indirect rule thus suggested a different means of achieving stability and gradualism in the management of colonial society. Those holding office under direct rule were not to have any say in important policy matters, of course. Theirs were the routine functions of maintaining everyday law and order, collecting taxes, organizing labour 'turnouts', enforcing cultivation and herding measures decreed by the colonial administration, and so on. That these functions and measures were often highly unpopular inevitably undermined any legitimacy that 'native' rulers and officials had, thereby defeating a major rationale for indirect rule.

The best known theoretical statement of indirect rule is *The Dual Mandate in British Tropical Africa* (1922) by Lord Lugard, the first Governor-General of Nigeria in 1914. Lugard had served his colonial apprenticeship in the conquest of Uganda, from which he derived the principle of dealing with Africans of 'thrash them first, conciliate them afterwards' (quoted in Low, 1973).

In outlining the concepts of direct and indirect rule, we have deliberately used terms like 'model', 'philosophy', 'theory' and the like, because the concepts are not necessarily an accurate guide to the real political practices of colonial states. Indeed, they are more likely to obscure analysis of these practices, because they present an idealized picture of colonial 'good government' and that from the perspective of the colonizers. In practice, the procedures, methods and activities of colonial states were shaped by the problems of effective rule they encountered in particular sets of circumstances, and their quest for solutions to those problems.

Such 'solutions' often contained elements of both 'direct' and 'indirect' rule. In Spanish America the Amerindian priesthood, a powerful source of ideological opposition to Spanish colonialism and its Catholic mission, was ruthlessly destroyed, while those of the Amerindian nobility willing to cooperate were incorporated in local versions of 'indirect' rule. As 'traditional' leaders they extracted the tribute and labour demanded by the colonial economy and its state. In return they were allowed to share in the proceeds of the exploitation of the population (and all this beginning four centuries before Lugard's codification of 'indirect' rule in Nigeria).

Britain's vast colonial territory in South Asia was divided between the administration of the Indian Civil Service (established after 1857–8, and the exemplar of a highly centralized and professional bureaucracy) and that of a multitude of 'princely states'. French colonial rule in Africa in practice rested on chiefs and headmen at the local level, rather than a cadre of salaried officials. The British colonial state in Nigeria contained quite different systems of administration in the north, where it reconstituted the autocratic rule of the Emirs, and in those areas of the south and east whose pre-colonial societies had been 'stateless'.

In conclusion, it can be suggested that different 'models' of colonial rule were more the *results* than the causes of different practices of domination.

That is, they were reflections on, and justifications of, specific methods and results of colonial state formation. While the latter had certain common conditions and features, these were necessarily manifested in historically complex variations from sixteenth-century Mexico to nineteenth-century India and twentieth-century Nigeria.

CHAPTER TWO

# Labour Regimes and Social Change Under Colonialism

## Colonial Political Economy

Whether the initial reason for the colonization of a territory was strategic or economic, few metropolitan governments were prepared to bear the financial cost of colonial administration for long. It was, therefore, necessary to organize the productive capacity of the area concerned in such a way as to generate sufficient income to sustain the administrative and military presence that maintained European control.

This was seen as a minimal requirement, though it was one that some colonial territories – poorly endowed with known natural resources, people, means of communciation or significant opportunities for profitable investment and trade – were barely able to satisfy. But beyond this requirement of being 'self-financing', colonies were expected to contribute to the economies of their metropolitan rulers and colonial states.

Both processes entailed integration in an international economy, initially formed by the expansion of Europe in its period of transition from feudalism to capitalism (chapter 1), and subsequently shaped and reshaped by the dynamics of capital development on a global scale. The making of colonial economies within the international division of labour occurred through the production of commodities for export, above all from extractive industries (mining) and tropical agriculture (sugar, cotton, palm products, tea, coffee, groundnuts, rubber, sisal, jute). The production of these commodities took very different forms. Mining and larger-scale agriculture (whether organized by plantation companies or individual colonial settlers granted large areas of land for this purpose) required some initial capital and a sufficiently large (and 'cheap') labour force. Alternatively, peasants were 'encouraged' to grow particular crops for sale and export, by various means ranging from direct coercion to more indirect pressures, including the need for a money income to pay taxes and to purchase the new kinds of goods and services introduced with colonialism.

The kinds of commodities produced in the colonies, and how they were produced, varied in time and place according to the interests represented in different colonialisms. Large-scale trade dominated by metropolitan companies and colonial entrepreneurs was a consistent interest throughout the history of colonialism, although (as noted in chapter 1) the composition and scale of that trade changed as industrial capitalism developed. In the sixteenth and seventeenth centuries, the mining of gold and silver in Spanish America and their transport to Europe provided the profits of colonial entrepreneurs, and of shipping and mercantile interests, and met the needs of the Spanish crown for revenue to finance its dynastic ventures in Europe. But as the growth of industrial capitalism in Western Europe and the USA accelerated during the nineteenth century, it required a more diverse range of products for processing and manufacturing, and in ever larger quantities: minerals like copper, and industrial crops like cotton, rubber, sisal and jute. The rapid urbanization that accompanied industrialization in the Western countries also resulted in a new market demand for tropical products that became items of mass consumption – sugar, tea, coffee, palm oils, and so on – and their production in the colonies was, consequently, expanded.

Changes brought about in the international economy as a result of the development of capitalism (and especially Western industrialization) also led to changes in forms of colonial exploitation. For example, the discovery of diamonds and gold in South Africa, and the subsequent massive development of the mining industry there in the late nineteenth century, was a very different matter from the earlier Spanish adventurers' colonization of Latin America in search of 'treasure'. In the late nineteenth century, gold was needed to support the 'Gold Standard', on which the stability of the vastly expanding international trade and international monetary transactions were held to rest. Diamonds were needed for new industrial processes, as well as continuing to be an item of 'luxury' consumption. The historian Colin Bundy (1979) has argued that prior to the discovery of diamonds and gold, a thriving African commercial agriculture had emerged in certain areas of South Africa as part of a previous phase of capitalist development. This was undermined by state policies to restrict African agriculture, and access to land and independent incomes, when the 'take-off' of mining (and the stimulus to settler or white commercial agriculture it provided) required a plentiful and continuous supply of 'cheap' labour power.

The variation and complexity of the economies created by European colonialism was, thus, partly a result of different stages in the formation of a capitalist world economy, and also of different forms of colonial incorporation and exploitation. The making of colonial economies required the 'breaking' of pre-existing types of economy and the social relations which governed access to resources, the recruitment and uses of labour, and the appropriation of the product, within them. In different cases, the rupture with the economic foundation and social organization of existing ways of life could be more or less abrupt, more or less brutal, and effected by more or less direct means, as the rest of this chapter illustrates.

## Colonial Labour Regimes

The term 'labour regime' is used here to refer to different methods of mobilizing labour and organizing it in production, and their particular social, economic, and political conditions. The essential mechanisms of four broad types of labour regime are described and illustrated briefly below, namely forced labour, semi-proletarianization, petty commodity production, and proletarianization. Connections between those labour regimes and the development of capitalism are then suggested, together with some comments on the 'labour problem' under colonialism which is also related to the 'land question' in different types of colonial economy.

### *Forced labour*

Of the regimes of forced labour, slavery in the Caribbean and the Americas is probably the most widely known because of its scale, its duration over more than three countries, and the intense violence of the slave trade and of the conditions of plantation production. There were two main historical factors that contributed to the development of the slave trade. The demand for tropical products (sugar, cotton, tobacco) increased with the expansion of production, trade and incomes in Europe associated with the development of capitalism (itself stimulated by the in-flows of precious metals and treasure acquired from colonial conquest in Spanish America, and subsequently from the plundering of large areas of Asia). But the indigenous people of the colonized areas of the New World were too few to provide sufficient labour to produce these commodities, or were resistant to enslavement, or were destroyed by European arms and diseases, or some combination of these factors.

Significantly, the slave trade and plantation production reached a peak in the eighteenth century, as northwestern Europe was completing its long transition to industrial capitalism. Slavery was profitable as long as a

FIGURE 4 Slaves on a treadmill in Jamaica (Mansell Collection)

plentiful and cheap supply of slaves could be assured. This might be met by the 'natural' (generational) reproduction of the existing slave population, although, reliance on this placed limits on the intensity with which slaves could be exploited: they could not reproduce themselves at the desired rate if they were literally worked to death after a few years (or less). Alternatively, plantation owners had to rely on continuing shipments of slaves from Africa at prices that suited them. This strategy was undermined by the abolition of the slave trade by Britain in 1807, which put considerable pressure on the profitability of slave production.

Two other factors in the eventual decline of slavery are worth noting. The first is that in the course of the nineteenth century new and superior technologies made available by the industrial revolutions of Europe and the USA were increasing the productivity of labour in agriculture as well as in manufacturing, thereby rendering slave production less competitive and, hence, less profitable in international markets. The nature of slave production on plantations, including the forms of brutal control and slaves' resistance to them, meant that it was very difficult to operate new and more sophisticated techniques of production with coerced and antagonistic workers. The second factor is that, as time went on, the social and political costs of maintaining control over slave populations grew as they themselves increased in number, both absolutely and as a proportion of the population in plantation colonies. The ratio of slaves to others was ten to one in Jamaica by the time of the abolition of slavery in the British Empire in 1833.

The major effects of slavery over this long period illustrate clearly the spatial dimensions and effects of processes contributing to the formation of a capitalist world economy.

1 In West Africa, slave raiding and trading brought about massive social disruption and depopulation. The raiding and warfare necessary for the provision of slaves was mostly carried out by indigenous groups (who consequently increased their own wealth and power by, for example, acquiring European firearms), in collaboration with the European traders on the coast.
2 In those societies it created (in the Caribbean, Brazil, the southern USA), the experience of slavery had profound consequences for social differentiation and cultural patterns that are still felt today.
3 For Europe, where the often vast profits of slave traders and shippers and plantation owners were directed, slavery contributed to the accumulation of wealth and facilitated the transition to industrial capitalism.

More or less contemporaneous with the long history of slavery was a variety of forced labour regimes in the Spanish colonies of the Caribbean and Central and South America, which were originally adapted from the feudal institutions and practices of Spain, and subsequently changed over time with the changing economic conditions and social and political struggles of the colonies. Only a few points are selected here from a

FIGURE 5 Carved ivory tusk depicting an African view of merchant capitalism as a hierarchy: slaves at the bottom, African producers in the centre and a European merchant at the top (National Museum of Denmark, Copenhagen)

complex history, a principal thread of which is how the Spanish settlers established themselves as a colonial aristocracy, in relation to the subjugated indigenous populations on one hand, and to the Spanish crown on the other.

In the first half of the sixteenth century, individual colonists, churches and agents of the Spanish crown were given rights to the labour of indigenous Indian communities, which they could extract as labour tribute (for agricultural production, porterage, construction, personal services, etc.) and/or tribute in kind (agricultural and craft products). Technically this system of *encomienda* did not bestow rights to Indian land, although individual grants of land could be made by the crown independently of the *encomienda*.

With the massive decline of the indigenous population (e.g. from about 11 million in Mexico in 1519 to 6.5 million in 1540 and 4.5 million in

1565), as the direct and indirect result of conquest and early colonization, and with the arrival of new colonists demanding their grants of Indian labour, there were conflicts over access to a diminishing labour supply. These were intensified by the discovery of massive silver deposits in Mexico and Peru in the mid-sixteenth century, requiring equally massive quantities of labour to mine them. The crown introduced new mechanisms of forced labour service, known in Mexico as *repartimiento* or *cuatequil* and in Peru as *mita*, through which colonists had to apply to the state for Indian tribute labour. In this sense, the allocation of labour was centralized and bureaucratized as an action of the colonial state against colonial settlers (who accumulated large numbers of Indians through *encomienda* and passed them on to their heirs). At the same time, the aim of the new tributory labour system was to 'rationalize' the supply of labour from wider areas for the concentrated demand brought about by the new mining boom. This was manifested in the long journeys undertaken by large convoys of Indians to work out their labour service at distant mines (and from which many of them never returned).

Without going into the intricacies of the gaps between the legal theory and the real practices of forced labour regimes in Spanish America, and of their changes in relation to changes in patterns of economic activity and to social and political struggles between settlers and Indians and settlers and the crown, it should be noted that when the new republics were established in the first half of the nineteenth century following wars of independence against Spain, their constitutions granted Indians equal citizenship and abolished forced labour. However, during the course of the eighteenth century many of the formal mechanisms of labour coercion had given way to other labour regimes based on debt bondage, to secure labour for the estates of what had become, in effect, a *landed* (rather than a purely tributory) aristocracy (see below).

Forced labour regimes were also features of other colonies at other times, particularly during the early stages of colonization. Throughout sub-Saharan Africa in the late nineteenth century, and in a number of Asian colonies, tribute labour was directed to the construction of railways and roads (the arteries of colonial commerce) and to work on European plantations. In both cases, the control over labour and the conditions experienced by workers were little different from those of slavery. Such forced labour occurred either by direct order of newly established colonial administrations or with their informal 'assistance'.

Another and distinctive type of forced labour regime was that of indenture. Indentured labour is a practice whereby people contract themselves to work for an agreed number of years for a particular employer. They did this because of destitution and desperation, lacking any alternative means of making a living. Indentured labour was an important device in the early settlement of British colonies in the Caribbean and the southern USA, those who were indentured as workers and servants coming from the poorest sections of the British population. Probably some of the small settlers in the Caribbean who were displaced by 'King Sugar' in the seventeenth and eighteenth centuries, had first gone there as indentured workers and had become small farmers when the period of their indenture had been worked out.

In the nineteenth and early twentieth centuries, indentured labour occurred on a far larger scale, drawing particularly on those masses of people in India and China whose poverty and destitution resulted from European domination (even though China was not formally colonized). Most of them were peasants driven from the land by crippling debt or hunger produced by intensified commercialization and exploitation, and craft workers like spinners and weavers, whose livelihoods were destroyed by competition from the cheap textiles of Britain's new factories.

Indian and Chinese indentured workers went to the plantations of the Caribbean and to other plantation islands like Mauritius in the Indian Ocean and Fiji in the South Pacific; to the rubber plantations of Malaya; to British East Africa, where the economically strategic railway from the port of Mombasa to Lake Victoria was built by Indian indentured workers in the first decade of the twentieth century; and to South Africa, as workers in agriculture and mining.

In principle, indenture was a contract 'freely' entered into by workers for a limited period, and in this sense it differed from slavery, where the body and person of the slave was exchanged and used as a commodity. However, given the circumstances of destitution that drive people into indenture, the tricks and coercion often employed by licensed labour recruiters to get them to sign the indenture contract, and the power of the plantation owners and other employers (backed up by the colonial state) in the countries where they went to work, the experiences of indentured workers were often very similar to those of the slaves of earlier generations (whom they replaced in the Caribbean), as has been amply documented by Hugh Tinker (1974) who termed indenture 'a new system of slavery'.

### *Semi-proletarianization*

Indentured workers who completed their contracts often stayed in the colonies they had been shipped to, some of them subsequently becoming semi- or fully proletarianized. The meaning of semi-proletarianization is often elusive (see, further, chapter 6) but two, somewhat different uses of it, can be suggested. The first can be illustrated by returning to debt bondage, which refers to a relationship whereby someone is forced to pay off their debts by providing goods or labour service to their creditor (or, not uncommonly, to a third party to whom the creditor may sell or 'rent' the debt). This kind of situation was (and still is) found among the poorest strata of peasants and rural semi-proletarians, caught in a permanent cycle of debt to their landlords and others with a claim on their labour. It was indicated above that in the eighteenth century, with the consolidation of the colonial aristocracy of Spanish America as a *landed* class, many of the former forced labour regimes gave way to debt bondage as a means through which landowners secured a 'captive' (and resident) labour force for their estates.

Significantly, the introduction of new and profitable commercial cr into particular areas was often accompanied by new types of debt bondag or the intensification of existing ones, by landowners and capitalists (fo example, the British trading interests involved in the Peruvian Amazon rubber 'boom' in the first decade of the twentieth century). The term 'semi-proletarianization' seems appropriate here to the extent that debt bondage is a way of securing labour for commodity production within capitalism, but labour that is clearly not 'free' in the full sense suggested by Marx (see chapter 5). In most Latin American countries, legislation to abolish debt bondage was passed between 1915 and 1920, but debt bondage as one type of labour regime established within capitalism (and not only colonial capitalism) remains widespread in many parts of the Third World today (see the excellent discussion by Brass, 1986).

Those who have to supply their labour because of debt bondage may also have some land of their own or other resources which contribute part of their livelihood through subsistence or small-scale commodity production. This is the major characteristic of the second form of semi-proletarianization in which periodic wage labour is combined with other economic activity (and especially subsistence agriculture) to provide a means of livelihood and household reproduction. This is discussed further in chapter 6; here it can be stressed that cyclical or periodic labour migration regimes were a major feature of many colonial economies, notably in sub-Saharan Africa where semi-proletarianized migrants supplied much of the labour for mining and commercial agriculture – both large-scale (particularly in southern Africa) and small-scale (particularly in West Africa) – and continue to do so. Like debt bondage, then, the regime of semi-proletarianized migrant labour is reproduced, or even recreated, more generally within capitalism beyond the specifically colonial origins it had in many cases.

### *Petty commodity production*

This last point is also true of petty commodity production, which is discussed in chapter 6, and considered further in parts III and IV. The important point to note in the context of colonial economies is that household production, especially in 'peasant' agriculture, presented another means of restructuring the economic activity of labour of colonized people to simultaneously meet the demands of capitalism for commodities and the demands of colonial states for revenues. Initially, then, the conditions of petty commodity production (or new types of petty commodity production) within both colonial and international divisions of labour were typically established by the need for a money income to pay taxes to the new states, and subsequently also to purchase new means of production and consumption that the extension of the capitalist market made available (and often necessary). In some cases, colonial states ordered particular cash crops to be grown and attempted to regulate their methods of cultivation; in other cases, peasants seized or created opportunities to pioneer new cash crops and ways of farming.

Generally, rural populations preferred to meet the new needs for cash imposed on them through petty commodity production, in which they could exercise some control over the uses of their labour, rather than periodic wage labour for others in the harsh material and social (control) conditions of plantations, settler estates and mines. There is a parallel here with *encomienda*, in which the payment of tribute in kind was experienced as relatively less oppressive than tribute paid in labour service.

In some colonial economies the preference of rural people to undertake petty commodity production, and their success in doing so, confronted capitalists requiring large numbers of workers at low rates of pay. An example was given earlier, in the context of the mining boom in late nineteenth century South Africa, which can be repeated for many other areas where the interests of powerful types of capital demanded a plentiful and 'cheap' supply of labour rather than commodities produced by peasants. In colonial Eastern, Central and Southern Africa (as in South Africa today), the 'solution' to the problem of competition over labour between (European) capitalist and (African) peasant production was to undermine the ability of the latter to generate an adequate income through growing cash crops. This was done by restricting African farming and rural residence to very limited and usually agriculturally marginal areas (the 'Native Reserve' system), and discriminating against peasant commodity production in terms of prices, transport charges, access to credit, etc. These various measures, directly imposed or facilitated by colonial states, institutionalized some of the conditions of semi-proletarianization.

### *Proletarianization*

Full proletarianization in colonial economies occurred when impoverished peasants and craft producers (the social groups from which indentured workers from India and China were mostly drawn) either lost access to land and other means of production, or were driven by debt or hunger (often the same thing) to try to secure a living through selling their labour power. From the side of capital, there was sometimes a demand for a more stable and skilled work-force than the labour regime of semi-proletarianization could provide – in some jobs in mining, in manufacturing (although this was very limited in most colonial economies), and in such branches as railways, ports, and road transport, which played a strategic role in the circulation of commodities and in the administration of the colonial state.

While the emergence of a stable working class in colonial economies was usually limited relative to the numbers of those proletarianized, that working class was able to develop trade unions and other forms of political action (both legal and illegal) which played an important role in the movements for independence from colonial rule.

### *Colonial labour regimes and capitalism*

The different types of colonial labour regimes discussed here are summarized in table 1, which is constructed in terms of the dimensions of the proletarian wage labour most characteristic of capitalism, 'freed' both from access to the means of production and from extra-economic (legal and political) coercion. The table does not represent a rigorous taxonomy or classification (consisting of mutually exclusive categories) which, in any case, is often misleading in social analysis. This applies particularly in considering the global history of capitalism, which has absorbed, created *and combined* such diverse social forms in the course of its uneven and contradictory development. Having said that, some comments on the table can clarify the links between colonial labour regimes and capitalism.

Firstly, the term 'labour regime' itself is used somewhat loosely: petty commodity production and capitalist production can incorporate different specific labour regimes. However, the term is still useful in its emphasis that the making of colonial economies entailed the breaking of pre-colonial economies and that the essential mechanism of this process was restructuring the uses of labour within a developing international division of labour.

Secondly, directly coercive labour regimes were more characteristic of the period of primary or 'primitive' accumulation on a world scale, during the sixteenth to eighteenth centuries when Europe was undergoing its long transition from feudal to capitalist society. Given the unevenness of capitalist development, this does not mean that directly coerced labour disappeared all at once in all colonies or former colonies. In Cuba, slavery was not fully abolished until 1889, and various forms of tribute labour were imposed on the people of 'new' colonies of Africa and Asia in the late nineteenth and early twentieth centuries (and which in the case of Portugal's African colonies, continued until the 1960s).

Nevertheless, from the turn of the nineteenth century, slavery began to disappear (though it was often replaced by indentured labour); the earlier plundering activities of the East India Company gave way to the systematic colonial administration of the British Raj in India; the originally 'feudal' colonialisms of Spain and Portugal finally lost their hold over Latin America, while the new capitalist colonialisms of Britain, France and Germany engaged in the scramble for African colonies; not least, the industrial revolutions vastly expanded the scale of international trade and changed its composition towards industrial crops and minerals, demanded from the colonies to supply the factories and growing urban populations of Europe.

These changes led to the establishment of forms of production in colonial economies based on semi-proletarian and proletarian labour (capitalist production) and household labour (petty commodity production). While the *initial creation* of these types of labour *within capitalism* (as distinct from, e.g. pre-capitalist and pre-colonial peasant production) often required direct and indirect forms of extra-economic coercion, the latter were replaced sooner or later by *economic compulsion*. That is, people came to depend on commodities as means of consumption (and in the case of petty commodity production, as means of production too) and, therefore, needed cash incomes to buy these commodities. Thus semi-proletarian, proletarian and household labour were all reproduced within capitalism as a result of economic necessity, and consequently have persisted in Third World economies after the demise of colonialism (see chapter 7).

TABLE 1 Colonial labour regimes

| *Labour regime* | *Separation of producers from means of production* | *Extra-economic coercion* | *'Free' wage labour* | *Examples* |
|---|---|---|---|---|
| 1 *Forced labour*: | | | | |
| Slavery | Complete | Yes | No | Caribbean, Brazil, southern USA, 16th–19th centuries |
| Tribute, tax in kind | No | Yes | No | Spanish America, 16th–17th centuries; Africa, 19th to early 20th centuries |
| Labour service | Partial | Yes | No | Spanish America, 16th–18th centuries; Africa, Asia, 19th to early 20th centuries |
| Indenture | Complete | Partial | 'Transitional' | Caribbean, East Africa, Malaysia, Mauritius, Fiji, 19th–20th centuries |
| 2 *Semi-proletarian labour*: | | | | |
| Debt bondage | Partial or complete | No | 'Transitional' | Spanish America, 18th–20th centuries; Asia 19th–20th centuries |
| Periodic labour migration | Partial | No | 'Transitional' | Africa, and Third World generally, 20th century |
| 3 *Petty commodity production* | No | No | No | India and Africa, 19th century; throughout Third World, 20th century |
| 4 Proletarianization | Complete | No | Yes | Some sectors of colonial economies: 18th century (Latin America), 19th century (India), 20th century (Africa) |

This is the reason why these three types of labour are shown in table 1 as not requiring extra-economic coercion as a condition of their reproduction. At the same time, one should not regard the 'freedom' of labour under capitalism too literally. Marx's reference to such 'freedom' was ironic: it consists precisely in economic compulsion rather than other types of compulsion. This does not mean, however, that capitalists are inhibited from trying to use political, ideological and legal means of coercion to structure, or to augment, economic compulsion in ways that will deliver the kinds of labour they want on the terms they want (levels of pay, conditions of control and discipline, etc.). This is evident in labour regimes using debt bondage to try to secure a captive and compliant work force, but it also applies to the class struggle more generally, including those circumstances in which labour power is 'freely' exchanged through the market.

A similar point applies to the separation of the producers from the means of production as a condition of 'free' wage labour, which should not be 'stereotyped' as Lenin put it. Semi-proletarian labour is generated within capitalism no less than fully proletarian labour, and is no less capitalist in the social relations of production it expresses (see chapter 6). Nevertheless, systematically generated and reproduced conditions of wage labour that include less than complete separation of workers from the means of production and/or direct coercion, are termed 'transitional' in a conceptual sense though not a historical one, i.e. such types of labour are not necessarily transitory or short-lived within capitalism.

### *Colonialism and the 'labour problem'*

Underlying the bare conceptual divisions of table 1 are the massive, diverse and complex histories of how colonialism and capitalism created the economies of the Third World. The labour regimes so briefly described here were the outcomes of processes of struggle – more or less brutal, more or less protracted – to impose new structures of economic activity on untold millions of colonized peoples, against their resistance or their attempts to adapt them to their own survival and needs. The 'labour problem' was a preoccupation of colonial officials and interest groups in many different places at different times. Why should labour supply have been so general a 'problem' for colonialism? The answer to this question suggests a number of connected factors.

The first is that the conditions of work in plantations and mines and on large-scale public works like railway construction, were extremely bad, and labour was exploited very intensively. Secondly, the payment for such work was minimal, sometimes barely enough to enable workers to survive from one day to another (or not even that). Thirdly, this kind of labour withdrew people from their customary farming and other productive activities, although this usually remained an important source of their subsistence and reproduction. But it was not only their productive activities and capacities that were materially undermined; so also were the social and cultural relations that were an integral part of their productive activities.

In short, their whole way of life was threatened – their ways of making and doing things, and the values associated with them.

This is particularly striking with respect to practices and ideas connected with *work*. While pre-colonial societies varied widely with respect to types of work – who did it, and how much of it – the performance of work was informed by very different principles and values from those imposed by large-scale colonial production. The development of colonial political economy almost invariably led to an *intensification* of work, as well as different (and frequently oppressive) kinds of work, for most of the people subjected to colonial incorporation. The intensification of labour sprang from the material interest of colonial states and settlers, but was also explicitly recommended in their ideologies of the 'civilizing mission' of European rule. In the ideological package of colonialism, hard work could conveniently be considered a moral (and specifically Christian) virtue as well as an imperative for economic progress (i.e. creating wealth for European colonists, capitalists, and states).

A Spanish decree on *encomienda* in 1513 stipulated that Indians 'were to work nine months a year for the Spaniards (i.e. without pay), and were to be compelled to work on their own lands or for the Spaniards for wages in the remaining three months'. The stated intention was '*to prevent them spending their time in indolence and to teach them to live as Christians*' (Kloosterboer, 1960, my italics). More than four hundred years later, the 1922 *Annual Report* of the Governor-General of the Belgian Congo stated that 'under no circumstances whatsoever should it be permitted to occur that a peasant, who has paid his taxes and other legally required obligations, should be left with nothing to do. The moral authority of the administrator, persuasion, encouragement and other measures should be adopted *to make the native work*' (Nzula et al., 1979, my italics).

As these quotations suggest, the other side of the colonial 'labour problem' was the equally widely expressed stereotype of the 'lazy native', which justified the use of coercion to get the natives to do more work as part of their apprenticeship to European 'civilization'. Certainly, people in pre-colonial societies had generally worked less than their colonial masters now wanted them to. Firstly, less labour was required to satisfy their needs (and even the needs of dominant classes in surplus-producing societies), and labour was spread unevenly over the year, according to seasons and modes of interaction with nature. Secondly, time not spent in directly productive work was used in social, ceremonial and creative activities that were an integral part of pre-colonial cultures. It is ironic too – and would hardly have escaped the attention of the 'natives' – that the virtues of intensive manual labour were advocated (and enforced) by groups of Europeans notable for their aversion to it, whether colonial officials, missionary 'princes' of the church, traders, land-owners or the managers of mines and plantations.

How disruptive of existing economic and social structures were the various labour regimes introduced with colonialism? This depended a great deal on specific conditions: the nature of the pre-colonial societies, the types of colonial state and interest groups, and the stage of development of the international economy. A further way of distinguishing the labour regimes described is to ask to what extent they destroyed existing forms of household and communal production, and to what extent they presupposed their continued existence (albeit in forms that were increasingly changed as they were incorporated in generalized commodity production; see further chapter 6).

The labour regimes of slavery, indentured labour and debt bondage presupposed the removal of alternative ways of earning a living. Slaves were forcibly removed from their homes in West Africa and shipped to the New World, where they were totally subordinated to the rights of their owners over them (as were also, of course, those born into slavery in the Americas). Indentured labour was recruited from the pauperized peasants and craftsmen of India and China, dispossessed of land or their traditional means of livelihood. Debt bondage presupposed the loss of (sufficient) land for subsistence production, and the indebtedness that ensued in an increasingly commercialized and monetized economy.

Other types of labour regime presupposed the continuing existence of household production, though with varying degrees of viability. Where the surplus product was appropriated in the form of a feudal-like tribute (*encomienda*) or taxes in kind, people were left in control of their land and of the organization of their labour to produce both their own subsistence and the surplus they had to deliver. This was also the case where peasant production of commodities was encouraged (as in India and West Africa), although pressure could be exerted to make peasants produce more for sale through imposing money taxation and paying low prices for their crops.

Those situations where labour on a large scale was demanded required some sort of balance between the amount of labour that could be compelled to work for the colonial state and settlers, and the amount of labour and other resources (e.g. land) necessary to reproduce the households of those performing labour service. The measures used to enforce the supply of labour ranged from straightforward legal compulsion by the colonial state (*repartimiento* in Spanish America, *chibalo* in Southern Africa) to economic necessity – when cash was needed to pay tax and could not be obtained in any other way. Economic necessity generally came to replace direct legal coercion as the need for a cash income extended beyond tax payments to include means of consumption which now had to be purchased as commodities, whether food, clothing, medicines, Western-style schooling, and new manufactures such as household utensils, farming implements, etc.

Colonial authorities could ensure that people had no means of buying goods and services (such as Western education) other than by working for wages. This was done by restricting them to overcrowded 'Native Reserves' (colonial Kenya and the Rhodesias, South Africa's 'Bantustans' today), preventing them from growing 'cash crops' and so on. Such policies effectively undermined what, in the terms of pre-colonial societies, had been a viable subsistence agriculture, and replaced it with a '*sub*-subsistence' agriculture that necessitated continuing periodic labour migration to make up for the shortfalls in subsistence. Moreover, as most labour migrants were men, their absence intensified the labour of the women left behind to try to maintain agricultural production.

It is hardly surprising, then, that there was a 'labour problem' under colonialism. This constant preoccupation and complaint of colonial rulers and settlers, and plantation and mining capitalists, further indicates that the making of colonial economies – with all their differences of time and place from sixteenth-century America to twentieth-century Africa – entailed a *common* process of breaking pre-existing ways of production and restructuring the uses of the labour thus 'released'. The resistance of the colonized to tribute and wage labour was particularly strong, and generally, when it was possible, they preferred what Ranger (1985) has termed the 'peasant option', that is, the attempt to retain at least some control over the uses of their labour in petty commodity production, even with all the pressures to which this too could be subjected.

### *Labour and the 'land question'*

Given that most people in pre-colonial societies gained their living from the land, the alienation of land to settlers and colonial companies by formal decree or other means (including outright land-grabbing), the restriction of indigenous people to agriculturally marginal (and sooner or later over-crowded) areas, and the competition for land as a commodity generated by commercialization, all contributed in major ways to the 'releasing' and the restructuring of the uses of labour in colonial economies. People were dispossessed of land, or their access to, and modes of using, land were radically changed. This has already been indicated in relation to debt bondage in Latin America, the recruitment of indentured labour, and processes of proletarianization. Some of the ways in which colonialism created a 'land question' with critical implications for labour, including peasant labour, can be briefly illustrated in the cases of India and Kenya.

In India, colonial land policy was seen initially as an aspect of revenue collection rather than as a method of (re)organizing agricultural production. There were no European settlers and peasant farming remained the main form of agricultural production, except in limited areas of North-East and South India and in Ceylon (now Sri Lanka), where tea plantations were introduced during the nineteenth century.

Under the Mughal emperors, the collection of taxes from agricultural producers (peasants) was conducted by an important class of intermediaries known as *zamindars*. They were not land-owners, as the concept and practice of private property in land did not exist, but they had the right of control over 'estates', some of which encompassed as many as 800 villages. Each 'estate' formed a hierarchy with the *zamindar* at its top and various levels of 'tenants' and 'sub-tenants' with different types of claims to the use of land. *Zamindars* collected an annual tax from their 'estates', based on a proportion of the harvested crop; this was subject to annual negotiation, according to weather and other conditions, and was generally paid in kind.

Lord Cornwallis's 'Permanent Settlement' of 1793 was designed to rationalize the collection of taxes via *zamindars* for the treasury of the East India Company, rather than for that of the Mughals. In retaining the role of the *zamindars*, the Permanent Settlement in Bengal conformed to the prevailing idea of 'non-interference' with indigenous social arrangements (see chapter 5). However, it contributed to the undermining of these arrangements by conferring on *zamindars* the status of 'land-holders' according to Western ideas of landed property, and by replacing a flexible annual tax paid in kind with a *fixed* annual tax paid in *money*.

These two measures had the most profound consequences, contributing to processes of commercialization of the rural economy. The legal establishment of individual property rights in land meant that, henceforth, it could be bought and sold: land became an exchangeable *commodity*. This allowed the development of a market in land as an object of speculation and profitable investment, yielding rent to land-owners. The monetization of taxes (and of economic transactions more generally) pushed the peasantry into producing cash crops for export markets, as British trading and industrial interests wanted (cotton, jute, indigo, and opium, introduced into Bengal by the East India Company to finance its tea trade with China). At the same time, the introduction of fixed annual taxes to be paid in money (rather than a share of the crop) led to peasant indebtedness in years of bad weather and poor harvests.

For peasants, the tyranny of fixed monetary obligations in relation to the variability of nature and of yields could lead to a cycle of debt-bondage through borrowing to pay taxes (and rents), and ultimately to eviction from the land they farmed. Bad harvests affected not only the peasants' ability to pay *zamindars*, but also the latter's ability to deliver the taxes demanded by the colonial administration. In this situation, the weaker *zamindars* were 'bought out' by the Indian merchants and financiers of Calcutta, while the stronger ones became absentee landowners living in towns, where they tended to merge wih the mercantile and money-lending class. The effect of the Permanent Settlement was, thus, to contribute simultaneously to the impoverishment and 'squeezing' of large numbers of peasants, and to the displacement of a local rural aristocracy in favour of an urban *rentier* class: that is, a class of landlords whose principal interest in the countryside was the income they derived from rents and from buying and selling land, rather than investment to enhance agricultural production. The formation of this *rentier* class also encouraged the conversion of rents in kind to fixed-money rents, parallel to the introduction of fixed-money taxes by the colonial state.

The Permanent Settlement and its effects provide a good example of a colonial policy which, while preserving the existing *form* of rural society (*zamindars* and peasants), profoundly changed its *content* in terms of property relations, the intensification of peasant labour through commercialization and monetization of the rural economy, and the appropriation of a surplus through taxes and rents.

The adaptation of the Mughal *zamindar* system was an attempt to build administration on an existing indigenous social structure. The same principle applied to South India led to the establishment of the *ryotwari* system, so-called because the basis of taxation was conferring land titles on *ryots*. According to Sir Thomas Munro, the architect of this system introduced in Madras in 1812, *ryots* were 'a crowd of men of small, but of independent property, who, when they are certain that they will themselves enjoy the benefits of every extraordinary exertion of labour, work with a spirit of activity which would in vain be expected from the tenants and servants of great land-holders' (Munro, quoted in Low, 1973, p. 46).

In Munro's conception – and by contrast with the aristocratic *zamindar* 'landlords' of Bengal – *ryots* appeared as small and 'improving' yeoman farmers on the model of those found in England at the time. In fact, those who benefited from the land titles bestowed by Munro's policy were local leaders and notables, often from powerful castes. With the possession of property titles, many of them were now able to constitute themselves as a land-owning class, similar to the *zamindars*, although on a more modest scale.

In effect, landlords used the opportunities presented by the *ryotwari* settlement in ways which had never been envisaged by Munro and the British administration in Madras. Because they were the major source of recruitment of local revenue officials, or were allied with locally influential persons, or even chose and paid for village officers, they had opportunities to shift many of their tax liabilities on to others. Madras revenue records provide hundreds of examples of land acquired by revenue servants or through family agents, and the use of torture and coercion in the collection of revenue was tacitly accepted by the administration (Stein, 1977, pp. 72–3).

In both cases, colonial legislation and administrative practice had profound effects quite unanticipated by the rulers, which often reflected their ignorance of important aspects of the indigenous societies they sought to shape. Together with other aspects of the commercialization of economic life brought about by integration with the international economy and the impact of a developing industrial capitalism in Europe, the colonial state in India contributed to new forms of exploitation of the peasantry, and the formation of new social classes (the urban *rentiers* of Bengal, the local landlords of Madras, the landless labourers resulting from the dispossession of the peasants).

In colonies like South Africa, Southern Rhodesia (now Zimbabwe) and Kenya, where large areas of land were alienated for use by European settlers, changes in existing patterns of landholding and land use in the process of the commercialization of agriculture resulted in other types of social differentiation. In Kenya, vast areas of the best land were appropriated by the colonial state and handed over to white settler farmers and landowners, while Africans were confined to Native Reserves and forbidden to grow cash crops such as coffee or to compete in the same market with food crops grown on settler farms. The 'land question' became very important in Kenyan politics and was a major factor in the Mau Mau revolt of the 1950s.

The taking over of land by conquerors was not a new experience for the main group in Kenya, the Kikuyu. 'What was novel, and produced great bitterness, was that the new white conquerors appeared to suppose that the rights of use conferred on them by victory were exclusive' (Kitching, 1980, p. 284). Traditionally, this concept of exclusivity did not exist. Land was abundant, with no fixed property rights in the Western sense; land settlement proceeded by the formation of new groups of cultivators based on kinship, and their movement into new areas. In some places two separate groups of people might use the same land for different purposes – Dorobo hunter/gatherers reaching a mutual agreement to share territory with Kikuyu cultivators, for example.

The alienation of land to Europeans transformed these former methods of land use by placing a rigid restriction on the amount of land available. By the time a Royal Commission on land was appointed in 1931, following decades of land alienation to European settlers, Africans were having to establish their claims to land in terms of Western concepts of 'ownership', 'purchase', 'sale' and 'tenancy'.

Kitching's account describes the way in which, from the mid-1920s onwards, household heads began to dispose of land by sale, or to rent it to tenants outside their own *mbari* (lineage). Colonial observers referred to this as the 'individualization' of tenure, but this again was based on a misconception, since household heads had always had very considerable latitude in land use once they were actually in possession of an area of land. The change was not one from communal to individual landholding and use, but from the concept of 'redeemable' to 'irredeemable' sale. This distinction had been of minor importance in a situation of land abundance but became central once land had become a relatively scarce *commodity* due to property titles, land alienation to settlers, and the increasing commercialization of agricultural production.

Once the concept of irredeemable sale had replaced the traditional concept of redeemability, sales of land increased, and a significant number of African 'land accumulators' began to emerge. Most sellers of land sold out of distress, to meet essential subsistence and other expenses. The increasing inequality of land ownership, combined with population pressure in Native Reserves with fixed boundaries, placed small landowning households in a vulnerable position. There were two additional important factors. Firstly, the transition from a livestock to an agricultural economy gave land accumulators the opportunity to buy land from others still oriented to pre-colonial notions of wealth in cattle, who used the proceeds of land sales to acquire livestock, which they could graze as squatters on European farms. Secondly, the 'chiefs' and headmen of the colonial state's system of indirect rule (see chapter 5) could use their positions to get land from others, by means of direct and indirect coercion.

Kitching's exhaustive historical study brings out the way in which changes in land tenure and land use and the beginning of land accumulation were instrumental in the creation of new social classes. On one hand, there was an embryonic African bourgeoisie which even during the colonial period was able to use its links with the colonial system (through mission education, government employment, headmanships, etc.) to increase income, saving and investment in land and business. On the other hand, a poor landless class developed, unable to take advantage even of the opportunities presented by the process of land reallocation after independence in 1963, and which came to form the basis of both a rural and urban proletariat.

## Colonialism and Social Changes

This chapter has focused on the historical creation and changes of labour regimes in the making of Third World economies. At the same time, restructuring the uses of labour was only one element, albeit a fundamental one, in processes of economic, social and cultural change under colonialism. Four aspects of these changes can be summarized, in conclusion.

1 The colonial experience involved resistance and adaptation (sometimes combined) by colonial peoples to the changes imposed on them. Two major instances in the sphere of cultural change concern the introduction of Western education and of the Christian religion (sometimes closely connected, as in most of Africa). Both illustrate contradictions of colonial rule, and the impossibility of ensuring its effective legitimacy over the colonized. Western education was introduced to train people for the lower ranks of the colonial civil service – as clerks, medical assistants, teachers – but those who acquired literacy in Western languages were able to continue their education beyond the limits set by their colonial (often missionary) teachers. They were able to articulate their resistance to foreign domination through turning 'Western' principles of democracy and justice (and sometimes the vocabulary of socialism) against their colonial masters.

Similarly, while Christianity was a central element of Western imperialism's ideology of its 'civilizing mission', and missionaries often functioned as informal agents of the colonial state, the meaning of Christianity could be assimilated and interpreted in different ways. It could facilitate the acceptance of colonial rule by preaching the virtue of hard work, sobriety and due deference to authority, both spiritual and temporal. On the other hand, its message of universal brotherhood and equality in the sight of God could be used to criticize the inherent racial oppression and inequality of colonial society.

2 Responses to colonial incorporation included initiatives and innovations by those who were colonized (often using their ability to draw on aspects of their culture and social organization of which colonial authorities were ignorant, or which they misunderstood). Within the (varying) constraints set by different forms of economic domination, some of the colonized became entrepreneurs and were able to accumulate through trade, land grabbing and renting, agriculture, and transport. In the sphere of religion, in Africa, many 'native' churches developed in opposition to the European

monopoly of Christianity (as also happened among the black populations of the Caribbean and the USA, themselves descended from African slaves). Whether overtly resistant to colonial rule in their teachings or not, these independent churches were necessarily subversive of the ideology that tried to justify European domination.

3 Colonial society was marked above all by ethnic divisions of labour, of legal status, political influence and social standing, between colonizers and colonized, justified by ideologies of European racial superiority. This was a potent factor contributing to the unity of anti-colonial movements, overriding (at least temporarily) many of the differences emerging among the colonized people themselves. This is taken up in chapter 5 in considering nationalism, where it is pointed out that such unity can be fragile and subject to intense strains following independence from colonial rule (decolonization).

4 The final point, then, is that the fundamental racial differentiation of colonial society could obscure the developing social differentiation among the colonized. The examples of the land question in India and Kenya provided glimpses of class formation and differentiation. These processes were often abetted, whether intentionally or unintentionally, by the policies and practices of colonial states, through their strategies of 'divide and rule' (contributing to the potentially explosive combination of extreme regional economic and social inequality with distinct cultural identities, including language and religion), incorporating and reconstituting ruling groups from pre-colonial society within the hierarchy of the colonial order (the offices of 'indirect rule', grants of land and taxes, educating the sons of chiefs and princes), and of conducting other experiments in 'planned' class formation. For example, the Tanganyika Agricultural Corporation was set up by the colonial government n 1953 to promote 'a healthy, prosperous yeoman farmer class, firmly established on the land, appreciative of its fruits, jealous of its inherent wealth, and dedicated to maintaining the family unit on it' (quoted in Cliffe and Cunningham, 1973, p. 134). This was partly a response to events in Kenya (Mau Mau), and partly an attempt to create social groups which, it was hoped, would underwrite social stability and friendliness towards the former colonial power (and the West more generally) following the inevitable moment of political independence.

In 1961, President Nyerere expressed the hopes of that moment of independence: 'This day has dawned because the people of Tanganyika have worked together in unity ... from now on we are fighting not man but nature.' In quoting these words at the end of his book on the history of Tanganyika, Iliffe (1979) noted 'but it was more complicated than that.' It proved to be more complicated precisely because the end of colonialism was not the end of capitalism. Not only did Third World countries still have to confront the unequal structures of the capitalist world market and international division of labour in efforts to achieve economic development, but the contradictory social relations and divisions of capitalism were now as much part of their societies as of those societies in which capitalism had its origins.

PART II

# Third World Economies: A Conceptual Framework

# Introduction

The first two chapters of this book have described the historical context of survival and change in the Third World. With a periodization of the expansion of Europe and a delineation of the ways in which new labour regimes broke pre-existing forms of production, they describe processes which 'made' the Third World. The four chapters in part II provide a framework for understanding processes of change in the contemporary Third World.

The framework rests on the analysis of production – which forms the basis for sustaining human life – and enables examination of the key question of how productive capacities can be increased. Basic concepts of the political economy approach are introduced in chapter 3. Ideas like productivity, the division of labour, biological and social reproduction, and the process of accumulation are explained. These are essential tools of analysis used in the rest of the book.

Chapters 4 and 5 build on this political economy framework by differentiating ideas about development, the process by which economies change and production may be increased. Chapter 4 discusses capitalist development and chapter 5 examines how socialist and nationalist ideas bear upon conceptions of development.

Chapter 6 provides ways of looking at the diversity of production within national economies in the Third World and the ways in which those diverse forms of production are integrated nationally and internationally. It discusses how capitalist development allows different forms of production to be combined in one economy and how their development may be markedly uneven, with one form of production advancing to the detriment of another.

Part II sets out a political economy of the Third World. It is abstract and condensed, and may, therefore, seem 'dry' to some readers, but it outlines a rigorous and consistent conceptual framework which will repay more than one reading.

CHAPTER THREE

# Production and Producers

## Some Concepts and Issues

### Production and Productivity: People and Nature

Economic life is concerned with production, the distribution of what is produced, and its consumption. The first involves such questions as which material goods and services are produced, in what quantities, and how their production is organized. In turn, the activities of production and how they are organized affect how the goods produced are distributed and consumed, and who consumes what. It is useful to think of the processes of production, distribution and consumption as interconnected aspects of a continuous cycle of activity necessary to the sustenance of human life.

At the same time, it is logical to start with production because one cannot consider distribution and consumption unless something first exists that can be distributed and consumed. Production in its simplest and most general sense involves interaction between people and nature. Nature supplies the raw materials for production. At one extreme, those raw materials can appear 'ready made', so to speak, as in the gathering of natural products by the Mundurucu Indians of the Brazilian Amazon (Murphy and Murphy, 1974). Alternatively, and more typically in human history, the raw materials that are used in a particular production process are the product of a prior production process. For example, the cotton used in the manufacture of textiles first has to be grown and harvested, then the harvested cotton has to be processed to separate the fibre from the other parts of the plant and, finally, the cotton fibre has to be spun into thread before it can be used in making textiles.

Both these examples involve an interaction between people and nature, and at the same time show that this interaction can occur in very different ways. These can be classified by different techniques of production used to extract raw materials from nature and to transform them into useful products for human consumption. In short, one way of distinguishing different types of production is by the different technologies they employ. 'Technology' is used here to refer to the combined 'package' of tools or instruments that people use in their interaction with nature, and the term 'technical culture' to refer to the knowledge and skills that their use involves. In the gathering activity of the Mundurucu, the 'tool' used may be the simplest of all, namely the human hand, or if a digging stick is used to get at edible roots, it serves as a kind of extension of the hand. The use of these elementary tools in procuring food from nature presupposes, however, a technical culture that contains a sophisticated knowledge of the natural environment.

An initial and general definition of production, then, is *a process in which human agency is applied in changing nature (through various means) to produce means of consumption*. As Marx (1976, pp. 283–4) put it:

> We presuppose labour in a form in which it is an exclusively human characteristic. A spider conducts operations which resemble those of the weaver, and a bee would put many a human architect to shame by the construction of its honeycomb cells. But what distinguishes the worst architect from the best of bees, is that the architect builds the cell in his mind before he constructs it in wax. At the end of every labour process, a result emerges which had already been conceived by the worker at the beginning, hence already existed ideally. Man not only effects a change of form in the materials of nature, he also realizes his own purpose in these materials.

Often associated with the idea of production is that of *productivity*. In effect, different concepts of productivity reflect notions of the efficiency of certain ways of doing things relative to other ways. Measures of productivity calculate the quantity of goods (whether for consumption or for use in further production) produced by the use of a given quantity of a particular resource, or resources.

One measure of productivity in agriculture is *yield*: the amount of the crop harvested from a given area of land (see chapter 10 on the Green Revolution, including the notion of high-yielding varieties of seeds). Another measure of productivity in agriculture, increasingly recognized with the growing interest in ecological issues, involves *energy* accounting. Starting from the other end of the process (i.e. holding output rather than input constant), relative efficiency can be calculated by the units of energy (calories), used to produce a quantity of crops of a given energy or calorific value. (Calculating the energy productivity of different techniques of production was initiated over a century ago – the pioneers of 'ecological economics' are only now being rediscovered, see Martinez-Alier, 1984, 1985).

By far the most widely used concept and measure of productivity, however, concerns the *productivity of labour*, which refers to the quantity of goods and services that someone can produce with a given expenditure of effort, usually measured or averaged out in terms of time spent working or labour time. The productivity of labour depends to a great extent on the tools or technology that the producer uses. For example, a farmer in the USA using a tractor and a combine harvester can produce, say, a ton of wheat with much less expenditure of time and effort than a farmer in India using an ox-plough. In turn, the latter can produce a ton of wheat using less time and physical effort than a farmer in Africa who lacks a plough and has to cultivate with a hoe and other hand tools.

Alternatively, one can imagine how much producers using different kinds of tools produce (on average) over a certain period of time. With respect to agriculture, a year is a relevant time-period because seasonality (of weather) is an important factor in agriculture almost everywhere. Then, say that the African farmer of the example produces 250 k of wheat in a year, the Indian farmer one tonne of wheat, and the American farmer 10 tonnes of wheat. This illustrates *differential labour productivities*; that is to say, the Indian farmer has a labour productivity four times that of the African, and the American farmer has a labour productivity ten times that of the Indian and forty times that of the African farmer. In sum, the productivity of labour is a ratio of output to the (average) labour time spent in producing it.

In these instances, increases in the productivity of labour are associated with the application of other forms of energy than human muscle power (the animal energy of the draught oxen, the energy generated by the fuel used in the internal combustion engine). Harnessing and applying other sources of energy, therefore, frees production and productivity from the limitations imposed by the energy of the human body alone, and in this case allows a larger area of land to be brought into cultivation relative to the number of those working on it. Thus, the mechanized production of grain is more efficient than hoe production in terms of the expenditure of human effort or time.

At the same time, it should be clear that different concepts and measures

FIGURE 6 Transplanting rice in West Bengal (Ben Crow)

of productivity may come into conflict with each other. For example, it is often argued that small farms are more 'efficient' than large farms, not least in Third World countries, because they obtain higher yields. On the other hand, it is often the case that those higher yields (output per unit of land) are achieved at the cost of a lower productivity of labour (output per unit of labour time), manifested in long periods of arduous and debilitating work on tiny plots. More generally it should be stressed that issues of technology, productivity, and efficiency, must be put in their proper context: the kinds of technology and technical culture that characterize a particular society can only be assessed in relation to the kind of society it is, and the ability of those who live in it to satisfy their needs.

Technologies and technical culture are encompassed in the *technical conditions of production*, conceived as the elements combined in a process of production and how these involve different types of interaction between people and nature. One crucial element is human labour in the shape of those engaged in production, and consisting of a variety of physical and mental capabilities and skills. In addition to quantity (labour time), labour should also be considered qualitatively in terms of its possession of the capacities demanded by certain kinds of tasks. If those capacities are not fully available, then this affects the productivity of labour adversely; for example, a producer who lacks the training or experience to use a complex piece of machinery efficiently, or those whose ability to perform arduous agricultural jobs in Africa or India is undermined by their low levels of nutrition and health more generally.

Another element of production is the tools or technology used – hoe, ox-plough and tractor in our example of the three farmers. A third element is the raw materials, which can vary a great deal too: soils, in terms of their fertility (and maintenance or enrichment through the use of the right kinds and quantities of fertilizer); the quality of seeds used (e.g. their resistance to disease); and the supply of water through irrigation or dependence on rainfall. They also affect the productivity of labour, and demonstrate that the original contrast between hoe, ox-plough and tractor is only one aspect of the technical conditions of production. The three farmers are all producing the same crop but in very different technical conditions which affect how much of it they produce, and most likely its quality too (in terms of nutritional content, for example).

So far, production has only been considered as an interaction between people and nature, and the activity of production as a relationship between an individual producer, certain tools or instruments of production, and raw materials. Nothing has been said concerning, for instance, how the farmers' activity involves them in relations with other people, whether the tools and raw materials they work with belong to them or to someone else, what sort of claim they have on the harvest they have produced through their efforts, how the crop is disposed of, and so on. These are questions connected with the *social conditions of production*, which encompass all the relations between people, or social relations, affecting how production is organized.

## The Division of Labour and Cooperation

We can assume that the farmers in our example did not make their own tools, an obvious assumption for the American farmer but also a realistic one for the majority of farmers in India and Africa today who use factory-produced ploughs and hoes. In that case, they had to obtain them from somewhere, ultimately from others whose work is to produce these different kinds of tools. This provides a simple example of the *social division of labour*, meaning that there are producers of different kinds of goods and services whose activities are complementary, and who are related to each other through the exchange of their products (exchange here does not necessarily mean exchange through the market). This, in turn, presupposes means of communications and transport that connect the various producers and their products (even if the producers do not meet each other directly). As the social division of labour increases in complexity, it makes available a more diverse range of goods and services.

We can still assume for the moment that the three farmers are working alone on their own farms (even though they depend on tools produced by others), which may be plausible for certain analytical purposes. It would be nonsensical, however, in the case of a car factory which is a very different kind of *unit of production*. This term denotes the social unit or institution within which the various elements of production are brought together and combined in the activities of the production process. As a unit of production, a car factory is a good example of a *technical division of labour*: the combination of different operations and tasks performed by a number of workers in the manufacture of a single product.

The social division of labour refers to the degree of specialization *between* different units of production, and how they are related through the exchange of their products, e.g. farms producing wheat, some of which goes to feed factory workers, and factories producing ploughs and tractors for use in agricultural production. The technical division of labour refers to the degree of specialization and combination of activities *within* any single unit of production or production process. At the same time, it clearly involves certain social conditions and relations, namely *cooperation* between the workers engaged in the production process and *coordination* of their efforts.

The technical division of labour within the production process suggests an enlargement of the *scale of production* beyond what would be possible for a single producer. The example of the car factory also shows that a particular social organization of production, involving cooperation and the coordination of specialized tasks, makes possible a higher productivity of labour than could be achieved by a single mechanic working alone and performing all the various tasks necessary to make a motor car. This was something like the situation in the early history of the production of motor cars before Henry Ford pioneered the techniques of 'mass' production.

Given the degree of specialization within production that modern industry typically involves, we can say that the technical division of labour in a car factory employs *complex cooperation*. But cooperation in the production process can have a positive effect on productivity even without major changes in the technologies used. In a book about *ujamaa* villages in Tanzania, von Freyhold (1979, pp. 22–5) suggests ways in which even *simple cooperation* between what are, to begin with, different units of production (peasant households) can help raise the productivity of labour, as it allows:

1 *planning*, by making performance more predictable, as the pooling of labour helps cancel out the qualitative differences between individual producers (of strength, skill, health, experience, and so on);
2 *economies of scale* in the construction of common facilities (e.g. grain stores, water tanks) and in guarding common fields against pests and vermin;
3 *complementation effects*, that is, 'adding individual labour to a project which only makes sense as a completed whole' (e.g. each individual digging a section of an irrigation channel, or building a section of a fence to protect crops);
4 *timing effects*, that is, concentrating effort to carry out tasks that have to be finished within a critical time (this relates to seasonality, above all periods of rainfall of uncertain duration);
5 *pooling of knowledge* and experience in collective decision making.

The main point about cooperation conveyed in these practical illustrations is that 'the whole is greater than the sum of the parts'. Even simple cooperation between a relatively small group of producers using the same technology as before (hand tools) but on communal fields, can result in a product larger than the aggregate of what they would each have produced working on their own. In this case, changes in the social conditions of production can help raise the productivity of labour directly (by protecting crops) and indirectly (by increasing the well-being of the producers). Moreover, von Freyhold (1979, p. 25) suggests that this kind of social change can facilitate the introduction of new technologies:

> Both the complementation and the timing effects are also useful when it comes to the transition to a higher technological level, for instance from hoe to plough. As long as certain operations are still done by hand (for instance clearing and harvesting), while some are already done with the help of oxen, the complementation effect can be employed to overcome the differences in the scale of the various operations (for instance when thirty people clear an area of stumps on which ten people can plough), while the timing effect can be used to level out labour peaks which the unbalanced technology entails.

## Reproduction

It has been implied that the various elements of the production process themselves have to be produced. Even the land used in agriculture, while originally a 'gift' of nature, is changed through people's interaction with it – its fertility can deteriorate or be maintained or enriched. Tools and machines used in production become worn-out after a time; raw materials tend to be used up more quickly, for example, seeds and fertilizers are used in each cycle of agricultural production. Therefore these elements of production have to be replaced, or *reproduced*, for production to continue in future. Here we want to concentrate on the production and reproduction of that most vital element of the whole process, namely the producer.

What has been said so far about production has contained no reference to, nor used the prepositions of, gender. Probably you did not notice this, nor then the achievement of writing so many sentences in English without referring to 'he' or 'she', and especially the former! (In the Turkish and Swahili languages, for example, there is one preposition for the third person singular, regardless of gender). If the example had described one of the farmers as 'he', or referred to 'his' labour or 'his' tools, probably this would not have struck you as significant because of the tendency to assume that certain kinds of productive activities are 'men's work'.

The significance of gender has been signalled because we are approaching an area which many people think of as self-evidently 'women's work'. The first and indispensable step, and also the most obvious, in the 'production of the producer' is that of *biological reproduction*. People have to be born for society to continue, and biology determines that only women can bear children. But this is only the first step. A child has to be cared for and raised until it reaches that stage of maturity when it can become independent, economically and in other ways. We will call this *generational reproduction*. A third aspect of reproduction is daily *reproduction or maintenance*. Adults as well as children need to replace or restore the physical and mental energies that they use up in the course of their daily lives. They have to eat and to rest, which requires the provision and preparation of food and drink, the maintenance of somewhere to live, clothes to wear which have to be washed, and so on.

Now, the 'facts' of biology do not exhaust what we need to know about biological reproduction, let alone the other aspects of reproduction. Biology imposes on us the need to consume a certain minimum amount of food and liquid at regular intervals in order to survive, but that does not tell us anything about the great variety of ways in which the production, distribution and consumption of food, drink and other necessities of life (shelter, tools, etc.) have been organized in different societies. Likewise, the biological status of women as child-bearers cannot in itself tell us anything about the variety of ways in which (hetero) sexual relations, as a precondition of human reproduction, have been organized in different types of societies, nor the necessary labour of raising children and of maintaining children and adults on a day-to-day basis. The range of social processes of production and reproduction cannot be deduced from, nor reduced to, a few biological facts.

It is necessary then to distinguish between 'sex' as a biological category, and *gender as a social category*. The latter refers to ideas about male and female roles, about the proper 'place' that each occupies in the scheme of things (whether that scheme is seen as 'ordained' by some or other deity, by 'nature', or whatever), about what constitutes appropriate or desirable (or inappropriate or undesirable) forms of appearance and behaviour for men and for women, and so on. Such ideas cannot be explained by physiological differences alone. Apart from anything else these kinds of ideas, and the social practices they inform or justify, vary enormously between different societies and cultures (and even within them), which means that they require some other explanation than what appears to be physiologically universal.

In other words, even child-bearing is a social practice, conditioned by social relations and ideologies. Sexual relations in different societies (and within them among particular social groups) are determined by different patterns of courtship and residence. The link between (hetero) sexual relations, conception and child-birth is regulated, among other factors, by the methods of contraception available. While it is 'ordained by nature' that only women can bear children there is nothing 'natural' about *whether* all women bear children, *when* they bear them, *how many* children they bear, nor that in many cultures there is a particular pressure on women to bear *sons*.

The same point about what is determined by nature and what is determined by social relations and ideologies (religious or otherwise) applies, of course, just as much to generational reproduction and everyday maintenance. There is nothing 'natural' about the fact that responsibility for bringing up children devolves on their mothers (or grandmothers, or aunts, or older sisters, or female servants, in different societies and social groups). Nor is there any 'natural' necessity that women should carry out the tasks of maintaining the current generation of producers as well as their children, who will provide the next generation. These tasks are often termed domestic labour. In so far as domestic labour is practised as 'women's work', it provides a special case of the social division of labour in which certain activities are carried out by a particular category of people. As it is a gender category, this is often referred to as a sexual division of labour.

The division of labour was defined above as the specialization of various kinds of productive activities, whether distributed between different units of production or coordinated within them. The sexual division of labour is a somewhat different concept which signifies that certain kinds of activities are allocated according to the position that people occupy in particular structures of social relations, in this case social relations of gender. Divisions of labour in this sense are not restricted to gender relations but are also widely manifested, for example, in racial or *ethnic divisions of labour* so evident in colonial economies (see chapter 2), and which as a result of colonial history still persist, or are reconstructed, in some parts of the Third World *and* in those Western countries which encouraged labour migration from the Third World.

Generally, sexual divisions of labour are accompanied and justified by ideologies of men's 'place' and women's 'place' in society, which go beyond the different kinds of work regarded as 'fitting' for them. The 'private' or 'domestic' domain tends to be seen as the province of women, and the 'public' domain that of men. The latter may include wage employment outside the home, and participation in 'public affairs' more generally, whether particular religious and ceremonial roles and activities, deliberations of village councils, holding office in a cooperative, or active membership of a trade union.

A Peruvian woman, Aida Hernández, has recounted her struggles to be taken seriously as a leader in an agricultural cooperative, including the struggle to convince the other women members of the cooperative that they could and should play a more active role in its affairs: 'the women, themselves, actually believe that we, the *compañeras* (sisters), are inferior beings' (Johnson and Bernstein, 1982, p. 186). This observation conveys a great deal about the power of ideology, which is not simply a set of abstract ideas but is lived through people's everyday practices and experiences. Ideology can reinforce – and reproduce – particular social relations, in this instance those of gender inequalities, above all when the ideology is 'internalized' by those who are subordinated by it – when they accept the 'place' in the world it defines for them. (Of course, other ideologies can contest and seek to transform the existing order and the social 'places' it prescribes).

In this discussion of reproduction with special reference to gender, our framework has broadened in several respects. It has been suggested that productive capacity should include not only technology and technical culture but also people's capacities to organize themselves to make decisions about production and carry them out. This was also indicated in von Freyhold's points about the advantages of cooperation in *ujamaa* villages. At the same time, the remarks about sexual and ethnic divisions of labour indicate that all these aspects of productive capacity, including the opportunity to participate in organizing production, may be distributed in different (and unequal) ways between various social groups and categories.

## Surplus Product and Accumulation

In all societies, those engaged in production must produce more than is required for their own immediate consumption, both to sustain those not involved in production, and to replace the tools and raw materials they have used up. Those not involved in production include children; therefore, part of what is produced is needed for generational reproduction. Replacement of tools and materials that have been used up may be termed material reproduction. To satisfy the requirements of both types of reproduction, there must be some quantity of goods produced that is 'surplus' to the immediate consumption needs of the producers themselves (i.e. 'surplus' to the satisfaction of their own daily reproduction or maintenance, as it was termed above).

Societies like that of the Munducuru are often termed 'subsistence societies' (Bujra, 1983) because whatever was 'surplus' in the sense defined above was used for the reproduction of subsistence (through the reproduction of the producers and of the material elements of production). Such societies were reproduced at more or less the same levels of subsistence (consumption) and of productive capacity, and they were also societies in which everyone was a producer, whether currently, in the past (the very old and the disabled), or in the future (the very young). This does not mean, of course, that everyone had an equivalent or equal status as producers, for example, because of the effects of sexual divisions of labour.

That they produced no 'surplus' beyond that required for reproducing the means of subsistence (at more or less constant levels of consumption) does not mean that those societies were 'poor' in their own terms. The modes of interaction with nature (technical cultures) some of them had developed enabled them to satisfy their needs with relatively little expenditure of labour time and effort. Thus the anthropologist Sahlins (1972) has provocatively termed hunting and gathering bands 'the original affluent society'. More generally, this relates to the point made earlier that 'the kinds of technology and technical culture that characterize a particular society can only be assessed in relation to the kind of society it is, and the ability of those who live in it to satisfy their needs'.

Bujra (1983; see also Wolf, 1982, chapter 3) distinguishes 'subsistence' from pre-capitalist 'surplus producing' societies, which had levels of material production and productivity beyond what was required for the subsistence of the producers (and its reproduction). What was 'surplus' in this sense was appropriated by classes of non-producers. 'Surplus producing' societies, therefore, are defined by *social relations of production through which one class systematically appropriates the surplus produced by another*.

The social relations of production in this context refer to the control over property – whether exercised by economic, political or military means or some combination of these – through which a dominant class of non-producers exercises its claims on part of the social product, i.e. the 'surplus product'. In pre-capitalist societies, agriculture was generally the major sphere of productive activity. Therefore, direct or indirect control over land also meant control over those who worked on it, and who had to deliver their surplus product as tribute, taxes or rents to those who ruled them. (In one type of pre-capitalist society, that characterized by slavery, the dominant class of non-producers actually owned the producers themselves as one form of property, in addition to owning means of production such as land, animals and implements).

The dominant or ruling classes of pre-capitalist 'surplus producing' societies consisted of royal dynasties or military or civilian aristocracies, religious or secular bureaucracies, merchant groups, or some combination of these. Their consumption and reproduction – as well as that of the often large retinues that served them (servants, soldiers, clerks, court painters and poets) – rested on appropriating the surplus product of those engaged in production (slaves, serfs, peasants, artisans). While some of these societies experienced periods of great expansion, sometimes associated wih changes in the techniques and organization of production (as well as communications, transport, trade, military power, etc.), the sphere of production was of concern to the ruling classes only in so far as it was the ultimate source of their wealth (through tribute, taxes, rents), their power (supplying arms and soldiers), and their glory (enabling them to consume luxuries, to build palaces, and act as patrons of religion and the arts). While pre-capitalist ruling classes often sought to regulate economic activity, and sometimes to stimulate it, they did not attempt to 'save' and reinvest the surplus product to develop the productive capacities of society in any generalized and systematic way, that is, by continuously expanding the scale and efficiency of production.

This last process of productive accumulation or *accumulation*, for short, made its historic appearance with the emergence of capitalist society on the basis of a unique set of social conditions of production. These included the separation of the producers from the means of production, the formation of labour power (or capacity to work) as a commodity, thereby giving rise to 'labour markets', and the generalization of commodity production (or production for the market). The social relations of production of capitalism produce two basic classes: one class that owns property in the means of production (the class of capital or capitalist class), and another class that, lacking means of production with which to produce its own subsistence, has to sell its labour power to those owning means of production in exchange for wages with which to buy its means of subsistence (the class of labour or working class). Under capitalism, by contrast with other (pre-capitalist) 'surplus producing' societies, all the elements of production tend to become commodities including, most critically, the labour power of the producers themselves, hence the term 'generalized commodity production'.

From the standpoint of the class of capital, the purpose of production for the market is to achieve profit, which brings capitalists into competition with each other to produce commodities as cheaply as possible. Lowering the unit costs of production of commodities is, thus, the most basic single criterion of 'efficiency' under capitalism, and typically involves reducing the unit cost of labour. The key to this is attempting to maximize the output of labour (its productivity) while minimizing its costs (wages), thereby increasing the amount of 'surplus' appropriated. This enhances the level of profits and hence the possibilities of accumulation: investment in even more 'efficient' ways of producing commodities (through expanding the scale of production, and the productivity of workers), to be able to compete more effectively, achieve greater profits, therefore accumulate more ... So continues the cycle in which accumulation is the key link connecting the distinctive social conditions of production of capitalism with its historically unprecedented (if highly uneven) growth of productive capacity, associated above all with industrialization.

The development of the productive capacities of societies depends on both the size of the product and the uses to which it is put. Both are determined above all by the social conditions and relations of production, and, it can further be suggested, by the struggles of needs and interests they give rise to. In all societies, the size of the social product is determined by the prevailing productivities of labour. In class societies, whether pre-capitalist or capitalist, the size of the surplus product (what is available for appropriation and, possibly, accumulation) reflects the outcomes of struggles between classes of producers and non-producers over the distribution of the social product, and often over its uses as well. This means that definitions of 'subsistence' are also involved in these struggles. Rarely do conceptions of adequate or 'fair' levels of subsistence ('standards of living') correspond to physiologically minimal criteria for survival, but such conceptions – and the extent to which they are satisfied in practice – express the relative strength and effectiveness of the social forces that contest them, and endeavour to raise or depress them.

## Not by 'Economics' Alone

In a preliminary way, this chapter has sketched some important concepts for understanding economic activity, and some connections between these concepts: production, productive capacity, and productivity, social divisions of labour and cooperation, production and reproduction, subsistence and surplus product, appropriation and accumulation. The concepts and issues introduced provide an initial checklist of questions concerning production and producers. As these are *analytical* questions, they can be addressed to any sphere of economic activity, and on any scale, whether a household or a village, a factory or an industrial sector, a regional or national economy, or the international economy:

1. what is produced, and how much?
2. in what ways is it produced, and by whom?
3. how is the product appropriated and distributed?
4. how does this affect the division of what is produced between consumption and accumulation?
5. how does this affect the levels of consumption of different groups and classes?

In practice, the investigation of such questions in relation to a particular farming household or industrial enterprise is likely to involve analysis of circuits of economic activity extending far beyond these individual units of production, of how their social and technical conditions of production are determined within broader structures of social relations and divisions of labour.

These questions provide a useful starting point for many of the issues with which this book is concerned, but it is only a starting point in at least two senses. The first is that answers to these questions tend to become more elaborate and complex when one addresses specific cases in the real world (and on an increasing scale). In fact, the questions suggest both an ascending order of analytical complexity and of their potential for controversy, which is the second sense in which they are only a starting point. The first question appears to be informational, whereas the others amplify issues of such general concern as 'Who does what?' and 'Who gets what?'.

The approach informing the above list of questions, and the various chapters of this book, is that of political economy, based on the recognition that there is no neutral or purely 'technical' discipline of economics free from cognitive and normative assumptions about how societies work, and without implications for the needs and interests of particular groups in society (Cole, Cameron and Edwards, 1983). In fact, the belief that there could be such an 'economics' is itself an ideological product of capitalism. A useful *political economy of production and producers* cannot, therefore, be reduced or restricted to 'economics' in the sense understood by many of its academic practitioners, that is, as an objective set of techniques for calculating the most 'efficient' ways of doing things abstracted from the historical circumstances, politics, cultures, and needs and interests of people occupying different places in social relations of production and divisions of labour.

This becomes all the more apparent if a further question is added: 'What is necessary to achieve economic change?'. In practice, this question takes the form 'What is necessary to achieve *desirable* economic change, and desirable for whom?', which is being debated just as fiercely in Britain in 1987 as in many Third World countries. The ways in which questions of desirable economic change – or '*development*' – are posed by the history and ideologies of the modern world, beyond the reach of 'economics' alone, are taken up in the next two chapters.

CHAPTER FOUR

# Development I

## Variations on Capitalism

'Development' means significantly increasing the productive capacities of societies, establishing new and better (more productive) ways of doing things and making things so as to make more wealth available. Development, in this sense, suggests major changes in the social and technical conditions of production, however protracted or uneven the historical course of such changes may be. The encompassing quality of social change associated with processes of development is conveyed in a distinction that Dowd (1967, p. 153) made between economic growth and development: 'growth is a quantitative process, involving principally the extension of an already existing structure of production, while development suggests qualitative change, the creation of new economic *and non-economic structures*' (emphasis added). Similarly, it has been suggested that the industrial revolution in Britain was a process of 'total' change – 'a change of social structure, of ownership and economic power in society; as well as a change of scale' (Kitching, 1982, p. 11).

Seers (1979) pointed out that development is invariably a normative as well as an analytical concept, and becomes synonymous with improvement or progress. In his view, the core of its normative content is the idea that development should satisfy 'the necessary conditions for a universally acceptable aim, the realization of the potential of human personality' (p. 10). The conditions Seers outlined are:

1 the capacity to buy physical necessities, in the first place food;
2 having a job (in the sense of some form of useful activity, not necessarily paid employment);
3 equalization of income distribution (as glaring inequalities in income distribution not only reflect the existence of mass poverty but are associated with, and underpin, social, political and cultural inequalities);
4 adequate educational levels (literacy);
5 participation in the political process (democracy);
6 'belonging to a nation that is truly independent'.

In short, for Seers the additional wealth created by enhancing the productive capacities of a society contributes to 'development' only if that wealth is used to satisfy 'basic needs', broadly defined as social, political and cultural needs, as well as material needs, essential to 'the realization of the potential of human personality'.

> The questions to ask about a country's development are therefore: What has been happening to poverty? What has been happening to unemployment? What has been happening to inequality? . . . From a long-term viewpoint, economic growth is for a poor country a necessary condition of reducing poverty. But it is not a sufficient condition. To realize the development potential of a high rate of economic growth depends on policy. A country where economic growth is slow or negligible may be busy reshaping its political institutions so that, when growth comes, it will mean development; such a country could develop faster in the long run than one at present enjoying fast growth but with political power remaining very firmly in the hands of a rich minority. (Seers 1979, p. 12)

In this conception, economic growth is a necessary but not sufficient condition of 'development', the distinction being an explicitly normative one in contrast with that of Dowd quoted above. Dowd's definition of development might include cases like the Brazilian 'economic miracle' of the 1960s and 1970s (see chapter 11), which for Seers provided an example of 'growth without development'.

Seers also suggested, in the extract above, that the relationship between growth and development can vary according to the time perspective adopted, and in conjunction with the political relations and structures prevailing in different countries. Underlying his observations are the major questions concerning any political system: Who wields effective power within it, by what means, and to what ends?' *and* How is that power, its means, and its ends, contested by others?. These questions bring together *interests* and *needs*, defining an area of analysis in which the interests (and needs) of some conflict with the needs (and interests) of others, above all in class societies where property, wealth, and political and cultural power are distributed highly unequally and tend to be concentrated in the same hands.

Some of the 'ways in which questions of desirable economic change – or 'development' – are posed by the history and ideologies of the modern world' can be usefully highlighted by focusing on three terms of overarching contemporary significance: capitalism, socialism, and nationalism. Their consideration in this chapter and the next is prefaced by some observations about the Industrial Revolution, which has provided the original and persisting framework of ideas about development over the last two hundred years.

## The Industrial Revolution as a Framework

The industrial revolution and the kind of society it produced has been the principal point of reference for debates about development for the following interconnected reasons, both historical and ideological.

1 The 'revolutionary' character of the industrial revolution refers to the

massive development of the productive forces and capacities of society it made possible. In this way, the industrial revolution is usually taken to be one of the most significant landmarks (or the single most significant) that defines *modern* history, demarcating the epoch we live in (say, the late eighteenth century onwards) from what had gone before.

2 It is understood to be definitive of modern *world* history. The international power and the wealth of Britain in the nineteenth century, not least as manifested in the extent of its colonial empire and its role as 'the world's banker', was associated with its status as the pioneer of modern industrialization. In this sense, Britain was seen as a model to emulate *and* to 'overtake' by the dominant classes of other countries for whom 'the primary goal of development, or more exactly of industrialization, was to protect or enhance the power and independence of the nation-states over which they ruled' (Kitching, 1982, p. 3). The rest of Western Europe, the USA, Japan and other countries (which form the membership of OECD today) industrialized in the wake of the 'first industrial revolution' in Britain.

3 What follows from this is that 'industrialized' and 'non-industrialized' became conventions for classifying the economies of different countries, and the place they occupy in the world economy or international division of labour. On this criterion, the countries of the Third World, which are mostly former colonies of European imperial powers, are often lumped together as 'non-industrialized'. Moreover, their (relative) lack of industrialization has commonly been taken as synonymous with their lack of development or their 'underdevelopment', not least by many people in the Third World.

4 No less important is the fact that Britain and the other countries mentioned above underwent a *capitalist* industrial revolution. That is, not only did they experience revolutionary transformations in the sphere of technology and its applications, and in the productivity of labour, but these occurred (and could only occur) through fundamental changes of a particular kind in the social conditions and relations of production. The potency of the industrial revolution as example, as the original and still pervasive reference point of modern history, thus combines social, political and ideological dimensions with those of an economic and technological kind.

5 The importance of the industrial revolution as original example and persisting frame of reference can be traced through the history of reactions to it, whether positive or negative or some more complex combination of the two. In a challenging book, Kitching (1982) distinguishes '*populism*' as one kind of response to large-scale industrialization. 'Populism', in Kitching's sense, applies to ideological currents and political movements rooted in the threat experienced by small producers (artisans, peasants, small farmers and businessmen) as a result of modern industrialization, and to the theories of various intellectuals who have identified themselves with the fate of small-scale production and have championed its merits as the basis of an alternative 'model' of development. It is extremely suggestive

that the populist thinkers and movements Kitching considers correspond to a historical sequence of areas that were successively and increasingly subjected to the effects of industrialization, *whether it was occurring in those areas or elsewhere*. In the latter case, its effects were transmitted through the increasing world market integration and changing international divisions of labour of the nineteenth and twentieth centuries (see chapters 5 and 6).

6 Even more important as a reaction to industrialization, and above all capitalist industrialization, is modern *socialism*, especially as influenced by Karl Marx. Marx lived in London from 1849 until his death in 1883 and remains the most influential of the contemporary observers and theorists of the new world created by industrial capitalism, among those who disagree with his ideas as much as those who have sought to develop and apply them. The final point, then, is that Marx's ideas were taken up by others who attempted to put them into practice, notably the Russian communists who carried out the revolution of 1917 and directed the subsequent industrialization of the Soviet Union. Leaving aside the (undoubtedly interesting) question of whether the methods of Soviet industrialization and the nature of Soviet society today are a true expression of Marx's ideas or not, it is important to stress that the Soviet experience presented itself in the twentieth century as an alternative, and in opposition, to capitalist development as represented by Britain's industrial revolution and those which followed it.

## Variations on Capitalism

### *Modernization*

> Historically, modernization is the process of change toward those types of social, economic and political systems that have developed in Western Europe and North America from the seventeenth century to the nineteenth and have then spread to other European countries and in the nineteenth and twentieth centuries to the South American, Asian and African continents. (Eisenstadt, 1966, p. 1)
>
> [Social scientists] persist in using the term [modernization] not only because it is a part of popular speech, but also because they recognize that these many changes (in individual attitudes, in social behaviour, in economics, and in politics) are related to one another – that many countries in the developing world today are experiencing a comprehensive process of change which Europe and America once experienced and which is more than the sum of many small changes. (Weiner, 1966, preface)

These statements are useful because they are quite explicit about taking the 'model' of what it is to be modern or developed from the historical experience of Western Europe and North America, *and* about generalizing that 'model' to the countries of the 'developing world' – those of 'the South American, Asian and African continents'. At the same time, this act of projection from Western history suggests a type of development that is both *viable* and *desirable* as a scenario for the countries of the Third World. In this usage, the term 'modernization' provides an apparently more universal, and less ethnocentric, wrapping for a package of ideas that a generation or two earlier was called more baldly '*Westernization*'.

What are the contents of this package? The brief extracts quoted suggest that they include economic, political and social systems, social behaviour and individual attitudes – all components of 'a comprehensive process of change' of the kind associated with development, as noted above (p. 00). In economic terms the key element is industrialization. The thoroughly modernized or developed Western countries which provide a 'model' for others to emulate, are above all industrial economies occupying the top positions in the 'economic league table' of national *per capita* income. In addition, they have political systems based on representative or parliamentary democracy.

At the level of social structure social organization, concepts of modernization (with all their specific variations and emphasis) contain two essential and related ideas. One is that of *structural differentiation*: that modernization entails an increase in the complexity (and typically the scale of interaction) of societies, the emergence of new kinds of institutions and roles with more specialized functions and activities. In effect, 'structural differentiation' is an application (and generalization) to social organization of the idea of the division of labour, discussed in chapter 3 in relation to production. The second, and closely connected idea, is that of '*rationality*', that the specialization of activities in particular institutions and roles makes the latter more 'efficient', hence 'rational', instruments for carrying out the social functions or tasks assigned to them.

This brief sketch of the content of modernization remains descriptive. It gives us a meaning of modernization as the process of change or transition from economic, political and social structures that are 'traditional' or 'underdeveloped' to those that are modern or developed (possessing the qualities industrial, democratic, and structurally differentiated). It has not yet been indicated what the connection of modernization with capitalism is (beyond the implied injunction to 'follow in the footsteps of the West'), what the agencies of modernization might be, or what is the content of 'modern' or 'modernizing' behaviour and attitudes. These issues can be addressed and brought together, first by considering the view of capitalism as a system of 'free enterprise'.

### *Free enterprise: the individual and the market*

Models of modernization that do confront questions of cause and agency, that is, attempt to provide some explanation of what or who brings about modernization and development, typically do so in *psychological* terms, in terms of the values and aspirations that inform the motivations of individuals. One expression of this is the idea of modernization as a process of diffusion, the spread of a desire to have the goods and services that modernity makes available to areas or sectors that are still 'traditional' or 'backward'. This 'revolution of rising expectations' provides the mechanism spurring people to acquire the means of obtaining these new goods and services, in short to endeavour to become modern, to 'develop'.

The emphasis on a psychological mechanism underlying processes of modernization and development, and on individual behaviour (moreover, behaviour of an acquisitive or 'maximizing' kind) as their key agency, is not surprising as a particular notion of *individualism* is itself a major ideological product of Western history. Analytically, individualism views societies as aggregates of individuals pursuing their own ends: society is simply the sum of its parts (individuals with their own motivations, goals, etc.).

FIGURE 7 Feeding the cities: a major grain market in North-West India (Courtesy: Sharma Studio, Lajpat Nagar, New Delhi, India)

Normatively, individualism views the free enterprise (or market) system as providing the best or most efficient mechanism through which the qualities that individuals possess and the efforts they make are rewarded. The 'logic' of the market, operating through the 'laws of supply and demand' rewards individuals for their efforts and skills in taking calculated risks. The merit of the market, in this view, is that it provides incentives for individuals to work hard and to invest their resources skilfully. Competition between them is socially beneficial as those seeking to sell goods and services have to find the most efficient methods of doing so ('supply'), in order to attract customers for their commodities ('demand'). In bringing together supply and demand in this way, the market allows for the effective allocation and utilization of resources such as land, labour, credit, raw materials, technology and other goods, according to the rationality of 'profit maximization'.

The impartial rationality of the market consists precisely in matching effort ('investment') with reward ('profit'). In this way, it is deemed to be both *efficient* in determining the allocation and utilization of resources, and *fair* in determining who gets what. It presents a formal equality of opportunity to all who enter it, but as they are unequally endowed with talents and act in the market with different degrees of effort and skill, then they leave the market with unequal rewards. The American psychologist David McClelland has expressed the logic of this process in a horticultural metaphor: 'The free enterprise system ... may be compared to a garden in which all plants are allowed to grow until some crowd others out' (McClelland, 1963, p. 90).

Individualist theories of market economy and market-led development rest on a fundamental psychological premise of assumed universal validity, namely, that self-interest is the driving force of human activity. This premise is then linked to another argument: that the market provides a unique mechanism through which individuals, in pursuing their own ends, thereby create wealth which benefits society in general as well as themselves in particular. According to Adam Smith (1723–90), the 'hidden hand' of the market functions to integrate and harmonize the competitive economic behaviour of individuals for the greater good of society, and to create 'the wealth of nations'. For others, the link between individual interest and social well-being is much more problematic, and the nature of this linkage has been one of the most enduring preoccupations of social and political philosophy. Thomas Hobbes (1588–1679), who lived when England was undergoing its long transition to capitalist society, argued that there would be a 'war of all against all' leading to chaos and social disintegration, unless there was a source of authority to regulate the pursuit of individual appetite and interest.

Even theories which assume or advocate the institutions of a (capitalist) market economy, therefore, need to posit some means of ensuring integration and cohesion in societies in which the pursuit of individual interest is the dynamic of economic progress. To achieve the latter without a 'war of all against all', requires some means of establishing rules of market competition and seeing that they are acknowledged and adhered to. For example, at the very least, there must be laws to safeguard private property, to define and enforce the terms of contracts concerning property transactions and other market exchanges. What is needed, therefore, is an agency believed to be impartial, that stands 'above the fray' of market competition, that regulates the behaviour of individuals in the interest of society as a whole.

For most people, as for Hobbes (who termed it 'Leviathan'), this agency is the *state*, an institution which is accorded authority to represent the interest of society as a whole precisely because it is deemed to stand 'above' the specific and competing interests of which society is composed, whether those of individuals or particular groups of individuals. The ideological authority of the state is associated with its role as the provider of laws regulating social conduct, and it is more effective to the extent that these laws (and the procedure by which they are arrived at) are regarded as legitimate by those subject to them.

This not only applies to regulating activities within the market. As noted above, the logic of this market is necessarily inegalitarian in its effects: some flourish while others are 'crowded out', and this is inevitably manifested in inequalities in the distribution of income, in access to economic resources, in political influence and social prestige, and so on. The state, then, must also be able to contain and manage the potential social conflicts generated by these inequalities.

If the 'order maintenance function' of the state is necessary to the stability and reproduction of societies in which a capitalist market economy is fully established, then it can be even more critical to societies undergoing modernization, and requiring new agencies of social integration to keep pace with the effects of growing structural differentiation. 'The state, the law, political groupings and other associations are particularly salient in this integration', and any failure of agencies of integration (above all those of the state) to regulate the more differentiated society produced by modernization and the development of market relations will result in 'social disturbances – mass hysteria, outbursts of violence, religious and political movements etc'. (Smelser, 1968, p. 127).

Beyond the 'law and order' and integration functions of the state, it can also be assigned a more active role in promoting development by making market institutions more effective, for example, removing 'obstacles' to the proper functioning of the market (such as modes of allocating resources based on 'traditional', i.e. non-market, principles), and enhancing the access of (at least some) individuals to market activity and competition, e.g. through credit, taxation, and trade policies that 'reward' entrepreneurship.

This can be illustrated by the kind of land reform advocated in Latin America in the 1960s by the modernizing strategy of the 'Alliance for Progress' (which was in part the response of the US government to the 'threat' posed by the Cuban revolution). The argument went as follows. A 'traditional' system of large landholdings farmed by peasant tenants prevents the efficient utilization of land and productive reinvestment of income derived from it. On one hand, large landowners have an interest in what happens on the land only because it provides them with income from rent. These *rentiers* are typically 'absentee' landowners who do not use their incomes for accumulation to boost productive capacities in agriculture, but spend them on 'conspicuous' consumption and perhaps on speculative investment, e.g. in urban property markets. On the other hand, their peasant tenants, who actually organize production on a small-scale, household basis, lack both the capital to develop productive capacities, and the incentive to do so because their returns on their labour are limited by what they have to pay in rent. In this situation, then, a land reform to break up large holdings and redistribute land can release the entrepreneurial energies of the former tenants who now become owners:

> a certain proportion of the new peasant beneficiaries will probably fail as entrepreneurs. Because some of these new entrepreneurs are going to fail

> does not mean that it will be unnecessary to carry out agrarian reform. But it will be necessary to caution against too rigid an institutional link between the beneficiaries and the land, so that a natural selection may take place later which will allow those who fail to be eliminated. (Chonchol, 1970, p. 160)

In this view, then, the rationale of land reform is, first, to free agriculture from the restrictions of 'traditional' land ownership, and, second, to allow for development through competition between those who receive land. Of the latter, those who are successful entrepreneurs will be able over time to acquire the land, and perhaps hire the labour, of those who are unsuccessful. What Chonchol refers to as a process of 'natural selection' embodies the same logic as McClelland's metaphor of the free enterprise 'garden' quoted above.

In addition, it is worth pointing out that 'obstacles' to the development of capitalism seen as a 'free enterprise' system may include not only those arising from 'traditional' modes of allocating resources and 'traditional' cultural traits, but also from tendencies to 'monopoly' arising from the workings of the market itself. It is argued, for example, that trade union organization promoting 'restrictive practices' (like the closed shop) obstructs the efficiency of the labour market, 'artificially' raising the price of labour power and hence inhibiting investment. Again, it might be argued that the concentration of capital in huge conglomerates (like multinational corporations) inhibits 'healthy' market competition between capitalists. In either case adherents of the free enterprise position might propose government intervention to limit the activities of trade unions and to regulate company mergers and takeovers. In practice, they are typically more preoccupied with the former than with the latter.

Western 'models' of the type outlined here combine ideas about the basic dynamic of change at the level of individual behaviour, with ideas about institutional conditions that allow the aspirations, motivations and energies of individuals to express themselves in ways that contribute to economic development, and modernization more generally (the institutions of the market and the 'free enterprise' system). Such models, of course, are not 'neutral', and embody a particular view of how Western societies (and Japan) developed, which is then recommended, as it were, to the Third World. Moreover, the general recommendation and the specific advice that often accompanies it, compete with other models presented by contemporary history, notably the development experience of the Soviet Union. 'East–West competition' (between the First and Second Worlds) has, of course, political, economic and military aspects as well as ideological ones, and acquired a new arena with the post-1945 process of decolonization in the Third World:

> Unless we (Americans) learn our lesson and find ways of stimulating that drive for achievement under freedom in poor countries, the Communists will go on providing it all around the world. We can go on building dikes to maintain freedom and impoverishing ourselves to feed and arm the people behind those dikes, but only if we develop the entrepreneurial spirit in those

> countries will we have a sound foreign policy. Only then can they look after their own dikes and become economically self-sufficient. (McClelland, 1964, p. 176)

How then do modernization theorists explain processes of change in Third World countries, and their contradictions, that frustrate the prescriptions of the Western model (when footsteps start to falter ...)? Is it because there is something wrong with the model, or because there is something 'wrong' with the Third World? The 'modernizing lands are societies-in-a-hurry. Emulating what the advanced Western societies have become today, they want to get there faster. Accordingly, they force the tempo of Western development. Even more serious, as a result of their hurried pace, they often disorder the sequence of Western development' (Lerner, 1967, p. 24). Daniel Lerner, a leading pioneer of modernization theory, is certain that the 'model' is right, and the Third World and its people 'wrong'. In another article, he expressed this in terms of 'The Want–Get ratio'.

$$\text{Frustration} = \frac{\text{want}}{\text{get}}$$

> Frustration rises in the measure that the numerator of Want exceeds the denominator of Get. In traditional societies, frustration remained fairly constant and at a relatively low level because wants (at least in the form of articulated demands) were relatively few and unchanging. Frustration is accelerating in transitional societies because articulated wants are increasing, diversifying, and spreading at very rapid and erratic rates ... Transitional peoples are accelerating their manifold demands beyond the supply capacity of their institutions and resources, including the capacity of individuals with increasing demands to adapt their personal behaviour in such ways as to increase supplies. (Lerner, 1968, pp. 392–3)

In short, Lerner is saying that people in the Third World want too much ('articulated wants') too quickly (thereby forcing the tempo and often disordering the sequence of development called for by the Western model). As well as this impatience, Lerner's last sentence seems to argue that people in the Third World who want more of the goods that development offers have to learn to work harder or more efficiently to get them. The underlying theme is that the 'revolution of rising expectations' can give rise to widespread and mounting frustration that manifests itself in social disorder. This was expressed very clearly by another American social scientist, Ithiel da Sola Pool, who was an adviser to the US government during the Vietnam war:

> In the Congo, in Vietnam, in the Dominican Republic, it is clear that order depends on somehow compelling newly mobilized strata to return to a measure of passivity and defeatism from which they have been aroused by the process of modernization. At least temporarily, the maintenance of order requires a lowering of newly acquired aspirations and levels of political activity. (Quoted in Chomsky, 1969, p. 33)

In conclusion, it is worth summarizing some of the criticisms levelled at Western models of development of the modernization and 'market-led' varieties. The first is that their view of 'traditional society' is a *caricature* (e.g. 'passivity' and 'defeatism'), presenting a prevailing image of Third World peoples as hitherto conservative, lethargic, and lacking in history, and currently unable to cope with the demands of modernization. The latter can be expressed as a reluctance to work hard or efficiently for what they want (Lerner), or mobilizing around anti-colonial and anti-imperialist politics (da Sola Pool). Both of these perceptions resonate stereotypes of a profoundly colonial (and racist) kind, respectively 'the natives are lazy' and 'the natives are restless' (see chapter 2). Moreover, 'traditional society' is a *residual* category, a sort of container in which everything defined as *non*-'modern' and *non*-'developed', i.e. non-'Western', is lumped together and explicitly or implicitly devalued, thus denying the historical and cultural differences between Third World societies, let alone their achievements.

A second criticism of Western models of modernization is that they present a falsely rosy picture of how Western societies work, how they came to acquire the prosperity and power that they have today, and how they (or their ruling classes) maintain that prosperity and power. This kind of criticism questions both the *desirability* of 'following in the footsteps of the West', and the *possibility* of doing so within the existing global distribution of economic, political, and military power, and the international divisions of labour that reflect and reinforce it.

Finally, it can be argued that the ways in which Western models define 'modernity' and 'development' in general (and as generally desirable) in fact incorporate features of capitalism, thereby denying the possibility of radically different kinds of development. This effect of Western models is all the more insidious and pervasive if the characteristics of 'modernization' are formulated through a mode of abstraction that makes no explicit reference to the mechanisms of the market and the agency of individual entrepreneurship, or appears to be 'detachable' from the latter. An example is the position that industralization imposes certain *universal 'imperatives'* of accumulation and organization irrespective of particular social and political conditions and whether, for example, it is pursued by a capitalist or socialist strategy. Such 'organizational imperatives' include a hierarchical structure of authority and decision-making dominated by 'élites' that concentrate expertise and the management of resources in their hands. Thus a 'model' of social organization derived from capitalist production is generalized as a necessary condition of *any* process of development.

### *Interventionism: the state and the market*

The picture of a 'free enterprise' system given above is an 'ideal type' in the sense that *laissez faire* capitalism with perfect market competition no longer exists, if it ever did, and however much it lives on in the fantasies of its ideologues. Capitalism produces associations and organizations of those who share similar positions (and interests) in the relations of production, i.e. class organizations (like political parties), and in its various markets. In practice, many organizations reflect both class and sectional (market defined) interests, for example, trade unions, employers' associations, industrial and trading federations. Moreover, the development of capitalism has resulted in the concentration of economic power in giant corporations and banks (increasingly international in their scale and operations). The importance of state economic regulation and government economic policies in capitalist societies both reflects, and is a response to, these tendencies.

It was noted that the advocacy of 'free enterprise' is not incompatible with state intervention in the economy, but that, ideally, it should be of a minimal kind to ensure 'healthy' competition. By contrast, there are arguments for more active and more direct state intervention in capitalist economies. These 'interventionist' arguments differ in their purposes and their emphasis.

A significant argument for interventionism early on in the history of industrial capitalism, was proposed by the German Friedrich List (List, 1941). Interestingly, List's argument was associated with the formulation of a 'National System of Political Economy' which he counterposed, as an organic or 'natural' sphere of economic activity, to the ('rootless') analytical individualism of the British economists he studied (Kitching, 1982, pp. 143–5). List put the case, in 'the national interest', for protecting the 'infant industries' of newly industrializing countries from competition by well-established industries elsewhere (above all in Britain, at the time List was writing). The argument for this kind of state intervention – 'protectionism' through tax concessions and other incentives to 'infant industries', ensuring them a national market through restrictions on imports (quotas, tariffs, etc.) – is also very widespread and influential in the contemporary Third World, where efforts to industrialize take place in a global economic context that includes already established and powerful industrial countries elsewhere, and multinational corporations with resources and sales greater than the national income of many Third World countries.

Another kind of argument for state intervention is associated with the name of John Maynard Keynes (1883–1946), probably the most influential economist of the twentieth century. Keynes' ideas were developed in the context of the great depression of the 1930s, which was a dramatic manifestation of the periodic slumps and crises that have marked the history of capitalism. He proposed state spending to off-set the decline in private investment occasioned by the depression. Large-scale state spending would increase employment and incomes and thereby restore 'effective demand' for the goods and services produced by the private sector. This would bring back into production the latter's unused capacity and, with economic recovery, stimulate new investment. While Keynes addressed himself to the cyclical problems ('boom' followed by 'slump') of already established capitalist industrial economies, his argument for the use of the state to stimulate private business investment has a wider significance, and has also influenced debates about development strategies in the Third World.

A third kind of interventionist argument derives from the 'meaning of development' proposed by Dudley Seers (pp. 67–8 above). The practical implication of Seers' view of the goals and criteria of development is that there must be proper, and if necessary extensive, national planning to link accumulation and investment to the creation of jobs, the eradication of poverty and inequality, and the satisfaction of other basic needs that are conditions for 'the realization of the potential of human personality'.

The first two arguments assume the institutions of a capitalist market economy, and aim to promote its national development through protection against international competition (List), and to safeguard its stability through 'demand management' (Keynes). Seers' argument is more ambiguous in relation to capitalism. If mass unemployment, poverty and inequality are *effects* of capitalism and the operation of market forces in Third World countries, then the logical conclusion of Seers' position is that, at the least, proper development planning should seek to direct private investment in ways that help satisfy basic needs. If this fails to work, then development planning would have to *replace* market forces as the principle of allocating resources, in order to achieve the desired effects of employment creation and a more equitable distribution of income.

The more general point is worth stressing, that historical and contemporary experiences of capitalist development show the opposition of 'market' and 'state' to be a false one in practice (and consequently an inadequate criterion for distinguishing capitalism and socialism as respectively 'market economy' and 'state economy'). Firstly, 'the market' is not a purely 'economic' institution, but its creation, reproduction and extension are continuing sites of social, political and ideological struggle. Secondly, in the historical emergence of capitalism, states played a leading role in facilitating the 'primitive accumulation' of capital in both metropolitan and colonial economies (see chapters 1 and 2). Thirdly, as Peter Worsley (1979, p. 108) has observed, 'a very high degree of *étatisme* (statism) exists practically everywhere, including the First World.'

It can be suggested that the extent and growth of state economic activity in contemporary capitalist societies reflect the following needs of the class of capital:

1 to 'manage' the social contradictions between capital and labour generated by the relations of production of capitalism (manifested, for example, in the emergence of, and struggles over, the 'welfare state', issues of unemployment, trade union rights, etc.);
2 to provide conditions for the operation and expansion of capitalist production on an ever-larger scale, and through ever-greater concentrations of capital in giant corporations, banks, etc. (these conditions include the continuous development of communications, of state administration to service the needs of capitalist companies, involvement in research and development, in education, and so on);
3 to negotiate conflicts between different sections of capital in the interests of capital in general;
4 to manage the links between national economies and the international economy. During the enormous expansion of the world economy in

the last three decades or so, its operations have grown in complexity and sophistication with development of new forms of international finance and internationalized production (through transnational corporations), and important changes in the international division of labour (see chapters 13 and 15).

These activities apply to capitalist states in both the First World and the Third World (each of the kinds of activity indicated is exemplified by the role of the state in Brazilian industrialization since the mid-1960s, see chapter 12). At the same time, to suggest that the extent and growth of state activity in contemporary capitalism reflects the needs (and interests!) of the class of capital (and of particular sections of capital), does not mean that it is necessarily successful in meeting those needs. If that were the case, then states would be imbued with an omniscience and omnipotence that in reality (and fortunately) they manifestly lack.

In short, even the most vigorous advocacy of market-led development, with all its ostensible advantage of harnessing the innate competitive and acquisitive energies attributed to 'human nature', is forced to confront the necessity of certain political and ideological conditions for the market 'to do its job properly'. In practice, state intervention is an intrinsic feature of all contemporary capitalist economies despite specific differences of ideology and policy between governments. The policies of all governments in the capitalist world today recognize and legitimate state economic intervention. The differences between governments (and the political parties from which they are drawn) reflect different views of what kinds of state economic intervention are desirable, and what particular forms they should take.

### *Class society: progress and contradiction*

The view of capitalism outlined here is associated with the ideas of Karl Marx, who considered it a particular type of class society constituted by antagonistic relations (relations producing opposed needs and interests) between different social classes, of which the most important are those of capitalists and workers.

Marx believed that the development of capitalism, above all in its modern industrial form, represented a massive advance in the progress of society. This is because the dynamic of capitalism – the pursuit of profit through the competitive production of commodities for the market – requires the continuous development of productive capacities, including the systematic application of science to methods and techniques of production. Together with this, capitalism brings about an ever-increasing scale of cooperation and integration in production processes, which are organized on the basis of *socialized labour*, as opposed to the small-scale 'privatized' labour of household production. Marx summed this up in the term 'the collective worker', meaning all those workers whose efforts are combined in a particular production process. The superiority of capitalist production over all pre-capitalist forms of economy means that the latter will be destroyed and replaced by capitalism in the course of its expansion: 'The country that is more developed industrially only shows, to the less developed, the image of its future' (Marx, 1976, p. 91).

On the other hand, Marx saw capitalism as a type of society constituted through relations of class exploitation and oppression, and the contradictions they give rise to. He was vehement in his condemnation of the conditions of life of the industrial working class in Britain and Europe at that time, and of the brutality perpetrated by British colonial rule in India. He was at his most scathing when discussing what he regarded as bourgeois hypocrisy, and the apologists of capitalism who hailed it as a new dawn of civilization while glossing over the extreme inequalities and suffering through which it developed. He was just as unstinting in his praise of the objectivity and fairness of the factory inspectors and other civil servants who produced voluminous reports on the shocking conditions of work, housing, nutrition and health in Victorian Britain's new industrial cities.

In short, Marx viewed capitalism as profoundly contradictory. While it has pioneered an historically unprecedented and revolutionary process of development of productive capacities, the latter are subject to the 'anarchy of the market' manifested in a particular economic cycle of expansion and boom, of recession and crisis in capitalist society. The organization of production requires a working class dispossessed not only of means of production but also of any effective control over the uses of its labour power, its strengths and skills, in production. In capitalist production, workers are 'an appendage of the machine', which results in their 'alienation' or incapacity to develop their full potential as human beings through productive and creative work.

Marx's view of the basic contradictions of capitalist society can be summarized at two levels. Firstly, the development of productive capacities under capitalism represents an enormous potential force for human emancipation and freedom from want and necessity, at the same time as the class relations through which the productive forces have developed deny their promise to the majority of people.

> The old view, in which the human being appears as the aim of production, regardless of his (or her) limited national, religious, political character, seems to be very lofty when contrasted to the modern world, where production appears as the aim of mankind, and wealth as the aim of production. In fact, however, when the limited bourgeois form is stripped away, what is wealth other than the universality of individual *needs, capacities*, pleasures, productive forces, etc., created through universal exchange? The full development of human mastery over the forces of nature, those of so-called nature as well as of humanity's own nature? ... In bourgeois economies – and in the epoch of production to which it corresponds – this complete working-out of the human content appears as a complete emptying-out. (Marx, 1973, pp. 487–8, my italics)

Secondly, these class relations embody a contradiction between appropriation based in private ownership and control of the means of production (profit), and increasing socialization of labour in the organization of production. Marx thought that when capitalism reached a stage in which private ownership began to obstruct, rather than promote, the further development of productive capacities, the conditions would be 'ripe' for the overthrow of capitalism. The latter is not an 'automatic' outcome, but the result of class struggle between capitalists and workers, organized in a political movement with the objective of dispossessing the capitalist class and reorganizing the productive capacities made available by capitalism to construct a different kind of society, namely communism.

CHAPTER FIVE

# Development II

## Variations on Socialism and Nationalism

This chapter provides an introduction to different interpretations of the meanings of socialism and nationalism, and how they bear on conceptions of, and debates about, development in the Third World. The discussion of socialism outlines and situates four major 'variations': (i) Marx's ideas of socialism and communism; (ii) the nature of the 'Soviet model' of state socialist development and its significance; (iii) the features of socialist ideas that have emerged from, or been combined with, national liberation struggles against foreign domination; and (iv) the claims of 'indigenous' socialisms to provide a 'third path' of development alternative to both capitalism and state socialism on the 'Soviet model'.

### Variations on Socialism

#### *From capitalism to communism*

As noted at the end of the last chapter, Marx believed that capitalism will be overthrown by a political movement based in the working class, which will go on to build a classless society free of material want and exploitation and providing the conditions for the full development of human potential. This is what he meant by communism, while socialism is a transitional stage between the overthrow of capitalism and the eventual realization of communist society.

Marx said that there is no way of providing a 'blueprint' of socialist or communist society because their specific forms of organization can only emerge from historically new types of social practice. At the same time, the construction of socialism and then communism, as the antithesis or negation of capitalist society, would have to be guided by certain principles and strategic aims. The most important of these include social ownership of the means of production and democratic control of the production process by the producers, rational planning and organization of production to satisfy human needs, the distribution of the product according to the needs of individuals, the elimination of forms of the 'division of labour' characteristic of capitalism, and the 'withering away of the state'. These last two merit further comment.

One of the features of the development of capitalism has been a division of social labour between manual and mental labour, generally detrimental in both material and ideological terms to the former. This is an extremely deep-rooted division in capitalist society, manifested and reproduced through the education system, the way that labour markets operate, the ways in which certain occupations are valued and rewarded and others denied such esteem. Manual labour is held to be 'disqualified' from those 'higher things' that mental labour is credited with. The division of manual and mental labour, and the denigration of the former, is one kind of obstacle, therefore, to the realization of human potential.

Another is the extremely specialized and routine nature of many jobs in capitalist industry, exemplified by assembly-line production and its equivalent in much of contemporary office work. At the same time as this development of the technical division of labour within capitalist production is associated with 'efficiency' (in the sense of raising the productivity of labour in the pursuit of profit), it necessarily represses the realization and development of human potential through productive work. The outcome of these points, Marx believed, is that the development of the productive forces under socialism would be directed to the liberation of work from drudgery and routine, as well as to the liberation of people from material want. In addition, no worker would be confined to a particular type of work or place in the division of labour, but would be able to move around between different kinds of work because of the development and democratization of technical and moral culture.

In the transition to communism the state would 'wither away' because it would no longer have any social function. In Marx' account of the state, it is an instrument of class oppression and control which arose historically with the formation of class society and becomes redundant in a society without classes (just as those pre-capitalist societies which were classless were also stateless). The state would be replaced by democratic assemblies at various levels, although how these could best be organized could only emerge through experience and practice, of a kind exemplified in Marx's lifetime by the Paris Commune of 1871 (Marx, 1974, especially pp. 206–19).

Marx and Engels saw themselves as 'scientific socialists', by which they meant that they had provided a scientific analysis of the emergence, functioning and contradictions of capitalism, identifying the social force that would carry forward from capitalism, and recognizing that this was only likely to be achieved through protracted and bitter class struggle. They termed 'utopian socialists' those who advocated 'turning the clock back' from the productive capacities and scale of organization made possible by capitalism, to what Marx and Engels regarded as a mythical pre-capitalist society consisting of self-governing communities of small producers (a recurring theme of 'populism' as discussed by Kitching, 1982).

### *State socialism: the 'Soviet model'*

It is a well-observed fact that there has been no successful socialist revolution in those societies in which capitalism is most developed. The first socialist capture of state power occurred in Russia in 1917 and led to the founding of the USSR, the subsequent experience of which has been probably the most significant influence on socialist ideology in the twentieth century, whether by acclamation, criticism or rejection. Capitalism in Tsarist Russia was 'underdeveloped' compared with Western Europe, the USA and Japan, and its working class, while highly concentrated in several major industrial cities and politically very militant, was a small minority in a still predominantly agrarian and peasant society. One reason that the Soviet experience has been so important for the Third World is that, while Marx generally saw socialism as a stage in the development of society *subsequent* to mature capitalism, the Soviet Union underwent a massive

FIGURE 8 The capitalist jeers at the Soviet Five Year Plan of 1928 with the words: 'Fantasy, Utopian nonsense!' Four years later he is crushed by the achievements of Soviet industrialization (poster by Deni and Dolgurukov; photo, Novosti Press Agency)

and rapid economic development under the name of socialism that has produced a 'model' of industralization *alternative* to capitalism. (The argument is presented in Shanin, 1983, that the 'late Marx' came to believe that a transition to socialism, *without* passing through the 'stage' of mature capitalism, is both possible and desirable, given favourable circumstances. Interestingly, the basis for this argument is Marx's studies of Russia and his correspondence with some of the Russian populists).

The success of the Soviet Union was bound to have an impact on those countries regarded as 'underdeveloped', or not yet industrialized, particularly if their experience of capitalism initially imposed from the 'outside' through colonialism is seen as a cause of their 'underdevelopment' (see chapter 2). As nationalist movements developed in the European colonies of Asia and Africa and became increasingly strong in the period after 1945, the USSR provided a double reference point for their campaigns for national independence.

Firstly, it presented a model of rapid economic development and social transformation alternative to capitalism; moreover, this model had the further appeal of suggesting a development process free from foreign control and interference and resulting in an industrial and military strength that could guarantee national independence. Secondly, the Soviet Union from its formation had opposed colonial imperialism and supported the aspirations of the colonial peoples to independence and national sovereignty.

It is a moot point whether those nationalist leaders who headed movements for national independence in Asia and Africa were attracted to the Soviet model because of its socialism, or because it presented to them an example of rapid development achieved through the state, rather than through the operation of market forces and the accumulation of private capital. Decolonization and national independence meant in the first place the 'inheritance' of the state in the former colonies, rather than control over their economies in which foreign capital tended to be dominant in such sectors as mining, plantation agriculture, manufacturing industry, banking, and large-scale export and import trade. From this point of view, perhaps more compelling than its claim to socialism was the Soviet state's control of the economy through the creation of state enterprises in industry and agriculture, finance, and domestic and foreign trade, and through centralized planning and the political means to implement it. It was the Soviet state that pioneered the theory and practice of economic *planning* on a large scale; today virtually every state in the Third World, regardless of ideological complexion, has some kind of national development plan.

Whether, and how, the Russian revolution of 1917 and the subsequent economic and social development of the Soviet Union conforms to or deviates from Marx's ideas about socialism, continues to be fiercely debated by (and among) Marxists, non-Marxists and anti-Marxists alike. One focus of debate concerns the 'inevitability' or otherwise of the draconian methods of 'forced industrialization', and their social and political effects, given the internal and external conditions of Soviet development. These included the relative 'backwardness' of Russia (its predominantly agrarian and peasant character); the problems of maintaining an alliance between the two political dynamics that had converged in 1917 – those of a working-class anti-capitalist revolution and a peasant 'anti-feudal' revolution; the devastation wrought by continuous international and civil war and military invasion between 1914 and 1921 (and again with the German invasion of 1941–3); the continuing threat of foreign intervention and the priority accorded to military and related industries.

For present purposes, we shall restrict ourselves to noting one type of criticism of Soviet theory and practice as an 'alternative' discourse of development, which is related to some of the issues posed in the previous chapter. The argument (well presented by Corrigan, Ramsay and Sayer, 1978) is that in the 'Soviet model', as conceived by the original generation of Bolsheviks and entrenched in the practices of Stalin and his successors, 'socialist revolution' consists primarily of the overthrow of an existing system of exploitation including the state which represented the interests of its ruling classes, and its replacement by a state representing the interests of the working class and the peasantry. This new 'workers' and peasants' state' is the principal agency of development: private property in the means of production is abolished and replaced by state property, production is organized in large-scale units, and development planned and directed through centralized state control of economic resources and activities.

What this represents, it is suggested, is a particular version or 'model' of modernization in the sense that, while the state 'substitutes' for the market, primacy is still accorded to an accumulation process determined by an overriding conception of developing the 'productive forces' (i.e. transforming the technical conditions of production). This conception, which assumes the intrinsic superiority of the economies of scale and external economies of large-scale production, has been termed the 'old orthodoxy' by Kitching (1982, who ably defends it against the critique presented by populism). Its theoretical power, of course, was demonstrated in practice by the material achievements (massive growth of production and productivity) of industrial capitalism. The argument then continues that because of its adherence to the logic of the 'old orthodoxy', the Soviet 'model' provides only a partial and incomplete alternative to capitalism, limiting the meaning of socialism as an ideology of human emancipation. The discourse of Soviet-style socialism involves the transformation of property relations, and of the state form, without providing a sufficiently revolutionary critique of the dominant forms of technology of capitalism and the organization of production they entail. In fact, the Bolsheviks were highly impressed not only by the material technologies of capitalism, but also by its 'social technologies' of organizing large-scale production, which reflect the technical and social divisions of labour of capitalist society. They tended to see both material and social technologies as 'neutral' dimensions of the productive forces which could be employed in building socialism.

In their view, the test of socialism was to develop the productive forces more efficiently than capitalism, and thereby demonstrate the 'superiority' of socialism according to the logic of the 'old orthodoxy'. For the Bolsheviks of the Russian revolution, and their successors in the Soviet Union, the success of socialism would be demonstrated by its ability, first, to 'catch up' with, and second, to 'overtake' the USA (by the beginning of the twentieth century, Germany and, in particular, the USA had replaced Britain as exemplars of the most 'advanced' industrial capitalism). As well as adhering to the economic logic of the 'old orthodoxy', this meaning of socialist development embodies a statist conception of politics, that is, a view of politics defined above all in relation to the activities of the state (Skillen, 1977, ch. 1). The 'seizure' of state power is seen as the decisive political moment in the transition to socialism, and the power thus 'seized' and reconstituted in a new class form (the 'workers' and peasants' state') is the primary agency of development.

This conception limits the transformation of the social conditions and relations of production to the abolition of private property and the creation of public property in the means of production, as the basis for state control and development of the productive forces. While the enormous significance of this change should not be underestimated, it is at best an incomplete foundation for socialist development understood as a process of collective organization of production by the producers themselves, and at worst can work against it in the name of targets and imperatives imposed from above by the state plan.

### *From imperialism to socialism*

Undoubtedly, Soviet society has been marked from the beginning by conditions highly problematic for socialist development. One type of constraint is presented by a hostile international environment in which both crises of international capitalism (as in the 1930s, and again in the 1970s and 1980s), and the tremendous expansion of the global capitalist economy (as in the 1950s and 1960s) produced different sorts of threats to any project of socialist construction. Regarding its internal social conditions, some argue that the 'backwardness' of Tsarist Russia, from which the Bolshevik revolution emerged, meant that Soviet development was bound to reflect the problems of a *'premature' socialism*. That is to say, attempts to build socialism in conditions that fall short of 'mature' capitalism, before the 'full stage' of capitalist development has been passed through, have considerable (and unnecessary) costs, for two reasons. One is that 'premature' socialism is not in a position to 'inherit' the highly developed productive forces of a mature capitalism, and to turn them to its own purposes. The second reason is that development in the sense of the 'old orthodoxy' requires a substantial rate of accumulation to achieve industrialization, which always has considerable costs for the majority of the population. 'Premature' socialism, therefore, has to take on the 'dirty work' of accumulation that capitalism would otherwise have carried out (Kitching, 1982, ch. 7; also implicitly, Warren, 1980).

This interpretation of the Soviet experience in the light of the inexorable 'logic' of the 'old orthodoxy' contrasts sharply, of course, with the position outlined above, which criticizes the Soviet model for failing to go beyond the conceptions of the 'old orthodoxy'. Without underestimating the problems facing the historical course of Soviet development, both internal and external, the latter position rejects any notion of 'premature' socialism for the following reason. While capitalism has indeed 'created' the modern world, it has done so through processes of 'uneven and combined development'. *Unevenness* is reflected in the extremely unequal distribution of economic power and prosperity, of productive capacities and levels of accumulation and consumption, in *spatial* as well as social (class) terms. These global inequalities are linked to each other, or '*combined*', through the distinctive international and other divisions of labour of capitalism (see, further, chapter 6).

The effect of this argument is, firstly, that capitalism *as an international system* is 'mature'; secondly, that the essential social conditions of its 'maturity' were established from the late nineteenth century with that phase of its global development that Lenin termed *imperialism* (see chapter 1); thirdly, given its characteristic processes of uneven and combined development, there is no reason to believe that the 'maturity' of global capitalism will be manifested in an equivalent 'maturing' of each of the national economies, sectors, branches or forms of production within it, but rather the opposite. While certain Third World countries at certain times undoubtedly 'develop' in the capitalist sense of the growth of the productive forces through large-scale commodity production (as in Brazil and the 'newly industrializing countries' or NICs of South-East and East Asia) the dynamics of uneven and combined development mean that capitalism is unlikely to fulfil its 'progressive' role in any uniform manner across the whole of the Third World. At the same time, the contradictions of uneven and combined development and the ways in which they are experienced by the workers, 'marginal', peasants and other small-scale producers of the Third World, create conditions of mass struggle that can provide a basis for socialist construction that is in no sense 'premature'.

Lenin suggested that the first successful socialist revolution took place in Russia rather than in any of the more 'advanced' capitalist countries because it was the 'weakest link in the chain of imperialism'. Ironically, Tsarist Russia was itself an empire but of a fundamentally *pre*-capitalist type in its origins and historical development, like others whose fate was sealed with the upheavals of the First World War (the Hapsburg and Ottoman empires; see, further, chapter 1 on the differences between pre-capitalist empires and modern or capitalist imperialism). This perception of Lenin's can be extended to another 'variation' on socialism arising specifically from twentieth-century Third World history, namely that associated with national liberation struggles against foreign domination in which socialist ideology and socialist or communist parties played a leading role.

Among other examples, China and Vietnam in Asia, Cuba and Nicaragua in the Caribbean and Central America, Angola, Guinea-Bissau, Mozambique and Zimbabwe in Africa, experienced protracted guerilla wars usually with peasant populations as the principal base of support for the national liberation struggle. While these struggles were directed against colonial rule and other forms of imperialist domination (e.g. the Japanese occupation of China in the 1930s, the massive American military intervention in

Vietnam in the 1960s), they were often combined with a 'civil war' against indigenous dominant classes, such as feudal landlords in China, and others who were seen as 'collaborators'a with imperialism (the Batista and Somoza regimes in Cuba and Nicaragua respectively).

It has been argued that the particular conditions in which national liberation struggles of this kind have been waged, and the forms of organization they have introduced, provide a model of socialist development alternative to that based on the Soviet experience. In this view, protracted 'peoples' war' necessitates the effective organization of production and distribution, of health services and education, and of administration, according to local conditions and through local initiative, improvisation and flexibility. The creation and organization of 'liberated zones' prior to eventual victory and the assumption of state power it brings, suggest ways of mobilizing energies and capacities which are not stifled by any centralized planning apparatus and the bureaucracy that often accompanies it, thus encouraging popular forms of organization to evolve.

It should be pointed out that the development of popular forms of organization in this sense need not be restricted to situations of 'people's war' (any more than the experience of 'people's war' guarantees the success, or even survival of socialism subsequent to national liberation). Processes of class and popular struggle in many contexts (rural districts, villages, plantations, mining communities, factories, shanty towns), at many different moments, demonstrate the 'energy, courage, capacity for solidarity for organization and leadership' among subordinated classes and groups (Johnson and Bernstein, 1982, p. 268). However, these more local or partial experiences of struggle often go unrecorded, and the possibilities of alternative modes of social organization they disclose are rarely the object of wider theoretical reflection. The tendency to focus on popular organizations developed during 'people's war' is connected with its scale (typically national or regional), the intensity and drama of armed struggle, and the demands this makes on constructing social bases of survival and support.

China is (or was, until the mid-1970s) regarded as the most significant example of an 'alternative' theory and practice of socialist development, because of its human scale and international importance, its long history of mass struggles before and after national liberation, and the influence of Mao Zedong as the major theorist of a 'mass line' of socialist construction. The 'mass line' was articulated as a critique of conceptions of 'modernization' and the imperatives of the 'old orthodoxy' in both their capitalist and Soviet ('statist') versions. The political theory and practice of the 'mass line' suggests an alternative conception of 'development by, for, and through the people' which can be summarized as follows:

1 It places a central emphasis on serving the needs of the people first. The satisfaction of daily necessities – feeding, clothing, housing and caring for everyone – is taken as the base line to be accomplished before other forms of development.

2 The achievement of this goal in the conditions of the contemporary Third World can only come about through the social and collective development of people, cooperating to augment their capacities in emancipatory forms. This process of development requires a critique – informed by theory and effected through the practice of struggle – of all those forms of social division that generate material and cultural inequalities, and give them ideological justification.

3 Because such social divisions (of class, gender, ideological and cultural domination and subordination) are so deeply rooted, and so strongly defended by those who benefit from them, they necessarily give rise to political struggle in its widest sense – the activities of maintaining, contesting, or transforming, more or less deeply, the forms of social existence. (Skillen, 1977, p. 43)

4 Those struggles may be shorter or longer in duration, more violent or peaceful in their methods. The overthrow of a landlord or capitalist class and the state which represents its interests may be impossible to accomplish without armed struggle. The historical connection between international or civil war (often combined, in fact) and the establishment of socialist regimes in the twentieth century, is well known. On the other hand, the development of a socialist agriculture through the collective self-organization of the producers is likely to be a much longer and more peaceful process, in which contradictions 'among the people' provide the dynamic of change, and ways are found to resolve these contradictions. (Those generated by the inequalities of gender relations are perhaps the most deeply rooted.)

5 The resolution of contradictions 'among the people' can be facilitated by political organization and leadership provided by the structures of party and state, which make available resources, ideas, and means of coordination, without imposing solutions 'from above'. In this conception of development, the state does not 'wither away' in some distant future when the material and social basis for socialism has been established. Rather, the state is actively 'deconstructed' as a vital part of the transition to socialism, as the powers and capacities hitherto reserved for the state are progressively taken over and fulfilled by popular organizations (in administration, education, defence, health care, and so on, as well as in the sphere of production).

Within this framework, issues concerning the promotion of large-scale or small-scale production in different sectors, the allocation of resources to accumulation or to individual or social consumption (e.g. education and health), whether to invest in (certain types of) industry or (certain types of) agriculture, how to develop technical skills and capacities, and so on, do not disappear. What is important is how such issues are formulated, that is, according to the primacy of meeting basic needs, and how decisions about them are made and acted upon, that is, through creating the conditions and practices of a participatory ('mass') style of socialist construction. What are so often presented, then, as 'technical' choices to be decided by those with the appropriate technical 'expertise' (a view encouraged, for example, by both capitalist and Soviet-type versions of the 'old orthodoxy'), in this conception are seen as fundamentally political in character, and subject therefore to decision through political processes in the widest sense (see above), and involving the widest numbers of those whose activities make up social production and reproduction.

### *Indigenous socialisms: the search for a third path*

In many Third World countries, the vocabulary of 'decolonization' combined nationalism with references to socialism as the desirable and appropriate mode of achieving development – a broadening, or dilution, of the meaning of socialism, according to one's point of view. For example, 'African socialism' was proclaimed as their ideology by regimes which subsequently did nothing to formulate or implement socialist policies, such as Senegal and Kenya, whose purely rhetorical allegiance to socialism was treated sympathetically by the US ambassadors to those countries (Cook, 1965, Attwood 1967). On the other hand, an ideology such as 'African socialism' can have a more serious, if not unambiguous content. For example, it can express an explicit attempt to find an ideology and strategy of development that is an alternative to both capitalism and socialism as represented by the Soviet Union. Capitalism was associated with the history of colonial rule (and continuing foreign economic domination after independence, or 'neo-colonialism'), and its destruction of indigenous societies and cultures. On the other hand, Soviet-style socialism is associated with a political system justified by an ideology of class struggle and proletarian class rule. Various political leaders and intellectuals in Third World countries have formulated philosophies of development that aspire to a 'third way' or 'third path' of national development that is appropriate to their own circumstances, and avoids models derived from the experience of others, whether of a Western capitalist or a Soviet (*or* other Marxist) socialist kind.

The aspiration to a 'third path' of development has its counterpart at the level of international politics in the notion of 'non-alignment', the desirability of occupying a position independent of both the Western and Eastern blocs, which is formally incorporated in the Non-Aligned Movement (NAM, to which many Third World states belong). The idea of 'non-alignment' has acquired a further political emphasis since the split between the Soviet Union and China in the 1960s, and Chinese commitment to the position that the USA and USSR (whatever their other differences) both confront the countries of the Third World as established 'super powers'.

A distinctive feature of many 'third path' socialisms is their view that the societies and cultures existing before colonialism contained principles of communal living and working, of cooperation and egalitarianism, in short a 'socialist ethic' with indigenous roots, that can be reclaimed for national development efforts in the post-colonial context. One of the best known statements of this position is associated with Julius Nyerere of Tanzania, (1966, 1968, 1973).

There are different versions of, and emphases within, this idea of a revival or retrieval of indigenous socialist or communitarian principles. One version is celebrated in Mahatma Gandhi's attempt to encourage small-scale production in agriculture and handicrafts so as to provide full and satisfying employment, and a 'human scale' in production and social life more generally. A better guide to the realities of indigenous socialisms than the Gandhian vision, however strong its ideological resonance, is the fact that their practices are likely to be informed by ideas of modernization and 'catching up', even if these are combined (with various degrees of tension) with 'populist' ideas. For example, the characterization of Tanzania's development strategy as 'populist' (as in Kitching, 1982, chapter 5) may be accurate, but is not sufficient unless it is made clear that this 'strategy' also contains a version of modernization, *and* has been pursued through highly statist ('top down') practices (see Bernstein, 1981, 1982a). More typical, then, of indigenous socialisms is the desire to combine those types of production made available by modern industrialization with their high labour productivity and economies of scale, with participatory, communal and egalitarian values attributed to an indigenous, pre-colonial past.

*"Join us. It's only a step."*

FIGURE 9 (Cartoon reproduced by courtesy of *South, the Third World Magazine*, London)

The principal point remains that attempts to formulate types of socialist ideology and strategy appropriate to the historical circumstances of Third World societies such as 'African socialism' or versions of 'Islamic socialism', take some other point of reference than class struggle and the leading role of a working class (itself created by capitalist development) that Marx and Engels stressed. For socialism of this 'indigenous' type the point of reference is the values that, it is claimed were represented in pre-colonial (hence pre-capitalist) forms of economic and social organization. Some tensions associated with this conception can be noted briefly. First, how accurate are such ideological reconstructions of pre-colonial society and culture? (for the case of Tanzania, see Mapolu, 1973). Even if their historical accuracy is not the real issue, but their ability to mobilize and organize energies for development, how successful are they in this respect? This relates to another – and, for some, the most important – source of tension, namely that if the contemporary societies of the Third World have indeed been 'created' by colonialism and capitalism (chapters 1 and 2) and are recreated through the places they occupy in a capitalist world economy (chapter 7), what head-way can appeals to indigenous 'tradition' make in the face of the class formations and class practices of capitalism so deeply embedded in these societies? (Again with reference to Tanzania, see the different analyses of its class structure and state presented by Shivji, 1976; von Freyhold, 1977; Bernstein, 1981; Gibbon and Neocosmos, 1985.)

This section has indicated that there are different, and diverging, meanings of socialism, and that those who consider themselves socialists, whether in the Third, Second or First Worlds, can hold very different beliefs concerning the nature and goals of socialism, the means of achieving it, and the social forces that can be mobilized for the struggle for socialism. At the same time, the term 'national' – signalled in the previous chapter by List's 'National System of Political Economy' and Seers' emphasis on national planning for development – has come increasingly to the fore in considering Third World 'variations on socialism' of both the national liberation and 'third path' types.

## Variations on Nationalism

> Nationalism is a doctrine invented in Europe at the beginning of the nineteenth century. It pretends to supply a criterion for the determination of the unit of population proper to enjoy a government exclusively its own, for the legitimate exercise of power in the state, and for the right organization of a society of states. Briefly, the doctrine holds that humanity is naturally divided into nations, that nations are known by certain characteristics which can be ascertained, and that the only legitimate type of government is national self-government. Not the least triumph of this doctrine is that such propositions have become accepted and are thought to be self-evident, that the very word nation has been endowed by nationalism with a meaning and a resonance which until the end of the eighteenth century it was far from having. These ideas have become firmly naturalized in the political rhetoric of the West which has been taken over for the use of the whole world. (Kedourie, 1960, p. 9)

This is the opening statement of a book written by a historian of the Middle East, in which his distaste for nationalism is quite clear. The book was first published in 1960, when the taking-over of nationalism 'for the use of the whole world' was dramatically evident: at that time India and Pakistan had been independent countries for over a decade following the division of the South Asian sub-continent, the 'jewel in the crown' of the British Empire; an independent communist China had been in existence for eleven years; nationalist struggles dominated the politics of the Middle East and Africa – in 1956 Nasser's Egypt had nationalized the Suez Canal, that striking symbol of imperial 'property' (and of imperial 'destiny', see Said, 1985, pp. 89–92) – and in 1957 Nkrumah's Ghana was the first British colony in Africa to achieve national independence. Kedourie's statement is a useful one to begin with, for several reasons (including its concentrated clarity). It starts by saying that nationalism has a history, and therefore has to be understood historically. Secondly, it suggests that nationalism as a political doctrine cannot be considered apart from questions concerning the state and the legitimation of the authority of the state. Thirdly, it implicitly contrasts the need to treat nationalism historically with the view that 'humanity is naturally divided into nations'. While much of Kedourie's book on nationalism is concerned with its formation as a set of ideas in eighteenth century European philosophy, I will focus on some of the issues nationalism raises for confronting the realities of the contemporary Third World, and the discourses of development that reflect them.

The idea of a nation, what I shall call *nationhood*, is that it provides a collective identity which defines those who belong to the nation on the basis of certain shared characteristics (and simultaneously excludes those who do not belong). These shared characteristics are 'cultural' in a broad sense: the notion of a common history and heritage to which are attributed distinctive ways of life, customs, values, tastes, form of aesthetic expression, and so on. The coherence of national identity in this sense is expressed above all through the use of a common language.

These, then, are some of the characteristics by which it is felt nations 'can be ascertained' (Kedourie). What, then, distinguishes nations from other cultural entities? Would the Mundurucu people of the Amazon forest consider themselves, or be considered by others, a 'nation'? These questions point to a problematic and highly charged area of modern history, namely the relationship between cultural identity and political organization, between nation and state, indicated by Kedourie's proposition that nationalism defines the nation as 'the unit of population proper to enjoy a government exclusively its own'.

Because the concepts of nation and state are so intimately, if uneasily, intertwined, I will dstinguish *nationality*, signifying the citizenship of a particular state, from nationhood in the sense defined above. Citizenship is a legal and political status that distinguishes all those who 'belong' to a given state from all those who do not (i.e. in a world territorially and politically divided between states, those who are – or 'ought' to be – citizens of other states).

It establishes simultaneously, therefore, the conditions of inclusion in *and exclusion from* the 'rights' associated with 'membership' of the state. In administering this legal and political status, the state has enormous power in deciding who can reside within its boundaries and on what conditions – a power that is experienced, for example, by two numerous categories of people crossing international boundaries, namely labour migrants, and refugees from political persecution, war or famine (phenomena which are often connected).

If the idea that humanity is 'naturally' divided into nations is rejected, then it is acknowleged that nations have emerged historically, and that perceptions of particular cultural entities and their claims to nationhood can change over time. This means that nations have to be investigated through the process of their *formation*, and its consequences, in the same way that historical investigation is necessary to understanding different processes of state formation. A critical area of contemporary history is thus defined by the ways in which the formation of nations and of states are related: the ways in which they have converged or diverged, and in which the claims of nationhood and nationality have reinforced or come into conflict with each other.

The area of problems and potential conflicts arising from the divergence of nation and state is by no means exclusive to the Third World. The association of a particular cultural identity with grievances over economic and social inequalities can result in assertions of nationhood, including the claim to a separate political sovereignty, in contemporary First and Second World societies as well (for example, in Britain, Spain, Belgium, the idea of a 'black nation' in the USA, the Baltic areas and the Ukraine in the Soviet Union, Yugoslavia).

On the other hand, the relationship of nation and state in the Third World seems to present a more generalized, and often more acute, potential for conflict. The principal reason for this has to be sought in the distinctive processes of state formation in the modern history of the Third World, in which colonialism played such a major role (chapter 1). For the moment, it is sufficient to emphasize that the boundaries of present Third World states were often drawn haphazardly in the course of European expansion, and as a result of the 'race' of European powers to acquire colonies. Consequently, there is no necessary correlation between the political 'space' constituted as the area of jurisdiction of given states, and the characteristics of the various peoples (including those with a claim to nationhood) who occupied those areas around which colonial boundaries were drawn. This pre-existing cultural diversity was frequently exacerbated by the extremely uneven nature of economic and social change under colonialism, and the predilection of colonial states for a strategy of 'divide and rule'.

The declaration of an independent Biafra and the Nigerian Civil War that ensued (1967–70) was one dramatic manifestation of a claim to nationhood in a particular region of a country, pursued to the extent of secession and a war to maintain a separate sovereignty. Moreover, the Ibo who seceded to establish the state of Biafra had been a 'stateless' people before the imposition of colonial rule; their sense of nationhood only emerged and was articulated as a result of the colonial experience in

Nigeria. This is one example, then, of a claim to a separate identity and self-rule by a 'nation' *within* the territorial boundaries of a state 'inherited' from colonialism. There are also political movements of peoples whose historical territory as a 'nation' was divided *between* several adjacent states, from which they may wish to secede to form their own state, for example, the Kurds of Iran, Iraq and Turkey, and the Somalis of North-Eastern Kenya and the Ogaden area of Ethiopia who want to join themselves to the state of Somalia.

The divisive effects of a divergence of nationhood from nationality are clear enough. On the other hand, one should note the *unifying* aspirations of nationalism as an ideology, including the powerful idea that nationhood and nationality express not only collective identities but also collective interests. Nationhood was defined as a collective identity, uniting people who may be differentiated in other respects, for example, by relations of class and gender. It is implicit in the discussion so far that identity can easily become associated with interest, as in the interest of those who share a collective identity to have their own state. The term *nationalism* is used here to mean an ideology of both collective identity and interest, based either in nationhood or nationality.

Attempts to construct a unity of identity and interest on the basis of nationality is likely to be more difficult than on the basis of shared nationhood. The processes of state formation in the Third World resulting from colonialism conferred the same nationality on people who may be differentiated not only by inequalities of an economic and political kind, but also by important cultural features such as religion, local and regional identities, and language. In many Third World countries, the population literally does not speak the same language. In sub-Saharan Africa, Tanzania is the only country that has a common language (Swahili) spoken by practically everyone.

Nationalism that appeals to a common nationality, therefore, has to find ways of transcending the more specific identities and interests of different social groups (including those sharing characteristics of nationhood) in order to realize 'the greater good'. The latter is customarily presented as 'the national interest', which exerts a unique claim on the support, commitment, hard work, sacrifice, and so on, of all those who share a common nationality. Some of the implications of nationalism can be indicated in relation to movements for national independence, 'nation building' after decolonization, and the uses of nationalism as a medium of political discourse through which different, and opposing, versions of 'the national interest' – and of 'national development' – are expressed.

The significance of nationalism as a reaction to foreign rule imposed by colonialism, and as a means of organizing movements for independence, is that it can bring together quite different social groups and classes for a specific purpose and against a specific target. At the same time, as noted above, national liberation struggles can also be aimed at indigenous social groups and individuals who are considered to be collaborators with the foreign enemy. In considering nationalist movements and their effectiveness in mobilizing people against foreign rule, one needs to assess the kind of unity they achieve. Does it provide the basis of a more fundamental and enduring national unity, or does it represent a temporary alliance which is subject to strain, and liable to disintegrate when the goal of national independence has been achieved? An example of the former is provided by the path 'from imperialism to socialism', discussed earlier, where the goal of national independence is combined with a programme of continuing economic, social and political change. The latter alerts us to the possibility that the unity derived from the struggle for national independence does not necessarily survive its achievement, that those with the same nationality are not necsesarily any closer to being a 'nation' in the sense of sharing a common identity, recognition of a common interest, and sense of purpose in pursuing it.

An awareness of this is expressed in ideas of 'nation building' *subsequent* to national independence: first, that such features of collective identity and commitment are desirable (and, indeed, a necessary condition of successful development), and, second, that they have to be actively constructed through policies and actions directed to this end. There is an interesting inversion at work here. The secessionist movements mentioned above seek to bring nationality in line with nationhood, as it were. The concept of 'nation building' expresses the aspiration to achieve nationhood on the basis of nationality.

There are two important implications of this. The first is that while independence brings political sovereignty, it is often argued that foreign domination continues in other ways, notably through the economic power exercised by industrialized countries and multinational corporations. This argument about 'neo-colonialism' can be used as a means of appealing to national solidarity against an 'external' enemy, in the same manner as the earlier movements against colonial rule. Second, the idea of 'nation building' in practice tends to assign a central role to state action for the reason already indicated: that common citizenship and accountability to the laws and policies of a given state may be the only basis for appealing to the unity of populations that otherwise are extremely differentiated in social and cultural terms.

The enlargement of the state in terms of economic and social management, the scope of the functions it assumes, and the claims on resources these involve, seems to be a feature of all contemporary states (chapter 3). In First World countries the experience of the depression of the 1930s, followed by state management of the wartime economy and of post-war reconstruction in Europe and Japan, was an important contribution to this trend (in which Keynes' ideas of state intervention also played their part). Concerning the Second World, the centrality of the state in the Soviet 'model' of development was stressed. In Third World countries the role of the state – in 'nation building', in articulating a national ideology (such as the varieties of indigenous socialism), and in its claims to the control of national resources to promote development – have been especially important because of the particular conditions and processes of state formation they have experienced under colonialism and capitalism.

In effect, those who control the state claim a unique ability to represent 'the national interest', which serves to legitimate their policies and actions. As Kedourie suggests, ideas of national interest have become 'naturalized' as the most common denominator of contemporary political rhetoric. This means that political differences are often expressed in terms of *competing* interpretations of the national interest and competing claims to represent it.

In conclusion, there is no single connection between nationalism as an ideological and political orientation and specific sets of policies. Secondly, following this, nationalism can be combined in different ways with ideas about capitalism and socialism. Thirdly, the issue of state control over national economies versus domination by foreign capital and imports looms large in debates about development in Third World countries (see chapter 14).

CHAPTER SIX

# National Economies

## Diversity and Integration

The title of this chapter contains an intentional ambiguity: does it mean diversity and integration *within* national economies or *between* them? The answer is both, as it is virtually impossible to make meaningful statements about *any* capitalist economy today (Third World or First World) without considering where and how it 'fits' in the international economy. Indeed, a very influential approach to Third World economies suggests that they are either actively 'underdeveloped' or their development is determined and limited, by the position they occupy within the capitalist 'world system' (see chapters 10 and 13). In this view, their place in the world market or international division of labour is the major determinant of the *internal* structures (including diversity) and processes (including integration or lack of integration) of Third World economies. As the possible scope of this chapter is so broad, it will be limited to introducing some key concepts for thinking about diversity and integration within and between national economies. The chapters in parts III and IV elaborate and apply these concepts in more detail, while part V concentrates on the international dimensions and determinants of Third World economies.

### Measures of National Economies

It is useful to begin with some of the conventions used to measure national economies, to see what they can and cannot tell us. The World Bank's annual *World Development Report* is a standard and accessible source of measures used in 'national income accounts' as they are termed by economists, for whom they provide an indispensable tool. The kinds of measures or indicators used in the *World Development Report* can be classified by their relevance to the size, wealth or poverty, structure, levels of welfare, and performance of national economies.

1 The *size* of a national economy is conventionally measured by its (annual) Gross Domestic Product (GDP) or Gross National Product (GNP). GDP represents the total value of goods and services produced within an economy, and GNP is GDP plus income accruing to the national economy from outside its boundaries (e.g. 'invisible earnings') and minus income payments 'exported' from it.

2 The relative *wealth or poverty* of an economy is evaluated by dividing GDP or GNP by size of population to get a per capita measure. The world economic 'league table' of countries is constructed by ranking them according to GNP per capita.

3 The *structure* of a national economy is indicated in national income accounting by the composition of GDP according to the shares of its various sectors, most commonly divided into primary or 'extractive' (agriculture, forestry, fishing, mining), secondary (processing and manufacturing industry), and the tertiary or service sector. An additional, and useful, indicator of economic structure is the distribution of the labour force between different sectors.

4 Levels of *welfare* are measured in such areas as health: daily calorie supply per capita, life expectancy, infant and child mortality rates, numbers of people per doctor/nurse/hospital bed, etc. and education: literacy rates, school enrolment by different levels of education and proportion of relevant age-groups, etc.

5 The most commonly used indicator of *economic performance* is growth (whether positive or negative) of GDP or GNP per capita over time. Other measures which might correlate with growth of GDP or GNP as indicators of economic performance include savings and investment as a proportion of GDP/GNP, and rates of value added (the value added to materials as they are processed or manufactured into further goods for intermediate or final consumption), both of which can also change over time.

The kinds of indicators listed present a number of problems, and always have to be treated with caution. Three general areas of difficulty concern their methods of valuation of economic activity, the levels of aggregation employed, and the ways in which average (per capita) indices obscure patterns of distribution.

*Valuation* of economic activity for international comparison is represented in the standard currency of international financial and trade transactions, the US dollar. This is problematic, firstly, because translating prices from national currencies into US dollars is subject to the vagaries and fluctuations of official exchange rates (and economists frequently argue whether particular currencies are 'overvalued' or 'undervalued' in relation to the dollar, particularly the former for Third World countries). Secondly, and partly related, valuation in US dollars is often a very misleading index of the real purchasing power of national currencies within their own economies.

A further issue is that the volume of goods and services not exchanged through the market (that is, produced for self-consumption or 'subsistence', see below) is notoriously difficult to put a market or price valuation on, and its notional value is generally very crudely 'guesstimated' (and typically underestimated), or omitted from national income accounts altogether. A clear example of the latter, missing from the data of economic activity in 'developed' no less than 'developing' countries, are the billions of hours of domestic labour (see chapter 3) expended each year, and without which no other kind of economic activity would take place.

One should also note the problem of comparable output value measures for the three sectors noted above. Monetary value in US dollars imputed to the production of goods is often an inadequate or misleading measure, but *physical output* data when available can indicate real trends in production. There is no equivalent alternative for services that are 'monetized' but not traded commercially, like government administration and certain other public services. Their 'value' in national income accounts is not represented by what they (notionally) 'earn', but by what they cost in salaries and other expenditure.

The second area of difficulty mentioned concerns levels of *aggregation*. In principle, and often in practice, this is not so serious because the imputed value of output of the three main sectors can be disaggregated by branches of production and the types of products they supply. For example, agricultural production may be broken down into food and non-food production, and industrial production into the various branches of the International Standard Industrial Classification or ISIC (the main ones are given in pp. 188–9 of chapter 10). This kind of disaggregation can be useful in giving a more detailed profile of the structures of national economies, including clues about their internal diversity (although the problems of valuation remain).

The third area of problems concerns the use of (per capita) *averages* which, of course, can mask extreme inequalities in the distribution of productive assets and real disposable income: who owns what and who gets what. Generally, the poorer a country the less likely it is to have reliable, or any, data on income distribution. The *World Development Report* for 1985 provides income distribution data for only 18 of 72 'low income' and 'lower middle income' countries (World Bank, 1985, pp. 228–9). Moreover the data used 'refer to the distribution of total disposable household income' (p. 241), which raises the following difficulties.

1 The definition of 'households' as units of income and consumption differs across cultures (and within, as well as between, countries); the difficulty this presents is compounded when part of real income consists of 'subsistence' goods as well as money income.
2 The measure uses household rather than per capita income. This means first, that a household which is poor but large and contains a number of income earners, would appear as 'better off' than it would in terms of per capita income.
3 Inter-household income distribution does not tell us about (systematic) inequalities of distribution *within* households that might exist, e.g. between male and female household members.
4 'Income' here does not distinguish between access to means of consumption and access to means of production (or other 'income bearing' property). The effect of this is to 'flatten out' considerably differences in the distribution of wealth particularly in capitalist societies.

The problems of per capita national income indicators apply equally to average measures of welfare. The latter, in any case, tend to be 'input' measures (supply of doctors, nurses, school places, etc.) and not measures of real consumption (the benefits gained from health and education facilities). The distribution of welfare 'inputs' and the real benefits from them are likely to reveal considerable inequalities between social classes, betwen urban and rural areas, and along gender lines.

Finally, and highly relevant to the concerns of this chapter and the rest of the book, are data on the international linkages of economies, which can be classified as in table 2.

TABLE 2 The international linkages of economies

| | *Inflows* | *Outflows* |
|---|---|---|
| Commodities | Imports of capital goods. Intermediate and consumer goods | Exports of capital goods. Intermediate and consumer goods |
| Capital | Private and public foreign investment, loans, 'aid', 'repatriated' profits from overseas investment, etc. | Funds invested in other countries, 'repatriated' profits of foreign companies, interest on loans, debt repayments, etc |
| Labour power | Migration from other countries | Migration to other countries |

In practice, national income accounts are strongest on commodity exports and imports, less strong on certain kinds of capital inflows and especially outflows, and do not refer to labour migrants at all (though they *may* feature in population and work-force censuses). The valuation of commodity imports and exports can be distorted by the 'transfer pricing' techniques used by multinational corporations in transactions between their subsidiaries in different countries. This can also affect the reliability of data on capital outflows, when the subsidiary of a transnational corporation (TNC) exports profits 'concealed' in the 'price' of import commodities it 'buys' from, or export commodities it 'sells' to, another branch of the same corporation elsewhere, thereby circumventing national laws limiting the repatriation of profits and/or avoiding paying taxes on its profits. More generally, capital outflows can occur in a variety of ways (including legal but shadowy, and plain illegal), some of which are very difficult to trace and record and, hence, measure properly.

As with the other indicators discussed, reasonably accurate and disaggregated statistics of different types of commodity and capital imports and exports (as well as international labour migration statistics for particular countries, when available) can provide useful clues about diversity and integration within and between national economies. Of these indicators, and the statistical relations between them, the most relevant to diversity and integration are probably GDP or GNP per capita, structure of the economy by sectors and branches and distribution of the work-force between them, and the value and composition of commodity and capital imports and exports. However, the best any of these indicators (individually or combined) can do is to provide clues: the *quantitative* (statistical) expression of the outcome or effects of *qualitative* (social) relations and processes of the kind discussed in chapters 3–5. Building on the latter, the rest of this chapter will present ideas for further considering these relations and processes in the context of national economies, as a 'bridge' between this conceptual part of the book and those that follow.

## Diversity: Types of Products, Types of Production

Diversity within national economies can be viewed in various complementary ways. One dimension concerns the types of goods and services that are produced, another concerns whether they are consumed by those who produce them ('subsistence' production) or exchanged for consumption by others, and a third concerns how they are produced (their social and technical conditions of production). Each of these dimensions are considered in turn, together with suggestions about how they relate to different and complementary dimensions of the social division of labour. The latter, as explained in chapter 3, is a key concept for the connections between different activities and thus the consideration of integration, which is taken up in the next section of this chapter.

A basic way of classifying types of products was already used for the composition of commodity imports and exports, that is, the distinction between capital, intermediate and consumer goods. *Capital* goods are those used to produce other goods (i.e. capital goods are tools and machinery), *intermediate* goods are materials (whether raw, processed or manfuactured) used in further production, and *consumer* goods are those ready for final consumption. (Both capital and intermediate goods are often termed producer goods to distinguish them from those ready for final consumption.) These distinctions represent a functional classification of products by their *uses*, which are very closely tied to their specific *material properties*. For example, components for motor vehicles are highly specialized products specifically designed for use in the assembly (or repair) of particular makes of vehicles. In other cases, the classification is not so precise. The material properties of sugar cane mean that it can be consumed directly as a foodstuff or as an intermediate good for sugar refinery or making rum and molasses.

This classification of types of products relates to the social division of labour understood as relations between those engaged in more or less specialized activities, producing goods and services with different specific uses. The central concept of integration in this context is that of *linkages* between such activities, often distinguished as *forward* and *backward* linkages. For example, cotton cultivation has a backward linkage with industries producing certain capital goods (hoes, ploughs, tractors, irrigation equipment) and intermediate goods (fertilizer, insecticides), and a forward linkage with industries using cotton as an intermediate good to produce cotton cloth and thread. The latter, in turn, can be intermediate goods with a forward linkage to the production of consumer goods (cotton garments). This represents a sequence in which each intermediate step has both a forward and a backward linkage, as shown in figure 10.

Agricultural equipment and chemicals ⟶/⇠ Cotton cultivation ⟶/⇠ Spinning ⟶/⇠ Weaving ⟶/⇠ Garment manufacture

FIGURE 10 Forward and backward linkages in cotton cultivation

The ability or inability (closely associated with resource and cost factors) to produce different types of capital, intermediate, and consumer goods, together with the density of linkages or exchanges between them within its division of labour, is often used to characterize the structure of a national economy, *and* to evaluate its relative 'strength' or 'health' by the extent to which that structure is simultaneously diversified *and* integrated (Amin, 1976). As no economy produces the whole range of goods it requires, what it does not produce has to be imported. In turn, the capacity to import depends on income from exporting goods required by others. The relationship thus indicated between, on one hand, diversity and integration in national economies (the types and density of linkages in their division of labour) and, on the other hand, export performance and import capacity (relating to diversity and integration within the *international* division of labour), is a central and controversial theme in the analysis of Third World economies, and their development prospects.

The second dimension of diversity arises from the distinction between 'subsistence' production and commodity production for exchange or sale. Subsistence goods are produced for their *use value* in direct consumption, and not to earn money through market exchange. When such goods are consumed, their use value is 'realized'. For example, when an African peasant family consumes its maize harvest it *realizes* the use value of the maize. What are the implications of subsistence production for considering the diversity (and integration) of national economies?

First, where subsistence goods are consumed by their producers and their families, the realization of their use values does not seem to entail any involvement in the wider relations of markets and the social division of labour more generally. To the extent that households or commodities are 'self-sufficient' in terms of meeting certain basic needs through their own production, they can 'resist' integration in the wider circuits of national economy. Both the goods they produce and the resources they use to produce them (land, labour, livestock, and so on) are apparently 'lost' from the viewpoint of the national economy, as they have no linkages with other producers or sectors of production. By the same token, subsistence production impedes specialization, hence the development of the division of labour. For example, if most rural households produce the food staples they eat, this inhibits the development of food staple production as a distinct and specialized branch of activity in the social division of labour (which it is in First World economies).

Second, the extent or relative 'weight' of subsistence production can supply an index of difference, or diversity, between national economies. For example, subsistence activities by the Munduruců Indians (see chapter 2) would not show up in the national income accounts of Brazil, of whose population they represent a miniscule proportion. By contrast, the weight of subsistence production in a national economy like Niger in West Africa is much greater. Twenty per cent of the population derive a substantial part of their livelihood from subsistence pastoralism. During the Sahelian drought of 1968–73 an estimated US$800 million of livestock perished in Niger, equivalent to about 40 per cent of the country's GDP in 1980. Following the previous point about subsistence production, it can be suggested that the greater its relative weight in a national economy, the less integrated that economy will be.

A third point, already noted above, is that the size and performance of economies with substantial volumes of subsistence production are more difficult to measure through conventional indicators. The authors of a World Bank report on sub-Saharan Africa noted that 'The data that underlie the national account aggregates, particularly for agricultural production, are very weak in most African countries. This is partly due to the large share of the subsistence sector in most of these economies' (World Bank, 1981, p. 187). They then present a table comparing estimates of the average annual rate of growth of GDP of six Sahelian countries (Chad, Mali, Mauritania, Niger, Senegal, Upper Volta) from 1960–70, according to seven different sources, which shows that for Chad, the highest estimate is eleven times the lowest, for Mali thirteen times, and for Upper Volta six times. The emphasis on agricultural production in this extract, and the examples of subsistence production given above, both suggest that it is likely to be more widespread in economic activity in the countryside than in towns and cities. In shanty towns, certain activities, such as building one's own house, have elements of subsistence production, but such activities can sustain urban life only to a limited extent compared, say, with peasant and pastoralist production of food staples for direct consumption. Consequently, there is also a sectoral dimension and 'bias' in the relative weight of subsistence production, and the degree of accuracy or inaccuracy of its representation in national income accounts.

A final and extremely important point about subsistence production is that everywhere it is combined with some form of interaction with commodity production, with markets and market exchange, whether through household production for the market or seasonal and occasional wage labour. Even the Munduruců seek to acquire certain commodities for which they need cash, which they have to obtain from selling products and/or working for wages, and the same is true of the pastoralists of the Sahel. The significance of this is taken up in the next section; for the moment the distinction between subsistence production and commodity production can be elaborated.

Goods and services produced for direct consumption or 'subsistence' were described as having use values. Goods and services produced for exchange as commodities must also have some utility or use value, or nobody would want to buy them. However, in addition to their uses for consumption or further production (capital and intermediate goods), commodities also have an *exchange value*. This means that they exchange in particular *ratios* with other commodities, for example, 1 tractor = X weight of raw cotton = Y finished cotton garments of a particular type. In practice, of course, commodities are not exchanged with each other in this way (which corresponds to barter) but are sold and bought for sums of money, expressing their relative *prices*. This includes the commodity labour-power, the price of which is the wage or salary paid to its seller, the worker.

It was noted above that the use value of a product is realized when it is consumed to satisfy, directly or indirectly (producer goods), a human need. This applies equally to an African family consuming the maize it has grown, or to someone in Britain or an African living in a city eating a loaf of bread she or he has bought. The critical difference, however, is that in the latter case *before* the use value of the loaf can be realized by eating it, its exchange value has to be realized by *paying* for it. In short, the exchange value of a commodity is realized when it is sold, providing its owner or seller with a sum of money, its price. Commodity production, therefore, assumes:

1 a separation of the realization of the use value and exchange value of commodities;
2 the existence of markets for commodities;
3 the existence of a medium of exchange (money);
4 the existence of a social division of labour between sectors and units of production making different kinds of commodities.

To briefly recapitulate: products were first classified by their types of uses, determined by their specific material properties. The second kind of distinction, between subsistence products and commodities, while necessarily retaining the idea of utility or use value, entailed a *social* criterion concerning conditions of production and realization, and their connection. In principle, there may be subsistence as well as commodity production of capital, intermediate and consumer goods, although their linkages will be restricted to divisions of labour within households or local commodities. The third dimension of diversity concerns the social conditions and relations of two basic types of commodity production, namely capitalist and petty commodity production.

In chapter 4, capitalism was defined as an economic system of generalized commodity production founded on social relations of production that generate two main social classes: the class of capital or bourgeoisie and the working class or proletariat. Capitalist commodity production is a process in which owners of capital invested in means of production buy the labour-power of workers to produce new commodities, which must have an exchange value greater than the investment in their production (expenditure on machines, materials, wages, interest on loans, etc.) for the capitalist to obtain a profit.

Petty commodity producers are, in a sense, both capitalist and workers at the same time: they have access to means of production which they 'put to work' with their own labour rather than the labour of others. While capitalists exploit workers to make profits, petty commodity producers employ and exploit themselves. If they are successful enough to accumulate savings from this self-exploitation that they can invest in expanding their enterprise by hiring other workers, then they are transforming themselves into capitalists, if on a small scale to begin with. If, on the other hand, they are unable to reproduce themselves simultaneously as labour (daily and generational reproduction) and capital (maintenance and replacement of means of production) then they are likely to lose their capital and be forced to seek their livelihood through working for others: they are proletarianized (see chapters 1 and 2).

There is great diversity among both capitalist and petty commodity enterprises which exist in a variety of branches of production in the social division of labour, producing a variety of goods by a variety of means. Both capitalist and petty commodity enterprises are also very diverse with respect to the resources they can mobilize, the levels of capitalization they can afford, the technologies employed and their associated productivities of labour, which in turn affect the income they achieve from their activities and its uses in reproducing and expanding enterprises.

At the same time, petty commodity production has certain limitations and sources of variation that distinguish it from capitalist production. The principal *limitation* concerns the supply of labour and its implications for the production processes that can be utilized. The kinds of technology petty commodity production can employ are limited by the amount of labour available to the individual unit of production (Friedmann, 1978), which may consist of a single individual or a household or family whose members contribute their labour in various ways. This does not mean, however, that petty commodity production is restricted to 'low technology' processes. While the 'family farm' in many African contexts may consist, say, of a dozen women, men and children cultivating five or six acres with hand tools, small engineering workshops found in many Third World cities may consist of two or three people operating sophisticated machinery (e.g. multi-purpose lathes) with considerable levels of skill, that makes the enterprise very flexible and competitive. On the other hand, some kinds of agricultural production (e.g. in plantations) and many kinds of manufacturing process (like vehicle production) cannot be undertaken by petty commodity production because of the numbers of workers they require (see chapter 10).

The source of *variation* that distinguishes petty from capitalist commodity production is that while the latter is always specialized, petty commodity production (especially in agriculture) can display various degrees of specialization. While some petty commodity enterprises in Third World economies may be as specialized as any capitalist firm, others are not and may combine a diverse range of commodity activities (cash crops, craft production, petty trade) with subsistence production, to varying degrees and in various ways. This has implications for 'development' in the capitalist sense of extending and intensifying commodity production, which entails increasing specialization and the development of more complex social divisions of labour.

The issues this raises are discussed in the next section. For the moment, it is worth noting that the distribution of economic activity between capitalist and petty commodity production (and between the wide range of types of production process within each of these two basic categories) represents another important dimension of the social division of labour in capitalist economies.

## Integration: Uneven and Combined Development

The preceding section about diversity also indicated some aspects and issues of integration. Firstly, the discussion of linkages concerned a central aspect of integration in terms of the use value dimension of the social division of labour: linkages between producers of goods and services with different kinds of specific uses. Secondly, the discussion of subsistence production and of the two basic types of commodity production under capitalism – capitalist commodity production and petty commodity production – introduced a crucial *social* dimension of the division of labour, namely the separation of the realization of the exchange value of commodities (through their sale) and the realization of their use value (through their consumption). It was suggested that subsistence products and the resources used to produce them are *apparently* 'lost' from the view-point of the national economy, as their circuits of realization are restricted to households or local communities rather than providing linkages with other producers or sectors of production in the national division of labour.

To explain the 'apparently' in the above statement, and to pursue the idea of integration further, it is useful to make a distinction between the *extension* and the *intensification* of commodity production in capitalist development. Capitalism was defined as generalized commodity production, but 'generalized' does not mean 'uniform'. In what follows, it will be suggested that the development of capitalism proceeds through *differential commoditization*, which reflects the process of uneven and combined development.

Firstly, let us deal with the extension of commodity production, the conditions of which were established historically through the processes outlined in chapters 4 and 5, and which may be summarized as follows. Generalized commodity production, established initially through the extension of commodity production and its social relations, exists when '*individuals are unable to exist and to reproduce themselves outside of circuits of commodity economy and divisions of labour generated by the*

FIGURE 11 (Top) Non-agricultural petty commodity production: an Asian boy preparing thread for home weaving; the spinning wheel has been made from a bicycle wheel (ILO photo). (Bottom) Petty commodity production of a peasant 'capital good': village blacksmith making a sickle, West Bengal, India (Ed Milner)

(Above) Spinning sewing thread in Ethiopia (ILO photo)

*capital/wage/labour relation and its contradictions*' (Bernstein, 1986, which draws heavily on the argument presented by Gibbon and Neocosmos, 1985). While this process was historically very uneven, incorporating different people in different places at different times within the capitalist international division of labour, it was completed on a global scale in the period of imperialism as Lenin termed it (the last quarter of the nineteenth century onwards). Moreover, the colonial expansion of this period – above all in Africa, but also in parts of western and East Asia – took place when industrial capitalism had become the major force in structuring the international division of labour.

Many people in the various indigenous societies of the Third World attempted to resist this process of incorporation in both its political and economic dimensions, the former manifested through colonial conquest, the latter through pressures (including direct coercion) to participate in new types of production and divisions of labour that were destructive of their previous ways of life. However fierce or protracted resistance was, once commodity production became an *economic necessity*, then the conditions of generalized commodity production (the extension of commodity relations) were satisfied.

> Once commodity relations are incorporated in the reproduction cycle of the [rural] household as an economic necessity, the question of how much of its resources (in terms of labour-time or of land) are devoted to the production of use-value and of commodities is secondary, though still important. Simple quantitative measures which might show, say, that only 20% of labour-time or 20% of land is devoted to commodity production, are misleading if they

> imply that the household is still basically a 'subsistence' unit (in the narrow sense), only marginally involved with commodity relations and therefore easily able to withdraw from them. (To the extent that a low degree of commodity production in this sense correlates geographically with labour reserve areas or socially with strata of poorer peasants, this is because the principal commodity produced in these cases is labour-power itself). (Bernstein, 1977, p. 63)

In Third World countries created as political entities by colonialism, and as national economies within the capitalist international division of labour (typically with considerable assistance from colonial states), some people were proletarianized, others were semi-proletarianized, many others became petty commodity producers in the sense defined above, and a mere handful became capitalists (to begin with, most commonly as traders and/or transporters, less so in agricultural production, and least in manufacturing). For the great majority who were either semi-proletarianized or became petty commodity producers, 'subsistence' production could contribute a significant part of their livelihood, as the statement quoted suggests, and for many of them it continues to do so. The critical point, then, is not that 'subsistence' production signifies a relative *lack* of integration in capitalist economy (national and international) but that different types and degrees of 'subsistence' production express *different forms of integration* in generalized commodity production. It can be further suggested that the different types and degrees of 'subsistence' production are *determined* by the different forms of integration in capitalist economy, rather than the other way round.

One illustration of this is provided by the situation of *semi-proletarianization*, introduced in chapter 3 and illustrated by regular (often cyclical) wage employment combined with household 'subsistence' agriculture. Many capitalist enterprises in Third World economies, notably in agriculture and mining but also in some branches of processing and manufacturing industry, employ workers at wage rates insufficient to reproduce them and their families (that is, insufficient to sustain generational reproduction). This both reduces the unit costs of production to the enterprise and forces workers and their families to supplement their wages with other sources of livelihood. If they have access to land, then food production may provide an important contribution to their survival, albeit at typically depressed standards of living. This can take different forms. For example, the mining sectors of Southern Africa historically have utilized fixed-period labour contracts with male migrant workers, whose wives, mothers and children remained in their rural areas and struggled to farm subsistence plots. Another widespread form of semi-proletarianization occurs when whole families engage in seasonal wage employment (often entailing temporary migration) in capitalist plantations and farms, for example, to work in the harvest, and the rest of the year engage in primarily subsistence farming on their own plots of land.

These examples show one kind of manifestation of uneven and combined development very well. Unevenness is expressed in the evident 'dualism' of highly specialized and often highly capitalized enterprises on one hand, and, on the other, family or mainly female subsistence farming in conditions of economic and ecological marginality. A 'snapshot' picture of the former would convey images of 'development', of the latter images of 'underdevelopment', 'backwardness', etc. But such 'snapshots' are wholly deceptive, as is any notion of 'dualism' suggesting that the two spheres of economic activity are quite separate from each other, because they are, of course, *combined*. Moreover, specific forms of combination express particular kinds of capitalist development, in which different conditions of wage employment *determine* the social conditions of 'subsistence' farming that helps produce and reproduce the labour power required by capitalism. In short, situations of semi-proletarianization show how the uneven and combined development of capitalism generates sectors of subsistence production within certain social divisions of labour, that simultaneously integrate differences in economic activity by type of production, by class relations, and by gender relations. (In the case of colonial economies and of contemporary South Africa, one should add the *racial* dimension of class relations to these differences.)

It was stated above that capitalist enterprises tend to be specialized in the commodities they produce (and the ways they produce them, i.e. their technical conditions of production). Indeed, such specialization (associated with growing complexity of the social division of labour) is characteristic of capitalist economic development. By contrast, it was suggested that petty commodity production varies a great deal in its degree of specialization, and the combination of commodity production with different types and degrees of subsistence production within the same unit or household. This applies especially to agriculture, as the following examples illustrate.

The first case is that of a peasant family that devotes most of its resources (land and labour) to growing food staples, and sells only that part of its harvest that is 'surplus' to its own needs. In a bad harvest year it needs to retain the whole of the crop for its own consumption, and therefore cannot acquire the commodities it can buy in a good year when it sells part of its crop. This means a (temporary) reduction in its consumption of commodities, but it also seems to indicate that the family is able to regulate its relationship with the market. This is possible because it is not engaged in specialized commodity production, but is concerned in the first place with the production of subsistence goods, which can be exchanged as commodities when they are 'surplus' to the household's needs.

The second case is that of a peasant household specializing, say, in the production of tea or coffee. The 'cash crops' of tea or coffee have no use value for their producers, who are therefore dependent to a much greater extent on the market to satisfy their needs. How much food (and other necessities) they can buy depends on the quantity of 'cash crops' they can produce and how much income they can earn by selling them (their 'realization' as exchange values). In this case, the tea- or coffee-producing household is more dependent on the market because it is engaged in more specialized commodity production, and also because it cultivates a

FIGURE 12 Uneven development in capitalist societies: views of São Paulo, Brazil (Alan Hutchison Library) and Marseilles, France (Jean Mohr)

'permanent' crop that only yields its fruits some years after planting. If prices for tea or coffee decline, it is a weighty decision for the households cultivating these crops whether to uproot the bushes and put the land they occupied to some other use.

In the third case, a peasant household specializing in an 'annual' cash crop like tobacco or cotton is, in principle, more adaptable to changes in market conditions. If prices are low or declining it may decide to plant

less tobacco or cotton and to grow more food for its own consumption, or to switch to a different cash crop.

These three examples illustrate different degrees of *intensity* of commodity production or 'differential commoditization' (within conditions of generalized commodity production, as defined above). On an increasing scale of intensity, the food producing household ranks lowest, the annual cash-crop household next, and that growing specialized 'permanent' crops, highest.

The main criterion implicit in this scale of intensification is *the flow of commodities in both directions*, that is, the quantity and type of commodities the household has to purchase for its reproduction, and the amount and type of labour and other resources it has to devote to commodity production to earn money to purchase the commodities it requires. Of the latter, it is useful to distinguish between producer and intermediate goods on one hand, and consumption goods (including food) on the other. This corresponds to the point above about petty commodity producers having to reproduce themselves both as capital (securing means of production) and as labour (securing means of consumption). It can be further suggested that another useful index of the intensity of commodity production is the cost of means of production that have to be purchased as commodities, relative to the overall value of production by the household.

In principle, one can expect at least a rough correlation between this index, the sophistication of the means of production used, the productivities of labour they make possible, and the degree of specialization of petty commodity production within the social division of labour. Such a correlation is evident, for example, if one compares 'family farming' of the highly capitalized 'Western' type (Friedmann, 1978) with, say, food-producing peasant households in Africa or India. At the same time, the vulnerability of the latter to the pressures exerted by integration in generalized commodity production should not be underestimated. Peasant families in Africa whose economic activity entails apparently little expenditure on means of production (limited to buying hand tools such as hoes and machetes) can experience severe crises if their monetary income is so depressed that they are unable to reproduce periodically even these means of production (this is graphically illustrated in Mamdani, 1986).

This African example corresponds to the first of the three cases given above, the least intense in terms of commodity production. However, an Indian Green Revolution example (see chapter 9) shows what happens when food staples are produced as a more commercial and specialized crop, increasingly dependent on purchased means of production (seeds, fertilizer, irrigation water, as well as tools, draught animals, and possibly rented land too). The dependence of even very small producers on the market increases, and problems of reproduction are experienced above all as problems of monetary income. The latter commonly lead to indebtedness with poor peasants 'mortgaging' their crops against loans, or otherwise selling much of their harvest to pay back what they have borrowed. Again, very commonly, they are forced to sell immediately after harvest when prices are lower and, when the food stock they have retained runs out, to buy the food they need at higher prics, necessitating further borrowing, and so on (for some indication of the scale of this process in India, and a very useful analysis, see Byres, 1974).

This last case illustrates how a particular combination of social conditions (relating to the intensification of commodity production) and technical conditions (Green Revolution technology) shifts the composition of commodity and subsistence production within a peasant household. As with the earlier examples of semi-proletarianization (wage labour plus subsistence activity), it can, therefore, be suggested that different types and degrees of 'subsistence' production combined with petty commodity production express, *and* are determined by, different forms of integration in generalized commodity production.

Non-agricultural and particularly urban petty commodity production in Third World economies also displays an enormous amount of variation in its activities and forms of integration, as the following suggests:

> The 'informal sector' of urban petty commodity production comprises the provision of personal and other services, as well as of goods, encompassing small-scale trading and hawking, the preparation of food for sale in the home or on the street, prostitution, the 'scavenging' of garbage for recycling and resale, and so on . . .
>
> The 'informal sector' is thus highly differentiated with respect to its activities, the resources that households and individuals can mobilize to pursue them, and the incomes they derive from them. Despite this differentiation, the large numbers of people struggling to gain their living through urban petty commodity production has the effect of intensifying competition between them, subjecting them to control by a hierarchy of 'middlemen' (such as larger scale traders and suppliers). This increases the precariousness of the ventures they engage in, and depresses their incomes and standards of living. (Johnson and Bernstein, 1982, pp. 260–1)

At the same time, even with this range of variation, urban 'informal sector' activities present some important contrasts with agricultural petty commodity production. The first, indicated above, is that urban economy presents much less opportunity for sources of 'subsistence' income, compared with farming or animal husbandry (which might be supplemented with hunting, fishing, gathering, and so on). Accordingly, urban petty commodity production is generally more intense in the sense of the flow of commodities in both directions that it typically entails.

A second point of contrast is provided by what are termed 'free entry' activities in the urban 'informal sector', which means ways of trying to gain a livelihood that require little investment of resources or technical skills. Such activities include small-scale hawking and trading, selling newspapers or cigarettes on the street, washing cars or clothes or other kinds of cleaning work, porterage around market places, the scavenging and 'recycling' of garbage, prostitution, and so on. These 'free entry' activities provide a minimal means of survival for large numbers of people in most Third World cities. They are often pursued by recent migrants to the city and others who are unemployed in order to 'get by' while they look for regular wage work. If one sort of activity is going badly, they can try to switch to another without losing precious resources in the process.

At the same time, the mobilization of resources for people in great poverty involves costs that contradict what an outsider may consider 'freedom' of entry into a particular sector of activity. The story of an unsuccessful attempt by an urban 'marginal' in Cali, Colombia, to establish himself as an 'independent' scrap merchant (Ruisque-Alcaino and Bromley, 1979), which involved selling almost all his household's meagre possessions to raise some 'working capital', has an epic quality of struggle reminiscent of the struggles of many poor peasants to cling on to a piece of land. However, the central importance of land as a means of production in agriculture, the value associated with land in peasant cultures, and the attachment of peasants to their land, are all very different from the intense spatial and 'occupational' mobility of urban 'free entry' activities.

Not all urban small-scale commodity production, of course, manifests this intense flux. Small-scale engineering and metal working, carpentry, building, shoemaking and tailoring, or the repair and servicing of machinery, require relatively high levels of resources: special premises and stocks of tools and materials, as well as specialized skills. It is from activities of this kind (as well as certain types of trade) that a minority of petty commodity producers might accumulate capital to the extent that they can themselves become small capitalists, expanding their scale of production through employing the labour of others, in the same way as the rich peasants/capitalist farmers of the Green Revolution.

The discussion in this section has focused mostly on petty commodity production, and to a lesser extent on semi-proletarianization, for two reasons. The first, implied by the reference to 'dualism', is that some types of petty commodity production and of semi-proletarian and subsistence activity 'look' as if they are less than fully integrated into generalized commodity production and wider (national and international) social divisions of labour. To consider them less than fully integrated is often to assume that they are also less than 'fully' capitalist (e.g. because they are held to combine capitalist and non-capitalist relations of production), and from here it is a short step to viewing Third World economies as 'underdeveloped' *because* they are characterized by the widespread prevalence of small-scale production and semi-proletarianization. The position put forward here (which is by no means uncontentious) is that Third World economies are characterized by generalized commodity production no less than those of the First World. At the same time, the concept of differential commoditization or intensity of commodity production recognizes that there are different types and degrees of 'development' *within* capitalism, which have some correspondence with different forms of integration in the market economy.

Whilst arguing against the optical illusion, so to speak, of viewing many types of production and producers in Third World economies as wholly or partly 'outside' capitalism, this chapter has also said little about capitalist commodity production because it is given much more attention in the chapters that follow. However, several points are worth making here in the context of the diversity and integration of national economies.

1 Capitalist enterprises and production processes display an enormous amount of variation, which can also be conceptualized in terms of forms and degrees of the intensification of commodity production, though with certain key differences from petty commodity production. For example, a central criterion of variation of petty commodity production in terms of intensification is the extent of the flow of commodities in both directions.

By contrast, in capitalist production all the elements of production are purchased as commodities, and all production is for sale as commodities (even though labour power itself is partly reproduced through non-commoditized activity: through subsistence production and domestic labour in the case of semi-proletarianized workers, and through domestic labour in the case of wholly proletarianized workers).

Variations in the intensity of capitalist commodity production can be conceptualized along two dimensions of the concentration and the centralization of capital. The *concentration* of capital refers to the *production process* itself: its levels of capitalization per worker, its uses of machinery, of economies of scale, of more or less complex technical divisions of labour, numbers of workers, and so on. It was indicated above that different levels and types of capitalization of the production process also represent a major source of variation in petty commodity production, but their upper limits are set by family or household labour supply. Capitalist production, however, is able to utilize economies of scale and complex technical divisions of labour far beyond the capacity of petty commodity production because of its ability to employ wage workers (i.e. its social conditions of production allow a much more extensive development of the technical conditions of production).

The *Centralization* of capital refers to the scale of operation of capitalist firms or *companies*, and the quantity of (particularly financial) resources they can mobilize. The application of these concepts can be illustrated briefly.

In the first case, let us look at those production processes that exhibit no particular economies of scale, hence no attraction in terms of competitive advantage to the concentration of capital. There may be, however, competitive advantages in economies of organization at the level of the firm. The garment industry and other branches of manufacturing utilizing 'outworkers' exemplify this situation, in which the firm consists of a capitalist and a number of scattered workers (individuals or families often working at home) whose production he or she organizes, supplying them with machinery and raw materials and collecting and marketing the commodities they make. Similar situations exist with 'contract farming' in agriculture in which a capitalist company operating, say, sugar mills, or tea processing factories, obtains its raw materials (sugar cane, tea leaves) from a number of contracted small farmers, to whom it advances inputs and credits and whose methods of cultivation it closely regulates.

In the second case, imagine a manufacturing process requiring a certain economy of scale, technical division of labour, and number of workers. Here the firm may consist of a single factory with, say, a hundred employees. The third case is the situation of transnational corporations which have large plants and subsidiary operations in a number of different countries.

The first case thus represents a certain degree of centralization of capital without any significant concentration of capital in the production process itself (the garment industry). The second case represents a greater concentration of capital in production but with a limited centralization (the two dimensions converging in a single firm/unit of production). The third case represents a very high level of both the centralization and concentration of capital which, of course, expresses the enormous economic power of contemporary transnational corporations. Other things being equal, the greater the centralization of capital, the greater a concentration of capital in the production process it makes possible. Interestingly, the case of agricultural processing integrated with small-scale farming might combine aspects of all three situations. That is, the sugar mill or tea processing factory represents a certain concentration of capital; it might be owned by a transnational corporation and integrated with its interests and activities (e.g. equipment manufacture, finance, transport, wholesaling) in other countries, while it draws its raw material supply from the small producers it contracts with.

2 The *second* broad point to be made here concerns the relationship between capitalist and petty commodity production as an important dimension of national economies and their integration. While it is impossible to offer any adequate empirical generalization about this relationship, given the enormous variation of both capitalist and petty commodity production, one may suggest as a somewhat crude generalization that, within the constraints of uneven and combined development, the more 'developed' the forms of capitalist production in a particular sector or national economy as a whole (above all in producer goods sectors), the more 'developed' many of the types of petty commodity production directly or indirectly integrated with them through the social division of labour.

3 The *third* and final point concerns the development of national economies. If, as has been argued here, diversity within and between national economies is associated with different forms (rather than degrees) of integration, and if the circuits of commodity economy are as determinant of the livelihoods of people in the cities and rural areas of the Third World as they are in First World economies, why are some national economies more 'developed' than others? There is no simple answer to this question, although some indications have been provided, involving relationships between:

1 the differential intensity of various types of both capitalist and petty commodity production (generally manifested in differential labour productivities);
2 the ways in which national economies are simultaneously diversified and integrated in terms of the backward and forward linkages between different sectors and types of production, at prevailing (and differential) levels of labour productivity;
3 the ability to develop productive capacity in different sectors and types of production and to enhance the developmental effects of their linkages.

All these considerations relate very much to *accumulation* in national economies. But what determines rates of accumulation and its effectiveness in expanding and developing various activities and capacities? Processes of accumulation both reflect and act upon diverse social and technical conditions of production in extremely complex ways, not least because they embody social, political and ideological struggle between, and also within, the different classes and other social categories of capitalism both nationally and internationally.

PART III

# Production and Producers in Agriculture

# Introduction

Chapter 6 (in the preceding part) asserts a particular view of Third World economies, that the incidence of forms of production (sometimes misleadingly referred to as 'traditional'), not found in developed economies, is a product of a particular relationship with capitalist production and not the continuation of pre-capitalist forms of production. There are no significant numbers of Third World peasants who are not dependent upon a system of generalized commodity production. These ideas are developed in the next three chapters, which examine production on the land.

Chapter 7 analyses the effects of different degrees of commoditization on the technical conditions of production for subsistence, petty commodity, and capitalist, production. It considers the ways in which both internal and external factors constrain or, alternatively, provide opportunities for increases in, agricultural output.

Chapter 8 focuses on small-scale production on the land as the dominant form of production for most of the Third World's population and a major concern, therefore, for any theory concerned with national development. Theorists have (broadly) viewed small-scale production as either an interim stage in the development towards large-scale (usually) fully capitalist agricultural production, or as an alternative form of development to large-scale production capable of generating increases in output. The persistence of small-scale production on the land is explored through analysis of the household as the unit of production and the divisions of labour within the household, especially those based on gender. It is the interaction between these conditions, internal to the household, and the wider socio-economic environment, that provides the dynamic of change. Many peasant households are kept at the margins of survival by chronic indebtedness until the loss of any access to land places them finally with landless labourers. Other households may be able to enter a 'virtuous circle' of increased output, improved technology and rising income, which allows them to accumulate and to begin to expand production.

Chapter 9 provides a case study of the application of 'Green Revolution' technologies to small-scale production in India which has, overall, exacerbated both these tendencies, increasing the pressures towards proletarianization for those households with the most tenuous hold on land, and providing new opportunities for growth for those able to get reliable access to the 'technological package'.

These and other examples are provided of the fact that while household production persists, both what is produced and how are changing, and survival in many circumstances requires the supplementation of household income from a variety of sources – casual labour, craft skills, services of various kinds, and so on. One of the most important effects of this process is the increasing differentiation among peasantries, with (in areas of India for example) the growth of a rich peasantry, in a position to consolidate their holdings from land lost by poor peasants and to rely on a growing pool of landless labourers to supply their labour requirements as they arise.

CHAPTER SEVEN

# Developing Production on the Land

Chapter 6 emphasized the diversity of production forms in the Third World and outlined ways of examining the processes of commoditization and capitalization which influence and integrate those diverse forms. In this chapter, the focus will be on the technical dimensions of diversity in agricultural production. Our intention is to show how differences between producers' use of land, labour and technology set constraints and provide opportunities for development. Although the focus of the chapter is the technical conditions of production, these will be examined in relation to a social change – commoditization.

## Development and the Commoditization of Agriculture

The development of agriculture in Third World economies is strongly linked to the extension and intensification of commodity production. Three important aspects of development (the increase of productive capacities) are frequently associated with the spread of commodity production. These are:

1 the increasing range of ways in which nature is transformed;
2 the increasing sophistication and power of the tools used in production;
3 the increasing scale and specialization of production.

As the various tools, inputs and products of agriculture, and the land and labour power used in agricultural production, become commodities, there is a tendency for productive capacities to increase. For that reason, an important focus of this chapter and chapters 8 and 9 is the differential commoditization of agriculture.

There are no readily accessible indices of the extension and intensification of commodity production in agriculture. There is, however, a related and widely documented change associated with the development of production on the land. This is the shift of labour power (and livelihoods) from the land to industry, a shift, as we shall see below, which is in part a consequence of the increase in productive capacities in agriculture.

In most (but not all) Third World economies, the central importance of agriculture, for both production and welfare, is indicated by the high proportion of the population gaining their livelihood directly from agriculture. In all economies, however, there has been a tendency for that proportion to decline. Table 3 shows the distribution of the labour force between the three sectors, agriculture, industry and services, for a selection of fifteen economies in two recent years. The economies include twelve from the Third World, exhibiting a range of size and other characteristics, and three industrialized economies for comparison. In all fifteen economies, there has been a reduction in the proportion of the labour force engaged in agriculture between 1965 and 1983. In the case of seven – Brazil, Chile, Peru, Nigeria, Philippines, Indonesia and the USSR – the reduction has been 10 per cent or more. So substantial a change in only eight years suggests rapid social change.

Figure 13 provides a crude indication of the shape, diversity and duration of labour force changes over a longer historical period. The ratio of the population engaged in agriculture to that engaged in industry is plotted for nine countries. It shows the long and continuing changes in those countries that industrialized first, Britain and the USA. The Soviet Union and Japan, by comparison, have experienced much more recent and rapid declines of numbers in agriculture relative to industry. In both cases their

TABLE 3 Sectoral division of the labour force in fifteen economies, 1965 and 1983 (percentages)

| | *Sectoral division of labour force* | | | | | |
|---|---|---|---|---|---|---|
| | *Agriculture* | | *Industry* | | *Services* | |
| | *1965* | *1983* | *1965* | *1983* | *1965* | *1983* |
| Brazil | 49 | 30 | 17 | 24 | 34 | 46 |
| Chile | 26 | 19 | 21 | 19 | 53 | 62 |
| Peru | 50 | 40 | 19 | 19 | 31 | 41 |
| Kenya | 84 | 78 | 6 | 10 | 10 | 12 |
| Niger | 94 | 91 | 1 | 3 | 5 | 6 |
| Nigeria | 67 | 54 | 12 | 19 | 21 | 27 |
| Tanzania | 88 | 83 | 4 | 6 | 8 | 11 |
| India | 74 | 71 | 11 | 13 | 15 | 16 |
| China | — | 74 | — | 13 | — | 13 |
| Philippines | 57 | 46 | 16 | 17 | 27 | 37 |
| Singapore | 6 | 2 | 26 | 39 | 68 | 59 |
| Indonesia | 71 | 58 | 9 | 12 | 20 | 30 |
| Britain | 3 | 2 | 46 | 42 | 51 | 56 |
| USA | 5 | 2 | 36 | 32 | 59 | 66 |
| USSR | 33 | 14 | 33 | 45 | 34 | 41 |

*Source*: World Bank (1985), pp. 214–15.

industrialization has been more rapid than was the case in Britain and the USA. The Third World countries in figure 13 are striking not only for the relatively high numbers employed in agriculture, but also for the unevenness of changes in the ratio of agricultural and industrial employment.

The development of commodity production (or, more generally, of monetized exchange), and these large shifts in the proportion of the population engaged in agricultural work, are connected through the expansion of productive capacities. In essence, the connection has four elements.

1 Commodity production enables a more complex division of labour. Thus, for example, the purchase of seeds may give a peasant household access to the work of agricultural researchers. The purchased seeds may have greater productivity than would have been provided by seeds selected by the household from its own previous year's harvest.

2 That division of labour has allowed greater specialization. In place of a population of peasant households producing their own seeds, this example postulates specialized seed producers whose work embodies the benefits of systematic investigation into seed production.

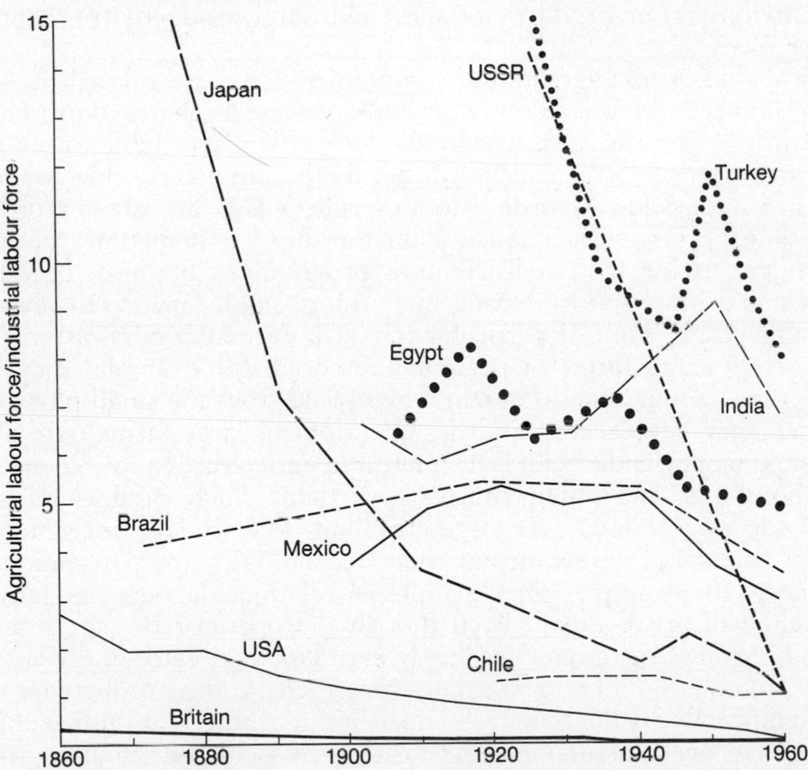


FIGURE 13 Changes in the ratio of the agricultural to the industrial labour force
*Source*: Crow and Thomas (1983), p. 31.

3 The new, specialized, division of labour allows the scale of production to be increased. The specialized seed producers will produce for more than one household. Seeds can then be produced with less labour per unit of production than would have been employed by dispersed, individualized, peasant production. In other words, economies of scale can be made.

4 The new division of labour fosters new groups of producers no longer directly engaged in agricultural production. In the case of our example, these are research scientists and a seed-production industry. Clearly, similar backward and forward linkages are developed for all manner of goods used in agriculture, from tractors and other tools to irrigation water and fertilizers.

The elements of the connection, that is commodity production leading to a new division of labour, specialization, new sorts of work, and a shift from agriculture into industry, are evident in a wide range of economies but they take different paths and have diverse consequences. One purpose of this chapter is to outline that diversity.

The next section of the chapter describes the technical conditions of three different production forms in order to examine the constraints and possibilities for increasing productive capacity. Before embarking on that description, a point should be made about the two main measures of productivity: labour productivity and yield (land productivity) (defined in chapter 3).

Many studies of agricultural economics have postulated a simple relationship between one or other (or both) of these measures of productivity and farm size (usually measured by the area of land available to the farm). Some investigations have concluded that there is an inverse rule connecting farm size and yield. According to this rule, yields are greater on small farms than on large farms. Such a relationship has sometimes been used as justification for land redistribution programmes because, if it holds, output could be raised by having many more small farms. However, this is not universally true. At particular times, in particular circumstances, the operators of small farms (a peasant household, for example) may invest considerable labour time to obtain a high yield from the small plot of land to which they have access, and the operators of large farms (e.g. a large trader and moneylender with little interest in agriculture) may expend much less labour time and obtain much lower yields. Such circumstances may prevail for long periods over large areas but they are still not general. As soon as the large farms deploy new technologies (new techniques or machinery, for example) then the simple relationship between farm size and yield will break down. Even though the operator of the large farm may still deploy little labour (probably even less than before), the adoption of new techniques and new machines may increase the productivity of the land significantly. If the new techniques and machinery are not within the grasp of the operator of the small farm, then yields on small farms may remain at their previous level.

Thus, the introduction of new agricultural technologies may change the relationship between farm size and yield. Before they are introduced, small farms may have higher yields because they use more labour time. After the introduction of new technologies, those farms which have successfully adopted the technologies will have the highest yields. In chapter 10 we shall examine an example of the introduction of new technology and see why it is most successfully adopted only by some farmers (often with larger farms).

## Three Production Processes

This section considers the technical conditions of production of three different forms of production on the land found in different parts of the Third World: (i) the economy of the Mundurucu society in the Amazonian forests of Brazil; (ii) small-scale production in India; and (iii) production on plantations in Tanzania. Within the categories of production forms introduced in chapter 6, these examples can be respectively categorized as subsistence, subsistence/petty commodity production, and large-scale, capitalist production.

### *The economy of the Mundurucu*

The case of the Mundurucu is taken from a study made of their community of 350 people in the 1950s (Murphy and Murphy, 1974). The Mundurucu villages of the savannah (grassland) regions in the Amazon forest were relatively untouched by Brazilian society, their main contact being through the rubber trade in which some of the Mundurucu participated for two or three months of the dry season. The combination of savannah and forest provided the basis for their subsistence which comprised gardening, hunting and fishing, and gathering wild fruits and nuts.

The production of manioc (cassava) was their main source of food and was also that which required the most labour. The Mundurucu practised slash-and-burn agriculture: clearing and burning areas of the forest which were then cultivated for two or three years before being left to return to forest. The gardens, which were about one hectare in area, were cleared by the men using axes and machetes. The cut vegetation was left to dry for three months and then burnt. The men then dug holes for the manioc shoots with hoes and the women followed behind planting them and covering them. When a garden was newly planted, manioc would take about eight months to grow to plants six to nine feet high with tubers (the main source of food) in the ground. After planting, the gardens took little weeding, which was done with hoes, and women would spend a few hours a week working there. When the tubers were about a foot long they were dug up by groups of women using machetes. Around the time of the rainy season, the stalks would be saved to cut into shoots for the next planting.

To make dry manioc flour, the tubers would be processed to remove poisonous acid and to make them edible. This involved peeling, grating, soaking, draining the pulp, sieving it and, finally, toasting it. An alternative process involved soaking the tubers in a stream for three to eight days to soften them and leach out the poison; the flesh would then be taken out of the skin and trodden into a pulp, after which it was sieved and toasted. This method was less laborious, but the soaking removed most of the starch while leaving the fibres and made this manioc flour less nutritious than dry manioc flour. Either method would be carried out by households of women including mothers, daughters and sisters. (Households comprised women, children and pubescent boys; men lived in a men's house.) The other crops that might be grown by women were yams, sweet potatoes, maize, squash, pineapples, cotton, beans, rice, sugar cane and bananas. Different soils were used for the different crops, for example, squash, beans and rice would be grown in the richest black soil, maize on the redder soils and manioc on the clay soils. Digging sticks would be used for planting seed crops and otherwise hoes were the main implements.

Hunting for game was carried out by groups of men using bows and arrows or old guns which they had acquired through trade with rubber collectors. Fishing was also done by men using bows and harpoon-tipped arrows. Men from the savannah region villages would only fish during the dry season when they were collecting rubber at the edges of the rivers. Women also went on fishing trips with the men but used small nets. Drugs extracted from roots and creepers were used to poison fish on collective fishing expeditions.

This provides description of most of the production processes and the techniques used by the Mundurucu. Certain productive activities, such as the processing of cassava, required the expenditure of considerable human energy. Other tasks, such as gathering wild fruits, required relatively little labour time partly because no effort was required to produce them, only to pick them. Nature was appropriated 'in the raw', so to speak.

*Land use* Using only simple tools, the Mundurucu were able to provide their own subsistence from a combination of a tropical forest and savannah environment. The type of *extensive* agriculture practised by them is particularly suited to areas where there is an abundance of land but where land is not very fertile and cannot be used for more than a few years at a time. (It takes about forty years in this case for the forest to cover the ground again in much the same way as it did before clearance.) The yield of this type of production is very low.

*Technical inputs* The simple tools used by the Mundurucu were an extension of their muscle power. But their technical culture, such as their knowledge of soils used in the growing of different crops, of poisons used in the processing of manioc and in fishing, was extremely important.

*Use of labour* While the growing of crops required only periodic inputs of labour, the harvesting and processing of the main food crop, manioc, was time-consuming and labour-intensive. Maintaining adequate supplies of manioc flour required continuous labour, particularly given the basic technology used. Carried out in groups, the process involved a technical division of labour, and is an example of *simple cooperation*. Task allocation was also organized around a clear sexual division of labour, in this case where women did the most continually arduous tasks in providing the main subsistence.

The kinds of production engaged in by the Mundurucu satisfied the consumption needs of the community, including securing what was needed in the form of tools, plant cuttings and so on required for the next production cycle. This limited form of production fulfilled the needs, therefore, of *simple reproduction*. Given their environment and level of technology, could the Mundurucu expand their production beyond satisfying consumption needs? It appears they were able to produce a small amount of surplus manioc flour which they traded with rubber collectors for tools and weapons. Thus they were able to improve somewhat on the quality of the technology they had through exchange relations with rubber traders.

The contact with the rubber trade led both to an increase in the productive capacity of the Munducruu community and to a dislocation of their society. Some Mundurucu were drawn more closely into the network of exchange relations with the rubber trade, as its activities encroached on the normal agricultural cycle. They settled at the edges of the river, where the rubber traders had penetrated by boat, and became integrated through mission stations into a different kind of life, as rubber became a more important element in their economy and fishing replaced hunting.

### *Small-scale production in India*

The technical conditions of subsistence and petty commodity production on the land in India provide our second example. The general characteristics of small scale agriculture in India are:

1 landholdings are small and fragmented;
2 tools are mostly simple;
3 access to irrigation is limited;
4 family labour is the principal source of labour.

The conditions required for growing particular crops clearly affect how the variables, climate, land, tools and labour are combined in any production process. The following account of some of the factors involved in maize production (abstracted from the Indian Council of Agricultural Research, 1980) gives an idea of what producers using new technologies have to take into consideration.

*Land* Maize preferably needs fertile, deep and well-drained soil but can be grown on any type of land, providing the soil can hold water and can be drained.

*Climate* It can be grown in a variety of climatic conditions but cannot stand frost and needs adequate water.

FIGURE 14 Hoeing in India (Ed Milner)

*Rotation* Maize is a short-duration crop maturing in 80–95 days and is usually rotated with other crops. For example, in the states of Punjab, Uttar Pradesh and Bihar, maize is rotated with wheat, potatoes and barley over the year, when these crops are under irrigation. Cotton and sugar-cane are also grown in a two-year rotation. Inter-cropping (growing other crops on the same land at the same time) is not so common but sometimes legumes or beans are grown together with maize and, in rainfed Central India, sugar-cane and *arhar* (pigeon peas).

*Cultivation* The land has to be ploughed two or three times with a wooden plough (but only once if a tractor is used) before sowing. To obtain high yields, the ground should be heavily manured and shallow drains made. The maize is sown, just before the monsoon starts, using a seed-drill or by dropping seeds behind the plough. Where there is inadequate rainfall, irrigation is required. The crop has to be weeded two or three times using bullock-drawn implements, between rows, and by hand between the plants.

*Harvesting* The ears of the maize are removed and dried in the sun before being shelled. This can be done by hand, by beating the ears with sticks or by using hand- or power-operated shellers. Seeds from the ears of the best plants are stored to seed the next crop.

There is no account of processing in this description but 85 per cent of maize grown is produced solely as a use value and is consumed directly as food in *chapatis* or porridge.

*Land use* Cultivation of land in this case is therefore *intensive* rather than *extensive*. That is to say, small areas of land are cultivated repeatedly (although part of the land may remain fallow to 'recuperate'). One way of trying to maintain the fertility of the soil is through inter-cropping as well as manuring. The simultaneous cultivation of appropriate crops can sustain soil–nutrient levels. Legumes, for example, 'fix' nitrogen, and may, therefore, replace some of the nitrogen consumed by adjacent cereal crops. Land is also used intensively, in so far as other crops are grown together with the maize.

*Technology* While the tools used by Indian peasants are basic, they are still more powerful than those of the Mundurucu. Animal-drawn ploughs, for example, can till soil much more effectively than hoes, and can till heavier soils. Such draught power can be used to draw other instruments, and is used to propel some water-lifting devices. Although such maize is rainfed, irrigation is being common. By contrast, the Mundurucu rely solely on rainfall.

*Use of labour* As with the Mundurucu, the technical division of labour involves cooperation within the household and is linked with the sexual division of labour. Limits to the availability of family labour, particularly during certain periods of peak activity, may set an important constraint on the increase of output in this form of production.

Chapter 9 describes the introduction of a 'new technology' in Indian agriculture, which has subsequently been termed the Green Revolution. The 'package' of fertilizer-responsive seeds, irrigation pumps, fertilizers, pesticides, and tractors has hastened processes of social change already underway in Indian agriculture. In places, the new seeds (principally wheat and rice) have displaced maize production. More significantly, the new technology has accelerated processes of commoditization. Whereas only some 15 per cent of maize output used to be sold, a much larger proportion of wheat is now marketed (60 per cent in the Punjab). The tools and inputs of this new agricultural technology are also increasingly purchased: seeds, fertilizer, pumps, pesticides. The limit to labour power set by family labour is being circumvented by the development of wage labour. The processing of the output, formerly carried out within the peasant household is, to a much greater extent, now undertaken by commercial mills.

In the maize production process described in this chapter, and to a greater extent in the use of Green Revolution technologies described in chapter 9, small producers are increasingly involved in petty commodity production for the market. The majority are still engaged in simple reproduction, but some of the producers with greater resources and social standing have been able to expand their production and approach the social and technical relations of capitalist production.

In general, however, limited access to land, to labour power and to investment resources constitute significant constraints to increasing productive capacities in peasant production. These are limits which capitalist agriculture is able to overcome.

### *Capitalist agriculture in Tanzania*

The final example is of sugar production on a plantation in Tanzania: the Tanganyika Planting Company (TPC) and its operation in Arusha Chini. The company started out as a relatively small sisal operation but gradually took over more land for the production of sugar. The following extract from a company report describes the technical conditions of the plantations production.

> The Arusha Chini Plantation
> Year: 1973
> Area: 12,000 hectares
> Output: 48,500 tons
> Labour force: 3,450
> Total population on estate: 10,200 (4,950 are children)
> Growing of sugar cane:
> After the fields have been prepared and the planting of the cane has taken place about 12 months will elapse before the cane is ready for harvesting ... as the cane needs about 5 times as much water as the annual rainfall to give satisfactory yields, irrigation is essential. Water for this purpose is taken from the Weru Weru river and lately also from a number of large-scale boreholes extracting water from underground. The water from the river is being directed to the fields through an intricate system of canals while the water from the boreholds is being pumped directly into overhead irrigation systems.
>
> When a field has been ripened and is ready for harvesting the sugar cane is being put on fire in order to burn away the dry leaves. The cane will then be cut, loaded mechanically into tractor-hauled trailers and later-on transferred to railway bodies for transport to the factory. As 10–11 tons of sugar cane are used for the production of 1 ton of sugar it will be necessary to harvest and deliver more than 550,000 tons of cane to the factory during the present season.

*Land use* Plantation agriculture clearly uses large areas of land. In this case, all the land is used for sugar which, under irrigation, is a perennial

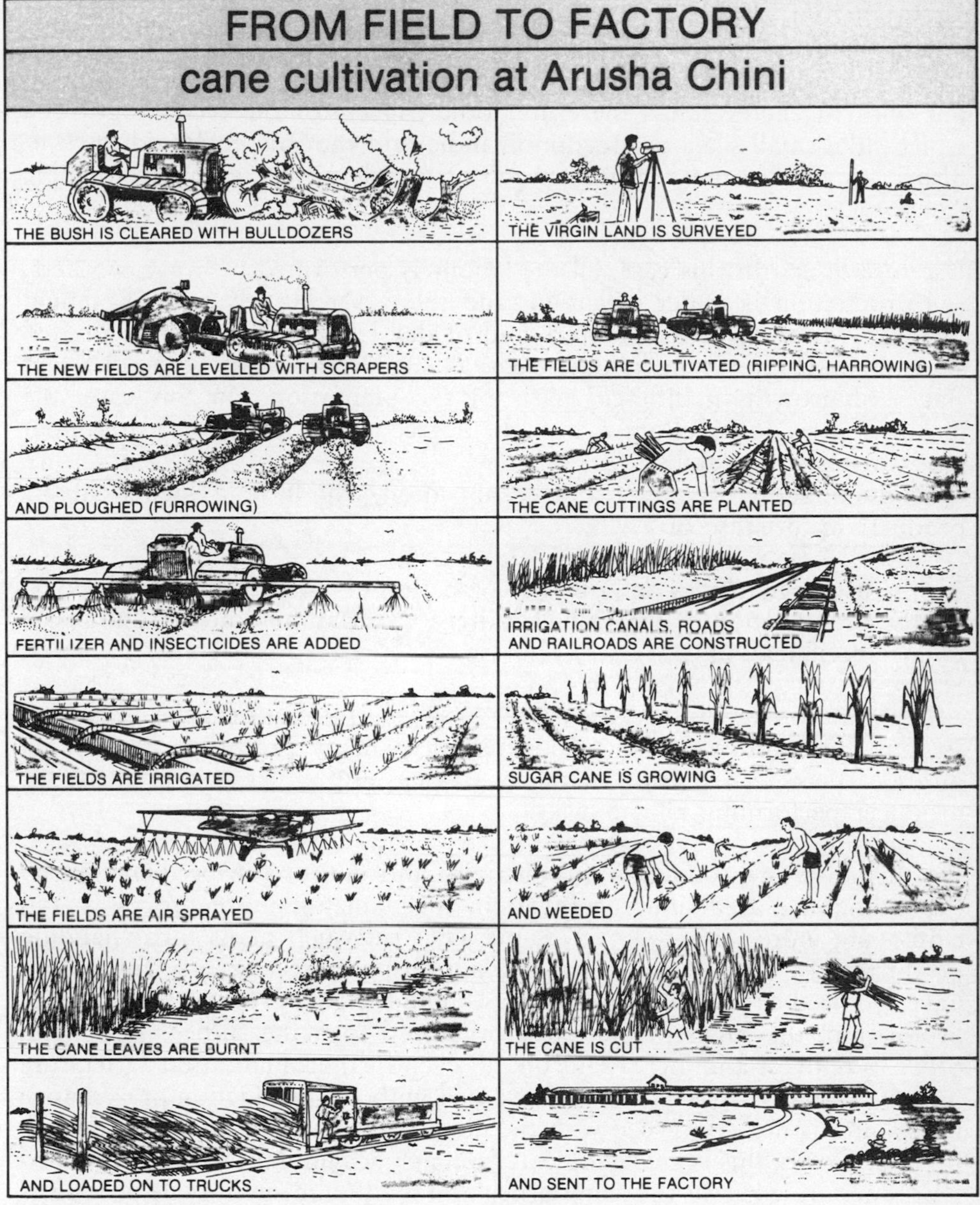

FROM FIELD TO FACTORY
cane cultivation at Arusha Chini
THE BUSH IS CLEARED WITH BULLDOZERS
THE VIRGIN LAND IS SURVEYED
THE NEW FIELDS ARE LEVELLED WITH SCRAPERS
THE FIELDS ARE CULTIVATED (RIPPING, HARROWING)
AND PLOUGHED (FURROWING)
THE CANE CUTTINGS ARE PLANTED
FERTILIZER AND INSECTICIDES ARE ADDED
IRRIGATION CANALS, ROADS AND RAILROADS ARE CONSTRUCTED
THE FIELDS ARE IRRIGATED
SUGAR CANE IS GROWING
THE FIELDS ARE AIR SPRAYED
AND WEEDED
THE CANE LEAVES ARE BURNT
THE CANE IS CUT . . .
AND LOADED ON TO TRUCKS . . .
AND SENT TO THE FACTORY


FIGURE 15 From field to factory: cane cultivation at Arusha Chini, Tanzania

crop. Thus a new factor in this example is that only one crop is grown. This is usually called monoculture.

*Technology* The level of technology used is much more sophisticated than in the previous examples and hence allows the large area to be cropped with much less labour input than if simple tools were used. Tractors are essential to plough and prepare such an extended area. Most of the tasks are mechanized but there are some exceptions. Firstly, planting is done by hand. Secondly, weeding is done with hoes, and thirdly, cutting is carried out with machetes. Thus there are some aspects of the technology used which, like small-scale production in India and that of the Mundurucu in Brazil, are carried out by an extension of muscle power, using very simple technology.

*Use of labour* In this case, all the labour is performed by wage workers. (As production is under irrigation, and there is relatively narrow annual range in variation of temperature and of day-length, there will be limited seasonal fluctuations in labour needs as sugar crops can be at different stages of growth in different parts of the plantation.) In this case, the technical division of labour reflects the degree of specialization by different kinds of tasks and skills.

Production on this scale and organization will have a higher labour productivity because of:

1 the use of machines and other technical inputs to substitute for labour;
2 the organization of the technical division of labour into specific tasks, or specialization.

In plantation agriculture, the degree of specialization of tasks is organized so that the coordination and cooperation of many producers performing different tasks can produce a much greater output per person than one producer performing all the tasks.

On this scale of production, productivity and output can be increased by expanding the area under cultivation, mechanizing more processes and employing more labour. In 1973, the TPC had such plans for expanding production by taking over more land and hiring more workers. This would have required substantial investment. Unlike the two previous examples of production, the sugar plantation is organized to make sufficient profit in order to reinvest and increase its output even further. Plantation agriculture (or any capitalist agriculture) is concerned with the production of exchange values and is not concerned with the direct consumption of the producers. In other words, this is an example of capitalist accumulation or of expanded reproduction, whereas the Mundurucu and the Indian small-scale producers were engaged in simple reproduction at either existing or new levels of consumption.

Sugar-cane is processed before being sold, and an essential contribution to the productivity of the TPC plantation is made by the location of a 24-hour refinery within the estate. The sugar content of cane deteriorates rapidly between cutting and processing, so there are technical as well as commercial reasons for situating a refinery near the land on which the sugar is grown.

TABLE 4 Technical conditions of different forms of agricultural production

| | | *Subsistence* | *Petty commodity production* | *Capitalist production* |
|---|---|---|---|---|
| Production | Use Values | Yes | Yes | Yes |
| | Exchange values | No | Yes | Yes |
| | Specialization of products | No | Yes | Yes |
| Land | Extensive or intensive land use | Either | Intensive | Extensive |
| Use of labour | Household labour | Yes | Yes | No |
| | Communal labour | Possibly | Possibly | No |
| | Wage labour | No | Possibly | Yes |
| Labour processes | Technical division | Yes | Yes | Yes |
| | Sexual division | Yes | Yes | Probably |
| | Specialization | No | No | Yes |
| | Simple or complex cooperation | Simple | Simple | Complex |
| Output | Labour productivity | Low | Low | High |
| | Yields | Varies | Probably low | Probably high |
| Character of production | Simple reproduction | Yes | Yes | No |
| | Expanded reproduction | No | No | Yes |
| Degree of commoditiza-ation | Land | No | Possibly | Yes |
| | Labour | No | Possibly | Yes |
| | Outut | No | Possibly | Yes |
| | Tools and other inputs | No | Possibly | Yes |

This example shows how labour and technology can be organized on a large scale to overcome some of the limitations (of land, labour power, seasonality, and investment resources) normally associated with agricultural production. In the sugar plantation, agricultural production and labour use are not constrained to seasonal patterns. The provision of year-round water and the organization of continuous-process production ensure that both labour power and machinery can be used steadily throughout the year. This form of production also incorporates more substantial linkages with industrial production, through its widespread use of machinery.

### *Summary*

Table 4 summarizes the technical conditions of each of these forms of production. The column headings – subsistence, petty commodity production, and capitalist production – relate to the general forms of production rather than to the specific examples described here. Peasant maize producers in India, for example, combine some subsistence production with greater or lesser volumes of commodity production.

## Developing Productive Capacities

The expansion of agricultural output is an objective shared by many Third World states and by most production units. Low levels of agricultural output in the Third World, and the vulnerability of output to climatic variation, are frequently perceived as causes of famine and poverty in Third World economies. There is an element of truth in this perception which justifies the widespread concern to raise output. A fuller explanation of the causes of famine and poverty requires consideration of the structure of consumption, as well as the level and vulnerability of output (production). We shall return (if only briefly) to the question of consumption later in the chapter. Here our concern is with production.

Table 5 provides some measures of how agricultural output has changed in recent years in the fifteen economies introduced in table 3. With the exceptions of Peru and Singapore, agricultural output and the output of food have increased in all the Third World economies shown. (Singapore is a city-state; agricultural production provides only a tiny proportion of overall production and of livelihoods.) The picture of agricultural and food production per capita is more varied. In five large Third World economies – Brazil, India, China, the Philippines, and Indonesia – which between them contain about half the world's population, both agricultural production and food production per capita have increased over the period in question. Of the remaining six (excluding Singapore), food production per capita has remained roughly constant or increased in three, and declined in three. Agricultural production per capita has declined in four of the six.

There is no way of explaining these changes (or interpreting their consequences) by comparing aggregated macroeconomic or historical descriptions of these economies. That explanation is to be found in the relative 'weights' of the different forms of production within each economy, the ways in which they are related, and the influences to which they have been subjected.

In general, agricultural output may be increased in three ways: by extending the land area used in production, by increasing the yield of each crop obtained from the land, and by overcoming seasonal constraints so that more crops can be grown each year.

Extension of the land area under cultivation may occur as a result of land colonization programmes where there is an abundance of unused land. Frequently, however, the extension of one form of agricultural production has been at the expense of another. Increasingly, pastoralism and hunting and gathering have been displaced by settled agriculture of one sort or another. Usually, the more extensive form of production is displaced by a more intensive use of the land. Examples of this process include the displacement of Amerindian pastoralists and hunter-gatherers from the plains of North America and from the rain forests of Latin America, the marginalization of pastoralists to arid lands in the African Sahel, and of 'Adivasi' (or tribal) producers to hill areas in South Asia.

Yields may be increased through technical improvements, such as new methods of cultivation, the use of new plant varieties, and the use of machines to enable certain tasks to be carried out more quickly or effectively than before. They may also be improved by increasing the input of labour,

TABLE 5 Indices of agricultural and food production, 1983 (1974–76 = 100)

| | *Agriculture* | *Food* | *Agriculture per capita* | *Food per capita* |
|---|---|---|---|---|
| Brazil | 133 | 134 | 110 | 111 |
| Chile | 112 | 112 | 98 | 98 |
| Peru | 100 | 97 | 80 | 78 |
| Kenya | 124 | 118 | 90 | 86 |
| Niger | 147 | 148 | 116 | 117 |
| Nigeria | 119 | 120 | 91 | 92 |
| Tanzania | 118 | 129 | 92 | 101 |
| India | 132 | 133 | 113 | 114 |
| China | 145 | 143 | 130 | 128 |
| Philippines | 133 | 132 | 108 | 107 |
| Singapore | 75 | 76 | 68 | 69 |
| Indonesia | 140 | 143 | 122 | 124 |
| Britain | 120 | 117 | 119 | 120 |
| USA | 98 | 94 | 90 | 92 |
| USSR | 108 | 109 | 101 | 101 |

*Source*: FAO (1983)

by intensifying the use of labour, by the mechanization of tasks previously undertaken by hand, and by reorganizing work patterns.

Since the Second World War, some of the largest increases in agricultural production have been associated with the partial liberation of cereal production from seasonal constraints.

There are both technical and social aspects of seasonality. The technical aspects include the growth conditions required by the plant, such as sunlight, water and soil nutrients, at the 'right' times and in the 'right' quantities, and a minimum season-length in which to grow. Agriculture involves human intervention to ensure that these conditions will encourage the plant to produce its maximum 'output' (of seeds in the case of cereals). The social aspects of seasonality relate to the need to provide interventions at particular times in the season. Tasks, such as irrigating, transplanting or harvesting, have to be undertaken at particular points in the season and within time constraints.

The technical aspects of crop seasonality are gradually becoming better understood. In the case of new varieties of cereal, significant advances have been made in respect to day-length constraints and minimum season-length. Many plant varieties have evolved so that certain phases of their growth are triggered by a biological 'clock'. Germination or maturation may not take place, for example, until both a minimum period has elapsed since sowing, and a minimum period of daily sunlight is available. (Soil temperature, soil moisture and other factors, including some yet to be discovered, may also influence these biological clocks.) The greater understanding of plant genetics is providing the means to influence these clocks in various ways. Some of the new cereal varieties are 'photo-period insensitive', that is not confined by signals from the length of the day, and come to maturity in a much shorter season. This has allowed more crops to be grown per year. In parts of Asia, two or three crops can now be grown where only one was previously cultivated. Freedom from day-length, temperature, and other triggers for the biological clock, also allows crops to be staggered, allowing sowing and harvesting to take place over a much longer period. This allows a steadier use of labour.

## External Influences on Productive Capacity

Both changes in yield and the extension of the land area under cultivation may be associated with several different kinds of influence on productive capacity. Chapter 8 will examine some theories about the dynamics of small-scale production in agriculture. Chapter 9 provides a detailed example of how productive capacities have been increased in Indian agriculture. Here we want to examine some general 'external' influences on productive capacity, that is, factors outside the control of the individual production unit. We have focused particularly upon the organization of production and consumption and the ways in which that may have been influenced by colonial rule and by the extension and intensification of commodity production.

A United Nations Food and Agriculture Organization document (FAO, 1978) on world food and agriculture states: 'In many countries, non-food crops occupy the best land, continuing the colonial pattern which favoured industrial crops for export. Much of the newly developed land is being used for such commodities, and indeed in many countries the proportion of land used for domestic food production may even decline.' Whilst it would be misleading to argue that the production of non-food crops necessarily leads to poverty or slow development, the changes in the structure of production introduced by colonial rule clearly have a bearing on the capacity to increase production.

Some of the consequences of colonialism on agricultural production were outlined in chapters 1 and 2 of this book. They included:

1 a 'redistribution' of land between classes of people and kinds of production;
2 the introduction of the European concept of private property in land through the issuing of land titles to particular groups;
3 money taxation;
4 the spread of commercialized markets in which peasant production had to compete with capitalist agriculture;
5 the recruitment of labour to work in large-scale agricultural units;
6 the introduction of new labour regimes, including degrees of proletarianization of rural labour;
7 migration to sources of rural employment on plantations, in extractive industries and towns.

Each of these changes had implications for the ability to increase productive capacities. We need more information in order to understand those implications. Was land, for example, redistributed to classes with more or less concern and ability to increase output? Were those who obtained title to land those who already cultivated it or outsiders from the cities? The answer to both questions is, 'Yes' and 'No'. In some cases, land was redistributed to classes able and concerned to increase production, and in some cases it was not. The introduction of monetary taxes provided a lever with which states (colonial states, initially, and now their successors) could exert influence upon agricultural production and extract some of its returns. The extension of commercial output markets, and the encouragement of production for exports, have a continuing and far-reaching influence on what is produced and the income it provides for farmers. New patterns of work and labour migration provide opportunities, which some production units will be able to grasp, to overcome labour constraints. For other production units, notably producers depending on household labour, new patterns of work and labour migration will place severe limitations on the availability of labour power, and hence upon the ability of these units to increase their productive capacities.

In the three examples of agricultural production processes described earlier in this chapter, some comments upon the structure of consumption have inevitably been made. Subsistence (or use value) production is, by definition, production for direct consumption within the production unit.

The production of manioc by the Mundurucu is for their own use. The production of maize by a peasant household in India may be primarily for its own use and, in smaller proportion, for sale. The production of sugar by the Tanganyika Planting Company is entirely for sale.

Clearly, subsistence production sets limits to the scale of both production and consumption. One reason why the extension of output markets is associated with an increase in production is because such markets release the consumption constraint set by the subsistence production unit. A subsistence household can only use as much maize (say) as its members can eat or store. Production above that amount will be wasted. In the case of food, output markets allow production to be directed to a larger group of consumers, and in the case of industrial raw materials, such as wood, rubber and palm oil, production can be directed toward a much larger range of production units. The addition of export markets to those available within an economy expands even further the number of potential consumers.

It is frequently assumed (as, by implication, in the quotation from the FAO report given earlier), that the diversion of land and labour from food production to export or 'cash crop' production leads to a decline in food consumption and food security. This may be the case but is by no means invariably so. To stretch an earlier example somewhat, an Indian peasant household might stop producing maize for its own use and produce, instead, mangoes for export as juice to Europe. This might enable them to increase their food consumption and their food security, or it might not. The household's ability to obtain food would now be dependent not on their ability to grow it but on their ability to purchase it. If the monetary returns from the sale of their mango crop are high (relative to food prices) then they will be able to obtain more food than before.

The security of their food consumption after the switch to mango production would depend upon the stability of the demand for mango juice, that is, it would depend on both the juice factory to whom they sold their output, and the world market for mango juice. If the Indian state wished to promote mango juice production it might guarantee the price paid to producers, juice-factory investors, and support the facilities necessary to create a mango juice market in Europe. In this case, the household's food supplies might be more secure with its labour and land devoted to export crop production than when producing its own food.

This is a very simple (and in its details, somewhat unlikely) example which, nevertheless, demonstrates some of the important principles involved in the diversion of land from subsistence to commodity production. Production for the market allows limits on the scale of consumption to be transcended. At the same time, it introduces new vulnerabilities. The production unit is now subject to the variability and level of prices both for its output, and for the foodstuffs it needs to purchase for its survival.

This leads to a related point about the commoditization of labour. In a widely acknowledged analysis, Amartya Sen has emphasized the importance of variations in household purchasing power in the causation of famine (Sen, 1981). If the prices of foodstuff rise significantly and the returns to labour (in wages or kind) remain steady or fall (either because output prices or wages fall), then households without reserves will suffer severe privation and may starve. One social group frequently caught as victims of a catastrophic collapse of purchasing power are agricultural wage labourers, those living in the countryside who have no land and only their labour power to sell. Sen (1981, p. 173) pointed out that the development of a landless agricultural labour class brings with it a particular vulnerability of famine:

> The growth of a labouring class with nothing but labour power to sell ... has led to a very widespread absence of trade-independent security, and ... the vulnerability to famine situation has much to do with this development. The phase of economic development *after* the emergence of a large class of wage labourers but *before* the development of social security arrangements is potentially a deeply vulnerable one.

## Conclusion

Strictly, what we have been analysing in this chapter are the consequences of change in production, rather than the process of change itself. The process is more complex and diverse than the (nearly linear) changes identified here. Those changes, nevertheless, provide a schematic outline of how production on the land can be developed.

The range of technical production conditions marked out by the three examples described in this chapter covers almost the complete spectrum of the appropriation of nature. It runs from negligible transformation of nature in the case of the Munducuru, to an extensive control in the case of the sugar plantation in Tanzania. The Munduruku have only limited control over the seeds and soil they use, and no control over water, solar flux, or the limitations of seasons. The maize-growing peasant household, by contrast, has some choice in the seeds it plants and, if it can gain access to new varieties of seed, can exercise some control in that respect. Some Indian peasants will have a degree of control over the water supply to their crops through irrigation and drainage, and some control over soil nutrient levels through the use of fertilizers. For most peasant maize growers, however, the limitations set by the seasons will be insurmountable. The sugar plantation has taken the process of natural transformation a stage further. Water control is almost complete, seeds and soil nutrients are carefully monitored and the limitations set by seasons have been largely overcome.

At the same time, the three examples illustrate some of the ways in which the social potential of production on the land can be realized. The Mundurucu have a technical division of labour and a substantial body of technical knowledge about the production of manioc. Their social organization, however presents some limitations to the supply of labour and to the scale of production. Both of these elements are limited by the size of the social group. It has to supply both the workers for the production process and the consumers to eat the product. Until that limitation can be transcended the scale of production cannot be expanded.

These social limits may be even more confining for the maize-producing peasant household in India. In that case, the household constitutes the principal supply of labour and, if it is producing for subsistence, also the consumption unit for the product. Even supposing that it is a large household, say 10 members, these are significant constraints on the expansion of output.

As has been noted, these three production systems have differential levels of commoditization. According to our descriptions, the Munducuru exchange only a small quantity of manioc with rubber traders. The level of commodity production for the Indian maize producer is higher. Overall, 15 per cent of maize output is exchanged. In this case, the limitation on labour power may have been mitigated by the hiring of wage labour, by exchange with other household or by some some communal labour initiative.

Almost all of the means of production required by the Tanzanian sugar plantation have been obtained as commodities – seeds, fertilizer, land, labour power. For these, the only limitation on scale is the capital to which the producer has access. That plantation has also transcended any immediate or simple limitation represented by the scale of consumption through the complete sale of output. Clearly world markets (and the actions of states) set constraints and opportunities for the expansion of this production unit's output. Those, however, are of a different order to the constraints set by the consuming household or the small, isolated social group.

The next chapter will be examining some of the social relations of production on the land, and particularly how those relations affect the ability of small producers to reproduce and expand their production.

CHAPTER EIGHT

# Survival and Change on the Land

Chapter 7 showed how the *technical conditions of production* influence output and productivity, and how the extension of commodity relations may be associated with overcoming technical and social limits on output. This chapter describes ideas about how change occurs, and why certain forms of production, such as peasant production, persist. It is focused on the *social conditions of production.*

After examining why it is necessary to study small scale agriculture, the chapter looks at the concepts of peasant and peasantry and examines one of the basic features of peasant or small-scale production, namely the household's economic structure and role. We then examine how and why some households are able to accumulate and grow, whilst others are dispossessed and have to seek wage work.

## Why Study Small-Scale Agriculture?

The prevalence of small-scale production on the land has made it an important focus of development theory. Any proposal aimed at economic growth or alleviating poverty in the Third World has to address the circumstances confronting the majority of agrarian producers.

One recent contribution to development debates (Kitching, 1982) usefully categorized large parts of development writing according to their portrayal of, and attitude to, small-scale production. Kitching termed *neopopulist* those theories that expected small-scale production to play the central role in economic development, and *orthodox* those theories that followed the tenets of classical economics by placing the expansion of the scale of production centre stage.

Orthodox theories of economic growth argue that the scale of production must be expanded, both in agriculture and industry. At larger scales of production, economies of scale accrue and new methods of production become possible. Chapter two in this book describes how complex cooperation and a technical division of labour allow task specialization and the use of sophisticated tools, leading to higher productivities. These innovations may only be possible with a greater scale of production and a greater investment of capital. Of the three examples described in chapter 7, the sugar plantation in Tanzania had the highest productivity because it was able to deploy powerful machinery and a complex division of tasks on a large throughput of sugar-cane.

Orthodox models of economic development also stress the importance of industrialization. Agricultural production as a whole has two important constraints on its expansion in an economy without industry (and without significant levels of international trade). Firstly, there are limits to the scale of production achievable within agriculture. Without the products of industry, such as machinery and chemical fertilizer, these limits are particularly severe. The development of industry can, therefore, provide inputs that enable production on the land to expand. Secondly, there are limits to the consumption of agricultural products in any non-industrial economy. Once industrial production is established, the range of products for which agricultural goods can be exchanged is increased and the range of products agriculture can produce (for example intermediate goods like rubber) is also increased. Thus, industrialization can allow an expansion in the output of agriculture. It is, therefore, seen as a prerequisite for economic growth in orthodox theories of development.

At the end of the last century, in Russia, the *populist* movement developed a critique of these orthodox ideas that rejected industrialization and large-scale production. It advocated small-scale production on the land as an alternative to capitalist development. The populists wanted to avoid the costs of primitive accumulation, that is, the dispossession of some producers in order that others might accumulate. In the first decade after the Russian revolution, populist ideas were developed and propagated as a critique of the socialist state's development strategy. The revolution had brought means of production into common ownership and introduced centralized economic planning, but in other respects it followed the tenets of economic orthodoxy described above. The resurgence of populist ideas encouraged more sophisticated investigation and debate about agrarian change. In the course of debate, two important theories were developed: for the populists, Chayanov suggested why small-scale production should persist and, from the socialist perspective, Lenin explained why some producers accumulate and others become landless. The ideas of Lenin and Chayanov are examined later in this chapter.

Kitching pointed out that the broad lines of this debate continue to structure contributions to thinking about development today. Many development theorists and practitioners (he cited, for example, Julius Nyerere, E. F. Schumacher and the International Labour Organisation) have criticized orthodox economic growth (industrialization and increasing the scale of production) and proposed small-scale, agricultural production as an alternative.

It is, therefore, necessary to study small-scale agriculture both because it provides a living for many in the Third World and because it is of central interest to debates about how development takes place. We shall also be examining some of the explanations for the persistence of small-scale production, orthodoxy notwithstanding.

## Peasants and Peasantries

Small-scale producers in the Third World are often called peasants. But, what are peasants? An anthropologist, Eric Wolf, has described them in the following way:

1 peasants control their means of production;
2 peasant production is aimed at subsistence;
3 peasants transfer their surpluses to a 'dominant group of rulers' (Wolf, 1966, p. 4).

Let me elaborate on this definition.

1 Peasants control their means of production. They have direct access to their means of production: land, whether owned or rented, and tools, whether owned or hired (as, for example, in the case of draught animals or tractors for seasonal use). Peasants also use their own labour or family labour. Many agricultural producers by contrast, are wage workers on large farms or plantations where the means of production are owned by the farmer or company. The wage worker only owns labour power.

2 Peasant production is aimed at subsistence. They produce to meet their own consumption needs and the needs of continuing production (paying debts, buying seeds, tools, and so on). They may also produce surpluses for sale over and above this but that is assumed in this definition not to be the motivating force of their production.

3 Peasants transfer their surpluses to a 'dominant group of rulers' or to a dominant class. By this is meant that a dominant class commands for its own use part of what peasants produce. This can take various forms. For example, it may take the form of rent, whether in cash or kind or in the performance of labour services for a landlord. The transfer here is from the peasant to the landlord. It may take the form of taxation which would involve a transfer to the state (although historically taxes may have been imposed by local 'lords' of one sort or another). The surplus labour of peasants may also be appropriated by money-lenders through high interest rates on debts, or by merchants through low prices given for peasant produce. The transfer of surplus in general may involve some combination of these mechanisms.

This third characteristic describes peasants as a category of producers who have a particular relationship to others in the society of which they are a part. These relations affect the terms on which they control their means of production and what happens to the product. Land may be held very precariously and a concern which often enters into land reform programmes is establishing security of tenure for producers. Further, the transfer of part of the product to others affects how it is distributed both within peasant families and between peasants and landlords or the state.

The location of peasants within a wider society distinguishes them from other agricultural producers such as the Mundurucu of the Amazon, described in chapter 7. Historically, transfers of goods and services have been largely within the boundaries of the Munducuru society and only with the spread of the rubber trade have the boundaries broken down. Peasants, however, are characterized by their relations to other classes within societies which today have commercialized national economies and are integrated into the world economy. Peasant production is linked through national economies to world markets.

Peasants are often referred to collectively as 'the peasantry', and in these three criteria from Wolf there is an assumption that peasants are a single entity with common characteristics and common interests. There are, nevertheless, important differences within the peasantry to which we shall return later in the chapter. Here it is sufficient to note the main dimensions of those differences:

1 access to means of production (peasant households have more or less land, for example, on better or worse terms);
2 extent of integration with commodity markets (this is the differential commoditization mentioned in chapter 6);
3 whether, and to what degree, household members sell their labour power or hire that of others.

## Household Production

Is there a way of explaining how peasant production takes place given the variety of circumstances in which it can occur? One approach is to look at the unit of production, the household.

The diversity in household structure and composition can be demonstrated by looking at household units in production forms already described. The Mundurucu, for example, lived in households divided on gender lines. The household dwellings comprised women and girls, and boys up to the age of puberty. While men lived separately in a men's house, they were regarded as attached to a particular female household through their wives or mothers. A peasant household in the Punjab, to take another example, may be an 'extended' family, which could perhaps comprise grandparents, a married son and family and other unmarried children. Even at this schematic level, one can see important differences in household composition between these culturally distinct groups of people. The differences are not only linked to customs about marriage and residence, but to how production is organized internally in the household unit.

In general, the role of the household head tends to be central to decisions within the household about who does what and who gets what. As most societies are patriarchal, the household head will usually be male. On death, divorce or desertion of spouses, male relatives frequently take on this role. There are many instances, however, where women do take on the role of household head, where circumstances, such as the migration of

FIGURE 16 The household head at threshing time, India (Sharma Studio, New Delhi)

men, permit or even oblige them to assume this role. The mechanisms whereby household heads exert their control, and the forms of internal organization of production, vary between cultures, as do the structure and composition of the family.

It is useful to contrast the organization of production in the household unit and in a more capitalist agriculture (see table 6). The household production unit may engage in both subsistence production and petty commodity production (both of which were introduced in chapter 6). The large-scale agriculture of the capitalist plantation is wholly devoted to commodity production and the accumulation of capital.

The internal relations of peasant households have provided a basis for theories explaining how peasant production works (or theories of simple

TABLE 6 The organization of production in household and plantation

| *Household unit* | *Plantation* |
|---|---|
| Primarily structured by the sexual division of labour in the household | Primarily structured by the division between labour and capital |
| Provides and reproduces its own labour through the family | Employs wage workers |
| Produces for direct consumption and/or the market, but to meet own consumption needs | Produces for sale to accumulate capital for reinvestment |

reproduction). One such theory is that of Chayanov the Russian economist, who based his analysis on how the economic calculations made by households relate to their internal composition.

In summary, Chayanov states that the two crucial factors in the calculations made by both peasants and capitalist farmers are labour and land.

1 For the capitalist farmer, labour can be hired and fired. The farmer will employ workers as long as is necessary for a profit to be made.

2 For the peasant, labour is provided by the family. Subsistence is the goal of cultivation, not profit. Overall output is the important determinant of labour input and the peasant family will continue to work until needs are met; thereafter labour input will decrease.

3 The farmer will also rent or buy land as long as a profit can be made; the peasant, however, must have enough land to meet subsistence needs and will continue to rent or buy until needs are satisfied.

4 Therefore, for peasants (unlike farmers) the size of holding and the intensity of cultivation will be determined by family size and composition; the labour/consumer balance (the balance between production and consumption) can be positive or adverse if there are many producing adults or many dependent children (and adults) respectively; the amount of labour input will be determined by the ratio of producers to consumers; this relationship has a longer-term 'equilibrium', however, as dependants grow up and households divide.

5 Peasants can, however, enter into competition with farmers because (i) they are prepared to work long hours for little return in order to meet subsistence needs, and (ii) they do not cost out their labour when they sell their produce and so can undercut the farmer; peasants may also be prepared to pay higher rents than farmers because they have to maintain themselves in production.

6 Peasants do not, therefore, disappear easily even with the spread of capitalist relations of production. The way in which capitalism affects peasant production initially is through the market, buying and selling produce, then through financial mechanisms such as the demand and supply of credit, all of which increase the control of merchants and financiers over terms of exchange, standards of produce and so on.

7 Peasants can become integrated into the wider economy through such vertical controls, whether under capitalism (private forms of finance and so on) or socialism (state promoted cooperatives).

The main point of Chayanov's argument is that because peasants are producing for subsistence rather than profit, and using their own family labour to do so, they use a different form of economic calculation from that of capitalist farmers.

The unit is sustained through the demographic cycle that also ensures (as households divide) the continued organization of production around the family. The implication of Chayanov's position is that small-scale production in household units can survive under capitalist development. This naturally begs a question for the Third World: will capitalist development in the Third World undermine small producers or not? Or will peasants, 'compete with' capitalist producers and become increasingly integrated into Third World economies? A further implication of Chayanov's thesis is that it is also possible to integrate household producers into economic structures other than capitalist ones (for example, cooperatives).

The debate in which Chayanov was engaged is, as has already been noted, still relevant to development debates today. A central element in that debate relates to differences between peasant households and the dynamics of peasant production. Chayanov's ideas led him to a theory of demographic differentiation, while the work of Chayanov's key opponent, Lenin, developed a theory of differentiation by social class.

Chayanov explained the wealth or poverty of a peasant household by its position in a cycle of household development. A 'new' peasant household consisting of few adults and many young children has a low ratio of producers to consumers and it is therefore likely to be poor, that is, to have low levels of consumption. As the children grow, the ratio of producers to consumers rises and levels of consumption may improve. At the third stage, when the young adults have left to form their own 'new' households, their parents are left alone with only a limited capacity to do the work of the farm, and their consumption levels may fall again, returning the household to poverty. This, in outline, is Chayanov's cycle of peasant mobility, the dynamics of peasant households, explaining why some households are rich and others poor according to their demographic composition (a thorough examination of Chayanov's theory can be found in Ellis (forthcoming)).

Lenin's study showed that change was not confined to the individual household; there was a strong tendency for change in the composition of the peasantry as a whole, with 'rich peasants' accumulating and 'poor peasants' losing their means of production. It is to this idea of differentiation of the peasantry that we now turn.

## Differentiation and Accumulation

### *Differentiation between units*

> There is not a single economic phenomenon among the peasantry ... that does not express a struggle and antagonism of interests, that does not imply advantage for some and disadvantage for others. (Lenin, 1899, in Harriss, 1982, p. 130)

With these words, Lenin emphatically summarized his conclusion that the peasantry did not constitute a homogeneous social group. He described a process which began with the emergence of 'property inequality', the uneven ownership of land and means of production, and ended with the dissolution of the peasantry. The 'old peasantry' was being replaced by 'a class of commodity producers in agriculture and a class of agricultural wage workers'.

In chapter 9, which follows, the process of differentiation in the Indian peasantry is described using Lenin's useful categorization of the main groups emerging from a peasantry in transition – rich peasants and poor peasants. As noted already, significant differences are apparent between peasant production units with respect to their access to means of production, the extent of their integration with commodity markets and the degree to which household labour is sold and wage labour used. Lenin termed 'rich peasants' those households with the ability to accumulate. The size of their farm requires that they hire wage labour to supplement or supplant the labour of family members. With that labour power and their preferential endowment of tools, draft-power and inputs, these rich peasant households are able to produce cheap commodities.

Poor peasants are not able to accumulate, their production is limited to simple reproduction and their ability to maintain their means of production may gradually decline. Their land may be too small, poor or fragmented, and subject to rent or sharecropping payments, their draft-power may be inadequate and their ability to purchase seeds and fertilizer too slight for their production to meet their own needs either through consumption or sale. In these circumstances, many peasant households sell their labour to others. The combination of different sources of income is typical of many such households in Third World countries today. These poor peasants tend gradually to lose their grasp on means of production and to become increasingly agricultural wage workers but in the process transitional forms of work emerge which are neither permanent wage work nor part of production by the household.

Between these two groups – the rich peasants from whose ranks agricultural capitalists emerge and the poor peasants tending to become wage labourers – Lenin identified a third group, the middle peasantry. These are the remnants of the 'old peasantry', maintaining an element of self-sufficient household production using family labour, and not needing to sell either their produce or their labour power.

These, then, are the three elements Lenin identified. They remain important concepts for understanding changes in small-scale agricultural production.

Differentiation between production units is, however, not the only source of differentiation in the peasantry. Differences also arise from issues related to gender.

### *Differentiation by gender*

There are certain tasks that seem to be strictly allocated to one gender or the other. For example, in India, only men plough. Men's work is basically only in production and scarcely involves processing or preparation of produce for consumption. In India, men would probably deal with market transactions (although not universally) and maintain wider social contact. This tendency is reinforced when rich peasants or landlords remove women from any kind of productive labour and employ servants.

TABLE 7 Allocation of tasks in peasant households in North-West India

| | *Tasks usually done by females* | *Tasks done by males or females* | *Tasks usually done by males* |
|---|---|---|---|
| *Children* | Occasional help with cooking and washing utensils; tending smaller children | Fetching water; minor purchases from shops; taking cattle to pasture or water | Helping to handle draught animals |
| *Adults* | Cooking; washing clothes; tending small children and babies; raising vegetables near the house; milking and feeding cattle; sewing and knitting | Fetching water; weeding; sowing; threshing (old method); harvesting; operating Persian well for irrigation; shopping | Ploughing; feeding threshing machine; operating tube-well; digging irrigation channels; operating farm machinery |
| *Elderly people* | Minding small children | Light agriculture work | |

*Source*: Sharma (1980), p. 90, table 2.

The productive work that women do is often connected with the work they have to do in the home to feed their families, such as tending and milking animals, harvesting and husking grain, and so on. Men's work, however, usually stops outside the fields or the market place.

Table 7 is instructive not only because it shows how the sexual division of labour works within the household but also shows that family labour can also be broken down by age as well as sex. Family labour, then, is not a homogeneous category.

In terms of economic calculations, different decisions may be taken as to how family labour is used depending on the composition of the household. This will not just vary in terms of adults and dependants (or producers and consumers), but also by how the productive capacities of the producing members are defined or determined by their age or gender. This may also affect who actually works in the household unit and who may be employed by others. In turn, this depends not only on the decision of the household (or head of household) but also on what kinds of labour are required by employers. This may have both a skill and a gender/age content.

Differentiation by gender is vividly illustrated by this extract from Sharma's description of circumstances in North-West India:

> Firstly, however large a role individual women play in decisions about the household resources, land is still held by men for the most part, and men are still the chief earners of cash. Most men, therefore, have a source of power in the household to which few women can ever aspire. If men share control of land and household income with the women ... this sharing takes place because the men have permitted it. Secondly, women continue to depend upon men to conduct transactions concerning the household in its relation to outside agencies, most importantly transactions which concern the household resources – marketing goods, banking savings, registering land. Women are implicitly debarred from this kind of function by norms which restrict their mobility in public places, their contacts with unrelated men, and frequently by their lack of education relative to men.
>
> Furthermore, there is one agricultural operation which women are explicitly debarred from performing – namely ploughing – and this renders every woman farmer dependent on her men-folk for carrying out this essential piece of work twice a year.
>
> Men depend heavily on women to cater for their domestic needs – to cook, clean, wash clothes, and care for their small children. These are tasks which few men would care to perform for themselves at home. But if a man's wife is sick or absent from home he is likely to be able to find a female 'substitute' to do the essential domestic work in her place from among female relations or neighbours. A woman whose husband is away will find it harder to manage without her man, although many are obliged to do so. She cannot just ask any male relative to do highly responsible tasks such as dealing with legal business, signing documents, marketing grain. Even finding someone to plough for her may not be an easy task. (Sharma, 1980, p. 113)

In these examples, Sharma is describing gender differentiation within the household. The point should be made that while the *effects* of gender divisions are experienced in households, by individuals, the system of unequal gender relations is not constituted at household level. Patriarchy, the systematic dominance of men over women, is established by widespread social arrangements awarding property rights and authority to men.

## The Social and Technical Conditions for Accumulation

A central consideration for understanding changes on the land is the ability of some small producers to accumulate. Following on from chapter 7 and from Lenin's analysis of differentiation, a number of social conditions can be identified that are prerequisites for accumulation:

1 private property in the means of production;
2 commodity production;
3 wage labour.

These three conditions have been introduced into peasant production to varying degrees and under different circumstances. Chapter 2 described how colonial rule introduced profound changes to many areas of peasant production in the form of new labour regimes, commodity production and elements of private property in land. Similar changes have continued since colonial rule under the impetus of rural development schemes, agribusiness ventures and the like. Chapter 6 stressed that the extension of commodity production and the development of wage labour has been uneven and, often, incomplete. The forms that accumulation and differentiation take, therefore, vary widely.

The three preconditions are necessary, but not sufficient in themselves, for production units to accumulate. Poor peasant households are not able to grasp opportunities to expand their production; even maintaining their output at a steady level (simple reproduction) may be beyond them.

A critical issue for poor peasants is debt. Indebtedness means that part of the product may go to a landlord or moneylender. The failure of poor peasants to repay debt provides one way in which some landowners and moneylenders can accumulate land – through default. Part of the product may also have to go in payment of rent. In many sharecropping arrangements, 50 per cent of what is produced will go to a landlord. Moneylenders often charge exorbitant interest rates. Then there may be other people outside the immediate households who expect to receive part of the product through familiar rights and obligations. A certain amount of what is produced may have to be stored, whether in money or kind, for festivals, ceremonies and emergencies. Thus, there can be many different 'funds' that have to be met from production and that limit the potential for 'accumulation'.

Poor peasants have to work their land very intensively in order to survive. When the costs of reproduction rise – through falling prices for that part of their output sold, or increasing obligations to others – survival may not be possible. In such circumstances, poor peasants may hire out their labour or may become displaced from their land. Many such households derive income from more than one source.

The uneven development of the three preconditions may provide other constraints on the potential for production units to accumulate. In many areas of peasant production, for example, land tenure arrangements may involve personal ties. The provision of land by a landowner may commit the tenant to 'reciprocate' with free or cheap labour. At times of high labour demand, such as harvesting, the landowners needs will frequently take precedence over the tenant's own production. The extension of credit may provide another route by which labour is 'bonded' to a master. Such labour arrangements may both disrupt the poor peasant's production and provide the master with ineffective labour.

As the conditions for capitalist production are (gradually and unevenly) realized, the potential for rich peasants to introduce new methods and new technologies is increased.

There are limits to the possibility of expanding production with constant land area, type of technology and use of labour. In particular, in land-scarce conditions which apply to many parts of Asia, the most widely used method of 'expanding production' is through technological innovation that

FIGURE 17 The wife of a rich peasant feeding the workers (Ed Milner)

can increase the potential for surplus accumulation. As new technologies are introduced, the use of labour changes. In particular, the proportion of family to wage labour may change.

Some elements of changes in labour use have been captured in a study of the impact of mechanization of wheat cultivation in the Indian Punjab (Agarwal, 1981). The research was carried out on 240 households in 1971–2. The plots held by these households were mechanized to differing degrees. Tables 8 and 9 show some of the effects of mechanization on labour time employed in production (only some operations and data in selected size ranges have been included for simplicity).

TABLE 8 Labour use on selected sizes of farm: percentage of labour time in wheat cultivation

| *Operation* | *Type of labour* | *Farm size in hectares* 0–4 | 8–12 | 20 |
|---|---|---|---|---|
| Ploughing | Family | 88 | 55 | 42 |
| | Permanent | 11 | 36 | 52 |
| | Casual | 1 | 9 | 6 |
| Irrigation | Family | 87 | 47 | 26 |
| | Permanent | 12 | 50 | 64 |
| | Casual | 1 | 3 | 10 |
| Harvesting | Family | 78 | 28 | 13 |
| | Permanent | 6 | 18 | 28 |
| | Casual | 16 | 54 | 59 |

*Source*: Agarwal (1981), p. 123.

TABLE 9 Change in labour time as a result of mechanization: hours per hectare

| *Operation* | *Type of labour* | *Farm size in hectares* *0–4* | *8–12* | *20* |
|---|---|---|---|---|
| Tractor ploughing | All | −91 | −81 | −79 |
| | Family | −81 | −51 | + 1 |
| | Permanent | −10 | −24 | −58 |
| | Casual | — | − 6 | −22 |
| Tube-well irrigation | All | +101 | +67 | +87 |
| | Family | +83 | +22 | + 6 |
| | Permanent | +17 | +40 | +59 |
| | Casual | + 1 | + 5 | +22 |

*Note*: The effect of mechanization has been measured by subtracting mean labour time for the modern technique from mean labour time used with the traditional technique; tractor ploughing is compared with bullock ploughing and tube-well irrigation with canal irrigation.
*Source*: Agarwal (1981), p. 123.

Firstly, looking at table 8, family labour varies considerably with farm size, the smallest farms using the most family labour. All tasks seem readily substituted by hired labour, but there are some important differences. For example, permanent labour seems to be preferred for irrigation, whereas casual labour seems quite crucial at harvest time.

Table 9 shows how types of labour time in particular tasks have been affected by mechanization. Ploughing uses less labour as a result of mechanization; tube-well irrigation requires more labour than canal-fed irrigation. While family labour is primarily used among the smaller farms, with larger farms, predominantly wage workers are hired. (With the exception of harvesting, permanent labour seems the preferred category, both with increasing farm size and where more labour is required.)

The introduction of mechanization has implications for the use of labour, both in the type of labour employed and the way it is used. Changes in the use of labour are closely linked with changes in the form of production. Firstly, household producers are able to increase their productivity by displacing certain tasks by machinery and reorganizing labour. The increase in productivity may allow them to buy more land and bring it into production using the machines and family labour already available and, if necessary, by hiring more labour. Hiring labour may then mean the withdrawal of some (or, in particular conditions, all) family labour. The owner of the land can accumulate surplus from the labour of those workers hired and reinvest it in further expanding production. But household producers can also improve their productivities and their yields to raise their levels of *consumption* rather than to accumulate more means of production. So the process of accumulation is not an *automatic* one for the *producers*, although accumulation of merchants' capital may be taking place through the trading of products on the market.

## The Changing Conditions of Petty Commodity Production

The extension and intensification of commodity production and change in the technical conditions of production occur against a backdrop of some elements of continuity. Many production units have no option but to use basic technologies and old cultivation practices. Production by households using family labour also persists, as does the production of food staples for direct consumption. Non-capitalist forms of land ownership (such as sharecropping) and use of labour (such as debt bondage), are also prevalent. There is, however, as chapter 6 explained, good reason to doubt that these continuities represent the persistence of 'tradition' or of 'pre-capitalist' arrangements. They are reproduced under changing conditions as capitalist production develops.

While the household persists as a unit of production, both what is produced, and how, are changing in many places. This extract from a newspaper article outlines the promotion of small-scale tea production in Kenya:

> Kenyan smallholders grow with London's financial aid
>
> A highly successful smallholder tea scheme, backed by British funds through the Commonwealth Development Corporation (CDC), has made the Kenya Tea Development Authority (KTDA) which runs the scheme, the biggest single supplier of tea to the world market.
>
> Until the early 1960s, Kenyan tea was almost entirely produced on large plantations. The plantations, owned by such household names as Brooke Bond or James Finlay, are still there, but smallholder farmers – averaging less than an acre of tea each – are already approaching the day when they will produce the bulk of Kenya's tea ...

> The KTDA operates by licensing individual tea farmers in a designated area who are then assisted through the supply of seedings, fertilizer and, above all, advice to become tea producers. When tea is ready for plucking (it is normally plucked by the farmer's own family, and not by hired labourers as on the large tea estates), the farmer sells it to a local buying centre. Here it is accepted by the KTDA, (or, if the quality is too low, rejected). The KTDA transports the tea to the nearest factory for processing, packing and shipment. The tea authority has 24 factories in operation, with another five on the point of completion and ten more under construction ...
>
> The farmer in Kenya receives an advance price of one shilling a kilogram for his green leaf, but he later receives a second payment related directly to the price his tea is sold for ...
>
> There are now about 127,000 acres of smallholder tea, tended by 130,000 farmers. Their average yield last year was 2,700 k of green leaf, and the average smallholder earned more than 3,000 shillings from his tea. This is a significant sum for a small farmer who also produces other crops on his land. (The *Times*, 10 February 1981).

This 'contract farming' is characterized by:

1 organization around households and family labour;
2 new techniques of production and new plant varieties;
3 marketing structures in which to sell the crop;
4 facilities for credit, agricultural inputs, transport, processing, packing and shipping;
5 industrial spin-offs (linkage) from the production of tea;
6 the organization of household producers into a national structure.

This example suggests a Chayanovian view that household production can be integrated into an economy on the road to capitalist development. What the long-term changes for these farmers will be is as yet unclear, although the provision of particular structures, facilities and technical innovations are an important part of support for the farmers' 'integration' and may, ultimately, change the nature of their production.

A different and widespread effect of the changing conditions of household production is described in the following example from Sri Lanka. In this example, production by the household on its own land is insufficient to ensure a living for the family:

> One household with 13 members had seven sources of income: (1) operation of 0.4 acres of paddy land by the adults, (2) casual labour and road construction by the head and eldest son, (3) labour in a rubber sheet factory by the second son, (4) toddy and jaggery making by the head and his wife, (5) seasonal migration to the dry zone as agricultural labour by the wife, eldest son and daughter, (6) mat weaving by the wife and daughter, and (7) carpentry and masonry work by the head and eldest son. Another household with 11 members and six sources of income, mostly agricultural: (1) home garden by the family, (2) a one acre highland plot operated by the wife, (3) labour on road construction on weekdays and on the plot on weekends by the head, (4) seasonal migration to the dry zone as agricultural labour by

TABLE 10 How one household uses its labour

| *Household production* | *Wage work* |
|---|---|
| Operation of paddy land | Casual labour/road construction |
| Toddy-tapping and jaggery making | Factory work |
| Mat weaving | Seasonal migration to agricultural work |

> the daughter and son, (5) casual labour in a rice mill in the dry zone by the eldest son, and (6) casual agricultural labour in the village by the head and his wife. (Tinker, 1979, p. 20)

The main feature characterizing the way these households make their living is the diverse sources of income. For example, the first household was engaged in both household production and wage work (see table 10). The family engaged in the production of commodities from the land and through artisan work, and earned wages through working for a variety of employers. Some members of this household are partially 'proletarianized'. While the household continues to survive as a production unit, its own production is supplemented by income derived from wage work.

## Conclusion

Small-scale agricultural production in the Third World is neither static nor isolated. New ways of organizing household agriculture are being introduced; some households are being forced to diversify their sources of income in order to survive; other households are able to accumulate and tend toward more capitalist forms of agriculture. Small-scale production persists but in changing circumstances and with increasing differentiation.

CHAPTER NINE

# New Technology and New Masters for the Indian Countryside

This chapter examines some aspects of agricultural change in one country: the introduction of what has become known as 'Green Revolution' technology in Indian agriculture. This new technology, centred on cereal seeds developed for their high potential yield, has been described as 'the most widely and rapidly adopted technology in agricultural history' (World Bank, 1981b).

In the 1960s, the Indian state chose to adopt Green Revolution technology as the focus of its 'new strategy' for developing the Indian countryside. This chapter describes the circumstances in which the 'new strategy' was implemented and its consequences. Our examination covers:

1 Indian agriculture preceding the Green Revolution;
2 the forms of agricultural change encouraged by the adoption of the new technology;
3 the effects of the new strategy, especially the rise of a rich peasantry.

## Peasant Agriculture on the Eve of the Green Revolution

The central concern of this chapter is the Indian peasantry, the major productive agents in the countryside, and how the 'new strategy' has been associated with changes in the peasantry. In this section, we provide a brief sketch of India's agrarian structure soon after independence in 1947, and the ways in which it was already changing prior to the introduction of the 'new strategy'.

### *Agrarian structure in the early 1950s*

At independence in 1947, the apex of India's agrarian structure was a *landlord class*, which leased out land to a subject peasantry from whom it extracted a surplus in the form of rent. Some landlords, in their capacity as moneylenders, drew interest from peasants as well as rent, often keeping peasants in debt bondage. Some landlords used hired labour, frequently in an unfree relationship with the landlord, to work the land that was not leased out.

Differentiation of the peasantry existed throughout India, but was most marked where commercialization had penetrated most deeply. Rich peasants accumulated capital to a certain extent, sold most of what they produced and were often employers of wage labour. Although they obtained significantly lower yields than poor peasants, they represented a nascent stratum of capitalism in agriculture. Rich peasants were not 'masters of the countryside' at Independence but they had in many regions waged a struggle against landlords that had achieved a considerable succss, and they were ready to continue that struggle. *Middle peasants* though more dependent on household labour, tended to be allied with rich peasants in any anti-landlord struggle.

*Poor peasants* were tenants to a far greater degree than other peasants and they were particularly likely to be sharecroppers. Among poor peasants, land fragmentation was rife, access to credit was through the village moneylender (who might also be the landlord) at usurious interest rates, and the level of indebtedness was high. They sold part of their produce, generally not because there was a surplus above their consumption needs, but because they were forced to obtain cash for pressing purposes. An important characteristic of poor peasants was the degree to which they had to supply labour to others, in order to survive. Such labour might be forced, unpaid labour, extracted by landlords as a condition of tenancy. Throughout India, the highest yields per hectare were achieved on the 'dwarf' holdings of poor peasants, by dint of very intensive application of labour to the land.

There had been *landless labourers* in India since Mughal times. In 1951, 15 per cent of all agricultural families were without land. They formed a class which was often in unfree relationship with those who employed labourers.

Moneylenders and traders were influential throughout the Indian countryside, constituting, along with landlords the 'unholy trinity' of Indian rural society. Historically, moneylenders had become landlords by dispossessing peasant proprietors unable to repay their debts. In the 1950s, 80 per cent of all rural credit came from moneylenders. Rates of interest were usuriously high, with far higher rates being charged to poor peasants, landless labourers and artisans than to rich or middle peasants or landlords. Access to institutional credit which carried a low rate of interest was effectively limited to rich peasants and landlords.

The critical point about *women* in Indian peasant agriculture was their economic dependence upon men. It was almost always the men who owned the land and the means of production and, among the dominant classes, women's dependence was intensified by the taboo upon women moving outside the home. Men dealt with all groups and agencies external to the household. A manifestation of upward mobility had long been the withdrawal of women from the fields and their confinement to the homestead.

### *Agrarian change, early 1950s to mid-1960s*

The agrarian structure identified above exercised a powerful constraining influence upon the development of technology and, therefore, upon the level of output, the productivity of Indian agriculture and its potential for growth:

> existing levels of production were low, and were kept low by the logic of the system. The landlord class was parasitic, uninterested in making or encouraging productive investment on the land. Within the peasantry the highest yields were achieved by poor peasants but given their position as sharecroppers, their lack of access to credit on reasonable terms, their crushing burden of unproductive debt, they were most unlikely to indulge in the risky, investments that would secure growth. Middle peasants were equally unlikely to do so, while rich peasants were as yet insufficiently strong and as yet not faced with adequately attractive profit possibilities (Byres, 1974, p. 237).

By the mid-1960s the agrarian structure had changed, but not so as to alter fundamentally the foregoing logic. The major change was a diminution (though most certainly not an elimination) of the power of landlords, and a significant increase in the economic and political strength of rich peasants. These shifts were hastened by land reform, introduced from the early 1950s.

In India, land reform has been largely unsuccessful in the ambitious egalitarian aims it has set itself; but it has allowed processes that were already afoot to develop more quickly.

The essential features of India's attempted land reform programme were as follows:

1 abolition of the landlord class;
2 the principle of *land-to-the-tiller* was enunciated, that is to say, as many peasants as possible should be owner-occupiers;
3 controlled and fair tenancy through the eradication of sharecropping, the setting of just rents and the provision of secure tenure;
4 ceilings on the amount of land a peasant could operate.

It was an ambitious programme designed to secure an agrarian structure that would have at its centre individual peasant farming for whom, it was argued, the way would be clear for the introduction of technological reforms that would lead to steady gains in agricultural productivity.

The largest landlords – the absentee, non-cultivating landlords, who had been the allies of the British in British India – experienced, through land reform, a blow from which they could never fully recover. Their capacity to resist land reform was not sufficient to the task. From among them, a small group emerged that was ripe for transformation into capitalist farmers. The medium to smaller landlords, who were often resident and sometimes cultivating, received no such blow. Their survival was assured, but on a rather different basis from their former condition.

The attempt to abolish all but fair and secure tenancy was unsuccessful. The smaller landlords, and some of the big ones, were able to devise new 'disguised' forms of tenancy (often oral rather than written), which successfully evaded the law. This evasion took place on a very large scale throughout most of India. The ability of these landlords to further their own interests was considerable.

There was a quite definite quickening of differentiation among the peasantry over these years. Agriculture grew at just under 3 per cent per annum, there was some extension of the irrigated area, and some rise in commercialization. By far the greatest beneficiaries of these changes, and of land reform, were the rich peasants. They were stabilized as independent proprietors, and were on the way to becoming, in many areas of India, the new dominant class in the emerging agrarian structure. Legislation, to the extent that it was successful, extended protection not to all tenants, but to richer tenants, and in the 1960s there was a rise in the amount of land rented by rich peasants, who gained control of a larger proportion of the tenanted area.

Middle peasants must have participated, to a degree, in any advancement, but poor peasants, landless labourers, and most village artisans and craftsmen gained very little from land reform or from the other changes that were afoot.

Between independence and the mid-1960s, the government also attempted to increase agricultural output through technical advance. In the early 1950s, methods of production were backward: instruments of production were primitive (wooden rather than iron ploughs); modern seeds and fertilizers were hardly in use; less than 15 per cent of the total arable area was irrigated; yields were very low and, by and large, stagnant. Significant investments were made in large-scale irrigation, but the percentage of arable area irrigated rose to only 17 per cent. This development was also regionally uneven, with states like the Punjab and Uttar Pradesh achieving far higher irrigation ratios than states like Gujarat and Maharashtra. Land consolidation, with the aim of eradicating fragmentation, was successful in only one state, the Punjab (where it occurred as a result of the Partition between India and Pakistan in 1947). Some improved seeds were developed and fertilizer factories were established. Some mechanization took place. It was all, however, on a relatively small scale, not constituting a significant technical advance. By the mid-1960s, Indian agriculture had entered a crisis of alarming proportions; its rate of growth was insufficient to sustain a significant rate of industrial growth or to lead to any rise in per capita food availability. Until then, Indian agriculture had grown at an annual compound rate of just under 3 per cent per year, a faster rate than the previous fifty years, but inadequate for India's situation and necessitating large food–grain imports, including US food aid.

## The New Agriculture

### *Introduction of the 'new technology'*

The genesis of India's Green Revolution or 'new strategy' may be traced to 1964. In that year, a dynamic new Minister of Food and Agriculture,

Chidambara Subramaniam, was appointed, after a successful term as Minister of Steel and Heavy Industry. India's circumstances were converging to make dramatic new policy initiatives a compelling necessity, for the old policies had failed, or, at best, had achieved only modest gains in productivity. Already, in 1964, there was some apprehension in India about the reliance on extension of the cultivated area and the near certainty that this could not be depended upon as a source of growth in the long term.

Yields, it was now realized, would have to grow far more quickly than they had done hitherto, and become the major source of growth. What was to *force* the issue, however, was the crisis of 1965–7 when what, in 1964 appeared desirable, suddenly become an imperative.

In 1964–5, as if to allay any gathering sense of urgency, Indian foodgrain production had reached an all-time peak of 89.4 million tonnes. But to anyone tempted to draw favourable conclusions from this, what was to follow was a savage reminder that Indian agriculture continued to be a precarious 'gamble on the rains'. The monsoons failed in 1965–6 and 1966–7 and, as a result of the worst weather since records began, output fell drastically, to 72.3 million tonnes and 74.2 million tonnes in 1966 and 1967, respectively, levels not experienced since the bad year of 1957–8. The results were devastating:

> Two successive droughts, unprecedented in their intensity, had produced conditions of severe scarcity in 1966, and a famine – the first famine since Independence – in 1967. The national economy received a severe setback, and the people passed through a traumatic experience. In the first year, the drought-induced scarcity enveloped peninsular India. In the second year, conditions of scarcity were far more intense and widespread, and an alarming situation developed in Bihar as a drought struck the populous Gangetic plains. (*Suresh Singh, 1975, p. viii*).

Indian imports of foodgrains had shown a steady tendency to rise since 1960–1: from 3.5 million tonnes in that year (4.8 per cent of net production) to 7.4 million tonnes in 1964–5 (9.5 per cent of net production). They now rose to 10.3 million tonnes in 1965–6 and 8.7 million tonnes in 1966–7 (16.3 per cent and 13.3 per cent of net production respectively).

India became heavily dependent upon the USA. An American agricultural economist tells us: 'nationwide disaster was mitigated only by the United States' heavy shipment of foodgrains to India' (Mellor, 1968, p. 87). However, the US government took the opportunity to use its apparent charity (the shipments in question were part of American aid to India) to exert powerful leverage upon the Indian state. Earlier, an agreement with the US had been concluded for aid for the period 1962–5. When war broke out with Pakistan in1965, only half had been received, but aid shipments stopped. In 1966, India, desperate for food imports, accepted one of the hardest bargains for aid ever driven by the US.

Among other things, India agreed to the following: that for seven years the government should no longer have control over the pricing and distribution of fertilizers by private fertilizer firms; that the Indian government should drop its demand for 51 per cent ownership of joint ventures in the fertilizer field; that greater latitude be allowed to American private firms operating in India; and that India should stop trading with North Vietnam. Apart from this, India's devaluation of the Rupee by 36.5 per cent on 6 June 1966 was strongly influenced by American pressure.

When, in December 1965, Subramaniam assured the Lok Sabha (lower house of parliament) that 'his Ministry had finally found "a formula [and] a program" which would take India to self-sufficiency in foodgrains by 1971' (Frankel, 1968, p. 693), he appeared to be making a bold claim indeed. (By 1966 and 1967 it was so much at variance with existing conditions as to seem foolhardy.) The 'formula and program' were the 'Green Revolution strategy', which was well under way by 1967. Desperate circumstances hastened its coming. They may at first have concealed its true nature, when the humiliation of the 1966 aid agreement was still fresh and the desire for self-sufficiency in food at all costs was paramount. But they could not do so for long.

The new strategy was a response to agricultural stagnation, famine and dependence upon food aid from the USA. It was required, therefore, to deliver self-sufficiency in food-grain production. But it had to do so within the constraints of the existing pattern of production and consumption of foodgrain, and to meet the goals set by the authors of India's development plans.

FIGURE 18 Weighing grain for sale in a North-West Indian market (Sharma Studio, New Delhi)

India's food-grain production is dominated by rice, which constituted 44 per cent of food-grain output in 1964–5. Wheat production accounted for only 14 per cent. In the short run, the two crops are not substitutes for each other. Neither production nor consumption can be readily switched from one to the other. Conditions and practices suitable for rice cultivation may be inappropriate for wheat cultivation; rice eaters will not easily switch to wheat as their staple food (or vice versa). A revolution in food-grain production was, therefore, principally required to be a dramatic increase in rice output.

The structure of Indian food-grain consumption delivered a second constraint for the strategy. Wheat and rice are known as 'superior' food-grains and provide the staple primarily for the better-off. Any increase in their production would not benefit the poor unless it were accompanied by a fall in their price or a rise in the income of the poor. If the new strategy were to benefit, or at least not worsen the lot of the poorest then it needed either to increase the production of inferior food-grains or to increase the availability of superior food-grains at the same time as increasing their output.

As stated above, Indian agriculture grew at 3 per cent per annum between 1950 and the mid-1960s. But by the start of the new strategy, Indian planners had set a target of 5 per cent growth per annum in order to sustain industrial growth and enable massive problems of poverty to be tackled. This was a rate of agricultural advance never before achieved in Indian history, and achieved by few countries in world history.

### *Characteristics of a technical strategy*

By contrast with previous state policies toward agriculture, which relied primarily upon social change, the spearhead of the new Indian strategy was the application of new technology to inputs.

These new inputs took two forms: biochemical innovations and mechanical innovations. The former comprised new high-yielding seeds, chemical fertilizers, pesticides, and the regulated flow of irrigation water. The latter consisted of tractors, threshers, seed-drills, mechanical pumps for irrigation, mechanical reapers, combine harvesters. Upon the distinction between the two a number of crucial issues turned. These issues influenced the extent to which the new strategy could be adopted by different classes of producer.

The first was whether the Green Revolution could be limited to biochemical inputs (and mechanical irrigation) because the biochemical inputs had been portrayed as having desirable attributes for the Indian context whilst those of the mechanical inputs were seen as undesirable. These attributes can be listed as in table 11. The implications of this are that biochemical innovations can, in theory, increase the output of all producers: poor peasants, on whose holdings they can be applied without difficulty; landless labourers who can benefit from increased employment; as well as rich and middle peasants, landlords and capitalist farmers.

The attributes are valid but there are two critical senses in which the

TABLE 11 Attributes of biochemical and mechanical inputs

| *Biochemical* | *Mechanical* |
|---|---|
| Labour absorbing, creating new employment opportunities | Labour-displacing, reducing employment opportunities by substituting for labour |
| Land saving, producing substantial increase in output without any increase in surface area and, possibly, even with a decrease | Land-using, creating the need for more land if they are to have their full effect, which is likely to mean the displacement of smaller cultivators from their land |
| Scale-neutral, generating their ouput increase on any size of holding, with no bias towards larger cultivators | Biased to scale, the larger the holding (up to a point) the greater their effectiveness |
| Economical on scarce capital resources | Capital-intensive, calling for large amounts of fixed capital resources, which absorb scarce capital. |

distinction breaks down. Firstly, the application of biochemical inputs alone, by allowing multiple cropping in shorter growing seasons, sets up pressures for mechanization to cope with the increased time constraint (transplanting must be done, or the harvest completed, within a specific and brief period).

The second sense in which the ideal description given must be strongly questioned derives from the fact of a *differentiated peasantry* and a *grossly unequal distribution of resources*. As one writer has commented, while the biochemical inputs may be scale-neutral they are not resource-neutral (Rao, 1975, p. 44). They may economize on scarce capital resources, but they still entail a *sizeable increase in working capital requirements*, by comparison with traditional inputs. They have to be *bought*, and to that extent their scale-neutrality simply becomes meaningless if poor peasants (and, indeed, middle peasants) do not have the means to buy them.

When, in 1965, the first formulation of the 'new strategy' was made in India,

> The Ministry proposed to introduce improved varieties of paddy [rice] and wheat developed in Taiwan and Mexico respectively, with reported yield capacities ... some six times the average all-India yield, and almost double the maximum potential output of conventional Indian varieties. They also proposed to extend the use of higher-yielding hybrid varieties of maize, bajra and jowar (sorghum and millet) development at Indian research stations in the late nineteen-fifties (Frankel, 1968, p. 694).

From a *technical* point of view (the viewpoint, perhaps, of a research station, where many of the ecological, social, political and economic factors may be ignored) it appeared that the new seeds might be the basis of a strategy that could respond to the various needs outlined above. But the seeds – if, indeed, they could replicate in Indian conditions what they had elsewhere – could not operate on their own. As had been found in Mexico, 'biochemical' inputs are to a certain extent *complementary*: that is, one of them will not significantly increase yields in the absence of any one of the others. So it was that they were seen as a *package* of inputs, in which irrigation occupied a key position.

The 'new strategy' could, however, apply only to those parts of India to which irrigation had spread or to which it might spread. Only 17 per cent of India's arable acreage was irrigated in the mid-1960s. Moreover, it was unevenly concentrated in states like the Punjab, Haryana, western Uttar Pradesh, Tamil Nadu, and Andhra Pradesh.

At the outset, then, at least 80 per cent of India's arable acreage was excluded from the Green Revolution, and any agricultural advance was limited to certain, specific regions. The most cursory inspection of the 'new strategy' revealed it as likely to be heavily unequal in its impact. Embedded in it was the certainty of an increase in *regional* inequality.

The policy-makers were conscious of the 'new strategy's' potential for increasing inequality in another, very potent sense: *within regions*, through the appropriation of its gains by the better-off, the *dominant classes* that we have identified above. Such a process, it was said, was to be strongly resisted. Thus, it was held that 'in areas selected for concentrated effort, there is to be no discrimination between cultivators on the basis of resources or the size of holding' (Government of India, 1966, p. 175).

Yet, despite such statements and assertions of 'scale-neutrality', there was from the beginning an apprehension, among many observers, that the realities of the Indian countryside were such as to make the 'new strategy' inevitably one of 'betting-on-the strong'. How, after all, did one ensure 'no discrimination' in circumstances of gross inequality and increasing differentiation? For the Indian state to secure this, indeed, would have been an unprecedented departure from anything *achieved* hitherto, although such statements of *intent* are legion.

### *State promises and private practices*

Whilst the Indian government made many commitments about the implementation of the new strategy in agriculture, much of the execution relied upon private agencies. The new seed varieties first introduced had been developed abroad, and the government took initiatives to see to the *breeding* in India of the relevant dwarf varieties and of *new* dwarf varieties which would be suited to the considerable diversity of growing conditions which existed. Arrangements were made to provide government certification for seeds grown by registered seed farmers. Trials and demonstrations were arranged to bring the new varieties to the attention of peasants.

There was early success with the new *wheat* seeds. The Mexican dwarf varieties (especially Lerma Rojo and Sonora 64) were suited, quite fortuitously, to the growing conditions and management practices which were prevalent among Indian cultivators and particularly those of the states of North-West India – the Punjab, Haryana, western Uttar Pradesh. After overcoming some initial problems, research in India has produced a succession of wheat varieties, with still higher yields than the original ones and 'better grain qualities of colour and taste than the original varieties' (Cummings and Ray, 1969, p. 148).

But the new seed varieties required new techniques and new social relationships. Principally, the harvest from one year could no longer provide the seeds for the next. This is because the new varieties were produced by hybridization, that is, the cross-pollination of two genetically dissimilar lines of wheat. Cross-pollination allows the desired characteristic of one line, a good response to mineral nutrient perhaps, to be combined with that of another. A strong, short stalk would be desirable to support the heavier wheat ears produced. But such hybrid plants do not breed 'true'. Their offspring are genetically heterogeneous and lack the 'hybrid vigour' of their parents. To avoid a rapid decline in yield after the first harvest, new seeds have to be provided for each planting.

So, instead of using seeds from last year's harvest, the peasants had now to buy the new seeds on the market. The government promised to extend credit at reasonable interest rates to make possible what for many peasants was an extension of their involvement in the market.

As with other government commitments, the seriousness of intent should not be doubted, but while government agencies and their officers were earmarked to play a role, *private* agents, not at all within effective government control, were very important from the outset, both as seed growers and as seed distributors. In India as elsewhere, government intention and private interests do not necessarily coincide. Also there may well be a gap between stated government intent and the capacity of government agencies and officials to take the needed action.

## Outcomes of the New Strategy

With the new wheat seeds there was early success. New rice varieties, however, proved susceptible to local plant pests or unsuitable to prevailing growing conditions. There have been successes in limited areas but new varieties of a sufficient range to suit India's varied environmental circumstances have not been available. Thus, regional inequality has been worsened by an uneven development of suitable seed strains.

Turning to the 'inferior' or 'coarse' cereals which are so important to India's poor, some hope was held in the early days of the 'new strategy' for *maize* and for the *millets*, although the expected increase in yields from new hybrid strains was never anything like as great as was predicted for wheat and rice. 'Coarse cereals' are predominantly rain-fed crops grown in drought-prone areas – areas which the Green Revolution has passed by. It is not that these crops have been completely untouched by the 'new strategy', for some of them have registered growth in certain pockets of the country with the good fortune to be irrigated. But they have been neglected to a very considerable degree, and their growth performance has been poor on the whole, as we shall see. This has been compensated for by neither a fall in the price of 'superior' foodgrains (on the contrary, their prices have risen markedly) not an increase in the income of the poor.

The 'new strategy' made no provision for *pulses*. Quite the contrary, the Green Revolution has increased the rate of decline of pulse production. In those areas in which the new technology has made the production of wheat relative profitable, there has been a diversion from the production of pulses to that of wheat. On this evidence, the 'new strategy' has, if anything, worsened the lot of India's poor. We will have more to say about the poor below.

### *Fertilizers*

To achieve their promise of significantly increased yields, the new seeds required greater quantities of mineral nutrients than the soil could provide. A great expansion of the provision of industrially produced fertilizer was needed.

The government pledged itself to take the necessary steps to promote the use of fertilizers – to guarantee their supply in sufficient quantity 'at reasonable prices and at proper time'. As with the new seeds, the pledge entailed activity at several different levels. It involved extensive publicity and action by a variety of government officers. It encompassed a scheme for scientific fertilizer tests, fertilizer demonstration in the peasants' fields, facilities for soil testing, and other services. It meant investment to secure a significant increase in Indian production of fertilizers, if necessary through encouragement of private foreign investment and, if domestic production were insufficient, the allocation of scarce foreign exchange to permit imports. It implied the control of prices and the supplying of subsidized fertilizers to peasants. It included the taking of fertilizers to points nearest to actual consumption centres, the opening of more retail outlets, and distribution to peasants through supply cooperatives. Not only that but, as with seeds, and to an even greater extent, the special provision of improved credit facilities was promised. Again, we must stress the importance of *private* interests. The government might have taken action at all of the levels noted, but the fertilizer market was still dominated by private traders.

The Indian fertilizer industry has also persistently underfulfilled its targets. It was observed by the planners in 1978 that 'the availability of fertilizers (from Indian sources) has almost continuously fallen short of the requirements and substantial imports have been necessary' (Government of India, 1978, p. 190). Supply has, indeed, been a problem. Moreover, India's capacity to *import* fertilizers was severely strained when fertilizer prices doubled within a short space of time, in the wake of the 1973 oil crisis.

While the inadequacy of fertilizer supply has not been an absolute obstacle to the new strategy, it has meant that the potential of the new seeds has not been fully realized. And had there been a breakthrough in the breeding of new rice seeds, fertilizer shortages might have become critical. Even without that breakthrough, India was importing one-third of its fertilizers and, with more foreign exchange, could have used more.

### Plant protection

It was pointed out that 'in the new agricultural technology plant protection has acquired an added significance ... [since] in the case of the high-yielding varieties, conditions which are conducive to the growth of plant population are also favourable for weeds, pests and diseases' (Government of India, 1970, p. 133). The chemical 'dressing' of seeds, the use of chemical weed-killers (because manual weeding was considered infeasible for high-density crops) and of chemical pesticides, were all to be promoted through state agencies. As with fertilizers, however, the government's promises here have not been realized in adequate supplies.

### Irrigation

The crucial importance of irrigation has been stressed. The new varieties of seed only produced their promise of high yields when grown in the right conditions with high doses of fertilizer and water both to provide the plants' water requirements and to transport dissolved fertilizer to the plants' roots. Without irrigation these new varieties were doomed to fail.

Before the Green Revolution the government had made heavy investment in large-scale canal irrigation. The irrigation element of the 'new strategy' was the consolidation of those schemes, through the construction, for example, of field channels, and a significant extension of private irrigation through the use of tube-wells. These are small-bore holes drilled down to the ground water, which can be pumped to the surface through tubular pipes by an electrical or diesel-powered pump.

This emphasis effectively restricted the new varieties to those who owned the tube-wells and those to whom they might sell the water. It was a policy that would obviously require a massive increase in initial expenditure for those contemplating investment in a tube-well, and in running costs. Once more, officially provided credit was to play a strategic role, through land mortgage banks, cooperative banks and a variety of government agencies.

By 1976, 25 per cent of India's land was irrigated, a significant increase, secured, for the most part, by the remarkable spread of tube-well irrigation. But 75 per cent of India's cultivated area was still excluded and the regional concentration of irrigation had also worsened. As table 12 shows, those states in which irrigation was most widespread in 1967–8 are also the states with the greatest increase in irrigated area since then. By 1976, the Punjab's proportion of cropped area irrigated had risen to a remarkable 74 per cent (and there were whole districts of the Punjab in which it was far higher). Punjab, Haryana, western Uttar Pradesh, and parts of Tamil Nadu and of Andhra Pradesh, states with irrigation ratios of between 35 and 74 per cent, are all areas where the 'new strategy' has had a significant impact. At the other end of the scale, we find in 1976 that Madhya Pradesh and Kerala, Maharashtra, Gujarat, Rajasthan, Assam, Orissa and West

Bengal, with irrigation ratios of between 9 and 19 per cent, have been touched to a far smaller degree by the new technology. There has been a *widening of inter-regional disparities* in Indian agriculture.

### *Mechanization*

In addition to the effects of the biochemical inputs, the mechanical inputs also exercised considerable influence. They have been monopolized by the dominant classes and have spread because their use has proved highly profitable for those who have been able to afford them: more profitable than the alternative technologies available.

The advance of *power-driven tube-wells*, the essential means by which the extension of the irrigated acreage has been secured, has been rapid. Thus, between 1966 and 1976, in India as a whole, energized irrigation pump-sets/tube-wells grew in number from 578,000 to 2,790,000. In as much as the *quality* of irrigation (that is, the need to obtain water at exactly the right time and in the correct quantities) exercises a decisive influence upon final yields, a considerable stimulus has been given to private, power-driven tube-well irrigation – where, of course, there is an adequate endowment with ground water. Tube-well irrigation gives to the

TABLE 12 Change in levels of irrigation in selected states, 1967–8 to 1975–6 (percentages)

| *State* | *Cropped area irrigated* *1967–8* | *1975–6* | *Change* *1968–76* |
|---|---|---|---|
| Andhra Pradesh | 27 | 35 | 8 |
| Assam | NA | 18 | — |
| Bihar | 24 | 30 | 6 |
| Gujarat | 11 | 15 | 4 |
| Haryana | 32 | 50 | 18 |
| Himachal Pradesh | 16 | 17 | 1 |
| Jammu and Kashmir | 40 | 40 | 0 |
| Karnataka | 11 | 15 | 4 |
| Kerala | NA | 9 | — |
| Madhya Pradesh | 6 | 9 | 5 |
| Maharashtra | 8 | 11 | 3 |
| Orissa | NA | 19 | — |
| Punjab | 58 | 74 | 16 |
| Rajasthan | 12 | 17 | 5 |
| Tamil Nadu | 43 | 47 | 4 |
| Uttar Pradesh | 32 | 40 | 8 |
| West Bengal | NA | 19 | — |

*Note*: NA = data not available.
*Source*: Government of India (1972), table 4.9 and Bharadwaj (1982), table 8.

cultivator who can afford it far greater control over the supply of water than does canal irrigation. The spread of tube-well irrigation long preceded the advent of the 'new technology'. There can be no doubt, however, that the new seeds (along with fertilizers), which brought 'the possibility of achieving very high yields with assured and controlled irrigation at regular intervals' (Raj, 1973, p. 116), have provided an especially potent impetus to that spread.

The use of tractors has also increased rapidly, particularly in the North-West of India. This increase, altogether more controversial than the spread of irrigation (because associated with labour displacement) has been given encouragement by the arrival of the biochemical inputs. These have markedly increased the time constraints on agricultural operations. By shortening the growth period, the new seeds enable two or more crops to be grown in one year. In these circumstances, the harvesting of one crop must be completed quickly to allow the land to be prepared for the next, and land preparation in turn has to be completed more expeditiously. In principle, these constraints could be released by a heavier input of labour at these seasonable peaks. But sufficient labour might not be available. If it is, it has acquired enhanced bargaining power. From the viewpoint of those adopting biochemical inputs, this is undesirable.

Tractors can cope with the land preparation constraint, and are a way of avoiding 'problems of labour management, discipline and supervision' (Binswanger, 1978, p. 75). Their spread has been significant in North-East India since the mid-1960s, without doubt as a result of the introduction of biochemical inputs on a large scale. Between 1966 and 1972, the number of tractors in use in Punjab and Haryana rose from 15,500 to 60,400.

Precisely how far mechanization of harvesting has gone is not clear. In Punjab and Haryana, there were 5,000 mechanical threshers in 1964, 10,000 in 1970 and, by 1979, there were 170,000 in Punjab alone. But let us not forget the relatively small part of India affected by these changes.

### *Credit*

The complementary nature of the new biochemical inputs has been stressed. They had to be supplied and used as a package if yields were to be raised substantially. The package meant, for those who adopted the new technology, a far greater dependence upon the market and the cash requirements were massive in relation to peasants' 'own' resources. It was a package beyond the means of many Indian peasants unless there was an extension of rural credit at 'reasonable' rates of interest (that is, lower rates than those charged by money lenders).

The government promised that credit would be provided through the banking system and cooperative credit societies. There has been an expansion of official or institutional credit but it has been inadequate to meet the needs of the majority of peasants who could otherwise have adopted the 'new technology'. It is significant that the dominant provider of rural credit, even in Green Revolution areas, is *still* the village moneylender, who continues to lend at exorbitant rates of interest (sometimes as much as 300 per cent per annum).

So long as moneylenders remain the major source of loans, the spread of the new technology is held in check. Most of the finance of the new technology has come from the resources of the peasants – strongly suggesting that access to the new technology is limited to rich peasants and landlords.

One of the commitments the government was able to keep was to hold agricultural prices high and stable. The prices of the main agricultural commodities – food-grains, sugar-cane, jute, cotton – were guaranteed. It has to be stressed, however, that the maintenance of this commitment has been the result less of an independent desire on the part of government to so act than of the organized pressure of the rich-peasant lobby upon government.

## Implications and Effects of the New Strategy

### *Overall agricultural growth*

It was the deceleration of India's agricultural output growth which provided the context in which the new strategy was adopted. What then has been its effect upon agricultural growth?

In *overall* terms, after the disasters of the mid-1960s, growth in agriculture appears to have returned to a trend compound rate of around 3 per cent per annum (Srinivasan, 1979). To have returned to the former trend growth rate after the apparent prospect, in the mid-1960s, of something not far from zero is, indeed, an achievement. But there has been no question of reaching the 5 per cent per annum that the Indian planners believed to be necessary. To that extent, India's 'agrarian question' remains unresolved.

In general, this return to 3 per cent has been secured by an acceleration in the growth of yields, with yield increase contributing something approaching 80 per cent of overall growth. That area expansion should still constitute 20 per cent or more of growth, when its *future* scope must remain doubtful, is disquieting. Indian agricultural growth remains problematic.

If we look at individual crops, we see that *wheat* alone has shown a speeding-up of growth in relation to the earlier period: between 1967 and 1978, it grew at about 5.5 per cent per annum, in contrast to the earlier figure of 3.9 per cent. *Rice* has shown no such acceleration, and has, in fact, slowed off somewhat (3.4 per cent per annum to 2.2 per cent). The 'coarser' grains have been most disappointing in their performance, with *maize* moving from growth of 3.8 per cent to an actual *decline* in production; *millet* from 2.3 per cent to more or less no increase; and *sorghum* from 2.5 per cent to 1.5 per cent. *Pulses*, too, have shown a deceleration from 1.4 per cent to 0.2 per cent. All of the coarser grains mentioned have actually lost area. These are figures which augur ill for India's poor.

### *Employment*

Until the mid-1970s, the effect of the biochemical innovations predominated over the effect of the mechanical innovations. With the result that, on the whole, there was an increase in employment opportunities in Green

Revolution areas. The effect should not be exaggerated, however. There has been a rise in *wage employment*, but that has been partially offset by a decline in *self-employment* consequent upon an increase in the number of non-cultivating labourers. In the early phase of the new strategy, the total of employment opportunities had risen.

But as mechanization spreads and intensifies, employment will be less. Once tractors and combines are deployed on the more labour intensive operations, such as harvesting and threshing, labour will be displaced. This would not matter if such labour could be absorbed in industry. Indeed, it would represent an ultimate increase in material welfare. In India, however, there is no prospect of that happening in the foreseeable future. Industrial advance has been and will be of the kind (essentially capital-intensive) and speed which generates remarkably few net employment opportunities. Industry's labour needs can be met quite comfortably (and with something to spare) through natural increase in the cities and towns. One scholar has written of labour in Punjab and Haryana being, for this reason, 'trapped in agriculture' (Bhalla, 1977, p. 1903). If this is true, it is a 'trap' which will become increasingly intolerable with an actual diminution in the level of employment in agriculture.

### *Accelerated differentiation*

As we have seen, by the mid-1960s a *rich peasant stratum* was well established, in certain areas particularly, as a powerful class. It was a class eminently capable of pursuing its own class interests relentlessly and with skill. As the 'new technology' became available it was effectively appropriated by the rich peasantry who thereby increased their own economic strength. Their capacity to do this, at first more or less exclusively among the peasantry, derived from several of their characteristics in relation to poor (and middle) peasants. This applies, also, to those landlords who adopted the 'new technology'.

1 Rich peasants (and landlords) had a greatly superior resource endowment and this, allied to their considerable class ties, gave them a massive advantage with respect to their ability to secure and to apply a scarce bundle of inputs. They had far greater access to information about the new inputs and their likely performance: again as a result of class ties, this time with block officials who disseminated information, control of village social clubs (which would exclude poor peasants), greater literacy, greater likelihood of ownership of a radio, and deliberate restriction of knowledge.

2 The degree of uncertainty attaching to new varieties was lower for rich peasants (partly because of their greater access to knowledge of new agricultural methods; partly because of a capacity, not possessed by poor peasants, to acquire and apply the inputs in correct proportions; partly because rich peasants, with their ability to store, can get higher prices), while they are better able to bear risk (given their greater resources).

3 Rich peasants (and landlords) could afford to purchase the new inputs – both biochemical and mechanical – because of greater command of resources and because they captured, to a very large degree, the institutional credit (supplied by both cooperatives and by commercial banks) that was made available at 'reasonable' rates of interest. Moreover, to the extent that rich peasants (and landlords) now used an increasing proportion of their own resources for productive investment rather than, as previously, for moneylending, this meant that less credit was available for poor peasants.

4 Where the available inputs were scarce (the high-yielding seeds, the fertilizers, canal irrigation water) and supplied through cooperatives and government officials, rich peasants were far better placed to acquire them.

Even if, after the initial stages, there was participation in the 'new technology' by those who were not rich peasants or landlords, there can be no doubt that the gains of these larger cultivators have been quite disproportionately large. Where smaller cultivators have so participated, it has been on terms that have been unfavourable. For example, given that tubewells are often concentrated in the hands of rich peasants and landlords, if smaller cultivators do participate they have to use more costly and less timely water. Indeed, late adopters are likely to derive less benefit than earlier ones, since latecomers, if they wish to have tubewells 'may have to incur higher cost for digging (boring) the wells because of the adverse externalities imposed, e.g. lowering the water table, by the early exploiters' (Rao, 1975, p. 202).

That the 'new technology' has hastened the process of differentiation seems beyond doubt. It has served to consolidate the rich peasantry as a powerful, dominant class: the rich peasantry has become stronger economically and has taken on more of the characteristics of a class of capitalist farmers.

Has the 'new technology' contributed to rural proletarianization and depeasantization, however? The processes are complex and incomplete, and the data imperfect. But it appears that the new technology has contributed to the creation of a class which survives and reproduces itself by selling its labour power and to the separation of peasants from their land and other means of production. As yet, the process of dispossession of the poor peasantry is incomplete. For example, in North-West India there is little evidence, so far, of any significant rise in the proportion of landless or any significant net sale of land by poor (or middle) peasants. There does, however, seem to have been some resumption of tenanted land. There has also been a rise in the proportion of the tenanted area worked by rich peasants. What has happened is that many poor peasants, finding that their small piece of land has become inadequate to provide the household's subsistence, have started to lease it out to rich peasants. This can be characterized as partial proletarianization: the 'new technology' has produced conditions in which, by a variety of means, the poor peasantry are, increasingly, being pushed out of *self-employment* into *wage labour*.

The poor peasant must, to a growing extent, sell his labour power in order to survive. But he does retain possession of a piece of land, however small. This has the effect of driving a wedge between the poor peasantry so affected and the completely landless wage labourers, making a political alliance between these two classes less easily attained.

A second form of partial transformation may be seen in North-West India and other parts of India penetrated by the 'new technology'. This relates to sharecropping. There has been a shift from traditional forms of sharecropping to new forms that we may describe as cost–share leasing. In the traditional form, the archetypal relationship was one in which the tenant supplied all of the inputs and, in return for the use of the land, handed over 50 per cent of the output to the landlord (though there might be many variations on this). In the case of cost–share leasing, however, the landlord supplies the new, bought inputs and, in return, takes a far higher share. The sharecropper is close to becoming a pure wage labourer (with the landlord taking a much greater part in decision-making with respect to the process of production), but does not quite do so. He retains possession of some of the means of production and continues to have the semblance of a stake in the land (and bears more risk than a wage labourer). Again, an identity of interest between poor peasant and pure wage labourer is forestalled.

### *The emerging rural proletariat*

If we examine further the nature of the emerging rural proletariat, we find that, in North-West India at least, some of its features are such as to blunt any concerted class action.

The first is a change in the structure of the labour force: away from a preponderance of *casual* labour (employed on a daily or occasional basis) and towards *permanent* labour (employed for a season, year or longer). This is a shift associated with growing mechanization.

Secondly, permanent or attached labour seems to be experiencing significant transformation in its relations with peasant (or capitalist) employers, in the wake of a qualitatively different way of organizing and paying for the work. Work is now paid mainly in cash (rather than kind), at a predetermined fixed money rate (rather than as a proportion of the crop) and according to *contract*, the length of whose term is increasing. These contracts have acquired quite new characteristics. They are now very formal in nature, they are finalized in the presence of three witnesses (who invariably are sympathetic to dominant class interests); and they have associated with them a system of borrowing for immediate consumption needs, the effect of which is to tie the labourer to the employer. Such contracts have been conceived precisely with the aim of countering any possible bargaining power that labour might attempt to acquire.

Further aspects of the stratum of permanent labourers are important. They are more or less exclusively male; a significant proportion of them come from households whose main income source is cultivation and which have more adults than the average of their class size; and of those households the great majority are in the size-group of one hectare plus, and many in the size-group of four to six hectares (that is, middle peasant households and the lower reaches of the rich peasantry, in this latter range). Such labour has a limited consciousness of shared interests with other labourers.

As far as *casual labour* is concerned, the 'new technology' has stimulated an increase in the use of *migrant labour* (in North-West India, from Rajasthan, Bihar, and eastern Uttar Pradesh); and among migrant labour, too, employers take steps to control the terms upon which labour is hired – basically, to prevent labourers from forming their own bargaining groups. Among casual labourers, the female component is far higher, and casual labour is far less likely to be totally landless than permanent labour.

It is certainly the case that there is an absence of militancy among agricultural labourers in North-West India, in contrast, with labourers in other parts of India. Moreover, this lack of militancy is reflected in the failure of real wages to rise appreciably in the years since the mid-1960s. The gains of the Green Revolution (or, more accurately, the 'wheat revolution') have not generally accrued to agricultural labourers, due, in part at least, to the factors identified above.

## Conclusion

This chapter has provided a case study of the development of agriculture in India since independence. It suggested some of the links between the extension of commodity relations, state implementation of a development 'strategy', and the rise of a 'new' social class. At the same time, it indicated the complexity of the process and its partial fulfilment in India.

In 1981, *India Today* wrote 'it is this cream of the Indian earth, the capitalist farmers delivered by the Green Revolution, who have made India a land of plenty amidst hunger and poverty.' According to that account, the new masters of the countryside were *delivered* by the 'new technology'. But this analysis of almost four decades of change in rural India suggests that it was not so sudden, so technologically determined, nor so complete. Undoubtedly though, Green Revolution technology has hastened and enhanced the rise to power of capitalist farmers.

PART IV

# Production and Producers in Industry

# Introduction

The focus of the next three chapters is on large-scale production, although aspects of small-scale production in the informal sector are touched on in chapter 12. The process of industrial production – the application of forms of non-human energy, mechanization, a complex technical division of labour, and so on – provides pressures towards large-scale production whether the process is applied to agricultural production (as in industrial agriculture) or to manufacturing.

Chapter 10 explores the extent of industrial production in Third World economies and provides evidence that, although output remains small by comparison with the First World, manufacturing industry has been growing faster (than for developed countries) over the 1963–82 period. There is no evidence to substantiate a dependency view of Third World industry as stagnating or in decline as a whole, although the degree of industrialization and rates of growth vary considerably across countries. The relationship between different types of industrial production and a broader social process of industrialization are explored. The contrast between Britain's industrial revolution and the experience of other European states is used to highlight the role of the state in providing conditions for generating and sustaining a general process of industrialization.

Two broad policy trends have been adopted variously by Third World States and Brazil is discussed in depth in chapter 11 as an example of successful application of import substitution industrialization to the vehicle industry. Export oriented industrialization is a strategy currently espoused most obviously by the newly industrializing countries of Singapore, South Korea, Taiwan and Hong Kong, although Brazil's history has for centuries also included dramatic periods of reliance on the export of single products (sugar, diamonds, gold, rubber, coffee). Brazil is currently able to build up exports based on the vehicle industry having developed a considerable manufacturing capacity from the stimulus created by initially supplying a large internal market for vehicles and road communication systems.

The social and the technical relations of production in the Brazilian motor industry are also taken up in chapter 11, and the political implications of state-led capitalism under the military which came to power there in 1964. The growing opposition to state-imposed restrictions on freedom were under strong challenge during the late 1970s, and mobilization of worker opposition was most effective within the vehicle industry. During

1978, the Metal Workers' Union was able to organize the first strike for ten years and has continued to make an effective challenge to the state's backing for repressive labour relations by firms in the vehicle industry.

Chapter 12 considers the implications of the uneven development of industrialization for particular industries (garments, engineering) and for Third World workers, whether car workers, urban 'marginals' or women engaged in household and other forms of production. This chapter looks both at the way small-scale and large-scale production coexist in some circumstances, and at the differential social valuation of worker skills, particularly the undervaluation of skills associated with gender issues. The chapter concludes with a brief review of qualitative aspects of 'making a living' in urban areas of the Third World.

CHAPTER TEN

# Industry and Industrialization

This chapter continues our focus on how people make their living in the Third World by analysing the growth and diversity of industrialization in the Third World and the increase in productive capacities this has brought about.

## Why is Industrial Production Important?

If agriculture is a proportionately larger contributor to economic activity in the Third World than elsewhere, and much the largest source of employment and livelihood, industry is often the fastest growing part of the economy, and the rapid growth of industry is a crucial characteristic of Third World development. Just as the British and later industrial revolutions gave, 'for the first time the real possibility of ending material want and suffering among human beings' (Kitching, 1982), so industrialization is often seen as the most important means of developing the Third World.

Three examples serve to illustrate the importance of industrialization.

1 Industrialization is central to issues of productivity and economic development. In previous chapters it has been argued that economic development requires the elevation of labour productivities, a process historically associated with increases in mechanization and the need for greater specialization. In this chapter, we will show that some Third World countries (like Brazil and South-East Asia) are industrializing rapidly. These are in the group called newly industrializing countries (NICs). But, are the NICs typical of, or relevant to, the majority of Third World countries? Some (like the neo-populists – see chapter 8) argue their irrelevance for Third World development, proposing, instead, types of economic development that use small-scale technology within both agriculture and industry to provide more employment.

2 Increasing output in agriculture sooner or later requires industrialization to reduce a country's dependence on imported industrial goods. Increasing output in agriculture has usually involved increasing productivity through machines and other inputs produced by industry. Chapter 9 showed the

importance of tractors, fertilizers and insecticides in increasing agricultural production in the Green Revolution.

This leads to a further issue: can industry be the driving force for more general economic development? Strong arguments have been made that investment in industrial production should be given priority over agriculture for the most rapid and long-term economic growth. Kitching (1982, pp. 6–18) contrasts 'orthodox' views of economic development through industrialization with 'populist' critiques of industrialization as a 'bad' way of developing.

3 Industrialization is also at issue in the broader concerns of the quality of life more generally. Industrial production is important in that it is about what goods are produced and who gets them? (Improvements in the quality of life depend on the production of goods such as clothing, footwear, agricultural implements and fuel). Industry is also a major source of employment and the technologies it uses affect the skills workers require, work organization and management control.

In summary, the study of industrial production is important because:

1 there are strongly held and influential opinions for and against the view that industrialization is a prerequisite for economic development;
2 development strategies must always engage with debates about what kind of balance to strike between (what kinds of) industry and (what kinds of) agriculture; and
3 it entails questions about how people live and work and thus about quality of life in the Third World.

## What is Industrial Production?

There are three distinct ways of defining industry in general use. The first defines industry as 'not agriculture'. It is a residual definition based on industry as the production of all material goods not produced directly from the land. The second, much used for statistical purposes, has a sectoral logic: industry as the mining, manufacturing and energy sectors of the economy (see Figure 19). Mining is that sector extracting minerals, energy is that producing energy. Manufacturing does not fit in so neatly because of its diversity. Manufacturing is the making of finished articles from raw materials by hand or by using tools or machines (at any scale of production). However, it is defined for statistical purposes in terms of the kind of output, not how goods are made. Neverthcless, this sectoral type of definition can be useful, because it does tell us what sorts of goods are being produced.

Manufacturing is divided according to the international standard classification into a number of quasi-independent sectors.

A Food products
B Drink and tobacco

C Textiles
D Clothing and footwear
E Wood products and furniture
F Paper and printing
G Chemical and petroleum products
H Bricks, glass and cement
I Basic metals
J Metal products
K Electrical machinery
L Transport equipment
M Others

The third definition of industry, based on the nature of the production process, is more satisfactory for analytical purposes. It provides a definition based on the idea of technical and social change, of industrial production as a particular way of organizing production with the capacity for continued increases in the quantity of goods made in society.

The choice of definition has important implications. For example, the first two definitions cannot encompass the idea of industrialized agriculture, given that industrial methods of organization and industrial inputs are of increasing significance in the Third World. The second definition suffers from its inability to distinguish small-scale handicraft production from large-scale factory production.

Although the use of more than one definition can be legitimate and useful, the last definition is the most useful here because it allows the construction of questions we need to explore. We shall now develop the third definition so that we can look at industrial production in two related ways: in terms of industrial production processes and the industrialization process more generally.

## The Industrial Production Process

Industry can be defined as a particular way of producing things, as a particular production process. In chapter 3, production was defined as a process through which human labour is used to change nature into goods for consumption. Industrial production processes are characterized by:

1 the possibility of utilizing complex techniques and sophisticated machinery associated with a large scale of production;
2 the utilization of a wide range of raw materials often already processed through the use of complex technologies and, therefore, of linkage with other forms of production;
3 a relatively complex technical division of labour within units of production;
4 a diverse range of skills within the work-force;
5 most energy provided by machines (including use of gas and electricity), not people.

WGV 794

FIGURE 19 Types of industrial production.
(Top left) Agricultural industry: Indian tea plantation (Camera Press, RBO)
(Centre) Mining: Peruvian tin mine (Alan Hutchison Library)
(Bottom left) Energy: Tucurui hydro-electric project, Brazil (Alan Hutchison Library)
(Top right) Manufacturing: electronics assembly in Hong Kong (Camera Press)
(Bottom right) Construction in China (Sally and Richard Greenhill)

This industrial way of doing things can be contrasted with artisanal production, also known as household handicraft production, for example, of textile cloth. In India, millions of handloom weavers, working in their own households, produce textile cloth to customers' orders. At the other extreme, India has many large textile factories with different types of machinery, complex systems of organization, workers doing many different tasks and producing a range of industrial products for the domestic and external markets. The contrast is not always so stark. In between artisanal and industrial production there are a variety of forms of organization of what could be called handicraft workshop production.

A research fieldworker, comparing small workshops weaving hammocks with a large textile factory in Brazil, wrote:

> Coming out of a modern spinning and weaving mill and entering a typical hammock 'factory' gives one the impression of going back in time, such is the similarity with a pre-industrial revolution workshop. The main types of production are carried out manually ... in some workshops the only source of power is human muscle. Work is based on the manual ability of the workforce, and in the words of one weaver 'energia feijao' [feijao, black beans, constitute a basic part of Brazilian diet] ... the looms are wooden and operated manually. A loom has two pedals on which the weaver stands; using his body weight he is able to change over the two sets of warp threads ... this work requires skill, especially when several different colours are being used. In all the firms visited, the looms were operated by men, given that strong arm and leg muscles are needed. (Schmitz, 1979, p. 11)

In this example, the handicraft production of hammocks operated nearby the industrial production of textiles.

## The Process of Industrialization

The other way of looking at industrial production is through the industrialization process. This includes both the study of the spread of industry and the resulting social modifications. It is important for our purposes here to consider the wider social and economic conditions within which particular industrial production processes develop, and in particular the extent to which these processes have become so widespread as to create a fully industrialized society.

The industrial revolution in Britain was the first example where such a complete penetration of industrial forms of production occurred that society was transformed at all levels: 'the first historical instance of the break-through from an agrarian handicraft economy to one dominated by industry and machine manufacture. The industrial revolution ... transformed in the space of two lifetimes the life of western man, the nature of his society and his relationship to the other peoples of the world' (Landes, 1969, p. 1).

Issues about industrialization require both micro and macro levels of analysis. For example, the analysis of the significance of multinational investment requires examination of the particular production processes it establishes in a Third World country, and also consideration of their effects on the process of industrialization in the country as a whole (the analysis of the vehicle industry in Brazil's industrialization is an example of this approach in chapter 11).

The two levels of analysis are not easily isolated from each other. Industrialization as a total process includes and subsumes within it the establishment of industrial production processes. But industrial production processes can be established without setting in motion an industrialization process. For example, many non-industrialized colonies contained important extractive industries, notably mining, such as copper in Zambia and tin in Malaya. Others had complex agricultural industries, for example, sisal in Tanzania and sugar in Guyana. These processes were established without linking with, or stimulating the development of, other industries in these countries. They were, thus, isolated from any more widespread industrialization process. If they had been set up in countries such as Britain, the USA or the USSR, their characteristics and effects may well have been very different. Such examples show the importance of looking both at production processes and at industrialization as a total process.

## Industry in the Third World: Growth and Diversity

How much and what kind of industry exists in the Third World? In this section, we shall present some statistical information to help answer this question. But statistical information by itself is not sufficient to understand the role of industrialization in Third World development. Facts do *not* speak for themselves. The data presented here have been used to support conflicting views on industrial production and its importance for Third World development.

We shall not then simply present statistical information in a theoretical vacuum (if, indeed, this is ever possible). We shall examine the statistics in relation to an influential perspective on Third World development known as dependency theory. The reasons for taking this approach are as follows: firstly, dependency theory originated in the Third World (in Latin America) and has become a very influential framework for considering national development in relation to the international economy. (These issues are the focus of chapter 13.) Secondly, a particular view of the importance of industry is central to dependency theory.

Unlike the populist views discussed in chapter 8, which give priority to agriculture and small-scale production over large-scale industrialization, dependency theorists favour rapid industrialization. But they also stress that Third World industrialization is not taking place rapidly enough to lead to development, and attempt to explain why not.

Below are two extracts from the work of dependency theorists, selected because of their view of industry. The extracts equate the statistical sector 'manufacturing industry' with industry in general. Although this is incorrect, 'manufacturing industry' and 'industry' are often used interchangeably because manufacturing is central to the process of industrialization and therefore conventionally seen as the most important part of industry. Manufacturing, therefore, is used as an indicator of industrialization in general, as in this chapter. There are problems associated with its use, however, and we return to these later in the chapter (pages 206–7).

> [In 1980] some nine per cent of the world's industrial goods were produced in the Third World. In only ten of the 123 countries of the Third World does manufacturing activity comprise more than 20 per cent of Gross Domestic Product and more than 20 per cent of total exports: Brazil, Argentina, Mexico, Colombia, Egypt, South Korea, Taiwan, Hong Kong, Singapore, and the Philippines. Manufactures make up between 15 and 20 per cent of the GDP in only 17 other countries. A very small number of countries export the bulk of the industrial production originating in the Third World: Brazil, Mexico, Hong Kong, South Korea, Singapore, and India. For the overwhelming majority of Third World countries, industrial activity remains a very marginal phenomenon ... The greater part of industrial production in the Third World is devoted to the food industry, textiles, ready-made clothes, beverages and tobacco. (Benachenhou, 1980, pp. 44–55)

> If ... the underdeveloped countries are developing significant heavy industry and their technology is becoming relatively sophisticated, we would expect to see this reflected in their ability to compete in the world manufacturing market. Yet when one examines the manufactured exports from the underdeveloped countries to the developed capitalist countries one finds the situation is not very encouraging. As late as 1968 five countries accounted for two-thirds of the exports of manufactured goods from the 'developing' to the advanced capitalist nations. Manufactured exports from the underdeveloped world have been and continue to be either processed foods (e.g. canned meats from Argentina) or more typically, based on assembly operations. Hong Kong (hardly a great industrial power) led the underdeveloped world in manufacturing exports!' (McMichael, Petras and Rhodes, 1974, p. 99)

The arguments regarding industry arising from these dependency theorists can be summarized as follows:

1 Third World industry is still very small in relation to global industrial production.
2 It is not increasing very rapidly in the vast majority of Third World countries.
3 Only a few Third World countries are industrializing rapidly.
4 *These few newly industrializing countries (NICs) are industrializing for reasons atypical of the Third World, for example their ability to offer low labour costs partly because they exert strong control over the working class; and because they are able to attract foreign investment. Their experiences cannot be generalized to the whole Third World. So the assertion that the Third World in general is industrializing is wrong. Even in the NICs the form of industry is 'distorted'.*
5 In the Third World, such industry as exists is concentrated in relatively few sectors – whether a few highly developed sectors for export rather than direct use in the national economy, or in consumer goods for

direct consumption rather than industries such as iron and steel, machine tools and electronics.

6 The consumer goods industries tend to produce 'luxury goods', which can be purchased by only a small proportion of the population.

7 *The lack of diversity of industrial production means that it is not possible for a 'total' process of industrialization, as occurred in Britain and the West, to take place; the 'blockages' on industrialization because of world market competition are too great to overcome.*

Arguments **4** and 7 are italicized because they are explanatory and cannot be derived directly from the information in this section. The other arguments are interpretations of empirical trends, and we shall focus more on these for the moment.

For completeness there are three further important arguments concerning industry to note, although we will not deal with them in this chapter. One is that the industries set up in Third World countries are relatively capital intensive so that, although they may be profitable, they are not able to employ all or even most of those looking for jobs. They also need skills that cannot be mastered easily by local workers. It is also argued by some that 'backward' agricultural countries in the late twentieth century, (so-called 'latecomers') cannot industrialize at all.

I shall test the arguments of dependency theory concerning empirical trends by working through a series of mostly statistical data presented in the following order: (i) the quantity of industrial output (arguments **1** and **2**; (ii) the growth of industry and differences between countries (arguments **3** and **4**); and (iii) diversity of industry (arguments **5**, **6** and 7).

### *The quantity of industrial output*

The total output of Third World industry remains small in comparison with that of the First World, as the above quotations suggested. One set of reasons for this arises from colonialism. The colonial powers typically discouraged industrialization in their colonies, for various reasons. For example, British policy in Egypt according to Lord Cromer, its Governor from 1883 to 1907, was not to encourage local industries. Cromer looked on the results of its policy as follows:

> The difference is apparent to any man whose recollections go back some ten or fifteen years. Some quarters [of Cairo] that formerly used to be veritable centres of varied industries – spinning, weaving, ribbon making, dyeing, tent making, embroidery, shoe making, jewellery making, spice grinding, copper work, the manufacture of bottles out of animal skins, saddlery, sieve making, locksmithing in wood and metal, etc – have shrunk considerably or vanished. (Quoted in Hayter, 1981, p. 49)

Later, in 1935, a Minister gave reasons for not encouraging industrialization in Britain's colonies in competition with Britain's own industry.

> The suggestion that the colonies should actively promote industrialization ... requires special consideration. It is obvious that manufacturing countries like

> ours could not afford to provide free or assured markets for manufactured goods in direct competition with their own. All questions of starting new industries in the colonies must be examined ... with regard to the welfare of the colony as a whole and as a primary producer. (Quoted in Brett, 1973, p. 273)

At that time, colonies were seen principally as producers of primary goods, that is agricultural and mining products used as raw materials in the manufacturing industries of the colonial powers, and as consumers of manufactured goods from the colonizing power. Note again the use of the word 'industry' to mean manufacturing industry. Colonial agriculture and mining did include some industrial production, such as plantation production of sugar and tea, and mining production of copper and phosphates. This is not included in manufacturing production.

Political pressure for a national industrial sector has generally been an important driving force for industrialization. In the main it was those Third World countries that were not formally colonized or were independent by the end of the nineteenth century that began to industrialize first. Brazil and Argentina are good examples. In Brazil, profits accumulated from agriculture were invested by Brazilian capitalists in manufacturing industry from the end of the last century onwards.

Table 13 shows that the quantity of manufacturing production in the Third World is very small relative to its population and area. The three continents of Africa, Asia and Latin America contained about one-eighth of the world's manufacturing production. It also shows, however, that the size and share of Third World countries have increased somewhat, a fact we deal with next.

To summarize, the small quantity of manufacturing output in the Third World seems to support the first arguments of the dependency view on

TABLE 13 Share of manufacturing production 1963–82 (percentages)

| | *1963* | *1980* | *1982* |
|---|---|---|---|
| Developing countries | 8.1 | 10.6 | 11.0 |
| Centrally planned economies | 14.6 | 22.9 | 25.0 |
| Developed countries | 77.3 | 62.7 | 64.0 |
| China | na | 3.8 | na |

*Notes*: *Developed* countries include Canada, USA, Europe (other than Eastern Europe), Australia, Israel, Japan, New Zealand and South Africa.
*Developing* countries include the Caribbean area, Central and South America, Africa, the Asian Middle East (other than Israel) and East and South East Asia (other than Japan, China, South Korea, Mongolia and Vietnam).
*Centrally planned* economies include Eastern Europe and the USSR.
NA = data not available.
*Source*: UNIDO (1983).

industry. I shall now look at the second, third and fourth arguments, concerning how quickly manufacturing is growing, and at the differences between countries.

### *Comparative growth of Third World manufacturing*

There has been a rapid growth in the establishment of industrial production processes in the Third World since the 1960s. The overall rate of growth of manufacturing in Third World countries has been greater than that of advanced Western countries over the period 1963–82, although growth has been from an initially low base (see table 14). However, growth has not been as great as in the centrally planned economies, including China. Moreover, during the 1970s, poorer countries have been faring much worse than 'middle income' countries.

Various reasons have been advanced to explain why the industrial growth rates of developing countries have been more rapid than those of developed countries. Decolonization and the winning of national independence in much of Africa and Asia in the 1950s and 1960s brought an increased political will to industrialize. Many Third World countries set up import controls to protect their home markets and encourage investors to produce goods to satisfy existing local consumers. The most important industries that were set up were those producing food, drinks, and textiles previously imported. This policy has been termed *import substitution industrialization*, for obvious reasons.

Transnational (and some local) companies have also been encouraged to invest in developing countries because of low wages and the possibility of making high profits. Some countries have been extremely successful at attracting such investment; examples are Brazil and the so-called 'gang of four' – South Korea, Taiwan, Singapore and Hong Kong. The information on Third World industrial growth in tables 13 and 14 seems to contradict the dependency position that industry is not increasing very rapidly. However, there are a number of problems with using such simplified data. One is that nothing is included on population growth rates so that we cannot estimate overall *per capita* increases in industry. Another is that, beneath the aggregated growth rates, major differences between countries

TABLE 14 Growth rate of manufacturing industry (percentage per annum)

| | *1963–73* | *1973–82* |
|---|---|---|
| Developing countries | 8.0 | 4.7 |
| Developed countries | 5.5 | 1.7 |
| Centrally planned economies | 9.8 | 5.4 |

*Note*: See notes to table 13, p. 00.
*Source*: UNIDO (1983).

exist. Table 15 has data on fifteen selected countries to illustrate the enormous differences, particularly between the Third World countries. For example, Brazil, South Korea, Nigeria, and Singapore had industrial growth rates of over 10 per cent per annum between 1960 and 1978. China (which does not differentiate manufacturing from other industrial sectors) had a 10 per cent growth rate. Turkey and India had growth rates significantly above their population growth. But Jamaica and Zambia had very low growth rates indeed. The table also shows the generally lower growth rates between 1973 and 1983.

Finally, if manufacturing value added (a measure of the product of the manufacturing sector of a national economy) is calculated per head of the population, a clearer divide is made between developing and developed countries at least for the fifteen countries in table 15.

In relationship to dependency, we have investigated arguments 2 and 3 (p. 194). Since fewer than 10 per cent of Thirld World countries had an industrial growth rate lower than their population growth rate, the general assertion that the Third World is not industrializing does not seem correct. However, the differences between Third World countries are large. The general level of growth has been relatively higher in middle-income than in low-income Third World countries, which grew at only 3.0% in 1973–82. That is, those countries like Brazil, that already seem to have relatively advanced economies, have proportionately higher rates of industrial growth. These differences need to be accommodated in any theory of Third World industry and Third World development.

The statistical information has been useful in gauging the extent of manufacturing industrial growth. But there are important questions that the information as it stands cannot help to answer. There is a strongly argued view that rapid industrial growth can still be 'dependent' if it is the result of foreign investment. The argument is that such investment cannot guarantee proper linkages between industries leading to further all-round industrial development in the future.

### *Diversity of industrial production*

In the last section, information was categorized by country, without reference to the composition of industry in each case. We need now to consider the kinds of products Third World industry produces, in order to investigate arguments 5 and 6 (pp. 194–5) of the dependency position, which lead to postulates.

1 that such industry as exists in the Third World is concentrated into a narrow group of sectors;
2 that it is concentrated in consumer, not producer goods production
3 that it is concentrated on luxury, not wage goods; and
4 that it has concentrated on producing goods for export, not to satisfy local consumption needs.

The meaning of these terms can be understood from figure 20.

TABLE 15 Some industrial indicators, selected countries

| | Manufacturing value added (US$ millions) | Population (millions) (1983) | Manufacturing value added per capita (US$) | Share of GDP | | Annual growth rate 1960–78 | | Annual growth rate 1973–83 | | growth rate 1973–83 (%) |
|---|---|---|---|---|---|---|---|---|---|---|
| | | | | All industry[b] | Manufacturing industries | All industry | Manufacturing | All industry | Manufacturing | |
| USA | 414,600 | 234 | 1,771 | 32 | 21 | 4 | 4 | 1 | 1 | 1.0 |
| Japan* | 252,581 | 119 | 2,123 | 42 | 30 | 8 | 8 | 6 | 6° | 0.9 |
| Britain | 52,963 | 56 | 946 | 32 | 18 | 2 | 2 | 0 | −2 | 0.0 |
| Brazil | 43,300 | 130 | 333 | 35 | 27 | 10 | 10 | 5 | 4 | 2.3 |
| India | 16,210 | 733 | 22 | 26 | 15 | 5 | 5 | 4 | 4 | 2.3 |
| South Korea | 11,492 | 40 | 287 | 39 | 27 | 17 | 18 | 4 | 12 | 2.5 |
| Turkey | 6,898 | 47 | 147 | 33 | 24 | 9 | 9 | 4 | 4 | 2.2 |
| Norway[a] | 6,181 | 4 | 1,545 | 42 | 14 | 5 | 4 | 4 | 1[c] | 0.4 |
| Nigeria | 4,049 | 94 | 43 | 34 | 5 | 13 | 11 | 0 | 11 | 2.7 |
| Singapore | 2,431 | 3 | 972 | 37 | 24 | 10 | 11 | 9 | 8 | 1.3 |
| Zambia | 427 | 6 | 71 | 38 | 19 | 2 | 1 | 0 | na | 3.2 |
| Ethiopia | 361 | 41 | 9 | 16 | 11 | 2 | 1 | 3 | 4 | 2.6 |
| Jamaica | 284 | 2 | 142 | 34 | 19 | 2 | 2 | −4 | −4 | 1.3 |
| Niger | 158 | 6 | 26 | 31 | na | 11 | na | na | 11 | 3.0 |
| China | na | 1,019 | na | 45 | na | 10 | na | 8 | na | 1.5 |

*Notes*: [a] Not Third World countries.
[b] 'All industry' means not agricultural or services.
[c] 1970–80.
na = data not available.
*Source*: World Bank (1985).

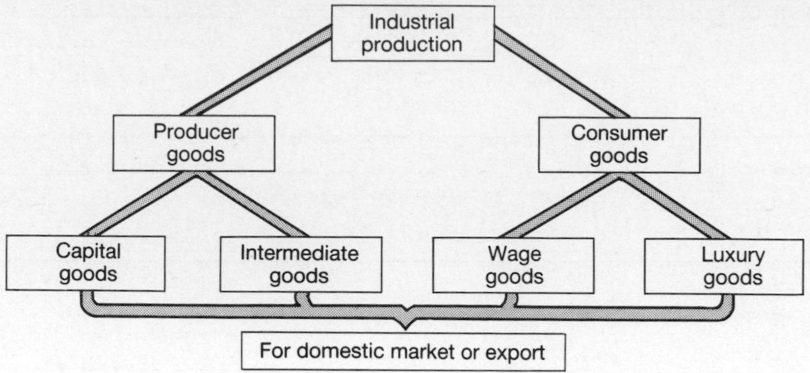


FIGURE 20 Diversity of industrial production

## *Producer and consumer goods*

The division between producer and consumer goods is based on a simple classification of industrial output. *Consumer industries* are those that produce goods for direct consumption, which may be designated either wage goods (considered essential for meeting basic living standards in the country concerned), or luxury goods (not considered essential). Examples of consumer goods are food products such as chocolates and bread, clothes, shoes, and washing machines. Specific examples from the Third World include processed tea and sugar. All are for direct consumption without further processing, although some markets, for example, those for tea and sugar, can be a long distance from the place of production.

*Producer industries* are those making goods for further industrial use. Producer goods are of two types – either capital goods, such as machinery, or intermediate goods, which are processed goods used as material for further production. PVC granules, for example, are used as the feed for moulding machines. They are, thus, producer goods since they are used as intermediate goods inputs for the production of plastic kitchen products (consumer goods) in another industrial process. Many Third World countries do not have facilities for making plastic, a complex product usually made from petroleum using large-scale processing. They, therefore, import plastic granules and use them in factories to make plastic kitchen products (see figure 21).

Obviously, to make consumer goods, both capital goods (machines) and raw materials or intermediate goods (or both) are necessary; for example, textile cloth needs cotton (raw material), spinning and weaving machinery (capital goods), and dyeing chemicals (intermediate goods).

The distinction between producer and consumer goods is important for industrialization strategies. For example, a government can decide to encourage investment in consumer industries, and to import the necessary machinery. Many Third World governments, especially of small or low-income countries, make this choice at least in the early stages of industrialization, attempting to substitute domestically produced goods for those imported. Others, especially centrally planned countries, have decided to give priority to producer, and particularly capital goods, industries.

If a decision is taken to concentrate on consumer goods, machinery must be purchased with foreign exchange. If the concentration is on producer goods, factories must still be imported that do not produce goods for direct consumption, leaving less available for investment in production for immediate consumption; in a nutshell, less consumption now for more consumption later – 'eating' less today to enable more tomorrow.

It has been argued that this strategy will lead, in the longer term, to higher production of both producer and consumer industries, of agricultural output, and to the more rapid growth of the national economic strength that comes from the productive capacity to build more machines. This was the argument behind Soviet industrialization that has been used as a model by some Third World countries.

Tables 16 and 17 give some indication of the recent balance between producer and consumer goods in Third World economies. Table 16 illustrates that the more economically developed countries in the list have more intermediate and capital goods. They also have stronger and more complex linkages between units and sectors of production (as we would expect from chapter 6). Table 17 shows the gradual move from dominance of consumer (light) goods to dominance of producer (heavy) goods over time.

The most advanced Third World countries have developed producer goods industries, although not up to the same level of capacity or sophistication as developed market or centrally planned economies. This does mean that consumer goods production has dropped. The overall

TABLE 16 Examples of consumer, intermediate and capital goods in various countries (percentages)

| | *Food, tobacco and textiles (mostly consumer goods)* | *Chemicals (mostly intermediate goods)* | *Electrical and mechanical machinery (mostly capital goods)* |
|---|---|---|---|
| USA | 20 | 12 | 31 |
| Japan | 16 | 12 | 36 |
| Britain | 23 | 13 | 29 |
| Brazil | 26 | 10 | 29 |
| India | 44 | 13 | 19 |
| South Korea | 41 | 8 | 24 |
| Nigeria | 54 | na | 16 |
| Zambia | 64 | 5 | 4 |
| Mozambique | 72 | 3 | 8 |

*Source*: UN Statistical Yearbooks

FIGURE 21 The plastics industry divided into: capital goods (top left); intermediate goods (bottom left, bottom right); and consumer goods (top right). (Top left and bottom right: courtesy of Shell International Petroleum Co. Ltd; bottom left: courtesy of ICI Plastics Division; top right: Mike Wells, Camera Press)

TABLE 17 The changing division between producer and consumer industries

| | *1960* | | *1980* | |
|---|---|---|---|---|
| | *Light* | *Heavy* | *Light* | *Heavy* |
| World | 40.7 | 59.3 | 33.5 | 66.5 |
| Developed countries | 38.0 | 62.0 | 32.3 | 66.7 |
| Centrally planned economies | 41.9 | 58.1 | 33.0 | 67.0 |
| Developing countries | 62.5 | 37.5 | 42.9 | 57.1 |

*Notes*: UNIDO (the United Nations Industrial Development Organization) uses the names 'heavy' and 'light industry' for what we have called 'producer' and 'consumer industries'. UNIDO statistics information is divided into: *Light industries* – industries such as foods, drinks, textiles, furniture; *heavy industries* such as cement, metals, mechanical and electrical engineering, cars. See also notes to table 13, p. 196.
*Source*: UNIDO (1983).

increase in industrial production has meant that the quantity of consumer goods produced has been rising, though not at the same rate as producer goods. We must also remember that producer goods sectors can become consumer sectors over time. For example, in electrical and mechanical engineering there has been rapid growth in the First World since 1945 of motor car, refrigerator, washing machine and television production. This seems to contradict the dependency argument (point 5) that industry in the Third World is concentrated in relatively few sectors and not in the important linkage industries like steel, machine tools and electronics. Clearly, developing countries are increasingly diversified in industrial production. However, again, we must take care not to over-generalize from our data. Some Third World countries are diversifying rapidly and others very slowly.

### *Wage and luxury goods*

Consumer goods production can be divided into luxury and wage goods (see figure 20). The importance of the division for us is that it is argued that a major limit to Third World economic development is the very low incomes of most of the Third World's population. This means that there is a low level of market demand for commodities, and that potential producers of goods cannot sell them profitably. This acts as a brake on the expansion of industrial production. The argument continues along the lines that, as only a small proportion of the Third World's population is rich enough to be able to buy a range of products, their needs – classed as luxury goods needs – dominate what is produced. The composition of industry is, as a result, skewed towards the production of luxury goods (for example, consumer durables) at the expense of wage goods (those necessities that everyone requires). This is point 6 on page 195.

The statistical problems of testing this hypothesis are considerable. First of all, the distinction between wage goods and luxury goods is difficult to establish. One possibility is to ascertain which goods the poorest classes in a country consume, for example, certain types of food and textiles, and call those wage goods; then we can term luxuries those commodities the poor cannot afford, such as refrigerators or cars. One problem with this approach, however, arises if the majority of poor classes do not buy food but grow their own. Then mostly the rich buy food. Is food, then, a luxury? From your reading of chapter 9 on the Green Revolution in India, you will see that rice and wheat have become luxuries for poor peasants because they cannot afford to eat these grains. Another problem is that such definitions can change. Some luxury goods may become wage goods over time, as cars have done in Britain over the last forty years.

Table 18 shows the changes that took place in consumption of fridges, televisions and cars in Brazil during the economic miracle years of 1967–74. Ownership is certainly skewed, with richer households consuming more of these consumer durables. However, what is striking over the period is that ownership, particularly of fridges and televisions, became much more widespread.

Wells (1977) used these data to argue against the view that consumer durables in Brazil were luxury goods, claiming that the market had expanded in all groups. So we must be careful not to assume that all products of industrial production go to the elites of the Third World.

### *Domestic and export markets*

Finally, we shall move to the distinction between production for export and production for domestic markets (see figure 20).

From the available information, it appears that the proportion of manufactured goods exported from Third World countries has not increased

TABLE 18 Percentage of households in each of five income classes owning a variety of durable consumer goods in Brazil, 1967 and 1974.

| | | *Household income as multiples of the current minimum wage* | | | | |
|---|---|---|---|---|---|---|
| | | *0–2* | *2–4* | *4–6* | *6–9* | *> 9* |
| Refrigerators | 1967 | 35 | 62 | 87 | 96 | 98 |
| | 1974 | 57 | 84 | 96 | 90 | 96 |
| Televisions | 1967 | 21 | 50 | 80 | 89 | 95 |
| | 1974 | 58 | 85 | 87 | 96 | 95 |
| Passengers cars | 1967 | 0 | 3 | 11 | 25 | 48 |
| | 1974 | 5 | 12 | 25 | 51 | 50 |

*Source*: Wells (1977).

significantly between 1965 and 1975. A recent survey of twenty-five selected Third World countries (UNIDO, 1980) showed that manufactured exports as a percentage of total manufacturing output had slightly decreased from 33 to 31 per cent between 1965 and 1985. But the overall quantity of manufactured exports had increased. If the trade in petroleum is omitted, the proportion of Third World manufacturing exports measured in terms of their value increased from 20 to 45 per cent of total exports between 1960 and 1976. That is, if we exclude oil, there has been a shift away from exporting raw unprocessed materials, such as agricultural crops and minerals, towards exporting already processed materials and finished goods. Although at the aggregate level these changes have occurred slowly, a few Third World countries have shown very large increases in manufacturing exports.

The distinction between production for local consumption or for export has been the centre of a major debate between advocates of two opposing strategies for industrialization: those advocating import substitution industrialization and those arguing for export oriented industrialization. This debate is taken up later in this chapter.

In summary, the data we have used so far has allowed us to throw considerable light on the growth and diversity of industry, even though we have had to concentrate on manufacturing industry alone. From an extremely low base before the Second World War, it has grown quite rapidly, both absolutely and as a proportion of world industrial output. The overall level of manufacturing industry remains much lower than in the rest of the world and growth has been uneven. A few countries' industrial growth rates have been slower than their population growth rates. However, only in a very few is it possible to argue that absolute production is stagnating or declining. The majority of countries have had relatively high growth rates. Thus, the dependency view that industry is not expanding very rapidly is difficult to substantiate. Also, blanket assertions that Third World industrialization is in a narrow range of sectors, and only for luxury consumption, are incorrect, though there are large differences between countries in the extent to which production is diversified.

The more economically advanced of the Third World countries, such as Brazil and South Korea, have developed strong producer goods industries and a wider range of interlinked industrial production processses. Some have been able to expand rapidly their exports of manufactures in a highly competitive industry. Here again, however, we must add the rider that it is impossible to generalize about the whole Third World.

It is important, then, that any theory of Third World industry and Third World development accommodates the clear differences we have found.

## Manufacturing Industry and the Process of Industrialization

There are two reasons why we have concentrated on manufacturing rather than on any other indicator of industrialization. Firstly, the range of production in 'manufacturing' is much greater than in any other industrial sector. Secondly, 'non-manufacturing industries' such as the extractive and agricultural industries do not *necessarily* have many linkages with other sectors of the national economy – for example, oil production and copper mining. One influential empirical definition of industrialization is that of Sutcliffe (1971). He put forward three tests of industrialization:

1 at least 25 per cent of GDP should be in industry;
2 at least 60 per cent of industrial output should be in manufacturing; and
3 at least 10 per cent of the total population should be employed in industry.

He includes the second test to avoid including countries with high mineral or other single-sector wealth. For Sutcliffe's categorization of countries by these tests of industrialization, see figure 22.

Still, there are problems associated with focusing only on manufacturing. We shall briefly look at two: (i) the danger of not considering other sectors; and (ii) the danger of seeing industry as only large-scale production. Table 19 gives information for a series of countries.

Even the limited information presented here indicates that 'non-manufacturing' industries can make up a much more significant proportion of GDP in Third World countries than in developed countries. Some countries have high mineral wealth, like Nigeria with its oil, and Niger with uranium, that statistically swamp the remainder of national industrial production. Agriculture has been included in table 19 to illustrate its relative importance but available statistics do not allow us to differentiate between industrial and non-industrial production processes used in agriculture.

As was argued at the beginning of this chapter, the best definition of industry was that based on the characteristics of the process, both technical and social, and on its capacity to increase the quantity of goods made in society. This involves economies of scale, energy provided by non-human forces, a wide range of raw materials and intermediate products, a complex technical division of labour and a diverse range of skills. However, the analysis of statistical information forces a return to less satisfactory definitions of industrialization, 'non-agriculture' and the 'sectoral' approach. There is no alternative with available statistics which, for example, do not allow us to differentiate between small-scale handicraft production and large-scale production, whether in the factory, the building site, the mine or the plantation. Chapter 12 deals with this issue in more detail.

## *The process of industrialization*

The distinction between production for national consumption or for exportation has been used in two strategic approaches to industrialization processes: Import substitution industrialization (ISI) and export oriented industrialization (EOI).

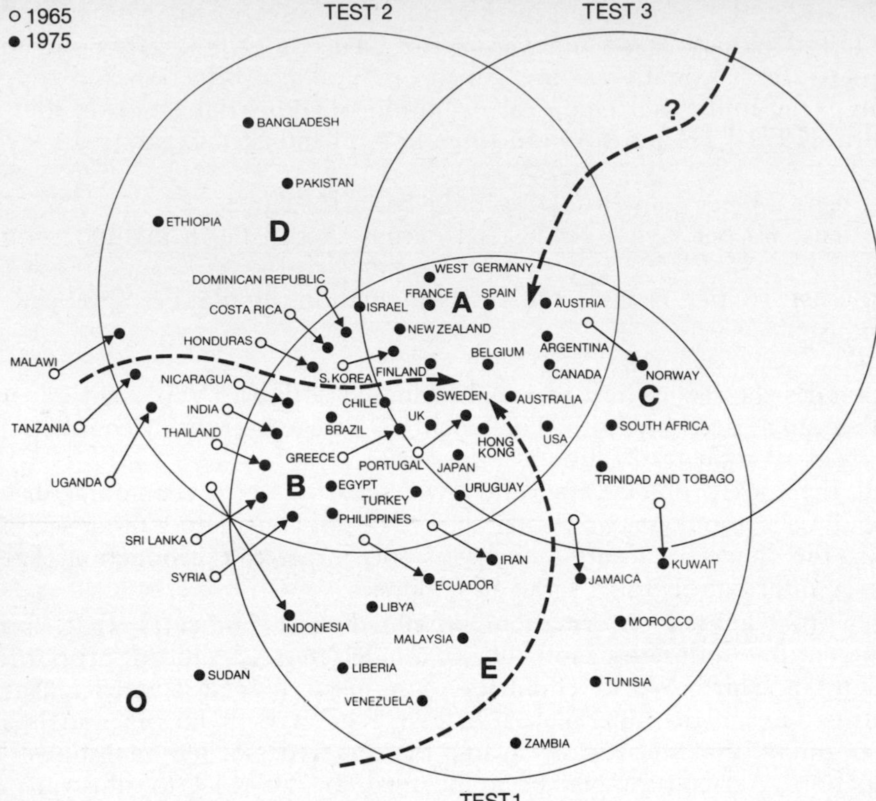


FIGURE 22 Sutcliffe categories of industrialization: the movement of countries between categories A–E and O, 1965–75

Sutcliffe's data were for the mid-1960s. A reworking of his calculations showed a substantial number of countries as having changed categories in barely ten years, as indicated by the arrows. The figure shows countries for which reliable data for all three tests were available in both cases.

*Notes:*

A Fully industrialized countries that pass all three tests: (i) at least 25% of GDP in industry; (ii) at least 60% of industrial output in manufacturing; (iii) at least 10% of the total population employed in industry.

B Countries that pass the first two tests. Manufacturing predominates in a substantial industrial sector that has not spread to affect the whole population.

A/B Borderline cases between A and B.

C Countries that pass the first and third tests. A large industrial sector (perhaps based on mining or oil) affects the population widely, but manufacturing is weak.

D Countries that pass the second test only. A small industrial sector is mainly based on manufacturing.

E Countries that pass the first test only. A substantial non-manufacturing-based industrial sector (again, perhaps, oil or mining) does not affect the population widely.

O Other countries, i.e. non-industrialized countries failing these tests.

TABLE 19 Share of GDP of industrial sectors and agriculture, 1981 (percentages)

| | *Manufacturing* | *Mining, electricity, water and gas* | *Construction* | *Industry*[a] | *Agriculture* |
|---|---|---|---|---|---|
| US | 22 | 7 | 4 | 33 | 3 |
| Japan | 31 | 4 | 9 | 44 | 3 |
| Britain | 20 | 9 (oil) | 5 | 34 | 2 |
| Brazil[b] | 23 | 1 | 5 | 29 | 11 |
| India | 15 | 4 | 4 | 23 | 32 |
| South Korea | 29 | 3 | 7 | 39 | 17 |
| Turkey | 24 | 4 | 5 | 33 | 21 |
| Norway | 15 | 20 (oil) | 7 | 42 | 4 |
| Nigeria[b] | 6 | 26 (oil) | 8 | 40 | 20 |
| Singapore | 29 | 3 | 7 | 39 | 1 |
| Jamaica[b] | 15 | 16 (Al) | 6 | 37 | 8 |
| Zambia | 18 | 9 (Cu) | 4 | 31 | 17 |
| Niger[c] | 10 | 17 (U) | 3 | 30 | 43 |
| China | – | – | 4 | 43 | 42 |
| GDR | – | – | 6 | 73 | 9 |
| USSR | – | – | 10 | 51 | 15 |

*Notes*: [a] Industry includes mining, electricity, gas and water, construction and manufacturing
[b] Data is for 1980
[c] Data for 1978
Al = Aluminium; U = Uranium; Cu = Copper.
*Source*: UN Statistical Yearbook

*Import substitution industrialization (ISI)* This is a strategy developed by a group of Latin American economists from the 1940s, including Paul Prebisch and Celso Furtado. Instead of concentrating production on primary goods for export, like minerals and agricultural commodities, they argued that indigenous industrialization as a replacement for imports should be encouraged by 'protecting' the home market at first in light industrial sectors producing consumer goods like food products and textiles, but later also producer goods production. This kind of industrialization process has a number of important implications.

One is the need for state intervention. Protection of infant industries demands tariff protection (like taxing foreign imports of similar products). This is not only an issue for Third World industrializers in the second half of the twentieth century. It has been an issue for all industrializers after Britain. All 'newly' industrializing countries after Britain have protected their industries, including Germany, France, the USA, Japan and the Soviet Union (as described in chapter 4, which referred to the arguments of List).

State intervention has not generally stopped there. After the first industrialization process, that of Britain, those wishing to industrialize had to do so from a position of relative backwardness. With the exception of the USA, the later industrializing countries tended to use a greater degree of state intervention to promote, protect and even finance industry.

There has been a similar tendency in countries wishing to industrialize in the twentieth century throughout the world, whether following an ISI strategy or not. In practise, ISI strategies have been more a way of mobilizing national opinion in favour of industrial investment than narrowly restricted to priorities for investment.

*Export oriented industrialization* Export oriented industrialization strategies have been articulated as a reaction to perceived blockages to further internal industrial growth in the 1960s and 1970s. The strategy is to break through these blockages by manufacturing for export. The prime examples of successful implementation of such a strategy have been the newly industrializing countries, particularly the 'gang of four' mentioned earlier (Hong Kong, Taiwan, South Korea and Singapore). South Korea and Taiwan had solid foundations for their export orientation. Their industrial expansion in the 1950s and early 1960s was largely oriented towards the domestic market, with import substitution for consumer goods playing a major role. During that period, vast quantities of aid from the USA made it possible to reconstruct the country's infrastructure, to improve education and health, and to reform and improve agricultural production. This aid, induced by the USA's commitment to what it termed 'the containment of communism', meant that South Korea had almost no foreign debt by 1965.

Contrary to ideas that South Korean development has been of the free trade variety, the state has been instrumental in executing economic policy. South Korea has been described as 'one of the free world's most tightly supervised economies, with the government initiating almost every major investment by the private sector' (*Financial Times*, 2 April 1979).

The change in policy towards export orientation was based on the knowledge that South Korea's natural resource base was very poor (like Japan's). It has no significant raw materials other than some low-grade coal. The conclusion was drawn in the 1960s that possibilities for further import substitution were confined to intermediate goods and consumer durables with a limited domestic market, which could not justify investment in large enough plants to realize economies of scale. Having made these decisions, based on specific conditions prevailing in South Korea, the state changed policy to encourage manufactured exports. It granted tax exemptions, reduced credit charges for export manufacturers, and later set up free trade zones.

Taiwan's industrial development was also initially concentrated on the home market, and the later export orientation was built on this base. Hong Kong's industrialization has a different history, one based on its status as a trading city 'state'. The separation of Singapore from Malaysia in 1965 reduced any possibility of Singapore's more advanced industry serving a larger local market. Singapore's export orientation dates from then. Thus, two of the four countries (South Korea and Taiwan) had sizeable local markets and industrialization first began to supply those. The other two (Hong Kong and Singapore) did not.

A recent tendency in the 1970s has been towards increased export manufacturing, not just as in Singapore and Hong Kong with their total export orientation, but in liaison with industrialization for the local market, as in South Korea, or for that matter Japan. Recent tendencies in Brazil, for example, are for the development of export oriented industries in areas where Brazil can be internationally competitive. South Korea has been shifting to export oriented heavy industries like chemicals, steel, shipbuilding and cars.

To encourage foreign investment, these and other countries have been setting up 'export processing zones' or 'free trade zones' where legislation gives preferential treatment to investors. Such laws generally include duty free entry of goods for assembly, fewer restrictions on profits transfer, reduced pollution restraints and constraints on labour organization. Chapter 16 will cover these developments in more detail.

## The State and Industrialization Processes

Polarization of industrialization strategies between ISI and EOI approaches is a rather narrow framework within which to study industrialization processes. Detailed differences between particular industrialization strategies are obscured. Crucial issues concerning the kinds of industry to encourage (consumer, producer), the types of production process most relevant and the role of the state in industrialization, are submerged in a narrow distinction between domestic and foreign markets.

One way of broadening our approach is to look at earlier industrialization processes, as in chapters 4 and 5. Chapter 4 showed the importance of the British industrial revolution, and chapter 5 describes 'statist' models of development. Here we shall pick up these models to show their importance for more recent industrialization.

The British industrial revolution has been a consistent 'model' for assessing the industrialization of other countries. Their industrialization has been compared with that of Britain (for example, in the range of industries, the time taken to industrialize, and the kind of state involvement) and, if found wanting, has been characterized as abnormal or incomplete industrialization. This is simply because Britain underwent the first industrial revolution, which was also a capitalist industrial revolution, 'followed' by those of other European countries, the USA and Japan. As these other countries became established industrial powers, their experiences merged into the more general 'Western' model referred to in chapter 4. We have, therefore, a 'British model' of industrialization, and a 'Western model' of industrialization. Sometimes the two models are used interchangeably, as if they are the same and have the same relevance for the industrial 'latecomers' of the mostly ex-colonial Third World. We shall look at the question of time for industrialization to occur, and unevenness of transformation.

Although the word 'revolution' implies something rapid, the changes in Europe took place over a considerable period of time.

> Since 1300 or so, when something clearly began to go seriously wrong with European feudal society there have been several occasions when parts of Europe trembled on the brink of capitalism ... Yet it is only from the seventeenth century that this taste became more than a seasoning to an essentially medieval or feudal dish. (Hobsbawm, 1954, p. 33)

> British governments from 1660 on were firmly committed to policies favouring the pursuit of profit above other aims, but the Industrial Revolution did not occur until more than a century later. (Hobsbawm, 1969, p. 38)

> The Industrial Revolution began in England in the eighteenth century, spread therefrom in unequal fashion to the countries of continental Europe and a few areas overseas and transformed in the space of two lifetimes the life of western man, the nature of his society and his relationship to the other peoples of the world. (Landes, 1969, p. 1)

Although Britain had been held up as the 'model' of total change, industrial transformation was not complete. There was not an even and balanced transformation of all branches of industry into large-scale factory production. Nor did industrial enterprises automatically begin by giving a living wage and stable employment to their workers. Technological development was also very uneven. In textiles, the first mechanized industry, handloom weaving, was destroyed by the early nineteenth century, throwing half a million weavers out of work, but clothing factories remained at a relatively low level of technology. Working conditions did not improve rapidly. Descriptions of the working conditions in industrial Britain in the nineteenth century could be compared with conditions in parts of the Third World today (see examples in chapter 12).

From the perspective of comparing industrialization processes, the most important feature of Britain's experience is that it was unique because it was the first industrial revolution. Others could learn from the British model, attempt to emulate it, adopting and changing their industrialization strategies depending on their specific conditions.

Although it is difficult to generalize, I shall point to four differences between British and later 'Western' industrialization.

1 The later industrializations, in Europe, the USA and Japan, involved a greater stress on large scale of production and on bigger enterprises. As the technical scale of production rose during the nineteenth century, so did the investments needed to establish production (Sutcliffe, 1971, p. 323). Industrialists turned to bankers for the finance needed, and banks in turn helped to coordinate companies' interests.

2 The later industrializers focused more intensively at the beginning on

producer goods and less on consumer goods. Still, they all attempted to set up a diverse range of interlinking industries.

3 The later industrializers had to protect their 'infant' industries against the British. All newly industrializing countries after Britain protected their industries through devices such as tariff protection.

4 The later industrializing countries tended to use a greater degree of state intervention to promote, protect and even finance industry. The USA was an exception to this tendency.

There may be purely economic and geographical reasons for particular industries to develop, such as locally available raw material sources or the 'natural' protection afforded local producers by transport costs for competing imports. But, very often, the main impetus toward industrialization as a whole is political; governments of independent nation states desire to have their 'own' industrial sector to decrease dependence on foreign suppliers, and to provide a base for an independent military capacity. They, thus, take steps to provide a favourable economic environment for local industrialization.

These differences, and others, have allowed some economic historians to argue strongly that there is not one simple set of 'stages' between 'backwardness' and 'modernity' common to all countries, nor a single set of mechanisms for moving from one stage to another.

From his study of the later European industrialization, Alexander Gerschenkron has proposed a scheme depending on the degree of 'backwardness'. The more 'backward' a country, the less likely it is that industrialization will occur and factories be set up unless the state intervenes and the banking system is geared to financing industrial production. He says, for example, that Russian backwardness (before the 1917 revolution) was the reason for much greater state intervention. The basic elements of backwardness appear in such an accentuated form as to lead to the use of essentially institutional instruments of industrialization where the state, moved by its military interests, assumed the role of the primary agent impelling the economic' (Gerschenkron, 1962, pp. 14, 16–17).

By 'backwardness', Gerschenkron meant backwardness in comparison with Britain in the nineteenth century, pre-revolutionary Russia being one of the most backward European countries. So far, I have referred only to capitalist industrialization processes. The industrial revolution in Britain and its 'followers' were processes of capitalist development, whether or not they involved strong state intervention and central banking coordination. The 'total' nature of the industrial revolution centres on the radical changes in social structure and culture as well as in technology and economy. Chapter 1 discussed the importance of the formation of a working class of 'free' wage workers; of 'free' markets and competition for private capitalist accumulation; and of state intervention and regulation of modern capitalist economies. Reading chapter 11 on Brazilian industrialization will allow you to study a Third World country's capitalist industrialization process with strong state direction and regulation of industrial growth.

Chapter 5 outlined the Soviet 'model' of industrialization as an alternative to capitalist development. Historically, the Soviet experience provides a 'bridge' between the capitalist 'followers' we have just considered, and the 'latecomers' to industrialization of the Third World. The Soviet experience has been extremely influential in Third World industrialization for various reasons. Here we shall mention four which are of particular interest in the study of 'latecomer' industrialization.

1 The higher economic growth and industrialization rates of the Soviet Union in comparison with those of advanced capitalist countries gave prominence to a model which was able to shake off the constraints of 'late' industrialization, constraints often used at the time as reasons for not encouraging industrialization in the Third World.

2 Third World countries were able to witness industrial growth rates in a country without colonies, without foreign investment, and which was economically 'backward' compared with Britain and the capitalist 'followers'. As Gerschenkron pointed out, even before 1917 Russian 'backwardness' was seen as a reason for much greater state intervention.

3 Soviet economic development, free from foreign control, depended on giving priority to the rapid development of producer goods rather than consumer goods industries. The need to defend the new Soviet state was considered to depend on building a strong machine industry and, therefore, strong metal and mechanical capital goods sectors. Table 17 showed that the centrally planned economies in general have concentrated on developing heavy (i.e. producer goods) industries.

4 Finally, the Soviet 'model' presented to the newly independent states in Asia and Africa an example of successful industrialization achieved through strong state direction of the economy and centralized planning.

It is a moot point whether those nationalist leaders who headed the movements for national independence in Asia and Africa were attracted to the Soviet model because of its socialism, or because it presented to them an example of rapid development achieved through the state, rather than through the operation of market forces and the accumulation of private capital. To repeat what we said in chapter 4: Decolonization meant in the first place the 'inheritance' of the state in the former colonies, rather than control over their economies. Perhaps more compelling than its claim to socialism was the Soviet state's control of the economy through the creation of state enterprises in industry and agriculture in finance, and in domestic and foreign trade, and through centralized planning. It was the Soviet state that pioneered the theory and practice of economic planning on a large scale; today virtually every state in the Third World, regardless of ideological complexion, has some kind of national development plan.

To summarize, the British industrial revolution was unique in the sense that it was the first case of capitalist transformation, 'the single most significant' landmark 'that defines modern history'. Many of the significant changes that took place during Britain's industrialization were replicated in later industrialization (for example, changes in the composition of employment, urbanization, the 'squeezing' of smaller and less productive units of production by more efficient enterprises). Those that industrialized after Britain had to compete with the pioneer. The scale of production increased; enterprises were bigger; integration between banks and industrial companies was greater; more state intervention and protection of national markets occurred. In the twentieth century, a strong alternative to capitalist industrialization emerged in the model of Soviet industrialization, which has been very influential in the Third World. A relatively small country, Britain – albeit with a very large colonial empire – was able to dominate capitalist development and industrialization for almost a century, gradually declining in economic power as 'followers', such as the USA, Germany and Japan, underwent their industrial revolutions. Finally, some Third World countries (for example, Brazil, Mexico, Taiwan and South Korea) have undergone rapid and substantial capitalist industrialization in the last twenty years or so, while others (North Korea, China) have industrialized rapidly along the lines of the Soviet 'model'.

Possibly the major conclusion from this chapter is that, contrary to the argument that Third World countries are doomed to agricultural backwardness too dependent on the First World to allow capitalist industrialization, such industrialization has and is taking place. We have also introduced some of the more important micro and macro concepts for the analysis of industrialization. This has allowed description and explanation of the considerable diversity and unevenness of industrial growth in different parts of the Third World: for example, the variety of producer and consumer goods production, the different ways of seeing wage and luxury goods production and distribution, the different strategies for industrialization based on production for internal and foreign markets. We showed that although some countries (the NICs) have made extraordinary changes, and industrial growth in most other countries has been relatively high, the overall level of manufacturing is still relatively low and growth has been uneven.

Finally, we would argue that it is difficult to analyse Third World industrialization as just one thing to be contrasted against First World industrialization. The industrialization of some of the NICs has been broad enough to make it impossible to lump them with the other Third World economies and write them off as doomed to backwardness.

CHAPTER ELEVEN

# Industrialization in Brazil

## The Miracle and its Aftermath

This chapter moves from the previous chapter's general analysis of industrialization to the particular example of Brazilian industrialization. It is designed as a case study that includes analysis at both macro and micro levels, using the example of the growth of the Brazilian motor industry, and its implications for economic development in Brazil. Concepts already introduced will be used in the analysis of a particularly interesting example of rapid industrial growth, which also illustrates concepts to be developed in later chapters.

The primary focus of this chapter is the period of rapid industrialization in Brazil following the military coup in 1964, with particular reference to the growth of the motor industry. However, it is not possible to examine the motor industry without an understanding of the overall process of industrialization and the strategies adopted to achieve it. Therefore, there is a brief account here of the development of the Brazilian economy from the colonial period right through to the end of the Second World War. Following this is a discussion of industrial policy in the period of democratic rule between 1945 and 1964. Then the period after 1964 is discussed, firstly, the military's doctrine of national security and the role of industry and transport within it and, secondly, the results of the rapid industrialization strategy.

### Growth and Decline in the Brazilian Economy

In Mexico, and Peru, the Spanish conquistadores found both mineral wealth and advanced civilizations. In Brazil, the Portuguese at first could only find limited agricultural opportunities. Even when Brazil's potential for sugar production was developed, a slave labour force had to be imported from Africa. However, sugar did not provide a lasting basis for economic development in Brazil. There was a gold and diamond boom in the eighteenth century, and a rubber boom in the late nineteenth century. Each boom was followed by a bust, and the regional economy at the centre of it fell into decline.

An important break with this cycle of growth and decline came with the development of coffee production in the nineteenth century. The development of coffee was on such a scale and had such ramifications in the fields of transport, commerce and banking that it laid the foundations for a profound change in the South-East region of the country.

Brazil became a major producer of coffee. This provided the resources and impetus for a limited industrialization and the development of transport and commerce. Coffee production required labour, and this was imported from Europe in large quantities at the turn of the century. It required banking and financial facilities, which were provided by both local and foreign capital. It required transportation networks, which were often built by the Brazilian capitalists. Fortunes were made and they were invested in both agriculture and industry. Inevitably, the wealth generated by the coffee boom created a high and rapidly rising demand for industrial products. Many of these were imported from Britain, but in the latter part of the nineteenth century a limited local industry also developed in the areas around Rio de Janeiro and São Paulo. In this situation, industrial growth was largely limited to the production of simple products that were in great demand in the local market. Consumer products – particularly food, clothing and textiles – accounted for the bulk of industrial output.

The Great Depression, which started in 1929, was a disaster for Brazil. Almost overnight export markets for coffee collapsed. Exports, and therefore the income needed to buy imports, declined catastrophically. Brazil's capacity to import fell by 35 per cent between 1925–9 and 1930–4 (Furtado, 1970, p. 41).

In Brazil, the immediate impact of the Great Depression was the overthrow of the old government based on regional landed elites and the coming to power of President Getúlio Vargas. In the fifteen years that followed, profound changes took place in the economic, political and institutional fabric of the nation. The state was centralized. Industry expanded to fill the vacuum left by the decline in import capacity, and while the state tried to ease the burden faced by the coffee sector, it began to foster industrialization actively. Vargas adopted a policy of diversification. Exchange controls, tariffs and credits stimulated industry, which was the destination of investment funds withdrawn from coffee production. To create the right conditions for industry, the state took on responsibility for basic inputs, developing energy resources and setting up the country's first integrated steel mill, at Volta Redonda, in 1943. By the end of the Second World War, Brazil had a much larger industrial base and a much more coherent industrial policy than had been the case in 1929.

## Post-War Development: The 'Democratic Interlude', 1945–64

Following the end of the Second World War, the reintegrated world economic system was effectively under the control of the USA. Brazil, in common with other Latin American nations that had industrialized through protectionist policies, had to decide how best to continue the process of economic and industrial development.

The Brazilian economy could no longer survive without industry and policies to support industry, but the path to industrialization was not easy.

The major Latin American economies had gone beyond the point where they could develop consumer non-durable and intermediate goods industries with little concerted action by the state. Post-war, the further development of industry required expensive state policies to promote new industries and provide the infrastructural base for more sophisticated production.

At this time, the choice for economic planners in Brazil was between further development of heavy industry or a policy of controlled integration and development of the consumer durables industries that could be implanted with the help of foreign companies and investment. After some vacillation, the government of President Kubitschek (1956–61) opted for the second strategy, promoting a policy of rapid industrial development, with special emphasis on the development of energy and transport. Foreign companies were given a major role, and massive government incentives were provided. The implantation of new industries was meant to provide the technological leap and impetus that would propel Brazil into the ranks of the developed nations.

In the short term, the strategy had some success. There was a construction boom as the government poured money into the construction of roads and to the building of the new capital, Brasilia, which was itself symbolic of the new age – a town without a rail link. Brazil was entering the age of the car, and the target plan was to give priority to road transport. From 1957 to 1961, output of manufacturing industry in real terms rose by 62 per cent (Singer, 1976, p. 63), and for the consumer durables sectors, growth was even more startling. Between 1955, just before the target plan strategy was implemented, and the end of Kubitschek's term of office in 1961, motor industry production rose by five and a half times, and electrical equipment (including domestic appliances) by three and a half times.

This boom was only bought at a price, and towards the end of the 1950s there were increasing economic and political problems surrounding the government. Firstly, the rapid industrial growth of the period had not resolved the inflation and balance of payments problems that all the countries involved in industrialization programmes in Latin America had suffered ever since the 1930s.

A second major problem for the government was the political conflicts that developed over the industrialization strategy. The target plan strategy had received support from the labour movement and left-wing forces because industrialization had been seen to provide both a chance to create a genuinely Brazilian economy, and jobs and rising wages for the working class. But at the end of the 1950s neither of these two effects appeared to be materializing. The foreign grip on the economy seemed to be reinforced by the expansion of transnational companies in the heart of the manufacturing sector. At the same time, the rapid industrialization strategy was not creating jobs in sufficient numbers to resolve the problems of employment and wages. By 1961, there were signs of a fall in industrial wages and a fall in the value of the minimum wage.

A period of mounting political unrest ensued as opposition to falling real wages and suggestions by the government for an IMF-linked stabilization policy fuelled political opposition to the industrialization strategy. This polarization of economic strategies and political forces led to a military coup in 1964. The coup produced not only a change in economic policy, but also a dramatic change in the political framework within which economic decisions were made. The technocrats drafted into the Ministries of Finance and Planning were given a free hand to develop economic policy.

## Strategy after the Coup

The most distinctive features of the military government's strategy after 1964 were:

1 its doctrine of national security;
2 its open collaboration with foreign capital; and
3 its determination to create conditions for renewed economic growth.

In other countries the military have taken political power but rarely have they pursued economic growth with such single-minded determination.

The doctrine of national security was defined by the Brazilian military before the events of 1964 and became a central determinant of the attitudes of the new military rulers. It combined three elements:

1 struggle against the internal enemy;
2 integration of the peripheral areas of the country; and
3 industrial development as a key to military might.

The threat of internal subversion was seen as a major problem in Brazil. The unrest of the early 1960s, the shock of the revolution in Cuba in 1959 and the development of armed resistance to the military government in the latter part of the 1960s all gave impetus to the notion that the war against international communism had become an internal guerilla war.

The military were also concerned about the security of frontiers and the power of Brazil's neighbours (particularly Argentina). Although the vast majority of the people live on or near the coast, the states of the northern region (those on the Amazon) combined with the state of Mato Grosso account for over half of Brazil's territory. The doctrine of national security demanded Brazilian colonization of these regions and their integration into the nation. The chosen method for this was the construction of a network of roads across the Amazonian region and around the north-western borders of the country. Road transport was seen by the military as part of national security, just as it had been a symbol of national integration for Kubitschek. More generally, the doctrine of national security argued that military strength depended in the long run on economic strength. As important, military independence would depend on the ability to create a domestic armaments industry. Economic and industrial strength were not merely desirable for the social welfare of the nation's population, but essential military objectives as well.

TABLE 20 Sectoral distribution of the economically active population in Brazil, 1950–80 (percentages)

| | *1950* | *1960* | *1970* | *1980* |
|---|---|---|---|---|
| Agriculture | 59.9 | 54.0 | 44.3 | 30.5 |
| Manufacturing; construction; public utilities; | 14.2 | 13.2 | 18.4 | 24.9 |
| Commerce; personal services | 15.4 | 18.6 | 19.9 | 26.1 |
| Transport and communication | 4.0 | 4.6 | 4.1 | 4.2 |
| Social services; public administration; other | 6.5 | 9.6 | 13.3 | 14.3 |

*Source*: Demographic censuses

The economic strategy introduced after 1964 was centred on the need to control inflation, increase productivity and keep down wage costs. Although in the short term the new economic planners adopted a fairly orthodox policy of credit control, restraint on government spending and wage controls, the new Brazilian economic policy was not the fore-runner of those of the conservative, monetarist governments of the 1980s. Credit and government expenditure were allowed to rise so that industrial production could be stimulated. The new policy tried to create the conditions necessary for rapid economic growth.

By any standards, the results were impressive. Economic growth rose from 1967, and there was a period of rapid development. For six years the economy, and in particular industry, expanded at break-neck speed. Output, investment and employment all rose sharply.

Table 20 shows that throughout the post-war period, the percentage of people in agriculture declined (even though the absolute numbers increased by over 40 per cent). This decline in the proportion of workers in agriculture is common enough in the Third World. What is less common is where they went. In the 1950s they were absorbed by commerce and the service industries and by the social services and public administration. In the 1960s and 1970s, however, it was industry that absorbed the major share of the economically active population. From 1960 to 1980, industry's share of employment (the share of manufacturing, construction and public utilities) rose from 13.2 per cent to 24.9 per cent. In employment terms, then, the economic miracle was a success.

The transformation that took place in the period of the economic miracle is startling. The two mainstays of Brazilian manufacturing in 1949 – textiles and food – employed just over 43 per cent of all workers in manufacturing. But, in the following two decades, employment in those industries stagnated. The new industries based on metalworking, mechanical engineering, electrical goods and transport materials (mainly the motor industry) accounted for 12.7 per cent of employment in 1949, but 33.4 per cent in

1975. The mechanical/electrical and transport group, in particular, expanded by over eleven times. This is the measure of the impact of the rapid industrialization programme introduced by Kubitschek and reformulated after the military coup in 1964. The nature of that employment altered dramatically – shifting to the consumer durables and capital goods industries.

However, the rapid rise in industrial output and employment was not achieved without costs and sacrifices. As the Brazilian ambassador in London succinctly put it, the choice was made by the regime in favour of production, not distribution: 'There appears to be, at least in the short run, a trade off between fast capital accumulation and the creation of the welfare state ... We had to make an option in favour of the productivist state as against the distributivist state.' By reducing real wages, the government effected a transfer of income from the lower-paid and the poor both to companies and to the higher-paid. The result was a worsening distribution of income, as can be seen in table 21. Tight control over wage increases was accompanied by control over the trade unions and remaining political opposition. The poor got relatively poorer. The top 5 per cent managed to secure a 72 per cent rise. Whatever the benefits of rapid industrial growth, they were not distributed equally.

The concentration of income did not cause any lack of demand for industrial products. The transfer of income to the middle and upper income groups combined with buoyant demand from industry, and the effects of rising working-class employment, ensured that there was adequate demand for the products of Brazilian industry in this period.

## Developing a New Industry: the Brazilian Motor Industry

In this section, we analyse the motor industry more closely. At the end of it you should have a clear idea of (1) how the industry was implanted and the role of the state in its development; (2) the factors that determined its

TABLE 21 Distribution of income in Brazil, 1960 and 1970 (percentages)

| *Population (from bottom to top)* | *Income* | | *Increase average real income of the group* |
|---|---|---|---|
| | *1960* | *1970* | |
| 50 | 17.7 | 13.7 | 1 |
| 10 | 7.5 | 6.2 | 8 |
| 10 | 9.0 | 7.2 | 3 |
| 10 | 11.3 | 9.6 | 10 |
| 10 | 15.6 | 14.8 | 23 |
| 10 | 38.9 | 48.4 | 61 |
| Highest 5 | 27.4 | 36.2 | 72 |

*Source*: Tolipan and Tinelli (1975).

long-term shape; and (3) the impact of the motor industry's growth on the rest of industry and on the balance of payments. Figure 23 illustrates how cars are made; this will help you understand what is involved in implanting vehicle assembly.

The term 'motor industry' refers to all those firms producing parts or assembling vehicles. All the vehicle producers, plus all firms producing components specifically for motor vehicles of all types – cars, vans, lorries, buses etc. – comprise the motor industry. The industry can be divided into two parts, the motor vehicle sector and the components sector. The motor vehicle, or vehicle assembly sector, consists of all those firms that produce and assemble completed vehicles or chassis. The components industry consists of those firms which produce only parts. Clearly, there is some overlap between these sectors, since assembly firms also produce components – engines, seats etc. In terms of the census classification, therefore, a plant owned by, for example, General Motors, that produces engines is part of the vehicle assembly industry. A similar plant owned by a firm producing only engines for vehicles would be classified as part of the components industry.

### Implantation

Until the end of the Second World War, demand for cars, buses and trucks in Brazil was satisfied solely by imports of complete vehicles or the assembly of 'kits' from the USA. By assembling kits alone, the two US giants, Ford and General Motors, gained access to the Brazilian market without having to make the major investment in plant and machinery necessary for the production of complete vehicles. However, after the Second World War, the situation began to change. Recurrent balance of payment problems led the Brazilian government to consider restrictions on imports. In 1951, motor vehicles accounted for 14 per cent of all Brazil's imports. New firms – both North American and European – challenged the market dominance of the two US giants, Ford and General Motors. Mercedes and Volkswagen both set up plants in the early 1950s, along with Willys-Overland, a small US company. The government began to consider adopting a definite policy on local production of vehicles.

The implantation of a complex and large-scale industry required considerable planning and investment but, by 1956, the Brazilian government was willing to make a firm commitment to a crash programme of development aimed at full local production of vehicles within five years. The immensity of the task can be seen from figure 23. Starting from almost nothing in 1956, the government planned the production of 490,000 vehicles in the three years 1958–60. By the third year of the programme, the government aimed to have 90 per cent of the weight of all locally assembled vehicles provided by materials produced in Brazil. In other words, the government wanted to replace a number of small-scale assembly operations by a fully-developed vehicle industry.

By the early 1960s, all the other parts of the industry had been established, together with most of the relevant industries supplying raw materials. This

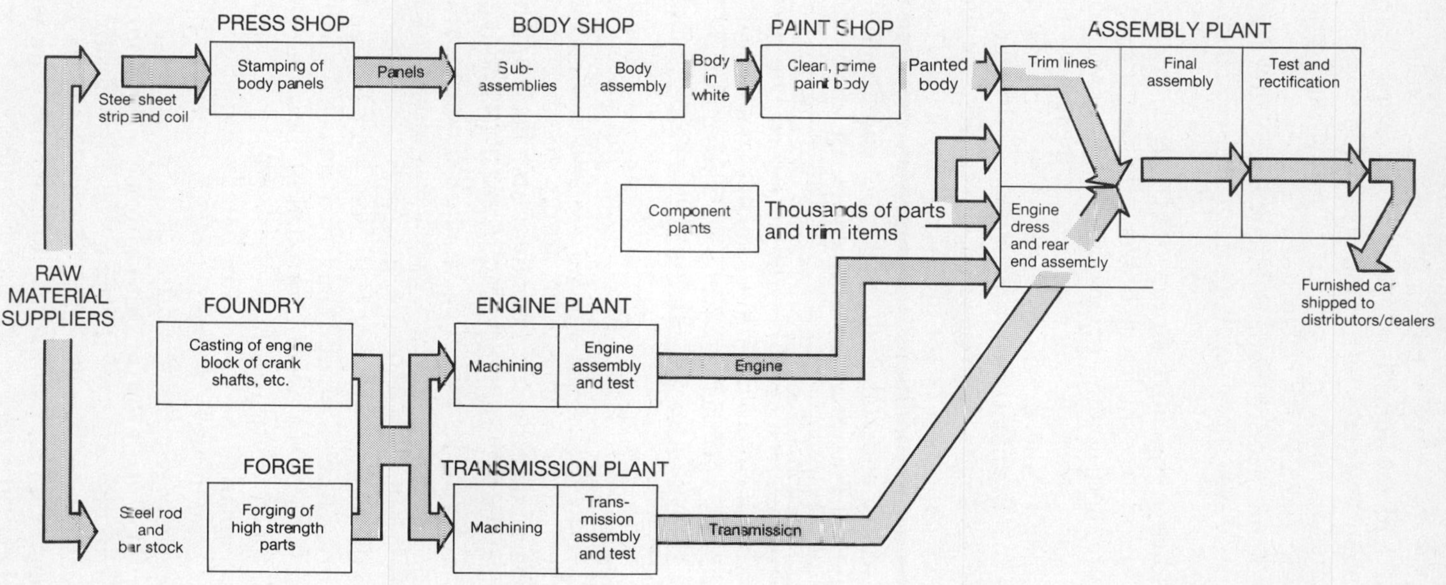


FIGURE 23 Motor vehicle production – the sequence of operations

meant massive investments by both component producers – to supply carburettors, mirrors, shock absorbers, locks, carpets, spark plugs, and the hundreds of other items that go into vehicles – and the assemblers themselves, who had to build body and paint shops, stamping plants, foundries, and engine and transmission plants. In addition, the new industry required raw materials, such as steel, glass, rubber and paint, as well as sufficient energy to run the new factories.

The massive commitment of both public and private capital needed for the motor industry was necessarily part of a broader plan for rapid industrialization.

The Motor Industry Executive Group (GEIA) laid down conditions for firms wishing to produce vehicles in Brazil, provided incentives for them, and tried to ensure that supplies, materials and labour would be available. The conditions were strict. At the same time, generous incentives were provided. According to the Brazilian writer, José Almeida, for every one dollar invested, the Brazilian government provided eighty-nine cents in assistance of various kinds. Such generous incentives, combined with the possibly even more important factor of exclusion from the market for firms not complying with the conditions, persuaded all the eight firms already committed to Brazil to undertake full local production. Another three firms were attracted into the market, making a total of eleven firms by 1960. Although Ford and General Motors were unwilling to undertake local production of passenger vehicles, they did so in order not to lose so large a market. The state, foreign vehicle companies and local producers of components combined together to create a viable motor industry. By the early 1960s, the transition to full, almost 100 per cent, local production had been achieved.

Once the vehicle industry was functioning, the government played a minor role. It was content to create the conditions for a motor vehicle industry and then allow competitive forces to determine its further development. The state provided incentives and back-up, but it did not determine the number of companies, the type of technology they should use, or the kinds of vehicles that they would ultimately produce. Instead, it encouraged an industry to develop which was almost totally in private hands and, in the assembly sector, dominated by large foreign companies. In 1960, five of the eleven firms were 100 per cent foreign-owned, while four had a majority foreign share. Only two small companies – both to be taken over in the 1960s – were controlled by Brazilian interests. Local firms and businessmen contented themselves with a role in the production of components. Similarly, the options of a fully state-owned firm (of the type found in the steel industry and in petroleum exploration, for example), or joint ventures between foreign firms and the state (as found in the chemical industry in Brazil), or the state-sponsored development of private local capital (as in the case of the state's heavy subsidy of the heavy industrial equipment sector in Brazil in the 1970s) were never seriously considered. Foreign capital, national capital, and the state were in general agreement about the structure of the motor industry.

The implantation of the motor industry was a major feat. Not only were most of the foreign companies successfully persuaded to switch to full local production, involving investment of US$0.170 billion between 1955 and 1960, but a similar amount was also spent on the development of the components sector. Starting from almost nothing in 1955, nearly 100,000 vehicles with over 85 per cent local content were produced in 1959. This development required a massive commitment by the state. It subsidized producers, ensured the supply of basic items such as steel, glass and paint, and provided facilities complementary to the production and consumption of vehicles, such as roads, electric power and petrol.

By the mid-1960s, Brazil had the largest motor industry in Latin America. To a large extent, it produced passenger cars. The original plan laid down by GEIA had given emphasis to lorries, buses and utility vehicles, but the firms followed market demand and, by 1964, over half the vehicles produced in Brazil were cars. Ten years later, cars accounted for over three-quarters of all vehicles produced.

### *The industry reorganized*

After the coup in 1964, the Brazilian economy was initially plunged into deep recession. This was a result of economic measures designed to restore fiscal and monetary order and control the rate of inflation. In the short-term, the motor industry suffered along with other sectors, and even the growth of output of passenger cars faltered, but this recession provided the basis for the period of rapid growth for the whole economy known as the 'economic miracle'. Government policy affected both the supply and the demand conditions for the motor industry. On the demand side, the government reformed the banking and credit system, making it possible to develop the extensive consumer credit networks necessary for the expansion of the consumer durables industries. The result was that when the first expansionary policies were pursued in 1966–7 and middle and upper-class incomes rose, the demand for cars increased rapidly.

On the supply side, advances were also made. The vehicle industry was rationalized during the recession, with some of the small firms being eliminated. There were advances in productivity resulting from favourable conditions for management control of labour after the coup (discussed in the next section). As a result of increasing demand and falling unit costs, the Brazilian passenger vehicle industry entered a 'virtuous cycle' of expansion. Sales rose, efficiency increased, and the cost of cars began to fall in relation to average incomes and other prices.

This further increased the potential market, encouraging expansion and additional increases in productivity. In 1974, the industry produced over 900,000 vehicles (see table 22), and yet exports only amounted to 5 per cent of all production. The internal market was entirely sufficient to support the output of rapid industrialization.

By 1974, Brazil was among the world's top ten vehicle producers and was well ahead of the other Latin American producers (table 22).

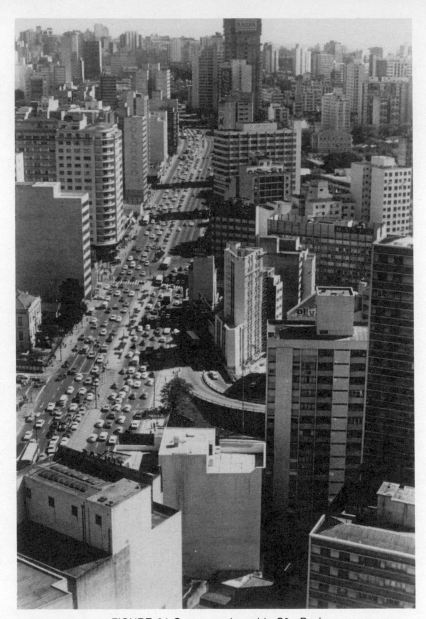

FIGURE 24 Cars now abound in São Paulo

## *The motor industry in the national economy*

As well as being a sizeable producer of vehicles in world terms, the Brazilian motor industry was also playing a significant role in the Brazilian economy. The automotive sector as a whole – the vehicle producers and those firms producing parts solely for the motor industry – accounted for 8 per cent of both industrial value added and industrial production in 1970, and also employed 6 per cent of all industrial workers. But the importance of the

TABLE 22 World production of vehicles, 1974 (top fifteen countries)

| | *Production 1974 (thousands)* | *Change 1970–4 (%)* |
|---|---|---|
| USA | 10,033 | 21 |
| Japan | 6,552 | 24 |
| France | 3,463 | 26 |
| West Germany | 3,080 | −20 |
| USSR | 1,950[a] | na |
| Britain | 1,937 | −8 |
| Italy | 1,772 | −4 |
| Canada | 1,562 | −31 |
| Brazil | 905 | 118 |
| Spain | 839 | 56 |
| Australia | 480 | 7 |
| Mexico | 387 | 104 |
| Sweden | 368 | 18 |
| Argentina | 286 | 30 |
| Poland | 207 | 82 |

*Note*: [a] Estimate. na = not available.
*Source*: *Automotive Industries*, 1 July 1975.

motor industry for the national economy lies not merely in its own output. It is also important both as a consumer of materials produced in other industries and as the producer of a series of products around which many other activities are organized. In many ways, the automobile and private road transport symbolized the economic miracle.

In a general sense, the automobile has become part of the Brazilian way of life – at least for the middle classes and the rich. Rapid urbanization and chronic deficiencies in public transport systems have made passenger cars a 'necessity' for many people. Public transport is both slow and uncomfortable. For industry and commerce, too, the transport of goods is concentrated on the roads, given the absence of an extended network of railways in Brazil. A far greater number of people are employed in the use and maintenance of vehicles than in their construction. In 1970, there were 191,000 workers in factories making motor vehicles or parts for them. But there were almost one million workers involved in the repair of vehicles, the construction of roads and road transport (passenger and freight).

Although this one million is small compared with the 17 million people in the economically active population working outside agriculture, it is a significant number of the total work-force in industry and transport. In a more direct manner, there are a number of industries closely tied into the production of vehicles. Firstly, the vehicle components industries are major sources of demand for capital goods. Twenty-seven per cent of all mechanical machinery, 14 per cent of electrical machinery and 20 per cent of all machine tools produced in Brazil in 1974 were consumed by the motor industry. In addition, the motor industry was a major importer of machinery and equipment. Secondly, the motor industry is a major user of raw materials and intermediate products produced by other industries. Eighteen per cent of non-metallic minerals production, 15 per cent of rubber production (tyres), and 12 per cent of steel production (20 per cent of rolled steel) went directly to the motor industry in 1974. Finally, the vehicle industry consumes other products from industries less obviously related to it. As well as small quantities of chemicals, textiles and plastics, it consumed one-quarter of the output of the furniture industry in 1974, through the purchase of car seats, for example (de Oliveira and Travolo, 1979.)

The motor industry, then, is closely tied to a series of industries which have been important for industrial development. As we saw above, the metallurgical industry (including steel) and the mechanical engineering industry (including machine tools) expanded rapidly in the 1960s and early 1970s, and with the motor industry and the electrical goods industry, they were the fast-growing heart of the economic miracle strategy. Largely because of the rapid expansion of the four metal-mechanical sectors in and before the period of the economic miracle, Brazilian industry was able to expand employment and create new jobs at such a rapid rate that its share of overall employment almost doubled from 1960 to 1976. In sixteen years the manufacturing sector's share of employment rose from 8.6 to 15 per cent, and the industrial sector as a whole increased its share from 14.2 to 23.2 per cent. This performance is impressive by any standards, but it did not mean that Brazil had found 'the answer' to the problems of underdevelopment. As we will show, the Brazilian model of development ran into problems in the latter part of the 1970s. In particular, the balance of payments posed a severe problem. The motor industry was deeply involved in this question.

### *The state and the working class*

When the military government came to power in 1964, it regarded the working class as a threat to political stability and a prime cause of inflation. Therefore, immediately after the coup, the new government imposed strict controls on unions and the labour movement. Within a few months of the coup, most of the important unions had been placed under the direct control of the Ministry of Labour. Elected union officials were suspended from office and, in some cases, were imprisoned or forced into exile or hiding. Three months after the coup the new regime introduced a law making strikes illegal in all but the most innocuous circumstances (e.g. workers could strike because of non-payment of wages, but not for higher wages). The new regime also imposed wage controls. Throughout the period of the economic miracle, wage increases were determined by government decree.

In the first three years after the coup, wage increases were kept well below the rate of inflation, and even during the economic boom, from

FIGURE 25 Men working in a São Paulo car factory (John Humphrey)

1968 to 1974, wage increases for many groups of workers barely kept pace with price rises. Low-paid workers were hit more harshly than the higher paid. Technical and managerial staff were largely unaffected by the wages policy, while for skilled manual workers recurrent shortages of labour forced firms to raise wages in order to attract the necessary numbers to their plants. But for the unskilled and semi-skilled workers, who were in plentiful supply, the wages policy led to falls in real wages.

Clearly, wage control and reductions in real wages, combined with control over the unions, created a climate in which firms could increase profits and finance new investment. But the state did not confine its support to these areas alone. A further major change took place in 1966, when the long-established law on stability of employment and compensation for dismissal from work was replaced by new legislation specifically designed to improve efficiency and productivity. It removed the special protection against dismissal previously given to workers employed by the same firm for more than ten years.

The government was reducing workers' rights while at the same time taking away workers' ability to protect their own interests through union organization. It gave employers much greater freedom to dismiss workers by removing legal and financial obstacles.

### The impact of the military regime on workers in the motor industry

There is no doubt that the new regime decisively shifted the balance of power towards the employers and weakened workers and unions. It is less clear, however, what impact these measures had on workers in the motor vehicle industry.

It has been argued elsewhere that workers in the motor vehicle industry enjoyed high wages and a series of other privileges that cushioned them from the impact of government policy on the working class as a whole. The claim is that workers in modern industry require social training and skills to do their jobs. Because of this they not only receive high wages, but are also secure in their jobs because employers will want to keep hold of trained workers. However, the majority of workers in the motor vehicle industry are not skilled (see table 23), even when white collar workers are included in the calculations. Real wages for the majority of workers in the motor vehicle industry probably fell after 1964, even though wage rates are relatively high in this industry.

Vehicle production will always conjure up images of the assembly line, but the genius of Henry Ford lay not only in the use of assembly line techniques, but also in the rational organization of work and discipline in all areas of production. The Ford plants combined the use of the moving conveyor with the application of modern methods to both production processes and the control of labour. This involves the use of machinery in the mass production of standardized products, the division of labour, the specification and control by management of all aspects of work, and the development of new methods of labour control. Among these methods was the famous 'five dollar day', which first gave the vehicle assembly industry a reputation for being a high-wage employer.

Productivity in the motor vehicle industry depends on many factors. The type of machinery used is clearly important, but as well as this factor, the cooperation of the work-force is a crucial element. Although, in principle, the jobs to be performed by workers are specified in advance and the discretion allowed to workers is reduced to the minimum, no production process can survive without the active cooperation of its workers. High levels of efficiency will be attained if workers perform the tasks specified

TABLE 23 Distribution of workers according to skill in two large assembly plants in São Paulo (percentages)

| | |
|---|---|
| Unskilled workers<br>(labourers, cleaners, canteen assistants) | 17 |
| Semi-skilled workers<br>(press operators, assemblers, machinists) | 42 |
| Skilled workers<br>(mechanics, plumbers, die-setters, toolmakers) | 24 |
| All white-collar staff[a] | 17 |

*Note*: [a] This is an estimate. It is the proportion of white-collar staff (including top managers and directors) in a major vehicle company.
*Source*: Management information obtained during research by J. Humphrey.

by management conscientiously. However, productivity increases also require that workers respond constructively to unforeseen circumstances and adapt to changing situations. In spite of detailed production planning, problems do arise in mass production processes and the cooperation and initiative of workers will have a significant impact on efficiency. In particular, a willingness to adapt and change quickly is essential for the continuity of production.

When output was rising at a rate of more than 20 per cent per annum for six successive years, a considerable amount of reorganization and dislocation occurred. The cooperation of workers was essential for the smooth introduction of new machinery and new models, which inevitably caused settling-in problems. In other words, the advantages of economies resulting from large-scale production and the introduction of new techniques and working methods could only be realized by obtaining the flexibility and cooperation of the work-forces in the motor plants. This was obtained by the use of relatively high wages and by high turnover policies. Such policies proved extremely cost-effective and generated the necessary funds for reinvestment, expansion and price-cutting.

> 'The wages are good. In other firms I've earned less, but you work harder here.' (Unskilled assembly line worker in a large motor vehicle plant)

> 'The worker in a large firm works more. I've already worked in small firms. The first time I went to work in ... I was taken aback. I'm now doing the work of two men and production has only gone down a little bit. The usual thing is for the output to go up and the number of workers to remain the same. They use time and motion to force the pace. At the moment it's getting worse. Very often you can't even go to the toilet ... It's got worse. For example, there are people who have to work while they have their coffee. (Assembler) (Humphrey, 1982, p. 82)

In return for wages which could be over 50 per cent higher than those in many other industries, workers were submitted not only to higher-than-average intensity of labour, but also worked extremely flexibly.

Government policy was extremely useful to firms in developing this type of regime in the plants. Firstly, the introduction of the wages policy allowed firms to keep wages down, which helped to control costs. Firms in the motor vehicle industry controlled their workers through the payment of relatively high wages. When wages for unskilled and semi-skilled workers in general fell, wages for motor industry workers could also be reduced. As long as the differential between motor industry and non-motor industry wages was maintained, the 'high wage' policy was effective. Secondly, the introduction of a new system for financing compensation for dismissal reduced the cost of dismissing workers and gave the employers much greater freedom to operate their turnover policies. Thirdly, the state's intervention in the field of industrial relations effectively prevented the unions from defending the interests of their members and also made conditions extremely difficult for rank-and-file activists in the plants. On the one hand, annual negotiations were bureaucratized and aggregated to such a high level (in effect only two groups to negotiate for all the metalworkers in the State of São Paulo) that it was impossible for unions to raise matters relating to specific firms or groups of workers. This meant that problems arising in the motor vehicle industry could not be negotiated through the official machinery, while the employers refused to negotiate in any other forum. On the other hand, the police and the military security forces actively intervened in industrial areas to dismantle opposition groups and activists in industry. The following newspaper report from São Paulo's most prestigious (and conservative) daily paper provides just a little of the flavour of the time:

> The imprisonment of workers is no new thing for the trade union leaders in ABC, who up to last night did not know what had happened to Manoel Fiel Filho. From the end of 1968 up until yesterday it is calculated that more than 800 workers from the region had been taken prisoner, and there have been allegations of several deaths, although it is impossible to give a precise number ... In ABC the imprisonment of workers intensified after the victory of the MDB [opposition party] in 1974. Soon after the elections, more than 200 workers at Volkswagen were put into jail at one time. There have also been innumerable imprisonments of workers at Mercedes, Phillips, and other factories in São Bernardo and São Caetano, mainly of metalworkers. (*O Estado de São Paulo*, 20 January 1976)

In ABC, the southern industrial suburbs of São Paulo where the motor vehicle plants are concentrated, the security forces could assist when the companies and the Ministry of Labour proved incapable of controlling workers and unions. The case of Manoel Filho in custody became a *cause célèbre*, and in some sense it marked the passing of the most difficult period for workers. By 1976, the idea of gradual, controlled democratization was being expounded by the government, and a new political situation was beginning to develop. In this the workers in the motor vehicle industry were to play a major political role.

## After the Miracle

Some criticisms of the Brazilian path to industrialization have focused on its failure to improve the standard of living of the poorer sections of the population. Others have drawn attention to the apparent need for dictatorship and repression to control internal opposition to the regime's economic policies. Yet others – particularly Brazilian businessmen – were alarmed and dismayed by the apparently inexorable expansion of the state sector and the strategic role of the transnational companies in the economy. However, none of these criticisms suggest that the model was not an effective route to rapid industrialization.

But is the Brazilian story really one of unalloyed success? In the 1970s, the Brazilian economy was beset by a mounting series of problems that made the 'miracle' look rather more tarnished. By the end of the decade, the phase of the miracle looked more like a brief interlude than a solution to the problem of underdevelopment. In this section, we concentrate on the adjustments made in the Brazilian economy after the 1973 oil crisis, the growth of political opposition to the military regime and the impact of these changes on the motor industry.

### *Balance of payments problems*

Problems with the balance of payments (importing much more than can be financed by export revenues) has been a recurrent problem in the course of Brazil's industrialization. Building up new industries often proves expensive in terms of imported machinery and equipment, and also because of the energy and raw materials required to keep them running. Thus, the rapid growth of the miracle period itself put strain on the balance of payments. However, in 1969 Brazil exported more goods than it imported – a balance of trade surplus of US$0.318 billion. There was a net outflow on the services account of US$0.630 billion, of which US$0.263 billion consisted of outflows of interest, dividends and profits. A relatively small inflow of long-term investment was not enough to balance the current account deficit, but over US$1 billion was raised in long-term loans, and even after some loans were paid back there was still a surplus.

This favourable situation quickly disappeared when the price of oil increased almost two-fold between 1970 and 1973, and then three-fold in the latter half of 1973. The immediate impact was to put a severe brake on growth and generate a large deficit on the balance of payments. Convinced that continued growth was the only answer to Brazil's economic problems, the government borrowed heavily – both to buy oil and to finance the new investments needed to sustain economic growth. Growth was, indeed, maintained, but at the price of increasing the external debt. The balance of payments became burdened by interest payments on the debt and loans due for repayment. The economy entered a vicious circle. Fresh long-term loans were raised to finance service payments on loans and repayments of old loans. Even with the trade account in surplus in 1977, net long-term loans of US$4 billion had to be raised. By 1980, total external debt had reached nearly US$60 billion.

In the course of the 1970s, the Brazilian economy ran into problems because of the rise in the price of oil and because of the increase of imports in 1974 and 1975 to continue the growth of the economic miracle. This, combined with the outflow of profits, dividends and interest from earlier loans, created a balance of payments problem that was resolved by more and more borrowing. Given the commitment of major world banks, and given its size and political importance, Brazil could not easily be forced to resort to the International Monetary Fund (IMF) and its 'stabilization' policies, as happened in Jamaica (see chapter 15). For a number of years, until 1980, Brazil merely carried on borrowing – hoping that a miracle, such as the discovery of vast oil deposits, would provide a solution. The miracle was, perhaps, that Brazil kept on growing until 1980 and managed to hold off the international financial community.

Some attempts were made during the course of the 1970s to reduce the balance of payments deficits, and the motor industry was forced to make changes.

For most of the miracle period the impact of the motor industry on the long-term capital and service accounts was not very great. The profitability of the industry and its great expansion meant that profits were generated and then reinvested. Therefore, inflows of new foreign capital were not massive, nor was there a massive outflow of profits and interest to parent companies. However, it can be argued that this period of expansion and reinvestment was exceptional. Once growth slowed down, one could expect investment to slacken and more profits to be remitted to parent companies. On the current account, the situation was less favourable. In the miracle period, the hectic expansion of industry led to shortages of raw materials and also imports of capital goods.

For this reason, the balance of payments contribution of the motor industry was decidedly negative throughout the miracle period. However, the effects listed above pale into insignificance compared to the question of oil imports. Two-thirds of the oil used in Brazil is for transport. Following the rise in oil prices in 1973, the oil-related deficit rose extremely rapidly. This amounted to one quarter of all imports. It was also equal to the total imports of all machinery and equipment (electrical and mechanical) in the same year. The rise in oil imports was not the only reason for a particularly bad balance of payments problem in 1974, but this meant that action had to be taken.

As part of the measures to curb the balance of payments deficit, the government intervened in the motor industry. An attempt was made to cut back on machinery imports by the motor industry by reintroducing import restrictions. A package of measures was introduced to promote exports of vehicles and components in particular, commitments to export were made a condition for new investment. Companies could only gain investment grants and exemptions from tariffs on imports if they promised to export part of the new production being created.

However, the major saving could only come from cuts in the consumption of petroleum and therefore from cuts in vehicle use. Although the government could raise the cost of motoring and road transport, it faced three major difficulties in pursuing this strategy. Firstly, cutting back on road transport could only be effectively achieved by offering alternative means of transport. This was a long-term and costly process and might require larger imports (the technology of underground railway systems, for example) that would be saved by cutting down on road transport. Secondly, the government ran the risk of crippling industry as a whole if it tried to put the brakes on the motor industry since it was a crucial sector for the other fast-growing sectors of industry. Thirdly, as we saw above, a slow-down in growth could lead to a fall in investment and an outflow of profit remittances, thus worsening the services balance.

The government's hands were tied. Although vehicle production did not grow as fast after 1974 as in the miracle period, the government did not make serious attempts to halt its growth. Faced with this constraint on policy, it is not surprising that the government sought a different solution – the search for an alternative to imported oil.

## The Oil Crisis and Alcohol

The worldwide oil price rise in 1973 created not only a Brazilian oil crisis but a more general restructuring of energy investment which has greatly affected Brazilian industrialization. The availability and use of cheap energy was a significant feature of the economic miracle. Continued industrial growth has depended on a continuing ability to mobilize adequate energy resources in the face of rising energy costs. In a similar way to state promotion of the motor industry, after the 1973 oil crisis the government moved rapidly to begin a programme to produce alcohol from sugar-cane as an alternative source of energy for transport. This was the most radical and innovative part of the state's energy policy. The gasohol programme put Brazil in the world lead for such technologies.

The National Alcohol Programme was established in 1975 so that the production of alcohol from sugar cane, cassava or other raw material would be stimulated. Special emphasis was put on modernization of existing farm units as well as installation of new plant.

A National Alcohol Council was set up with representatives from various relevant industries to coordinate the various participants in the programme, to decide on new projects and to plan output totals. Finance would come from one of several state banks.

Most of the alcohol would be used for two purposes:

1 to add 20 per cent alcohol to petrol, producing gasohol; This could be done without changes to petrol engines;
2 to fuel specially modified cars which would run on 100 per cent alcohol.

The plan was to produce 10.7 billion litres of alcohol per annum in 1985, an equivalent of 160,000 barrels per day (bpd) of petrol. Total petrol consumption in 1980 was 1,000,000 bpd. (One barrel contains 34 gallons.)

There were a number of factors that gave Brazil an advantage over most other Third World countries.

1 a large sugar industry;
2 considerable technical expertise in distilling alcohol from sugar-cane;
3 technological expertise to manufacture most of the industrial equipment required.

The government took full advantage of these features by adopting strong state control over the alcohol programme. Agreement had to be reached with the motor companies so that new car models would be fuelled by both petrol and 100 per cent alcohol. At the beginning of the programme, the target was to convert petrol cars to take 20 per cent alcohol. Garages were licensed to convert 100,000 cars a year. The conversion is simple, requiring only more protection against corrosion. In 1975, an agreement between the government and manufacturers allowed for the production of 900,000 new 100 per cent alcohol-run cars. By 1979, the first alcohol cars were coming off production lines. Fiat, Volkswagen, Ford and General Motors now all have alcohol powered cars, and are exporting them to other countries. There were close to a million conversions and new cars on the road by the end of 1981.

So the Brazilian government was able to increase alcohol production through its coordinated programme. The programme was able to call on some specific advantages of Brazil, on tight state control over motor manufacturers, and on a wide range of incentives to users, including massive price subsidies. However, the alcohol programme had a number of drawbacks.

*Pollution* The main by-product of alcohol distillation is highly concentrated organic 'stillage'. It could be a raw material for fertilizer but this requires further investment. Stillage is dumped into rivers destroying the habitat of fish in many rivers of São Paulo state. Recent legislation may lead to a reduction of this problem. Air pollution from alcohol use is probably less than from petrol.

*Corrosion* There is a danger that the small quantities of water left in the alcohol will lead to corrosion in car engines. There are reports that this is already a problem, and petrol tanks are now made of stainless steel.

*Land use* The growth of the alcohol programme has been such that it was using one million hectares of new land for sugar in 1982; this new area given over to sugar was expected to grow to three million hectares by 1985. The two million hectares of good land which will be used could produce 500,000 tons of black beans, 1,500,000 tons of rice and 1,500,000 tons of corn – representing roughly 20 per cent, 17 per cent and 8 per cent of the present production of such crops. The production of alcohol could, therefore, be at the expense of these basic crops.

*Investment requirements* The alcohol programme is funded and subsidized by the government, which uses the credit facilities given by foreign sources. It is an expensive and relatively long-term project – ten years to 1985 for the first stage – initiated during a period of economic crisis and rapidly increasing foreign debt in Brazil. Investment costs are high and subsidized prices are paid to farmers and distillers to encourage the programme. Alcohol at the pumps is also subsidized, so that the price of alcohol is about 60 per cent that of petrol.

The cost of the programme might have been acceptable when oil was expected to rise to over 40 dollars per barrel. With oil costing about half this price in 1987, the economics of the project are totally altered. Brazil will have to slow down or reverse the trend to alcohol-powered cars.

## Liberalization, Democracy and Trade Unionism

One of the reasons for the regime's economic success in the 'economic miracle' period was its single-minded pursuit of growth, unfettered by political opposition. Control of the working class, cooperation with foreign capital and willingness to expand the state sector were all ingredients of the recipe for rapid industrialization. However, just as the economic strategy of the regime faltered in the 1970s, so, too, did its political strategy. There were two main reasons for this. Firstly, the military themselves were unsure about what political form they wished to impose. Secondly, economic difficulties led to opposition from within the ranks of the regime's own supporters.

During the period of the economic miracle, the government had gained the support of businessmen and the middle classes. Salaries had risen markedly and rapid growth and unequal distribution of its benefits had been to the advantage of both industry and middle-class consumers. But when economic conditions began to worsen and the government began to apply corrective measures, the business community became very anxious about policy-making. In 1977 the government faced a rising tide of criticism from industry, expressed in the newspapers, on which censorship had been relaxed. Industrialists feared that the 'tough decisions' needed to stabilize the economy would fall on them, rather than on finance or the state sector.

From 1977, an irreversible process of liberalization was underway, and although democratization was still some way off, the political climate had changed significantly. This, too, had a significant impact on the motor industry.

In the early 1970s, the demands of the Metal Workers' Union were limited to matters relating to the wages and working conditions of its members and its own ability to perform effectively as a trade union. Even in the most difficult circumstances of the early 1970s, the union voiced its demands for the right to negotiate directly with employers without the mediation and control of the Ministry of Labour and the Labour Courts, the right to take strike action, and the extension of union organization into places of work. The union tried to avoid making directly political demands, but demands for a major overhaul of the trade union structure were inevitably laden with a political content. To some extent, the union compensated for this by being markedly uncritical of (indeed, by expressing some limited support for) government policy in general. Later in the 1970s, the situation became more favourable for the union. From about 1976 onwards, the combination of increasing economic difficulties and doubts within military circles about the desirability of the continuation of non-democratic government led to pressure for democratization. Inevitably, a commitment by the government to liberalization, a reining-in of the security forces, the ending of direct media censorship and the introduction of democratization at some point in the future allowed for a relaxation of state controls over society in general. The unions were not slow to take advantage of this.

The organization and mobilization of workers advanced most rapidly in the motor vehicle industry. Building on the work carried out in the major plants earlier in the decade, and taking advantage of both the concentration of the industry and the inability of the official industrial relations structures (both inside and outside the plants) to begin to resolve workers' grievances, the union campaigned for higher wages and union reform in 1977. Its central message was that workers would only get higher wages if they stopped work and demanded them. The union campaigned for wage rises to compensate for the falls in wages experienced between 1972 and 1974. The union's President, Luis Inacio da Silva (usually called 'Lula'), summed up this campaign: 'It was a campaign of practically five months, showing the worker that he could only recoup this money if he got tough. And when we workers use this language of "getting tough", we don't mean start fighting, it simply means stopping the machines.' (Lula, interview, March 1978; Johnson and Bernstein, 1982, pp. 143–52).

Following this, in May 1978, workers at the Saab-Scania plant downed tools in support of a wage claim. In contrast to the situation in 1973–4, the whole plant stopped work, and its example was quickly followed by the Mercedes and Ford plants in the area. After ten years without major stoppages, the industrial relations picture changed almost overnight. Within a month, more than 250,000 workers, mainly in the metalworking industries, had been involved in stoppages. In the following two years, the same workers in the motor vehicle industry set the pace in the confrontations between workers and government over wages, stability of employment and the reform of the union structure. Wanting to negotiate with the employers, but forced to confront the state, the local union became the focus of a remarkably rapid development of working class politics in Brazil at the end of the decade. It challenged not only government control of the unions, but also entered the political sphere by launching a new political party, the Workers party.

Motor vehicle workers took full advantage of the less authoritarian policies of the post-1973 Geisel government. The strikes in 1978 and 1979 produced not only rises in wages, but also a shift in the balance of power between workers and management. Hire-and-fire policies were sharply curtailed or abandoned, and the metalworkers union in São Bernardo began to attack the basic elements of the motor industry's previous employment strategy: insecurity of employment, extensive power in the hands of the first-line supervisors, and lack of union representation in the plants. However, the gains from 1978 to 1987 have been uneven and subject to reverses from time to time.

## The 1980s

In the preceding sections, we studied the background to the economic miracle, the miracle period, and the adjustments following the first oil price shock in the early 1970s. We have studied the changes wrought on the motor industry by both economic and political factors. In the 1980s, these changes have become even more pronounced. In the economic sphere, the debt crisis has led to severe disruption. Following the first strikes in 1978 and 1979, the motor industry went through a prolonged period of industrial instability as the emergent union organizations came into conflict with the employers and the state. Even after the new civilian government took office in 1985, the uncertainty and instability continued on both the economic and industrial relations fronts.

Following the first oil crisis, Brazil borrowed in order to finance both its balance of payments deficits and its ambitious plans for heavy industry. In terms of a strategy to maintain growth, borrowing was a great success for seven or eight years. The economy grew at a rate of over 7 per cent per annum in the 1970s, and even in the final three years of the decade, 1978–80, industrial production rose at an average rate of 7.2 per cent per annum. The motor industry continued to grow and diversify, albeit at a lower rate than in the miracle period.

However, this growth strategy required an increasing external debt. At the end of the 1970s, Brazil was faced with two major external shocks. Firstly, a doubling of the price of oil in 1979, combined with a fall in export prices, led to a significant deterioration in the terms of trade (export prices relative to import prices). Comparing 1975–8 with 1979–81, the terms of trade fell by 29 per cent. Secondly, the interest rates charged on Brazil's external debt (owed mainly to the commercial banks of the developed world) rose from around the 8 per cent level of the 1970s to a peak of more than 16 per cent in 1981. This represented a major drain of foreign currency, and together these two shocks far outstripped Brazil's export earning capacity. In the years 1978–80, Brazil was forced to borrow US$10 billion to finance the gap between exports and imports, and a further US$10 billion to pay interest on its foreign debt. In the same two years, loans worth US$13 billion came to maturity, and Brazil needed to negotiate their renewal or replacement with the banks. Faced with such a massive demand for new finance, the banks demanded stringent economic policies designed to control inflation and cut the drain of foreign currency.

The policies adopted by the government in 1981 led to a sharp fall in industrial output. Output as a whole fell by 10.1 per cent, but in the consumer durables industries, particularly the motor industry, the fall in production was much greater. Vehicle production fell by one-third, from 1,165,000 units in 1980 to 781,000 units in 1981. Domestic sales fell even more sharply, by 40 per cent, and overall production was only bolstered by a rise in exports of over 50,000 units. Employment fell sharply, too. In the six major vehicle assembly firms, employment dropped by over 20 per cent. Although output rose by 80,000 units in 1982 and a further 36,000 units in 1983, employment remained more or less stable at its new, low level, and the industry as a whole remained in difficulties. Even so competition remained fierce. Investment in new plant and machinery went ahead, and the big firms introduced Brazilian versions of their 'world' cars such as the Uno, Escort, Cavalier and Santana. The major firms were both jockeying for position within the internal market, and also looking to Brazil to play an increasing regional and global supply role.

Industrial relations in the early 1980s were also rather eventful. In 1980 itself, the wave of conflicts in the industry which had been building up in 1978 and 1979 erupted into a forty-day strike which resulted in defeat for the workers, expulsion from office of the leaders of the Metal Workers' Union in São Bernardo do Campo, and the union being administered by a Ministry of Labour official. The union was still under Ministry control when the economic crisis hit the industry, and one major company, Volkswagen, had already used this opportunity to introduce an employee representation scheme whose aim was to provide an alternative to the union.

The sudden onset of the crisis in 1981 could have weakened the nascent union organization in the motor vehicle plants quite considerably. Workers were sacked in thousands in the first months of the year with little protest, but from April onwards resistance increased. Volkswagen was forced to abandon plans for either a 20 per cent cut in hours and wages or 5,000 redundancies in the face of both union and government pressure and, following a weekend-long strike at Ford in July 1981, redundancies were reduced and then stopped altogether.

From this point on, the union gained in strength. One important outcome of the strike at Ford was the formation of a factory committee. Early in 1982, this committee was formally constituted by an agreement signed by the union and the company in São Bernardo. Later in the same year, Volkswagen abandoned its employee representation scheme in favour of a similar agreement with the union. The introduction of such committees (extended later to all four of Ford's plants, and also seen at General Motors in São Jose dos Campos) marked a major shift in industrial relations. At Ford, the factory committee had a broad range of actvity, including participation at all levels of the disciplinary procedure. Many of the managerial powers described earlier were curtailed.

However, this institutionalization of management–union relations did not bring lasting peace. There were short strikes in 1982 and 1983, and, in 1984, General Motors suffered its first strikes in twenty-five years. Finally, in 1985, there was a further major strike in the metalworking industries that lasted intermittently for about two months. The employers refused concessions on the main demand, a forty-hour week, and in a number of factories large-scale sackings took place. In the two General Motors plants, the factory committees and internal accident prevention committees were sacked, along with hundreds of other workers. Industrial relations continue to be tumultuous. Both workers and employers seem inclined to trials of strength in order to gain advantages where they can.

This chapter has focused on the example of Brazilian economic development during two decades of predominantly military rule. The Brazilian national economy is one of the most developed in the Third World. Indeed, it contains the highest level of industry of any Third World country. The chapter has concentrated on state policies for, and the consequent growth of, a key industrial sector. But it has also shown the strengths and diversity of the Brazilian economy that cannot be simply described as 'backward'.

The use of Brazil as an example, apart from detailing the development of a relatively strongly industrialized national economy, was also aimed at showing the dangers of making simplistic generalizations about the level and diversity of industrialization in the Third World. As was discussed in chapter 6, all national economies have peculiarities, with different forms of integration both internally and in the international division of labour.

We hope that this case study has shown both the importance of industry in Brazilian economic development, and illustrated the possibilities and importance of detailed national studies.

CHAPTER TWELVE

# Making a Living

Chapter 10 identified five characteristics of industrial production processes:

1 enlargement of the *scale* of production;
2 the growth of complex and wide-ranging *linkages* berween production processes;
3 a technical division of labour and coordination of tasks within units of production;
4 the replacement of human energy by machines; and
5 the development of a more diverse range of human *skills* and specialization.

This chapter focuses on the implications of these characteristic features of industrial production processes, for the livelihood of Third World producers and for economic development more generally.

## Scale

Scale of production has been discussed in earlier chapters. Chapter 3 introduced the idea of productivity of labour, contrasting the productivity of the African farmer with a hoe, the Indian farmer with an ox-cart and the farmer in the USA with a tractor. The Indian farmer had a labour productivity four times that of the African, whilst the US farmer had a labour productivity ten times that of the Indian and forty times that of the African farmer. These increasing rates of productivity require (amongst other things) increasing amounts of fixed capital. But with this capital a 'quantum' leap in output *can* be obtained, giving returns proportionately much greater than the capital investment needed for the ox-cart or the tractor. These economies of scale arise from increasing the scale of production and are a crucial tenet of 'orthodox' growth models of development. Nevertheless, quantum leaps are by no means always obtained and fiery debates continue over the relative merits of the large or small scale in industrial production. The following examples show something of the range in scale of production in Third World industry and the extent to which it is possible to achieve economies of scale in different production processes.

*Vehicles*

Chapter 11 analysed in detail the increasing scale of production in the Brazilian vehicle industry.

At the end of the Second World War, Brazil had a number of vehicle factories importing kits of vehicle components and assembling them into vehicles on a relatively small scale (a few thousand per annum per factory). By 1974, full production of a range of vehicles had been achieved; for example six models of passenger cars were being produced on a scale of 100,000 per annum or more each. Setting up the motor industry involved establishing

1 the vehicle factories;
2 components factories, producing a wide range of metal and other products, such as mirrors, spark plugs and batteries;
3 raw material processing factories, for example, glass (for windows), rubber (for tyres), and paint; and
4 production of energy for the factories, and to run the cars.

Even if we look only at the vehicle factories, there is a complex specialization of tasks in each unit of production (requiring a large recruitment operation and different types and levels of skills). The productivity of labour is many times greater than that achievable by a craft car workshop at the beginning of the century, or even Henry Ford's model T assembly line of 1926. Indeed, the concept of increased scale of production often conjures up a picture of Henry Ford's assembly line or a later development of it, a clear indication of the importance of a large scale of production in the vehicle industry in twentieth-century development.

One implication of such wide-ranging and large-scale investment in Brazil was the need for investment by transnational as well as local companies. Local companies concentrated on establishing the components industries, rather than the vehicle industry. Transnational investment was encouraged for the vehicle industry because of:

1 the large scale of investment required to achieve the economies of scale associated with assembly line production – local private companies did not have sufficient capital for this investment and the Brazilian state decided not to invest directly even though it was centrally involved in the planning and subsidy of the industrial investments;
2 the transnationals' monopoly control over the complex technology of vehicle production, for example, doing their own research and development and design; and
3 the technical complexity of the industry, which involved associated technical skill and organizational requirements not available to the Brazilian companies in the 1950s.

Not only in the Brazilian case, but more generally, we can say that the rising scale of production has implications for the size of investment, and thus for the size of company. The motor industry globally has relatively few companies. Only a few Third World countries have tried to set up independent motor companies complete with their own research, development and design. All have needed the support of the state and could not rely only on private initiative. Some of the experiments have failed, like the attempt of Sanjay Gandhi, Mrs Gandhi's son, to make an Indian car.

In some cases, the control on a world scale of a very few companies over one industry has demonstrably slowed down the growth of that industry in Third World countries. One example is the case of petroleum refining. Many newly independent countries were unable to persuade the big oil companies to set up refining operations that involved some national control. The Italian company ENI–Agip supported many of these countries and expanded Agip activities in Tunisia, Iran, Tanzania, Egypt, Morocco, Zambia and Zaire. It earned the hostility of the big British and American oil giants, but did allow local refineries to begin production in these and other countries.

### *Garments*

The motor vehicle industry is perhaps an extreme example of concentration and scale. Not all processes have been successfully automated and organized to enable similar economies of scale. The hammock weaving industry in North-East Brazil described in chapter 10 is one example – described there as handicraft workshop production rather than industrial production. Another example is the garment making industry, where electrical machines and other technical advances have increased the efficiency of production, but without being able to break the basic unit of one operator per machine. It is possible, therefore, for the unit of production to be a household, a workshop, or a factory. Designing patterns and cutting cloth can be done centrally, so use of *industrial production processes* has increased. Still, the use of 'putting out' techniques persists, with household production processes linked to industrial ones.

Labour productivity in this industry has traditionally increased by raising the intensity of labour rather than investing in new technologies. The industry is also traditionally strictly divided on gender lines. Often, men have been employed in the earlier parts of production processes involving pattern making and cloth cutting. Women have almost exclusively been the sewers. Their work has been strictly controlled on the factory floor – often in 'sweat-shop' conditions – with piece-work payment methods.

Garment manufacturers have also been able to achieve strong *labour flexibility* through the 'out-work' system. Home working systems provide clothing factories with a work-force recruited through family ties or from previous women factory workers with children. They are, thus, largely dependent on the clothing factories, although only used by them at times of peak demand. Their employers recognize little if any responsibility to provide them with work at other times.

### *Engineering workshops*

There are still plenty of other production processes that are difficult to automate. In developed countries there is, at the moment, a massive research and development effort to improve productivity in what is called small-batch engineering production. Much engineering production is of small batches of products, (up to fifty say), not like motor vehicles that can be mass produced. Many industrial workshops still exist with a small number of lathes and milling machines *flexible* enough to produce a wide range of intermediate products. Research on flexible manufacturing systems aims to improve productivity through changing the organization of production, using computer systems to keep tighter tabs on the batches between machines, and robots and other automated systems to handle materials.

Small-scale engineering workshops abound in cities of the Third World, mending, changing, rehabilitating all kinds of machines. Ghosh describes a workshop area in Howrah, part of the Calcutta conurbation, as follows:

> As one walks along the crowded Belilious Road teeming with small factories and workshops on all sides, the first impression is one of complete anarchy ... A moulding unit is situated right amidst a cluster of a few turning shops; a precision grinding works is almost choked with the heat and smoke of the surrounding forging units. In the different workshops there are all kinds of machines – lathe, capstan, shaping, milling, punching, slotting, grinding; but there is an utter lack of systematic co-ordination and planning ... [to the] inexperienced eyes of a newcomer. (Ghosh, in Johnson and Bernstein, 1982, p. 126)

### *Large-scale agriculture*

These three examples are sufficient to illustrate that very different scales of production continue in the whole world, not just the Third World, although there is, overall, more small-scale production in the Third World, most easily observable in agriculture. In chapter 7, a sugar plantation in Tanzania was compared with Indian peasants involved in the agricultural changes of the Green Revolution. TPC (Tanganyika Planting Company) is an example of a large-scale capitalist enterprise operating for profit. Many large-scale capitalist farms in the Third World are owned by large transnationals with household names like United Brands, Del Monte, Geest or Brooke-Bond–Liebig. These companies and many other smaller, often locally owned enterprises, are part of the process of industrialization of agriculture or *agribusiness*, as it is sometimes called.

Large-scale agriculture also permits economies of scale, because high capital investments on technical inputs like tractors and fertilizers *can* be employed effectively on large land areas, and because of the more complex technical division of labour in the organization of workers in specialized tasks. The enterprise can achieve high output and productivity, and accumulate profits for further reinvestment through the sale of the product. This economic logic is the same as that of capitalist manufacturing industry.

There are various consequences of the dynamic of this kind of production. One is the increasing concentration of land ownership. Another is the centralization of productive facilities (for example, processing and packaging) around the production unit. A third is the development of other business activities, such as transport and production of agricultural implements, which are linked with the production of crops.

There are certain limits on economies of scale in agriculture which do not exist in manufacturing.

1 An important factor is the absolute limit on land: the scale of production cannot be increased indefinitely because total land area is limited.

2 The quality of land is an important factor in production. Farmers and companies may therefore have different yields from farms of the same size even if other inputs are the same.

3 The soil cannot be replaced as easily as machines and has to be regenerated through the use of fertilizers, by leaving it fallow or by using it for other crops or livestock.

4 Agriculture is subject to climatic and seasonal variations as well as to pests, diseases and general crop failure. The decline in genetic variation of plants because of the development of high-yield varieties may make crops more susceptible to pests and diseases.

5 Because of these factors, it is not easy to 'relocate' agriculture in other areas if the existing conditions of production no longer give as high profits as necessary or desired. So in agriculture, there are *physical* limits on production and its expansion which do not exist in industry.

There are also other kinds of limits. For example, it is more difficult to mechanize certain tasks in agriculture than in industry and, because of seasonal variation, labour and machines often cannot be used to their 'full capacity'. Nevertheless, the expansion of production on the land, particularly where new land is not available, requires more capital investment or 'rationalization' of the use of existing resources. That is, there have to be improvements in technology and the use of labour. For this investment to be worthwhile, it has to bring in a higher rate of return than rent. The internal organization of large-scale production units is therefore important for their success in terms of profit.

### *South African gold mining*

Mining is one industry which has a relatively large scale of production in the Third World and elsewhere, witness the large coal mines, oil complexes and aluminium mining operations dotted over Asia, Latin America and Africa.

One interesting example is gold mining in South Africa. Only at the very beginning, in the early 1890s, was it characterized by single small mines operating on or near the surface. The gold of the South African Witwatersrand is located deep underground in narrow seams and brittle rock. Within a decade, mines were being sunk several thousand feet deep. The mining industry had to contend with two other constraints. One was that although the Witwatersrand contains the largest concentration of gold bearing ore in the world, the grade of the ore is low. In the first decades of this century, South African gold ore contained only about half the gold of Australian and Canadian ores. The other 'problem' was that gold was no ordinary commodity since the international financial system depended on its price stability. Gold producers could not determine its price – until 1972 its price has remained constant for decades at a time. This led to two unusual characteristics.

1 The mining industry required large amounts of capital to sink the mines and keep them operating. The industry rapidly became one of very large scale, and highly concentrated. Anglo-American, much the largest South African company, grew from this concentration.

2 Very cheap labour was needed to keep costs down and make mining of low-grade ore feasible under fixed-price constraints and bad technical conditions. A massive migrant labour force developed under the monopoly recruiting organization set up by the South African Chamber of Mines to stop competition for labour. As a result, African wages fell by 25 per cent between 1889 and 1897 and remained at that level in real terms until the 1970s.

So South African gold mining needed both very large scales of production and very cheap labour to survive against other gold producers.

### *Large-scale or small-scale?*

These five examples illustrate that scale of production is about concentration (or lack of concentration) of at least the following elements: capital, technology and labour. The examples remind us that, although there is a tendency to increased scale of production at any one period and in any one place, there will be specific conditions, both technical and social, that are important determinants of the kinds of production processes established. These conditions change constantly and are often difficult to analyse. They make decisions about new investments difficult and dangerous.

Understanding these different conditions is all the more important in the Third World because fewer people are employed in larger-scale enterprises. More generally, a lower proportion even in urban areas are employed in the so-called 'modern' or 'formal' sector of large-scale enterprises in industry or services where conditions of work, pay and social insurance are observed more closely, and workers have more opportunity to organize themselves in trade unions.

This contrasts with conditions in the so-called 'informal' sector of self-employment, casual and irregular wage work, employment in personal services or in small-scale enterprises in manufacturing and services. In Latin America, the term 'marginalization' has been used to 'refer to the effects of "modern" capitalist industrialization (and agricultural development) which, it is argued, provides fewer and fewer jobs relative to the numbers of those seeking them. Those unable to find (or retain) regular wage employment – the "marginals" – consequently swell the ranks of the "informal sector", forming an increasing proportion of the urban population' (Johnson and Bernstein, 1982, p. 92).

The difference between the 'formal' and the 'informal' sector is one reason for the emergence of a critique of large-scale industry similar to the populist critique of large-scale agriculture. Perhaps the best known is that of Schumacher (1973). In his book *Small is Beautiful*, he presents a critique together with a plea for a new kind of labour intensive, smaller-scale industry that he calls 'intermediate technology'. Schumacher not only argues in favour of a technology that uses more labour but one that produces better (i.e. more humanized) work. He writes in favour of a wide-ranging craft approach to work and against fragmentation of work that produces alienation. He is against mass production since it involves 'idolatory of giantism'. Kitching (1982, p. 98) argues that Schumacher's mixture of looking back to a period of smaller, less industrialized society and his argument that modern science and technology could be used to scale down production to lower social disruption and instability puts him squarely in the 'populist camp'.

Schumacher's book has been the most influential in this area. It has been the focus of an extended debate between advocates of 'intermediate' technology and those of orthodox development approaches. A number of criticisms have been made of his approach. One (presented in the early chapters of this book) argues that overall wealth creation depends on increasing the capacity to produce things, which requires increasing the productivity of labour. Another is that it tends to place the blame for unemployment and underemployment on capital intensive technology rather than on political decisions and the social relations of production. Others have pointed to the 'sweat-shop' conditions of small-scale industries and contrasted this with the 'romantic' view of the self-employed, skilled, craft worker which is often assumed by the proponents of 'small is beautiful'.

At the heart of this debate is the question of whether small enterprises have growth and employment potential. As Schmitz (1982) coherently argued, this question cannot be answered in the abstract. In fact, small enterprises do exist and can spread but only under certain conditions, often without assistance from development policy makers. So called 'informal' sector enterprises often grow in the interstices of 'formal' sector enterprises, whether in the rural or, more likely, rapidly growing urban areas of the Third World. Sometimes they have been made to grow or at least survive through massive state assistance. But there are less optimistic conclusions about the potential of small enterprises. One famous study (by Amartya Sen) investigated the productivity of the Indian hand spinning wheel. An improved version of the traditional wheel, so important to Gandhian ideology, and still the symbol of the Congress Party of India, had been developed and encouraged by the Indian government. Sen showed that this innovation 'far from creating any flow of surplus produces a flow of output value less than even its recurring costs. For the Ambar Charkka [improved spinning wheel] to have ... no recurring adverse effect on the national capital stock, the workers would have to be paid [less than 2p] per eight hour day, which is quite absurd' (Sen, 1972, p. 110).

There is, thus, no generalizable positive or negative answer to the first question of whether small enterprises have the potential to create growth or employment. A more reasonable question then is not *whether* small enterprises have growth and employment potential but *under what conditions they might do so* (Schmitz, 1982, p. 445). Interestingly, much less research has been completed on this (superficially easier question) than on the first. What results exist suggest:

1 that conditions differ dramatically depending on the industrial sector (say between garment making and chemical fibre production); and
2 that conditions are strongly related to the kinds of *linkages* between enterprises: linkages between small enterprises like the engineering workshop example, but more importantly between small enterprises and larger enterprises; and
3 that polarization on the basis of scale may be an inappropriate way to look at different forms of production.

## Linkages

What is meant by linkages? The concept of linkage can be used to consider the relationship between different production processes in an analogous way to the idea of connections between units of production. In chapters 6 and 10, the concept of linkage was used to explain the interdependence of producers of different kinds of goods (the social division of labour), for example between capital, intermediate and consumer goods (chapter 10). They rely on others for some of their 'inputs' and for transport. The energy to activate machinery also usually needs to be brought in from outside, as well as the transport to take out the products when they are ready for distribution. The more industrialized a production process becomes, the more complex, generally, are the linkages that evolve between it and other processes (chapter 6). This has major implications for resource use, giving new opportunities to use natural resources (for example, rubber for tyre production, and copper minerals for electricity cables), and to substitute for other natural resources (chemical synthetics for rubber, nylon for cotton). The car industry provides a wide range of such examples. Setting up a car industry has clear implications for industrialization as a whole, since it requires many other industries and can consume a large proportion of a country's financial resources. For example, the establishment of the motor industry in Brazil required a large number of 'inputs':
1 steel, glass, rubber and paint;
2 components such as batteries, spark plugs, lights, locks, carpets, seats;

3 machinery for the assembly lines, foundries, press shops, and so on; and
4 energy to fuel production.

These are called *backward* linkages because they link backwards in the sequence of production processes from the motor industry to other industries. Each one of these backward linkages has its own backward linkages leading eventually to the natural resources it derives from (steel to iron ore, glass to various minerals, processed rubber to natural rubber trees or synthetic rubber to oil, paint mostly to oil).

In order for motor vehicles to be useful, other investments are required. For example, roads, car parks and garages, industries that require the transport equipment and, crucially, petrol or diesel fuel to power the vehicles. These are called *forward* linkages from the motor industry to other industries. (For a more detailed analysis, refer to chapter 10).

### *Linkages and uneven development*

This example concentrates on the linkages between relatively large-scale production processes. Chapter 6 demonstrates the crucial importance for national economies of links between and within production processes of all kinds, whether capitalist (like the Brazilian car industry) or petty commodity production forms (like small-batch engineering, workshops or shoe making).

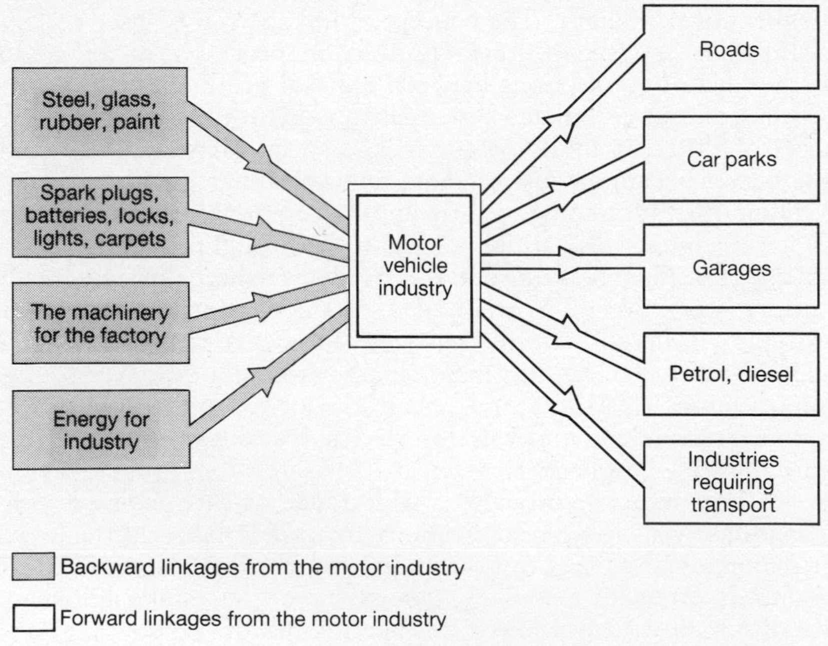


FIGURE 26 Linkages in the motor vehicle industry

It also demonstrates that development from one type of production to another is typically uneven. This is a very important conclusion and not only for Third World economic development. The first industrial revolution, in Britain for example, was not an even and balanced transformation of all branches of industry into large-scale factory production. In textiles, the first mechanized industry, handloom weaving, was destroyed by the early nineteenth century, throwing half a million weavers out of work, but clothing factories remained at a relatively low level of technology.

Using this approach earlier, in chapter 6, it was possible to move from the conclusion that development is *uneven*, and characterized by the coexistence of different types of production, to ask, *In what ways* do these different types of production interact with and affect each other? Thus, for example, it was possible to explain the importance of subsistence forms of agricultural production in migrant labour reserves. Chapter 6 also showed why some 'informal' sector activities persist in urban areas under certain conditions. 'Free entry' activities requiring very low investment of resources or technical skills provide a means of survival for those lacking regular wage employment.

Schmitz (1982) looked at a series of constraints on the growth of small-scale manufacturing, and his observations are also very useful in looking at reasons for the survival of small enterprises. Frequently, he discovered that the reasons for their survival related directly to their linkages with large organizations. Such linkages had contradictory effects, since they were crucial for small enterprises but also constrained their growth and tended to keep them small.

One example Schmitz gave was of subcontracting work done by smaller enterprises for larger ones. Much construction work, garment making and leather work is subcontracted. Schmitz's work on the hammock industry found that small subcontractors took the brunt of market fluctuations because their production was cut in slack periods. He concludes that this does not give the small producers a solid base from which to expand. But neither does it automatically lead to the demise of small-scale production. Small producers are usually available for recall in an upturn in the economy.

Although it is true that large-scale production has tended to take over sectors once characterized by the putting out system, the process of take over has been uneven. Schmitz quotes Schmukler's (1977) study, which stresses the heterogeneity of forms of production in Argentinian industry. Schmukler concludes that small firms used for subcontracting 'do not constitute transitional forms towards more mature capitalist relations of production nor do they become an obstacle to the development of capitalism in the [formal industrial] branch' (p. 16).

Subcontracting can be an important continuing element in industrial growth assisting other large-scale production processes to expand. This is just one kind of relationship between small and large enterprises, but one that well illustrates the kinds of constraints on the independence of small-scale enterprises. Constraining influences include: access to markets that larger enterprises control; access to raw materials controlled through the 'putting out' system, and even access to credit for production or expansion.

FIGURE 27 Women workers in Shanghai (Sally and Richard Greenhill)

Schmitz felt that much government assistance for small-scale activities could end up killing it by taking insufficient account of why small firms survived. For example, increased government inspection might reduce clandestine employment within enterprises and improved conditions of work or wages might make smaller enterprises less competitive.

On the other hand, firms could improve their stability if government assistance were able to improve the links between smaller enterprises and their markets, raw materials and credit. Evidence that government agencies have done this is weak even in countries with governments that appear to support small-scale producers, like Tanzania. One exception is China, where small enterprises have been encouraged to link to larger ones both during the 'walking on two legs' period of the 1960s and in the present modernization period.

The Chinese example leads to arguments for planned national industrialization. That is, to be industrialized, a nation needs not just one or two industries, but requires a whole range of interlinked industries as a prerequisite for their efficient operation. Although this industrial structure must include and be led by large-scale production, it can also contain small enterprises.

That survival of small-scale enterprises is not necessarily a constraint on rapid capital accumulation is shown by the Japanese experience, where small enterprises and industrial subcontracting still play a crucial role in

Japan's industrialization. This is particularly apparent in the modern industries, such as electrical and electronic engineering, where subcontracting coexists alongside the low stock or no stock 'just-in-time' policy of the large manufacturers.

Clearly, the small-scale can survive under certain conditions, but how it survives and whether it prospers depends on how it interacts with the wider social division of labour. Linkage of production processes is obviously important for industrialization and the integration of national economies.

## Skills

The third implication of establishing production processes is often taken for granted: the need for a greater and more diverse range of human skills and specializations.

It is surprising how often the term 'skill' is used as a static concept – an unchanging characteristic of people. Chapter 3 asserts that the technical culture characteristic of a particular society can only be assessed in relation to the kind of society it is, and the ability of those in it to satisfy their needs. Skills need to be conceptualized in a dynamic way, as capacities that can be increased (or decreased) – capacities such as the knowledge and skills to use instruments and/or machines. Skill requirements can change dramatically with technical change and with economic development.

The example of the motor industry in Brazil again allows us to illustrate that a complex set of industrial production processes requires a large number of specialist skills – the effect of a sophisticated technical division of labour.

The ability to establish and operate a complete motor industry requires more than the skills to set up a vehicle factory. For example, the research and development and design requirements involve a wide range of high-level specialist skills.

In the production process, management and financial skills are required, as well as the technical skills needed to operate and control the machinery. Each part of the production process requires different skills: press operators, assemblers, machiners, and painters (semi-skilled workers); keeping the machinery running requires mechanics, plumbers and toolmakers (skilled workers).

To these must be added the less tangible skills of being able to withstand working in an industrial production process. Chapter 11 noted that although high levels of efficiency can be obtained if workers perform the tasks specified by management, productivity will be increased if workers respond constructively to changing situations: advantages of economies resulting from large-scale production could only be realized by obtaining the flexibility and cooperation of the work-forces in the motor plants. This was obtained by the use of high-wage and high-turnover policies.

In some industries it is not that skills are less tangible, but that they are taken for granted as natural, not formally recognized, and not remunerated. Important examples are to be seen in women's manual work. The answers that companies give when asked why they employ women, as well as the statements made by governments trying to attract world market factories, show that there is a widespread belief that it is a 'natural' differentiation, produced by innate capacities and personality traits of women and men, and by an objective differentiation of their income needs in that men need an income to support a family, while women do not. A good example is the following passage in a Malaysian investment brochure, designed to attract foreign firms:

> 'The manual dexterity of the oriental female is famous the world over. Her hands are small and she works fast with extreme care. Who, therefore, could be better qualified by *nature and inheritance* to contribute to the efficiency of a bench-assembly production line than the oriental girl'. Sewing skills can be readily extended into industrial work because they 'already have the manual dexterity and capacity for spatial assessment required'. (Elson and Pearson, 1981, p. 93)

Elson and Pearson point out that such skills largely result from training received as part of domestic labour which is 'socially invisible and privatized [so] that the skills it produces are largely attributable to nature'.

But if these are socially derived differences in skills when women arrive in the labour market, why are they perpetuated at work and why are they remunerated at levels below those of men's work? The answers lie partly in the segregation of men's and women's work, the means by which this is sustained, and the way in which the concept of skill is perceived and defined. Employers operate systems of recruitment and of training, upgrading and promotion, which control access to opportunities for learning and progression to better jobs. But it is not only a matter of employer action. Phillips and Taylor have drawn attention to some of the consequences of the deskilling effects of technological change:

> Men workers have fought long and hard against this process, fought to retain their craft position, and, failing all else, at least their craft labels. And in these struggles, craft has been increasingly identified with masculinity, with the claims of the breadwinner, with the degree of union strength. Skilled work has been increasingly defined *against* women – skilled work is work that women don't do. (Phillips and Taylor, 1980, p. 86)

The classification of jobs as skilled, unskilled etc. is anyway often less a reflection of objective differences in content than of the weighting of criteria such as strength or manipulative ability according to prevailing social values and attitudes. Defence of the male position in the labour markt, emphasis on the need of the 'breadwinner' for a 'family wage' and consequently, assertion of the 'secondary' nature of women's earnings, have produced the effect that 'It is the sex of those who do the work rather than its content which leads to its identification as skilled or unskilled' (Phillips and Taylor, 1980, p. 85).

These examples of less tangible skills (general industrial skills such as attention to detail, flexibility of work, and the ability to concentrate on continuous process monitoring) and of unrecognized skills (like women's sewing abilities) serve as a reminder that skill development is not only in (largely male) craft skills and in skills gained from formal education.

What is not at issue is the need to increase skills if industry is to be established. Once machine processes are installed, they require skills to operate them. There is a whole library on 'the transfer of technology to the Third World', meaning both the movement of machinery and also the development of skills and knowledge of industrial production processes. Many books in this 'technology transfer' literature argue strongly that a smaller scale of technology would be more appropriate for many Third World needs, on the assumption that the skills they require will be more easily found or created within Third World countries. Others argue that it is the lack of skills that holds back Third World industrialization and that smaller-scale technology will further perpetuate backwardness. The best solution, they argue, is to set up industries that require skills, so that these will diffuse into the national work-force and increase the capacity for future development.

## Making a Living

This section explores more general points about making a living and includes autobiographical accounts by individuals in the Third World who make a living in very different forms of production: an urban 'marginal'; the wife of a tin miner; and a wage earning car worker. These examples have been chosen to illustrate the heterogeneity of capitalist production and the consequent variation in ways of coping with the struggle for survival and improvement.

### *Urbanization and urban work*

Most generally, industrial growth implies a broader range of changes than those at the point of production. One is the concentration of population. The first industrialization – that of Britain – illustrated dramatically the changing social conditions of people undergoing a general process of industrialization where in the space of a century from 1750–1850 the number of cities rose from 2 to 29. (Hobsbawm, 1969, p. 86)

One myth about the Third World is that its population is rural. It is increasingly urban. Although less than one-third of Asia's and Africa's population is urban, the Latin American urban population approaches 70 per cent. Not all live in shanty towns, by any means. But the image of the Third World shanty dweller is both a powerful and common one, often linked to precarious casual work in the 'informal' sector.

A powerful description of a poor urban marginal is that by Ruisque-Alcaino and Bromley (1979). They interviewed 'Miguel' as part of a project on the urban poor in Cali, the third city of Colombia. Their conclusions are a powerful counter to those who argue that the poor remain poor because they don't try to help themselves.

Miguel's autobiography serves to illustrate the weaknesses of two conventional 'caricatures' of the poor; that the poor are poor *simply because* they have too many children and that the poor are poor because they *all* don't work hard or show initiative. Miguel only has one child of his own whom he never had to support, and one adopted child whom he has supported since 1973, hardly a large family by any standards . . . There is no doubt that they work very hard to make a meagre living. They are far from underemployed in terms of hours worked or effort expended, though clearly they are under-remunerated in relation to average incomes in urban Colombia.

. . . Most importantly, Miguel's autobiography illustrates the continuously precarious nature of enterprises, work, and even existence itself, for the very poor. Poverty is not only associated with low incomes, but also with lack of savings and capital, meaning that 'reserves' are very limited, even taking account of what can be obtained through sales, pawning and appeals to friends and relatives. Severe instability of work and incomes, and even of health and housing, are common characteristics of the poor, and are typical of 'the poorest of the urban poor'. Poverty is not simply a condition of insufficiency or deprivation, but also one of insecurity and instability. (Ruisque-Alcaino and Bromley, 1979 quoted in Johnson and Bernstein, 1982, pp. 124–5)

### *Women's work: the double day*

Another neglected element of how people make a living is the importance of women's work.

A vivid description of how a woman spends her day is that of Domitila Barrios de Changara, a women's leader and miner's wife in the most important tin mining community in Bolivia. There have been continuing struggles between the miners and the army in Bolivia. When union leaders were imprisoned in 1961, their wives mounted a successful hunger strike and subsequently formed a housewives committee in support of the miners' union and to agitate over political issues.

'My day begins at four in the morning, especially when my *companero* is on the first shift. I prepare his breakfast. Then I have to prepare the *saltenas* [a Bolivian small pie, filled with meat, potatoes, hot pepper and other spices] because I make about one hundred *saltenas* every day and I sell them in the street. I do this in order to make up for what my husband's wage doesn't cover in terms of our necessities. The night before, we prepare the dough and at four in the morning I make the *saltenas* while I feed the kids. The kids help me: they peel potatoes and carrots and make the dough.

Then the ones that go to school in the morning have to get ready, while I wash the clothes I left soaking overnight.

At eight I go out to sell. The kids that go to school in the afternoon help me. We have to go to the company store and bring home the staples. And in the store there are immensely long lines and you have to wait there until eleven in order to stock up ... So all the time I'm selling *saltenas*, I line up to buy my supplies at the store ... From what we earn between my husband and me, we can eat and dress. Food is very expensive: 28 pesos for a kilo of meat, 4 pesos for carrots, 6 pesos for onions ... Considering that my

> *companero* earns 28 pesos a day, that's hardly enough, is it?
>
> Clothing, why that's even more expensive! So I try to make whatever I can. We don't ever buy ready-made clothes. We buy wool and knit ... Well, then, from eight to eleven in the morning I sell the *saltenas*, I do the shopping in the grocery store, and I also work at the Housewives' Committee, talking with the sisters who go there for advice.
>
> At noon, lunch has to be ready because the rest of the kids have to go to school. In the afternoon I have to wash clothes. There are no laundries. We use troughs and have to go get the water from the pump.
>
> I've also got to correct the kids' homework and prepare everything I'll need to make the next day's *saltenas*.
>
> Sometimes there are urgent matters to be resolved by the committee in the afternoon. So then I have to stop washing in order to see about them. The work in the committee is daily. I have to be there at least two hours. It's totally voluntary work.
>
> The rest of the things have to get done at night. The kids bring home quite a lot of homework from school. And they do it at night, on a litle table, a chair, or a little box. And sometimes all of them have homework and so one of them has to work on a tray that I put on a bed ... So that's how we live. That's what our day is like. I generally go to bed at midnight, I sleep four or five hours. We're used to that.
>
> I think that all of this proves how the miner is doubly exploited, no? Because, with such a small wage, the woman has to do much more in the home. And really that's unpaid work that we're doing for the boss, isn't it?' (Chungara, in Johnson and Bernstein, 1981, pp. 234–335).

Domitila de Chungara describes her daily domestic grind as the wife of a miner and cynically notes that 'in spite of everything we do, there's still the idea that women don't work ... that only the husband works because he gets the wage.' (Chungara, in Johnson and Bernstein, 1982, pp. 124–5) But poor women in the Third World rarely just do domestic work. They also earn an income whether through producing food on their farms, through wage work or producing and selling commodities. Women are thus subjected to 'double work' combining domestic work with earning a living either to supplement family income or to provide entirely for the family. The division between the two spheres is, however, often blurred.

Another way in which women's subordination is made most apparent is through relations between the sexes, in marriage and the family.

> This is double-edged: on the one hand, women are subjected to forms of male domination within the family itself; on the other, marriage and family relationships are often unstable which imposes an economic and psychological burden on women who are usually left to care for the children ... Husbands prevent their wives' independence ... For many peasants, rural and urban workers, the material conditions for marital stability do not exist ... Instability is also reflected in the casual liaisons that characterize many family relations, particularly between those who are often on the move looking for work. Social and cultural factors are also involved: desertion and divorce often result from men going off with other women. (Johnson and Bernstein, 1982, p. 161)

## *'Privileged' workers?*

It is examples like these that strengthen arguments that those workers with regular wages and relatively more stable employment are 'privileged', a 'labour aristocracy' or even that some workers *exploit* others. Even when we know that these relations are not exploitative, and that divisions between those struggling for a better life strengthen those who do exploit, the material differences between groups of exploited people cannot be wished away.

Brazilian motor workers are the kind of group of workers who could be accused of being 'privileged' since their wages are relatively higher than in other industrial sectors. Chapter 11 argues that their employment in a fast-growing, capital-intensive modern industrial sector does not thereby make them a privileged stratum. Above average wages were paid for an above average intensity of work. Also management were confident of obtaining new workers when needed, and so operated a policy of high turnover as well as high wages. In 1974 they cut the work-force in one plant by 25 per cent in one month.

Managements have the policy of gradually weeding out less able workers and also firing long-serving workers (with higher wages) and replacing them with workers at the bottom of the scale. Wages were high but employment was far from stable.

Even so, workers were able to organize. Industrialization in and around São Paulo, especially, involved a large concentrated industrial work-force, where relatively strong unionization grew even under such an authoritarian regime. Union membership ranged from around 45 per cent to just over 30 per cent for hourly paid workers. Before the strikes of 1978, the Metal Workers' Union, under the leadership of Luis Inacio da Silva (Lula) had built up an effective organization, particularly through the work of members of the union executive who were full-time organizers in the factories. As a result, the union was well placed to play a leading role in the wave of strikes. During May 1978, much of the southern industrial belt of São Paulo was affected by total or partial stoppages, in which workers attended the factories but refused to operate the machinery. Subsequently, a whole series of strikes occurred throughout 1978. In the course of the strikes from 1978 to 1980, with which he was closely associated, Lula was deposed by government intervention in the running of the trade unions. He then devoted his energies to the *Partido dos Trabalhadores* (Workers Party) which he helped to establish at the end of 1979, and which was permitted under the cautious reforms of the *Abertura* ('opening') introduced by President Figueiredo. Lula was subsequently tried under the National Security Law and sentenced to three years' imprisonment. Humphrey suggests (1979) that far from being a privileged group insulated from the harsh conditions faced by other workers, these workers' struggles have inspired working class organization and action more generally.

In an important question and answer interview, the workers' leader, Lula, made an eloquent argument that workers struggle can integrate with other struggles, such as that for democracy in Brazil, whilst keeping its emphasis on organization of the exploited.

> *Q*: *How does the working class look at the fight for amnesty, for a constituent assembly, and for democratic liberties? What do you think today really mobilizes the working class?*
>
> *A*: Let's start with the democratic liberties. I think that this demand is important not only to one or other group of Brazilian society, but to all groups. As for amnesty [for people accused of political crimes, or stripped of their rights], I believe that in good conscience, no citizen could be against it. And I go further than amnesty for just the politicians thrown out of office and deprived of their political rights. I support the amnesty that the working class needs: the right to live with dignity, because the working class is the eternal prisoner, the eternal thrown-out-of-office; it doesn't participate in anything in this land except in the process of production. So I defend more emphatically a broader amnesty which would give the working class what belongs to it. This is why people are frequently confused, because it's not just a question of amnesty for political prisoners and people deprived of their political rights. I think it is legal to cancel a person's political rights if it is done by the courts in a legally constituted regime with civil rights, where it is determined that a person acted wrongly and must pay for it. But I'm against depriving people of their rights arbitrarily. In conclusion, I am in favour of these demands as long as they involve the proportional participation of the working class.
>
> *Q*: *Should the labour movement work by itself, or should it try to establish relations with the other sectors of the Brazilian opposition like the student movement, the medical interns' movement, the bank workers, etc? If it should establish these relations, how can they be made concretely?*
>
> *A*: I have maintained the following: to participate in a movement that is outside of labour before participating in our own movement would be to do the impossible; it would be putting the cart before the horse. The type of freedom that we workers want, if it is the same type of freedom that the students want, that the middle class wants, that all groups want, then I think it will be impossible to refuse the common aspirations after each specific struggle has developed. (Lula, in Johnson and Bernstein, 1982, p. 150–1)

Lula here is emphasizing an important conclusion: it is through collective organization (in his case of workers, students, the middle classes; in Domitila's case, of women and mine workers) that different groups improve their ability to control their lives. His view is that wider movements have to build from these concrete experiences.

## Industrial Struggles and Lives of Struggle

In this chapter we have travelled from the meaning and debates over *scale of production* – its importance in industrialization and its unevenness, to *linkages* between production processes and their importance for integration of national economies, to *skills* of people involved in industrial production and how these not only change over time but are not always recognized and rewarded. This led to a final section about the capacity of people to organize their lives and struggle to improve them.

The three examples in the last section were chosen to reflect the unevenness of capitalist production and the different struggles for survival and improvement that result: from Miguel Duran's extreme instability to Domitila's need to engage in cash earning activities to supplement male wages insufficient for family reproduction; from the burdens of 'double work' for women and 'triple' work for Domitila with her organizing commitment with the housewives committee to the gradual growth of a strong union among Brazilian car workers; from the solitary struggles for survival of the marginals to the growth of collective organization of women in a community and among car workers, after a military coup.

These examples show that there are no easy answers to the 'problem' of economic development and who shares and benefits from it. The process of industrialization is not one that is separate from development more generally – it is a *total* process. Industrial growth creates new forms of employment, as well as unemployment, urbanization, proletarianization, increased consumption, new forms of collective work and collective organization. These consequences cannot be wished away. Kitching (1982, p. 179) writes:

> Industrialization cannot be avoided or run away from, either in theory or practice. Those who try to do so, in the name of loyalty to the peasantry and the poor, are likely to end up offering no effective help to 'the people', and seeing the process of industrialization occur in any case under the anarchic sway of international capital.

Similarly, we cannot run away from the struggles that emerge. 'People change as a result of participation in struggles, and acquire a new self-confidence in their collective ability to organize and control the conditions of their lives' (Johnson and Bernstein, 1982, p. 267).

One should not underestimate the capacity of working people to learn from their experiences, of victories and defeats, and to organize in attempts to control and, thus, to transform their lives.

PART V

# Integration in the World Economy

# Introduction

Parts III and IV have focused primarily on the internal dynamics of production in Third World economies. Part V shifts the focus to the international economy and to recent changes in the international division of labour. This section examines, particularly, the roles of transnational corporations (TNCs) and the International Monetary Fund (IMF), integrating national economies through trade, investment and finance with the world economy.

Chapter 13 describes TNC investment in the Third World and examines the proposition that foreign investment constitutes a barrier to development. Whilst such investment may create an unequal relationship, the chapter rejects the deterministic view that First World investment in Third World economies prevents development. It describes how state policies in the Third World have tended to evolve from attempts to nationalize TNCs to more supportive measures, providing the financial and labour force conditions encouraging foreign investment. In the newly industrializing countries following the latter path, TNC investment has been associated with the development of productive capacities and rapid industrialization.

Chapter 14 examines the new international division of labour that is emerging as a result of industrialization in the Third World and deindustrialization in the First. It looks at two alternative theories of what is happening. The chapter concludes that the relocation of manufacturing industry to the Third World cannot be explained solely as a result of TNCs seeking a cheap and docile labour force. It is part of a more fundamental international restructuring of industry.

The International Monetary Fund plays an important role in determining the conditions for this international restructuring. Chapter 15 examines the way in which the IMF structures the integration of Third World economies with the international economy and how it has contributed to the creation of a world economy dominated by private banks and TNCs.

CHAPTER THIRTEEN

# Dominance and Dependency in the World Economy

---

Third World economies are part of an international economy. Each Third World country is integrated into the international economy through trade, investment, financial flows and migration. The most important international economic links of the majority of Third World countries are with First World countries. In general, such links are quantitatively and qualitatively more important than links with other Third World countries, and more important than links with Second World countries.

Such links are not new, as will be clear from chapter 2, but their significance has increased with commercialization and industrialization in the Third World. Today, there are very few parts of the Third World where people make a living untouched by international economic links.

According to orthodox economic theory, these are mutually beneficial links that promote development and are evidence of harmonious interdependence between First and Third Worlds. Many people in the Third World reject that view, however. They see the links as means by which the First World asserts its dominance, and confines the Third World to a subordinate position in the world economy. One school of thought, often called the dependency school (Palma, 1978), sees international links as presently constituted as a barrier to development. Far from promoting development, international trade and investment are seen by many dependency theorists as means for perpetuating underdevelopment.

In this chapter, we analyse trade and investment links between First and Third World countries, to see to what extent they are equally beneficial to both parties or whether Third World countries would be better off without them, as some dependency theorists have suggested. We need to bear in mind that there is a third possibility: the links may be extremely unequal, and vehicles for domination of the international economy by the First World, and yet they may be necessary to Third World countries and, at least in some cases, permit development. We do not have to agree with either the interpretation given by orthodox neo-Classical economic theory or the interpretation given by dependency theory.

## Transnationals Corporations (TNCs)

The integration of Third World countries into the international economy takes place to a very large extent under the auspices of First World firms.

The channels of international trade and finance are organized by First World banks, trading houses and shipping lines (Clairmonte and Cavanagh, 1985). The activities of transnational corporations have been seen as especially significant by many Third World writers. Radical economists have described the TNCs as a modern form of imperialism (Radice, 1975).

Many of today's TNCs grew out of the small family businesses of nineteenth-century Europe and the USA. (Japanese transnationals have a different history and structure, but limitations of space will prevent us from considering their differences in detail here.) The first stage was the development at a national level from a family business, typically tightly controlled by a single entrepreneur or small family group who possessed all the information and made all the decisions about the firm, to a national business corporation with a formal administrative structure, with division of function (finance, personnel, purchasing, production, sales, etc.) and a hierarchical division of responsibility and power (field offices to manage local operations, head office to supervise field offices). The second stage was movement abroad. As large national firms, they had developed the capacity to go abroad, in the form of a suitable administrative structure, and financial strength. What pushed them into using this capacity was the competitive struggle with other large national corporations. Competition became a much more complex affair once a firm was competing against a limited range of known alternative suppliers, rather than against a large number of unknown alternatives. It was much more feasible to collaborate with competitors, for instance to organize cartels to keep up prices. On the other hand, there were very rich pickings for the corporation that could outwit its competitors by controlling sources of supply of inputs, or sales outlets, or by developing new products that would make the old obsolescent. Some firms invested abroad to get the security of control over their raw material requirements; some to control marketing outlets; some invested abroad as a pre-emptive measure to forestall other corporations gaining control of raw materials or markets. US corporations led the way.

## The Growth in TNCs

The first wave of direct US foreign investment occurred around the beginning of the twentieth century, followed by a second wave in the 1920s. This movement slackened during the depression of the 1930s, and resumed again after the Second World War, accelerating rapidly.

Between 1950 and 1969, direct foreign investment by US firms expanded at a rate of about 10 per cent per annum. It is in this twenty-year period that direct foreign investment by transnational corporations became a world economic phenomenon of great importance. Before 1914, between two-thirds and three-quarters of the value of all private foreign investment took the form of portfolio investment, that is, it took the form of purchases of financial securities, such as bonds issued by foreign institutions, governments or business firms. The City in London played a key role in these transactions. Although a few large American and European companies, such as Lever, Singer, General Electric, Courtaulds and Nestlé already owned sizeable foreign manufacturing plants in 1914, these were the exceptions rather than the rule. However, by the mid-1960s, the greater part of private foreign investment took the form of direct investment by transnational corporations.

US TNCs remain the most important, though their share in the total stock of direct foreign investment was estimated to have falled from about 54 per cent in 1967 to about 48 per cent in 1976 (United Nations Centre for Transnational Corporations, 1978, Table III-32, p. 236). A recently released report by the US Department of Commerce estimates that, in 1977, 3450 US transnationals (in all industries except banking) owned or were connected with 24,666 foreign affiliates, who controlled US$490.02 billion in assets and employed 7.2 million people.

An important feature of foreign investment by TNCs is the disproportionate role of a quite small number of very large firms. For instance, United Nations estimates published in 1973 showed over 70 per cent of direct US foreign investment to come from only 250–300 firms; in the case of Britain, over 80 per cent was controlled by 165 firms. Eighty-two firms controlled over 70 per cent of direct foreign investment by the Federal Republic of Germany. One way of grasping the sheer economic size of the largest transnational corporations is to compare their 'value added' with the gross national product of national economics ('value added' means the value of sales minus the value of purchases of material inputs). A United Nations report estimated that, in 1971, the value added by each of the top ten TNCs was greater than US$3 billion, which was greater than the Gross National Product of over eighty Third World countries. The value added of all TNCs was estimated to be US$500 billion, which was approximately 20 per cent of the combined Gross National Product of the First and Third World (United Nations, Centre for Transnational Corporations, 1973, ch. 1).

Perhaps the single most important characteristic of TNCs, and the key to their power and influence, is their ownership and control of knowledge, including the technology of production, as well as organizational systems, marketing systems, and financial systems. Though *basic* knowledge tends to be produced by government-financed research and training centres, the applied development of technology is generally undertaken by business firms, and a large part of commercialized technology is in the hands of the TNCs. For instance, nearly all of the world's patents are held by the TNCs.

## The International Distribution of Investment by TNCs

Table 24 shows the distribution of flows of direct foreign investment by TNCs. This makes clear that, since 1965, about three-quarters of foreign direct investment has, on average, gone to First World countries. Typically, the pattern within the First World is one of cross-investment, with US firms investing in Canada and Western Europe, and Western European firms investing in each other's economies, and in North America. Japan

TABLE 24 Direct foreign investment in selected country groups, 1965–83

| Country group | *Average annual value of flows (US$ billions)*[a] | | | | *Share of flows (%)* | | | |
|---|---|---|---|---|---|---|---|---|
| | *1965–9* | *1970–4* | *1975–9* | *1980–3* | *1965–9* | *1970–4* | *1975–9* | *1980–3* |
| Industrial countries | 5.2 | 11.0 | 18.4 | 31.3 | 79 | 86 | 72 | 63 |
| Developing countries | 1.2 | 2.8 | 6.6 | 13.4 | 18 | 22 | 26 | 27 |
| Latin America and the Caribbean | 0.8 | 1.4 | 3.4 | 6.7 | 12 | 11 | 13 | 14 |
| Africa | 0.2 | 0.6 | 1.0 | 1.4 | 3 | 5 | 4 | 3 |
| Asia, including Middle East | 0.2 | 0.8 | 2.2 | 5.2 | 3 | 6 | 9 | 11 |
| Other countries and estimated unreported flows | 0.2 | −1.0 | 0.6 | 4.8 | 3 | −8 | 2 | 10 |
| Total[b] | 6.6 | 12.8 | 25.6 | 49.4 | 100 | 100 | 100 | 100 |

*Notes*: [a] Figures converted from billions of SDR to billions of US dollars based on average IMF exchange rates.
[b]Total includes IMF estimates for unreported flows.
*Source*: World Bank, 1985, p. 126.

does not follow exactly the same pattern. There is very little direct foreign investment in Japan itself, and Japanese firms have, until recently, concentrated the bulk of their overseas investment in the Third World, especially in Asia. But Japanese direct investment in North American and European countries rose rapidly in the 1970s, so that at the end of the decade the largest stock of Japanese direct investment was held in the USA. Indonesia and Brazil were the next largest recipients, but in fourth place was Britain, followed by Australia in fifth place. An important factor leading to Japanese investment in the USA and Britain has been the desire to jump over the trade barriers (such as voluntary restrictions on car exports) which have been increasingly erected against Japanese exports to other developed countries.

## TNCs and the Third World

Direct foreign investment within the Third World has been highly concentrated in a limited number of countries. As the Brandt Report (1980) points out, 70 per cent of the direct foreign investment in the Third World has been in only fifteen countries. Over 20 per cent is in Brazil and Mexico alone, and much of the rest is in other middle-income countries of Latin America (such as Argentina, Peru and Venezuela), and in South East Asia (such as Malaysia, Singapore, Hong Kong). About one-quarter is in oil-exporting developing countries. In the poorer countries, direct foreign investment is mainly in minerals and plantations, or in countries with large internal markets, like India. But this concentration of direct foreign investments in the richer developing countries does *not* mean that the activities of TNCs are only of interest to these few. There is *some* investment by TNCs in virtually *all* Third World countries, and though in the case of many countries the amount of such investment is a drop in the ocean by world standards, it is highly significant in the context of their small domestic economies.

Until recently, investment in the Third World by transnational corporations has been mainly in oil, mining and plantations. But manufacturing now accounts for about half the current flow of foreign direct investment in the Third World. There is a strong tendency for transnationals to invest in the areas where the cultural and political influence of their 'home' countries has been greatest. The exception to this is recent large-scale Japanese investment in Latin America, but most Japanese investment in the Third World is still in Asia.

## Nationalization: Ownership and Control?

In any serious conflicts with Third World governments, TNCs tend to rely on their home governments' ability to exert leverage to change the policy of Third World governments. Where TNCs have been in dispute with independent governments of Third World countries, they have often been

*'Upon my word — the only solution to the distressing misery of this poor shopkeeper is self-evident! He and yonder oil merchant must give those lowly beggars a share of their profits that they may make a habit of purchasing his goods . . .'*

FIGURE 28 A comment on the Brandt Report's argument that the economies of the Third World and the First World are mutually dependent. (Cartoon by Gibbard, reproduced in the *Guardian*, 13 February 1980)

able to persuade aid agencies to cut back on aid flows. For instance, the attempts by Peru and Chile in the later 1960s to exert greater control over American transnationals were met by very large cuts in the aid channeled to them by the Inter-American Development Bank.

In the last decade, outright conflicts have in any case become far less common. The hallmark of the 1970s has been increased cooperation between Third World governments and TNCs. Joint ventures, in which an enterprise is owned jointly by a Third World state agency and a transnational corporation, are one important expression of this cooperation. Some joint ventures in the mining and oil sector were created through a process of partial nationalization. Typically, Third World governments bought 51 per cent of the shares of companies owned and operated by TNCs. For instance, the Zambian government bought 51 per cent of the shares in the companies operating the copper mines, previously wholly owned by two giant multinational mining corporations, Anglo-American and Amax.

A recent report on TNCs and world development argues that Third World governments increasingly possess the capacity to ensure a more equitable relation with the TNCs, and have achieved some success in persuading the corporations to accept more participation in decision making, and in minimizing the influence of the corporations on their domestic political process (United Nations Centre for Transnational

Corporations, 1978). But other researchers are less optimistic and claim that many developing countries have learned by painful experience that nationalization does not put an end to foreign control.

When the Zambian government nationalized the copper mines in 1969 it did not possess the knowledge necessary to run the mines. It, therefore, negotiated a management contract with the TNCs that had owned the mines – Anglo-American and Amax – whereby they continued to supply all managerial, financial, commercial, technical and other services needed to run the mines. In return, they got 0.75 per cent of the sales proceeds and 2 per cent of the consolidated profits (before income tax, but after mineral tax). They also continued to market the copper. The contract contained no legal obligations to train and employ Zambian personnel nor to use the profits to diversity into other industries.

This kind of arrangement, of 51 per cent ownership of shares and a management contract with the existing operators, is often unsatisfactory since it is expensive and does not give control over the most vital decisions. In the Zambian case, the government agreed to pay a total of US$296.5 million in foreign currency for the shares it nationalized. Payment was to be out of future profits on the government's 51 per cent share. This meant that the government's ability to pay depended on the mines being run at a profit, which in turn depended to a considerable extent upon management, which it did not control. After five years, the Zambian government concluded that it did not have sufficient say in the development of copper production and the management contract was terminated on 15 November 1974, at enormous cost, at a time when the industry was facing difficulties.

A well-known Canadian researcher concludes that 'Minority ownership, technology contracts, management contracts, marketing contracts, etc., may be just as effective as indicators ... of the potentiality for foreign control of productive assets as majority ownership' (Helleiner, 1979, p. 75.) So why have more Third World governments not pursued the path of total nationalization, or outright expropriation, breaking off all contact with transnational corporations? One of the few that did is Cuba, earning in return the implacable hostility of the US government and loss of the US market, Cuba's major traditional outlet for its main export crop, sugar. Cuba was only able to survive because knowledge of sugar-refining technology is not a monopoly of the TNCs, and because the USSR offered an alternative market for its sugar exports. But this reliance on another powerful foreign country was not without problems. By 1980, Cuba had a deficit of US$890 million on trade with Comecon countries (mainly the USSR and Eastern Europe) and a stagnating economy, to set against undoubted progress in health and education. So Cuba has decided to open the door once more to private foreign investors, inviting them to form joint ventures with Cuban state-owned enterprises. Cuba hopes to gain foreign exchange, jobs, and expertise in activities such as nickel production, citrus fruit exporting, and oil exploration.

The case of Angola, another country whose present government is intent on pursuing a socialist development strategy, also illustrates some of the difficulties of trying to do without TNCs. Crude petroleum is Angola's most valuable export, followed by coffee and diamonds. When the present MPLA government took over from the Portuguese colonialists in 1975, oil extraction was in the hands of foreign companies, the most important of which was the Gulf Oil Corporation of the USA. Coffee was produced for export on plantations run by Portuguese settlers; and diamonds were mined by a company called Diamang, whose major shareholders included Belgian, British and South African firms. The marketing of these diamonds was controlled by the international diamond cartel, the Central Selling Organization, run by the South African firm of De Beers, part of the giant Anglo-American Corporation.

At the time of independence, many of the coffee plantations had been abandoned and their Portuguese owners had fled back to Portugal. These were nationalized and plans were made to turn them into state farms. But the oil and diamond transnationals had not abandoned their lucrative assets. Gulf Oil began to pay rent, royalties, and a tax on its profits, to the socialist Angolan government, as it had to the Portuguese administration. But the US government backed a rival Angolan organization, UNITA, which has been fighting against the MPLA government in some areas of the country.

On 19 December 1975, the US State Department ordered Gulf Oil to cease both payments and production. Gulf complied by immediately ceasing all production and paying their outstanding taxes and royalties into a US account in the name of 'Angolan Government', to be held until an Angolan government existed which was recognized by the US government. The immediate priority of the government was to get production going again, because this was its major source of foreign currency. No one in the government had the expertise necessary for this, so they tried to find an alternative foreign source of that expertise. They held discussions with Nigeria, an oil-producing African country, and with the Italian State Oil Company. They also received help from the Rumanians and the Algerians. But it quickly became clear that, in the short run at least, there were grave difficulties in replacing Gulf. The main production was offshore, which involved more difficult technology and Gulf, having closed down production, had also removed or destroyed the relevant technical documentation containing the information needed to restart operations. There was a danger of the oil wells clogging-up if production was stopped for as long as six months. There was little alternative but to open up negotiations with Gulf, who were ready to cooperate since they were themselves not at all keen to lose their Angolan assets, despite pressure from the US State Department. The outcome in February 1976 was a new arrangement with Gulf, in which the Angolan government bought 55 per cent of the shares in Cabinda Gulf, the Gulf Company running its Angolan operations; and was paid by royalty of 16.5 per cent on all oil produced; and a profit tax of 65 per cent. In return, Gulf released the payments it had been holding and restarted the oil fields. This new arrangement was certainly an improvement on the previous one, in which no shares in Cabinda Gulf were owned by the government, and royalties were only 12.5 per cent and profit tax 50 per cent. But it must be remembered that the oil price rise of 1973 had vastly increased the profitability of Cabinda Gulf.

The production of diamonds involved nothing like the same level of technology as did oil. The problem here was on the marketing side. For most of this century, diamonds have been marketed internationally only through the Central Selling Organization, run by De Beers, which effectively regulated the supply of diamonds in order to keep up the price. Even the USSR, which supplies about 20 per cent of the world market, has used the Central Selling Organization to market its diamonds in the West. De Beers were very successful in 'policing' all international diamond sales, so that buyers were reluctant to buy from outside suppliers, for fear of offending the Central Selling Organization. Expropriation of Diamang would have cut Angola off from the Central Selling Organization, and there was little possibility of developing a powerful enough alternative. Accordingly no action was taken to nationalize Diamang.

The problem of marketing is at its most extreme in diamonds, but it arises to some extent for many other minerals. It has provided a basis for TNCs to maintain a dominant position:

> The TNCs counter-reacted [to nationalization] by promoting alternative control mechanisms over the nationalized enterprises ... governments of developing countries that nationalized TNC assets at the raw materials level often found they had to sell their output to foreign-controlled processing and distribution outlets frequently owned by the same parent firms whose assets had been nationalized. (Vaitsos, 1979, p. 37)

## State Support for TNCs

Increasingly, independent Third World governments have been drawn into deploying their state power to aid, as well as to control, the business operations of TNCs. This is particularly the case in the manufacturing sector. A study of the role of TNCs in production of manufactures for export from the Third World suggested that there are two basic factors that influence the choice of which Third World country to invest in: political stability and labour docility (Nayyar, 1978). Many governments in Third World countries have shown themselves quite ready to oblige by restricting or banning the organization of trade unions and outlawing strikes, if necessary implementing these measures through the use of force. There is a good deal of evidence to support the view that many independent Third World governments have, to a great extent, taken over the role colonial governments used to play with respect to the labour force. The TNCs have no need to directly mobilize the power of their 'home' governments when they can rely on Third World government to smooth the path of their operations.

## Mechanisms of Surplus Appropriation

The core of the dependency school's economic case against the operations of TNCs in the Third World is that they extract a surplus from the Third World and transfer it to the First World. The most obvious way in which TNCs withdraw surplus from the Third World is by remitting profits back to their head offices in the First World. For instance, it has been estimated that, between 1960 and 1968, US TNCs took, on average, 79 per cent of their declared net profits out of Latin America (Barnet and Muller, 1974, pp. 153–4).

Third World governments can retain some of the surplus by requiring payments of rent, royalties and taxes (as we saw in the case of Angola and Gulf Oil). Rent is mainly important for mineral and agricultural products where national resources are a key factor. So are royalty products by TNCs to Third World governments. Whereas rent is a payment for access to the natural resource, royalties are payments related to *utilization* of the resources. For instance, royalties paid by oil companies are typically a specified percentage of the price per barrel of oil produced, whereas rent has to be paid irrespective of the level of production. The term is also used for payments for the utilization of other resources. TNCs also get paid royalties *by* Third World governments for the use of their technology and trade marks. Taxes can be levied on company profits, or on the value of company sales or the value of company exports. The nominal tax rate of a certain percentage of profits, sales, or export value, is often not indicative of the amount of tax actually paid because there may also be all kinds of tax concessions, such as allowances for new investment, allowances for depletion of mining assets, accelerated depreciation and tax holidays.

In many cases, Third World governments have successfully raised the rate of royalty and tax payments though not always without a struggle, as is shown by the so-called 'Banana War' of 1974 between the Central American countries of Panama, Costa Rica, and Honduras and the TNCs engaged in banana production for export, including Del Monte, Castle and Cook, and United Brands. The three countries attempted to introduce a tax of US$1 per box on all banana exports (a box containing 40 pounds net weight of bananas is the physical unit in which most international trade in bananas is carried out). The TNCs resorted to a number of different tactics to try to get the tax removed. Initially, they argued on two basic grounds: firstly that the taxes were illegal because the companies were operating under long-term contracts with the governments concerned, in which there were specific clauses stating no further fiscal measures could be introduced within the time limit of these contracts; and, secondly, that the taxes were counter-productive because they would price bananas from Panama, Costa Rica and Honduras out of the market.

When these arguments failed to get the taxes removed, they resorted to other measures, such as cutting back on exports, or even stopping them altogether, and bribing high government officials. General Oswaldo Lopez Arellano, head of the Honduran military government, was forced to resign in 1975, when it became known that he had accepted a US$1.25 million bribe from United Brands in return for lowering the export tax from US$1 a box to 25 cents a box, with provision for a rise to 50 cents by 1979. The governments of Costa Rica and Panama also bowed before the pressure and reduced their taxes; in the case of Costa Rica to 25 cents a box in 1974, raised to 45 cents in 1975; and in the case of Panama to 35 cents a box in 1974, raised to 40 cents per box in 1976. Besides the immediate pressure from the companies, there was also the fear that perhaps there was something in their arguments that the tax would make banana production in their countries uncompetitive. To judge this, the governments needed information on the costs of production which only the companies had.

Lack of alternative sources of information on costs of production is often a critical factor in negotiations about the level of payments a TNC should make to a Third World government. Typically, what a government wants to do is get more of the golden eggs without killing off the goose. That is, it does not want to price the country's exports out of the market; nor render production so unprofitable that no company will undertake it; nor remove all incentive for new investment. But the government rarely possess the knowledge required to judge the rate of payment which will secure these goals. Generally, it has neither sufficient *technical* knowledge to judge accurately the physical potential of a mine or a plantation; nor sufficient *economic* knowledge to judge the assets' profitability.

## Transfer Pricing

The difficulty of making an assessment of the economic value of the operations of a TNC in a particular country is, to a large extent, the result of the fact that there is often no 'open market' price for the inputs used or the outputs produced. Frequently, the inputs are supplied by different branches of the same firm; and/or the outputs are bought by different branches of the same firm. The inputs and outputs are not bought and sold between independent sellers and buyers who transact at 'arms length'. Instead they are intra-firm transfers, and the prices at which they are transacted are known as 'transfer prices'. A large TNC has considerable discretion in deciding the level at which it sets its internal transfer prices, and can manipulate such prices in order to reduce the payments it makes to governments. For instance, it can transfer funds from a particular country by raising the prices it charges for inputs to its subsidiary in that country; or by lowering the price it pays for outputs from that subsidiary.

This ability to decide, within rather wide limits, the pattern of internal transfer prices, means that a company can afford to concede higher rates of royalty payment or profit tax. It can then minimize the impact of the higher rates by setting internally transferred output prices low and input prices high.

It is much easier to estimate the *potential* for manipulation of transfer pricing than it is to estimate the actual extent of such manipulation. This is because it is often difficult to establish a market or arms-length price of a particular product with which to compare the transfer price: the product in question may be specific to one particular corporation, with nothing else exactly like it produced by other sources.

To gain some idea of the potential for transfer pricing, we need to look at the proportion of international trade that is intra-firm trade: that is, the proportion of imports or exports that are transferred internationally *between* countries but *within* one TNC. Unfortunately, in most countries, data on intra-firm trade is only sporadically collected. Only the USA regularly collects and reports two different sets of data indicating the extent and composition of US intra-firm imports. These are data on imports from majority-owned affiliates of US companies, and data on imports from 'related parties', i.e. from firms in which 5 per cent or more of the shares are owned by the importing firm. In 1975, nearly one-third of all US imports originated from majority-owned affiliates. The proportion was somewhat higher for US imports from developing countries (35 per cent from majority-owned affiliates) than from developed countries (28 per cent from majority-owned affiliates). However, these figures do include oil imports. If oil is excluded, then the figure for imports from developing countries drops to 11 per cent.

The data for related-party imports shows that, in 1977, nearly 54 per cent of US imports from developed countries came from related parties, and about 43 per cent of US imports from developing countries. If oil is excluded, the figure for imports from related parties in developing countries falls to 28 per cent. If we consider only international transactions with majority-owned affiliates, then we leave out all those joint ventures where TNCs have a minority of the shares. On the other hand, some 'related-party' transactions are not between a US transnational and its overseas affiliates, so the proportion of US non-oil imports from developing countries which are 'intra-firm' is somewhere between 11 per cent and 28 per cent (Helleiner, 1981).

To what extent is the potential for manipulation of transfer prices actually used to the detriment of Third World countries? It *is* difficult to get evidence on transfer prices and their appropriateness, but the verdict of Indian economist Sanjaya Lall is that the few investigations that have taken place have *all* shown that transfer prices are used against Third World countries (Lall, 1981, p. 62). One of the most thorough studies is that carried out by Constantine Vaitsos on the impact of transfer pricing in Colombia, Peru, Chile, Bolivia and Ecuador. He found that manipulation of transfer pricing, especially the over-pricing of imported inputs, is used extensively by TNCs as a way of repatriating profits from those countries. Here is an example: in the pharmaceutical industry in Colombia, Vaitsos found that reported profits accounted for 3.4 per cent of effective returns; royalties for 14.0 per cent; and over-pricing for 82.6 per cent (Vaitsos, 1973, p. 319). He estimates that the loss of surplus to Colombia in 1968 could have been as much as US$20 million (Vaitsos, 1974).

Some estimates have also been made of the impact of transfer pricing in Kenya. An International Labour Organisation Employment Mission which went to Kenya concluded that the over-pricing of inputs probably more than doubled the real outflow of surplus from the manufacturing sector as compared with the declared outflow of profits and dividends (International Labour Office, 1972, p. 455). A detailed study of the operations of a very large TNC producing pineapples in Kenya suggests that in this case there is manipulation by under-pricing of exports by about 20 per cent (Kaplinsky, 1979). This has a similar impact to over-pricing of imported inputs, in that both reduce the apparent profitably of the company, and its liability for taxes and royalties.

## Payments to TNCs

There are some other, less obvious, ways in which a transfer of surplus can take place. Payments to TNCs for patents, product and technology licences, brand names, trade marks, and management, marketing and technical services, have all been growing rapidly. A United Nations estimate puts the growth rate at 20 per cent a year (Colman and Nixson, 1978, p. 229). One of the reasons for this rapid growth is the trend to nationalization in the mining and agricultural sectors. The other is industrialization in the Third World orientated towards producing the kind of products, with the kind of technology, that TNCs have developed. But why should payments for patents, licences, trade marks, brand names and management marketing and technical services, be regarded as transfers of surplus rather than as payments for a necessary input? This depends on the indeterminacy of the price of such items; the fact that such prices are not determined on an open market with independent and competing buyers and sellers. Particularly important is the fact that, in many cases, the buyer is not in a position to know enough about what is being purchased, nor how necessary it really is for the production and marketing process. As Vaitsos has put it:

> a prospective buyer needs information about the properties of the item he intends to purchase so as to be able to make appropriate decisions. Yet in the case of technology, what is needed is information about information which could effectively be one and the same thing. Thus, the prospective buyer is confronted with a structural weakness intrinsic to his position as a purchaser, with resulting imperfections in the corresponding market operations. (Vaitsos, 1975, p. 190)

The same argument applies to management and marketing contracts. From the point of view of the TNC, an important aspect of income from these new sources is the way they diminish risk. There are many circumstances that can have an adverse effect on profits – bad weather, low demand, geological difficulties, labour unrest – so income in the form of profit is subject to considerable risk. But payments for licences, management contracts, etc. have to be made whatever the level of profits; and know-how is not subject to nationalization in the same way as physical assets. So there is considerable evidence that TNCs withdraw a surplus from the Third World, and are capable of finding ways of circumventing some of the efforts of Third World governments to retain more surplus within their countries. But does that mean that the activities of TNCs in Third World countries lead to a polarization with underdevelopment in the Third World (or periphery) and development in the First World (or centre)?

## TNCs and Development

Many economists who accept that there are costs to the operations of TNCs argue that there are also benefits; they claim that TNCs make contributions to the creation of a surplus, as well as withdrawing a good part of it, once it has been created; and that in the process of surplus creation there are 'spin-offs' that aid development, such as wages and salaries paid to Third World workers, dividends paid to Third World shareholders, foreign exchange from exports, physical assets – mines, factories, plantations – and some transfer of technology. They make the same kind of point that Marx made about British investment in colonial India that foreign investment does contribute to the development of the productive forces of Third World countries.

How valid is this argument? What kind of contributions might TNCs make? One obvious suggestion is that they are a source of finance, that they bring finance into the Third World when they set up their operations there, helping to close the gap between finance required for investment and the savings available within the Third World. However, TNCs do not necessarily *transfer* large quantities of capital *to* the Third World, even though they may *own* large quantities of capital *in* the Third World. The activities of TNCs within the Third World may, to a considerable extent, be financed from local sources within the Third World. TNCs borrow from local banks, sell shares to local shareholders and take over already established local firms. They do reinvest some of their profit within the Third World, but these reinvested earnings have often been derived from investment financed by local sources. One United Nations study estimates that, in Latin America, during the period 1957–65, US TNCs financed 83 per cent of their total investment from local sources, either from reinvested earnings (59 per cent) or local borrowing (24 per cent). In the case of the manufacturing sector, a larger proportion of finance came from local borrowing (44 per cent) than from reinvested earnings (38 per cent) (Colman and Nixson, 1978, p. 224). In 1973, the US Senate Committee on Finance reported that less than 15 per cent of the total financial needs of US-based manufacturing subsidiaries abroad originated from US sources (United States Senate Committee on Finance, 1973, p. 38).

The most important contribution that TNCs make is the provision of know-how, whether in the form of 'hardware' such as machines and components, or 'software', such as managerial and marketing skills. Not all this know-how is necessary and appropriate for the people of the Third

World. We may doubt whether the knowledge of transnational food corporations about how to produce and market dried milk for bottle feeding babies helps mothers and babies in the Third World. Lack of sanitation and clean water, lack of refrigeration, illiteracy, and low incomes, result in over-diluted and contaminated bottle feeds, with terrible effects on the health and survival of babies receiving them.

However, we must not forget that elite groups within the Third World play an important role in selecting what kind of know-how TNCs contribute to their countries, particularly in their choice of the type of goods they wish to consume. It has been argued that TNCs cannot be directly blamed for the lack of development (or the direction that development is taking) within the Third World. Their prime objective is global profit maximization and their actions are aimed at achieving this objective, not developing the host Third World country. If the technology and the products that they introduce are 'inappropriate', if their actions exacerbate regional and social inequalities, if they weaken the balance of payments position, in the last resort, it is suggested, it is up to Third World governments to pursue policies that will eliminate the sources of these problems (Colman and Nixson, 1978).

Some Third World governments have done just that, carefully regulating the role that TNCs are allowed to play in their development. For instance, the Indian government has always been cautious about foreign investment. Several industries are reserved to the public sector and closed to both private domestic and foreign investment. In other industries, foreign ownership is normally restricted to 40 per cent of a company's equity, though a higher percentage may be allowed if the venture is largely export oriented or brings with it highly desired technology. Royalties and fees paid by Indian firms are subject to close scrutiny by the authorities. The royalty allowed in a technical collaboration depends on the nature of the technology but will normally not exceed 8 per cent of the ex-factory value of production. Rather than relax their vigilance, the government of India has preferred to do without investments from big companies, like IBM, which insist on setting up wholly owned subsidiaries. TNCs play a more important role in South Korea than they do in India but, again, they are subject to careful state direction. They are discouraged in sectors where they would compete with South Korean firms, and are generally allowed in only on a joint venture basis. Wholly Korean owned enterprises account for 75 per cent of manufacturing output and 90 per cent of manufacturing employment (Barone, 1983).

So, there seem to be some reasons to doubt a simple argument that the activities of TNCs in the Third World are a barrier to development. Frequently, the relationship between the corporation and the country is very unequal; frequently the TNCs play a dominant role. But the quality of the relationship depends a great deal on the policies of Third World governments and the skills at their disposal. In the case of many of the poorer countries, it has been suggested that their problem is not too much, but too little, investment from TNCs. For, in allocating their resources, TNCs certainly obey the biblical maxim: to them that hath shall be given.

If we want to understand the barriers to development, we should look not just at transfers of surplus out of Third World countries, but also at the factors that prevent the investment in the first place.

There is certainly a correlation between high rates of growth and a high share of TNC investment in the Third World. Most of the investment in recent years has gone to the newly industrializing countries (or NICs) of Latin America and Asia. The NICs include large countries – Brazil, Mexico and India – city states like Hong Kong and Singapore, and medium-size countries like South Korea and Taiwan. With the exception of India, their industrialization over the last fifteen years has been export-oriented. They have rapidly expanded their exports of manufactures to the First World, leading to talk of a new international division of labour replacing the old international division of labour, in which Third World countries exported mining and agricultural products.

Most of the manufactures exported to the First World are labour intensive products: textiles and garments, footwear, toys, televisions, radios and watches. The labour intensive stages of production of high technology goods like semi-conductors (more familiarly known as micro-chips) are also carried out in many NICs. Some of the NICs are now competitive in the export of cars, and even of heavy industrial goods such as iron and steel and ships. South Korea's shipbuilding industry ranks in the world second only to that of Japan.

The role of the TNCs in the newly industrializing countries has been variable, both across industries and across countries. The TNCs have been very important in high technology industries like electronics. But in more traditional industries they have been far less important. Locally owned firms, especially in Taiwan, South Korea and Hong Kong, have produced most of the exports of clothing and textiles, though often operating under sub-contract to First World firms. In general, the transnationals have played a more dominant role in Latin America than in East Asia (Lall, 1981, p. 218).

## Responses to Changes in the International Division of Labour

One response from the dependency school to newly industrializing countries is that what is going on in them is not development at all. Andre Gunder Frank argues that it is not development at all because it involves 'super-exploitation' and oppression of the work-force in the export oriented industries responsible for rapid growth. He argues that export oriented industrialization in the Third World is based upon making industrial workers work harder and for lower wages than they do in the First World. It is this, he claims rather than skills or technology, that enables Third World factories to compete successfully in world markets. He cites evidence that the working day and working week have been extended in the NICs well beyond those common in the First World. In South Korea, for instance, he claims weekly working hours are twice as long as in the West, and annual working time is 50 per cent higher. He also claims that the intensity of work is higher than in comparable industries in the First World, and he points to wages that are only 10 per cent or 20 per cent of those in the First World countries. He suggests that workers can only be got to endure such onerous conditions if employers are backed up by armed police or troops. Thus, he concludes, successful integration into the new international division of labour entails oppression to keep labour sufficiently cheap and docile (Frank, 1981).

Frank's argument is no longer that integration into the international economy prevents the development of the forces of production in the Third World, and leads to stagnation. Here he argues that the growth of industry that integration into the world market fosters is 'super-exploitative' and unable to bring people in the Third World the increase in living standards that industrialization has brought to people in the First World. This argument is not accepted by all writers working within the general dependency approach. Some of them, such as the Brazilian, Fernando Cardoso, argue that in at least some NICs export oriented industrialization does not necessitate 'super-exploitation' but is compatible with 'the production of relative surplus value'. This last phrase is a Marxist term meaning, roughly, the production of a surplus through continued improvements in technology, which render profitability quite compatible with improvements in the workers' living standards, such as higher pay and a shorter working week.

Rapid capital accumulation in a particular industry usually creates a tendency for real wages to rise in that industry, either because workers have enhanced bargaining power, or because employers need to attract labour, particularly skilled labour, away from other employment. There is certainly evidence of this tendency at work in East Asia. For instance, in South Korea, real wages rose on average by 16 per cent between 1977 and 1981 (*Financial Times*, 27 April 1981). In Singapore, standards of living have risen dramatically. The percentage of households with income below the minimum subsistence requirement level fell from 30 per cent in 1973 to 8 per cent in 1982 (Kirkpatrick, 1985). Frank himself quotes evidence of rising wages from an article in the *Wall Street Journal* (20 September 1973). The article reports that labour in Hong Kong, South Korea, Taiwan and Singapore had become scarce and costly, so that the electronics transnationals were looking elsewhere for sites for new investment: mainly to Malaysia, occasionally to Indonesia.

Frank suggests that these improvements will be short-lived. He claims that export oriented industrialization is of a temporary enclave variety. When wages rise and workers become less controllable, First World firms will simply move their factories and their sub-contractors to another country. Little permanent contribution to development will be left, Frank suggests, because there are few linkages to the rest of the economy from the export oriented industries, either in terms of requiring inputs from the rest of the economy, or producing outputs for the rest of the economy, and there is little transfer of technology. Is there any evidence to support this view?

## Underdevelopment or Dependent Development?

It is true that the export industries which are sited in free production zones (sometimes called free trade zones or export processing zones) have very limited links to the rest of the economy and do not operate in such a way as to be good vehicles for the transfer of technology to the rest of the economy (UNIDO, 1980). It is true that large electronics TNCs have sought out new and cheaper locations within South East Asia, though to date they have been relocating *expansions* of capacity in cheaper areas, rather than closing down existing plant completely. In the older established locations, such as Hong Kong and Singapore, electronics transnationals have been upgrading the skill and technology content of their work, for instance including testing, as well as assembly, of micro-chips. Nevertheless, there are worries in the long-established Asian NICs about the potential for relocation to cheaper countries. South Korea is now rated as the least desirable site for new investment among the nine fastest-growing Asian nations by leading Japanese companies (*Financial Times*, 27 April 1981). There are also worries about declining markets for goods like textiles and garments due to protectionism and recession in the First World. Taking a more long-term perspective, there is also the possibility of technical innovation in labour intensive assembly processes leading to a return to production in the First World.

It is not the case that labour intensive assembly processes in the semi-conductor industry or in garments are *impossible* to automate. They were not automated in part because there were no *economic* incentives to do so. In the semi-conductor industry, the main reason for this was the rapid change in product design that made equipment obsolete very fast. In garments, the main reason was also rapid change in product design. Labour's advantage is that it is generally more *flexible* than machines. However, the flexibility of machines is increasing, not least as a result of the micro-electronics revolution, and so is the emphasis on quality control, where an automated process often has an edge.

A recent report, by Kurt Hoffman and Howard Rush of the Science Policy Research Unit, on the impact of micro-electronics on the nature of production and patterns of international trade in the clothing industry, found that radical innovations have been introduced into the design, pattern-making, and cutting stages of clothing production. But in sewing, micro-electronics as yet has had only limited impact. However, major research and development efforts on automated assembly are underway in the EEC, USA and Japan that are expected to bear fruit in the 1990s. Hoffman suggests that newly industrializing countries like South Korea, Taiwan and Hong Kong may themselves invest in the automated equipment, and maintain their competitive position. But the prospects for other Third World countries wishing to follow in the footsteps of the NICs are likely to be seriously affected by automation (Hoffman, 1985).

Computer-based automation is now being introduced in practically all stages of the production of electronic components and equipment. The most automated equipment is being introduced in First World countries (Goldstein, forthcoming). Even in the Third World, the levels of automation have been rapidly increasing, with the result that employment in electronics in the 1980s has been stagnating, in comparison with the rapid growth in the 1970s (Ernst, 1985). Countries like Singapore, Taiwan and South Korea are now shifting out of production of consumer electronics goods and components like semi-conductors, and into production of computers and peripheral equipment, such as terminals and disk drives. In future, their comparative advantage may not lie in supplying relatively cheap female labour for 'nimble-fingered' assembly operations, but in supplying relatively cheap but highly skilled computer engineers and programmers. It seems likely that the newly industrializing countries will retain their competitiveness in the electronics industry but, as with clothing, the prospects for other countries wishing to follow in the footsteps of the NICs are far less certain (Ernst, 1985).

In any case, industrial development in the NICs is not confined to free production zones, and is also not confined to labour intensive products such as semi-conductors, textiles and garments. Undue emphasis on these features leads to an underestimation of the depth and breadth of industrialization in the leading NICs. Countries such as Brazil, South Korea and India have export capacity in heavy industry, such as iron and steel, shipbuilding and machine tools, and in consumer durables, such as automobiles. Moreover, the NICs are showing an increasing capacity for innovation in production. For instance, there is now growing production of fashion clothes completely designed and made in Hong Kong. Producers have shown themselves capable of moving beyond tailoring clothes to the design and specification of Western firms, from Levi-Straus to Pierre Cardin, and to get their own designs accepted by international fashion buyers (*Financial Times*, 3 April 1981). A Taiwan research and development firm has developed the world's first personal computer with Chinese language, as well as English, capabilities (*Financial Times*, 6 June 1982). Some NICs are now appearing as competitors on international technology markets, with their local enterprises vying with the established TNCs in selling turnkey plant, consultancy services, and other types of manufacturing know-how in industries with stable technologies (Lall, 1981, p. 217).

So, there is considerable evidence that the NICs are moving beyond the stage where cheap unskilled labour working longer and harder than anywhere else is the main basis for their growth. The evidence seems to support Cardoso's view rather than Frank's: the new international division of labour does not necessarily entail 'super-exploitation' of Third World workers. However, Cardoso does not suggest that the new international division of labour means a more equal relationship between First and Third World. He describes the development of the newly industrializing countries as 'dependent development'.

Cardoso argues that technological innovation, especially in the critical capital goods industries, remains 'in the central nuclei of the transnational firms'; and that the industrialization has only been achieved at the cost of

FIGURE 29 Female worker in a Hong Kong factory (Camera Press)

massive indebtedness to the First World banks. This may be true of Cardoso's home country, Brazil, but it is not true of the Asian NICs. Recent research suggests that a significant amount of technological change is taking place in those Third World countries with a relatively long experience of manufacturing and with a broad-based capital goods sector, such as India and South Korea (Lall, 1981; Fransman and King, 1984). India has no debts to the First World banks. South Korea has very large debts, but no debt problem, because her export earnings are high enough to cover interest and amortization payments. It is quite normal for rapidly developing countries to have a high level of international debt. This is how the USA and Canada financed their development.

## Third World TNCs

There is a further factor to consider – the emergence of Third World transnationals. According to data produced by the United Nations Centre on Transnational Corporations, a pattern of cross-investment has developed in Latin America in which firms from the larger, more developed countries such a Argentina, Brazil, Chile, Mexico and Venezuela, are engaging in direct investment in each other's economies, and in the small economies of the region. The products involved are mainly consumer goods, especially electrical products, food products and metal products. In Asia, Hong Kong firms are major investors abroad within the region. Taiwanese, South Korean and Singaporean firms also invest in other Asian countries. Indian firms had, by mid-1976, 134 direct investments abroad, the largest number of them being in Malaysia. At the moment, it is difficult to quantify the value of direct investments by Third World TNCs, but it is clear that capitalist development in the NICs has reached the stage, which we noted at the beginning of the chapter, where large national firms have developed the capacity to go abroad, and are being impelled to do so by the competitive struggle. The struggle to retain or gain access to markets is a key factor propelling Third World firms to internationalize, particularly to get around the barriers to imports into developed countries from the NICs, which have been growing in strength. For instance, firms in Hong Kong, Taiwan and South Korea have invested in garment production in Sri Lanka because garment exports from these countries have reached the limits set by quotas under the Multi Fibre Agreement (which regulates international trade in textiles and garments), while exports from Sri Lanka have not yet done so.

## The Potential for Interdependence – and Inter-imperialist Rivalry

It is not only within the Third World that Third World firms are engaging in direct foreign investment. Samsung Electronics of South Korea has begun manufacturing television sets in Portugal, mostly for export to the EEC, Africa and the Middle East. Tatung, Taiwan's leading electronics group, has purchased a colour television factory at Bridgnorth in Shropshire in Britain. It also has wholly owned subsidiaries in Japan, Hong Kong, Singapore and the USA. A leading Hong Kong textile and clothing firm, Yangtzekiang Garment Manufacturing (YGM) is to start production of trousers, shirts and blouses at Knowsley, near Liverpool, in 1986. Large firms from South Korea and Taiwan have also begun investing in North America.

Here are the beginnings of cross-investment by each others' firms between the leading NICs and some First World countries. This may create the conditions, which have not hitherto existed, for a kind of interdependence between some Third World and some First World countries. For interdependence means more than links; it implies a reciprocity of obligations, especially a reciprocity of obligations to uphold the international economic order, the 'rules of the game' (both legal and political) that constitute the environment in which investment takes place. Such a reciprocity is not constructed at the political level alone. It requires reinforcement from a foundation in the international economic system. A key source of such reinforcement is cross-investment, whereby investors from *each* country have a stake in the economic order prevailing in the *other* countries, because they have assets at risk there (whether financial or productive) and have an interest in the harmonization of the various national economic orders into an international economic order. It is important to note that cross-investment by capitalist firms is not simply a matter of two-way flows of investment resources. After all, in the colonial period there was such a two-way flow between Britain and India, in the sense that here was both an inflow of investment resources from Britain to India and an outflow of investment resources from India to Britain. But the outflow from India was not the result of decisions made by Indian capitalists, but the result of decisions made by British colonialists. The kind of cross-investment significant for reciprocity is an interpenetration of capital that requires sufficient capitalist development to produce indigenous investors in *both* countries wishing to internationalize their operations by investing in the other. There is reported to be a wholly Indian owned assembly plant for machine tools in Luxembourg, and a number of private Indian enterprises are actively exploring the possibility of investing in the Irish Republic.

The experience of the Asian NICs cannot be easily fitted into the dependency perspective. This conclusion has been reached by researchers working in the framework of radical political economy (Browett, 1985; Bernstein, 1982b; Hamilton, 1983). This does not mean we have to agree with Warren's view, that internal, not external factors, are the main barrier to development (Warren, 1980). Nor do we have to agree with the view that the Third World would be better off moving towards free trade and unrestricted foreign investment, which many neo-Classical economists suggest. Rather, it means coming to the conclusion that though international links between First World and Third World may operate very unevenly, and distribute their benefits very unequally, they do not necessarily prevent development. Detailed empirical research is required to understand the relation between development and international trade and investment in particular countries and in particular periods of time. It is the *quality* of the links that is vital.

Policy in Third World countries has to focus not on how to withdraw from the international economy, but on the best way to restructure the necessary links with the international economy so as to maximize the development benefits. The best policy cannot be prescribed abstractly, whether on the basis of dependency theory or neo-Classical economic theory. It can only be derived for particular circumstances.

In case this conclusion should be thought too optimistic, it should be added that it seems unlikely that other, less developed, Third World countries will easily be able to emulate the success of the NICs, regardless of the policies they adopt (Cline, 1982). This is because of changes in the operation of the international economy in the 1980s compared with the 1960s and 1970s. Growth is much slower; protectionist barriers to exports are on the increase; the net flow of international investment funds is from the Third World to the First World, as payments of interest, amortization, profits and dividends continue to flow out of the Third World, while new inflows have slowed to a trickle. There is high unemployment in the First World; fears for the stability of the international banking system; talk of a crisis in the international economy.

The international economy does not adapt smoothly to changes in the underlying relations of production. Changes in the productivity of resources and profitability of capital accumulation in different parts of the First World led to a break down of the post-war system of fixed exchange rates and reductions in trade barriers at the beginning of the 1970s. The dominant economic position of the USA was challenged by the strength of the West German and, especially, the Japanese economies. The General Agreement on Trade and Tariffs (GATT) was breached as 'voluntary' quotas were imposed in USA and Western Europe on imports from Japan and the Multi Fibre Agreement restricted imports from the Third World. In the second half of the 1970s, the response to the rise of the Organization of Petroleum Exporting Countries (OPEC) and the four-fold increase in the price of oil led to recession as First World countries cut back on demand for other goods. The recycling of the petro-dollars through the international banking system appeared to work smoothly but by 1982 it was apparent that this had simply built up a debt problem in Latin America and Africa. The possibility of default by a major debtor or a run on a major lending bank was no longer a remote possibility (Lever and Hulme, 1985). The international 'rules of the game' (both political and legal) that had underpinned the post-war boom in the First World countries began to look rather precarious. In the ultra-cautious words of the World Bank's Development Report:

> There are, more over, new reasons for concern about the protectionist trends emerging in industrial countries. The costs of such policies to industrial countries' consumers and developing countries' exports are well documented. The recent debt service problems have added a new dimension to these concerns ... Servicing of the resulting foreign debt would be impeded seriously if increased protection in industrial countries were to deny developing countries access to industrial countries' markets. This in turn would jeopardize the effective functioning of the financial system. (World Bank, 1985, p. 42)

But protectionist pressures in the First World show no signs of abating. The USA is likely to demand a tightening up of the next Multi Fibre Agreement. The USA and Japan are discussing an international cartel to regulate international trade in semi-conductors.

Continued growth in the NICs, and the attempts of other Third World countries such as Malaysia to join their ranks, will intensify the disruptive pressures in the international economy. The more successful Third World countries are in challenging patterns of trade and foreign investment that kept them dependent in the past, the greater the threat of crisis in the international economy. The ways in which Third World countries are integrated into the international economy may not necessarily impose underdevelopment on all of them: given favourable combinations of internal and external social and economic forces, a process of development can get underway, as it did in Japan. But the international economic system as currently constituted may be unable to withstand the shock. Development in the Third World is more likely to intensify the rivalry between capitalist countries than to lead to a harmonious interdependence. This is a dimension of patterns of dominance in the world economy which is present in Marxist theories of imperialism (Elson, 1984) but which dependency theory has tended to ignore. The interdependence of capitalist countries is a dialectic of cooperation and conflict, punctuated by crisis, requiring for its stability the hegemony of a dominant power: in short, a system of imperialism. Escape from dependency does not mean escape from imperialism.

CHAPTER FOURTEEN

# Divisions of Labour or Labour Divided?

## International Relocation of Industry

In this chapter we shall look at the implications for the Third World of recent changes in the world economy. Rapid industrialization in some Third World countries in the 1960s and 1970s occurred at the same time as the phrase 'deindustrialization' was coined to describe the widespread closure of old industrial plants and the stagnant and sometimes falling industrial production in some advanced countries, particularly Britain and the USA. At the same time, there has been significant relocation of industrial production processes to low-wage countries. As a result, some observers believe that a new international division of labour is being created, in which labour intensive work is moving from some advanced industrial economies to cheap labour locations. These cheap labour economies attract capital investment in industries producing goods for export – export oriented industrialization. In certain sectors, like garments and electronic assembly, this is taking place at a time when there is a growing surplus of world production capacity, and it is argued that this part of a conscious strategy by transnationals to reassert control over labour costs and over their employees. It is alleged that production in cheap labour economies substitutes for local production in First World countries. In this chapter, we shall be investigating three issues: (i) the extent of this 'new' international division of labour; (ii) its characteristics and implications for both Third World and First World economies; and (iii) whether it is a permanent change in the global economy.

### Industrialization and Deindustrialization

Is there a new international division of labour? Is relocation of manufacturing actually taking place? To attempt an answer, we shall summarize the information on tendencies in industrialization in the First World and Third World and the evidence for a link between them.

#### *Third World industrialization*

The data in chapter 10 showed that Third World countries are industrializing at a higher rate than First World countries. Indeed, between 1963 and 1973 manufacturing in Developing Countries grew 2.5 per cent over the

TABLE 25 Annual growth rates in manufacturing and industry more generally, 1965–83

| | *Industry* | | *Manufacturing* | |
|---|---|---|---|---|
| | *1965–73* | *1973–83* | *1965–73* | *1973–83* |
| South Korea | 18.4 | 11.2 | 21.1 | 11.8 |
| Hong Kong | 8.4 | 8.2 | na | na |
| Singapore | 17.6 | 8.5 | 19.5 | 7.9 |
| Mexico | 8.6 | 6.2 | 9.9 | 5.5 |
| Brazil | 11.0 | 4.7 | 11.2 | 4.2 |

*Note*: na = not available.
*Source*: World Bank (1985).

rate in developed market economies (UNIDO, 1983, table 14). This gap grew to 3.4 per cent between 1973 and 1980. Even during the heavily depressed years 1980–2 the difference was 1.7 per cent per annum (that is a growth of 0.7 per cent per annum compared with a decline of 1 per cent).

The aggregated data disguise even greater differences. For example, table 25 shows five countries with much higher than average industrial growth rates and which figure in most lists of newly industrializing countries (NICs). The NICs of Asia – South Korea, Taiwan, Hong Kong and Singapore (the so-called gang of four) – have been particularly singled out as posing a threat to the international competitiveness of certain industries in advanced countries. The NICs' international competitiveness is much greater than that of the vast majority of Third World countries. For example, the nine NICs in figure 30 were responsible by 1976 for 77 per cent of Third World manufactured exports.

### *Export orientation and export processing*

Those who postulate a link between Third World growth and relative decline of First World industry point to the relocation of production for First World markets from the First to the Third World.

The early industrialization strategies of many Third World countries revolved around import substitution (see chapter 10) but, from the late 1960s, there has been an increasing tendency towards export oriented industrialization (EOI). In particular, EOI is directed to the First World where large markets already exist. EOI policies have been advocated by international agencies like the United Nations Industrial Development Organization (UNIDO) and the World Bank, as well as interested groups in Third World countries. The argument is that, by establishing or attracting export oriented industries and by competing in international markets, Third World countries are able to generate employment and acquire experience of up-to-date methods of work organization and production technology,

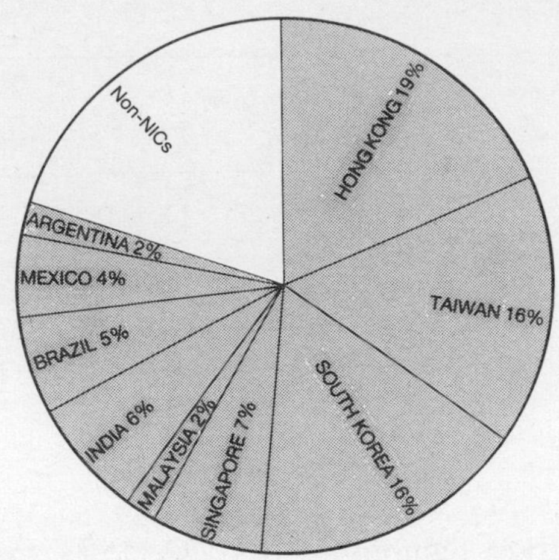


FIGURE 30 NIC's share of Third World exports 1976 (by value)

of suitable efficient methods of work and quality control, and of contemporary design and marketing. This and the associated broadening of the skill and experience of the work-force are held to make a significant contribution to further industrialization.

How do countries pursue an EOI policy? In part, governments have sought to develop the export potential and capacities of industries that have already been established, by subsidies and other forms of incentive. In addition, established Third World firms may increase exports by producing orders on a sub-contracting basis for trading and manufacturing firms based in the First World. Third World countries have also sought to develop their exporting potential by attracting new investment by firms based in the First World, many of them the transnational corporations (TNCs) discussed in general terms in chapter 13.

Even allowing for unevenness of industrial growth between Third World countries, there is no doubt that some have used a variety of methods to increase production rapidly and to do so they have increased their exports to advanced countries, clearly changing at least to some extent, the trade relationship between some Third World and First World countries. Some Third World countries have also been successful in linking to other Third World economies through attracting foreign investment. Kaplinsky argues that much export expansion was caused by the location decisions of TNCs: 'In South Korea the share of transnational corporations in production in the mid 1970s was 11 per cent but they accounted for 28 per cent of exports; in Singapore the respective ratios were 30 per cent and 70 per cent' (Kaplinsky, 1984, p. 153).

Some early attempts at attracting new industry utilized the concept of a free port or free zone. In such areas – Singapore and Hong Kong are two examples of free ports – goods could be brought in for storage, grading, grouping and part processing for subsequent re-export, all without payment of export or import dues or other taxes. Free ports were often linked to the export of primary products: Singapore, for example, originally developed around the trade in products from Malaya. To attract a broader base of manufacturing capacity, it then became necessary to offer a wider range of incentives to attract inward investment, the scale of incentives being driven upwards by competition between countries. In essence the requirements are:

1 the provision of infrastructure such as docks, airports, roads of high standard and reliable power resources;
2 the provision of suitable industrial sites and buildings;
3 the availability of financial incentives such as freedom from local taxation and export and import tariffs for an agreed period, and possibly some element of direct subsidy.

Additionally, a fundamental factor is abundant supplies of compliant and low-cost labour, largely unhampered by protective legislation relating to working conditions, safety and health, or by union organization.

These conditions are essentially those also needed for world market factories whose production is almost totally, if not exclusively, concerned with exporting. In some countries, these factories are often located on special industrial estates. In others, they may be grouped in free trade zones (FTZs) or export processing zones (EPZs), which are sometimes carefully segregated from other areas in the countries in which they are located.

> The 'free trade zone' is like a country within a country. Cut off by barbed wire or concrete walls from the rest of the country and guarded in some cases by 'zone police', the zone is 'an enclave in terms of customs-territorial aspects and possibly other aspects such as total or partial exemption from laws and decrees of the country concerned' as a survey on FTZs for the Asian Productivity Organization (APO) [1975] describes. The zone has its own authority to which the central government functions are largely relegated ... Workers employed in the zone are often subject to special regulations (prohibition of labour disputes, for instance), have to show special passes to enter it and must often undergo body checks when they finish a day's toil. This latter is to prevent 'smuggling' of the zone's products into the workers' own country. (Takeo, 1977, p. 1)

The case in favour of establishing EPZs has been summarized by Frobel et al. (1980, p. 366). EPZs are said to provide:

1 the creation of new jobs and consequent elimination of unemployment;
2 the training of a skilled industrial work-force and access to modern technology;
3 access to increased foreign exchange receipts and a wider scope within which developing countries can conduct their foreign trade policies.

Attempts to attract export oriented investment have been particularly successful in four countries in Asia – Taiwan, South Korea, Hong Kong and Singapore. This has triggered the setting up of FTZs or EPZs in other Third World countries. There is considerable competition between countries to attract firms to these zones, visually evident in the related advertisement brochures, but also expressed through competing tax concessions and other incentives.

How significant are the EPZs? EPZs are not the main source of export production. For example, in Hong Kong there are 59,000 people working in the seven industrial estates. But much of the rest of the Hong Kong labour force of two million is also involved in export manufacturing activity. UNIDO estimated that, overall, 645,000 were employed within EPZs in 1978 and one million in 1980 (UNIDO, 1980b, quoted in Elson, 1982).

However, the importance of EPZs cannot be measured solely in terms of the volume or value of output, or of the growth in the numbers employed. They are important as indicators (or symbols) of an approach to the problems of Third World industrialization. Furthermore, labour conditions, patterns of economic activity, and organization in the zones, have a wider influence on forms of organization and employment conditions elsewhere. The very existence of competition from countries in which labour costs are low, and in which other working conditions are below standards in industrialized countries, can be exploited to pull down labour costs in the industrialized countries. This is particularly potent when there is surplus productive capacity in many industrialized countries. Thus, the significance of EPZs is greater than their immediate level of activity, and has been used to support the argument that industrial growth in the Third World has been at least partially at the expense of growth in the First World. In its most extreme form, the argument implies a 'zero sum' game that Third World industrialization will liquidate First World manufacturing.

### *First World 'deindustrialization'?*

Against the background of economic depression since the early 1970s, the growth of the NICs has been contrasted with the lower growth in many First World countries. Overall industrial growth in industrial market economies dropped from 5.1 per cent per annum between 1965 and 1973 to 2.3 per cent in 1973 and 1 per cent in 1980–2. This includes the industrial performance of Japan, with growth rates of 13.5 per cent between 1965 and 1973 and 5.5 per cent between 1973 and 1983. Britain's industrial decline is particularly significant in manufacturing, which fell in volume by 8.7 per cent between 1979 and 1983 (World Bank, 1985).

Some of this decline has been blamed on imports from Third World countries. Table 26 illustrates increases in the proportion of manufactured imports from the Third World between 1962 and 1978. To put these data into perspective, it is important to note that, even in the USA, with the highest import penetration, imports from non-Third World countries still accounted for almost three-quarters of all imports. In clothing and shoes, for example, Italy is a major exporter to the rest of Europe and the world but, in the EEC, is not subject to quotas as are the NICs.

TABLE 26 Percentage of imports of manufactures coming from Third World countries

| | *1962* | *1970* | *1975* | *1978* |
|---|---|---|---|---|
| All industrial countries | 5.3 | 6.8 | 10.0 | 13.1 |
| Europe | 4.2 | 4.8 | 7.5 | 9.6 |
| West Germany | 4.6 | 6.3 | 10.8 | 12.9 |
| Japan | 5.9 | 11.4 | 21.4 | 25.1 |
| USA | 12.3 | 14.7 | 21.0 | 26.7 |

*Source*: World Bank (1982), cited in Kaplinsky (1984), p. 152.

Cable (1983, pp. 14–15) has estimated that, for Britain in 1978, Third World imports account for the loss of about 200,000 manufacturing jobs. However, he also noted that Britain's manufacturing exports to the Third World accounted for about 650,000 jobs. First World manufacturing is still absolutely predominant and continues to have a strong place in world capitalism. Transnational corporations are in the middle of a hectic restructuring of their productive capital in the First World and not simply liquidating or protecting it.

## *First World protectionism*

One reaction to manufacturing decline has been to blame 'low labour cost imports' and to impose quotas and protective barriers particularly against imports from Third World countries. These are drafted so as to appear to be not exclusively directed towards Third World importers, but in practice they largely are. From the 1950s, the USA has gradually introduced restrictions against imports of clothing and textiles, and these have primarily affected Third World exporters. The restrictions were extended in 1972 and, in 1977, the EEC countries joined the protective arrangements against Third World clothing and textile exports in the Multi Fibre Arrangement. There is pressure to extend protective measures to other industries and it is sometimes suggested that there is a 'new protectionism', that will increasingly restrict trade. Third World countries are particularly vulnerable. Their exports are already being limited by such means as 'voluntary' quotas, in which a powerful importing nation establishes quotas by agreement, to be 'voluntarily' observed by the exporting nation.

Since 1980, protectionist pressures have generally grown stronger, with 'voluntary' agreements against Japanese imports to the USA and Europe, against European imports to the USA, and against steel from NICs and industrialized countries to the USA. Thus, it is not just that NICs are seen as a threat by governments and workers in the First World; they are often singled out as the main kind of 'unfair' competition. Is this new protectionism simply paranoid or do these Third World exporting industries constitute a threat to First World economies?

## A New International Division of Labour?

The previous section suggests that there has been a shift in the international division of labour as work in labour intensive production is moved to the Third World. What changes in the new international division of labour can be observed?

We shall, firstly, consider the kind of production processes being relocated, and why; then look at the changes in investment and marketing patterns, as corporations and bankers influence world patterns of investment. These two ways of investigating the changes relate to two kinds of explanation of the changes in the international division of labour (Jenkins, 1984, Elson, 1986). One kind of explanation emphasizes those factors allowing *international fragmentation* of production processes, i.e. relocation only of those processes needing cheap unskilled labour, that leads to a new international division of labour based on super-exploitation and immiseration of Third World workers. The other explanation sees the changes governed more by a more general *internationalization* not only at the level of fragmentation of production, but also an internationalization of investment and marketing. In chapter 13 it was argued that the latter can lead to technical change in Third World production allowing increased wages and better conditions and a broader and more diverse industrialization process.

### *Fragmentation of production*

Industrial production processes with an export orientation located in the Third World are concentrated in certain sectors of industry, principally clothing, textiles, leather and shoes, and electrical equipment, which make up almost three-quarters of First World manufactured imports from the Third World (see table 27). This average conceals even greater concentrations in some products, making protectionist pressures much greater. For example, in the EEC in 1978, imports from Third World countries accounted for 49 per cent of the market for men's shirts and 42 per cent of that for women's blouses (Keesing and Wolf, 1981).

Apart from blouses and shirts, there is very significant production of electronic watches, radios, TV sets, toys, electrical and electronic components, footwear, car components, basic metals and chemicals, and basic engineering goods. The range is diverse, involving complex and simple products and processes, labour and capital intensive industries, growing industries and declining ones. What factors can explain a superficially random assortment of production processes? One answer can be found by looking more closely at the types of product. In some cases, certainly, integrated industrial processes have developed, from the processing of raw materials through to the production of comprehensive product ranges, often as a consequence of import substitution policies. The textile and clothing industries provide good examples, as in India. In other cases, such as the production of steel and steel products, in South Korea, Taiwan and

TABLE 27 First World countries manufactured imports from Third World countries by sector, 1970–8

| | *Value (US$ million)* | | | *Rank order by value (N = 15)* |
|---|---|---|---|---|
| | *1970* | *1978* | *Annual growth (%) 1970–1978* | *1978* |
| Major traditional manufactures | | | | |
| Semi-finished textiles | 1,815 | 9,610 | 5.3 | 1 |
| Leather | 183 | 950 | 5.2 | 9 |
| Clothing | 1,181 | 9,502 | 8.1 | 2 |
| Shoes | 151 | 2,033 | 13.5 | 7 |
| Major higher-technology manufactures | | | | |
| Chemicals | 588 | 2,282 | 3.9 | 5 |
| Metals and metal products | 319 | 2,223 | 7.0 | 6 |
| Machinery except electrical and business | 81 | 1,136 | 14.0 | 8 |
| (of which farm machinery) | 2 | 29 | 14.5 | 15 |
| Electrical machinery | 372 | 4,463 | 12.0 | 3 |
| Business machines | 81 | 600 | 7.4 | 12 |
| Scientific instruments | 24 | 359 | 15.0 | 13 |
| Motor vehicles | 23 | 603 | 26.2 | 11 |
| Aircraft | 18 | 737 | 40.9 | 10 |
| Shipbuilding | 40 | 355 | 8.9 | 14 |
| Consumer electronics | 214 | 2,391 | 11.2 | 4 |
| Other manufactures | 401 | 2,922 | 7.3 | |
| Total major traditional manufactures | 3,330 | 22,095 | 6.6 | |
| Total major higher-technology manufactures | 1,762 | 15,178 | 8.6 | |
| All | 5,493 | 40,195 | 7.3 | |

*Source*: Kaplinsky (1982).

the Philippines, export oriented policies have resulted in the development of comprehensive manufacturing processes. But most products are produced by assembling different components.

Thus, a mix of complete manufacturing processes and of stages within manufacturing processes is found in Third World export production. These have the following factors in common.

1 They are predominantly *labour intensive*. While capital intensive and 'high technology' industries are among those attracted by export oriented policies, it is often only the labour intensive parts that are located in the

Third World. In such industries, the total production process may be international, sometimes involving complex transfers of raw materials, semi-processed materials, components, part-finished items and assembled products between locations. This may be carried out within a single TNC or by sub-contracting work out.

2 They use *'unskilled' or 'semi-skilled' labour* (or rather, work which has traditionally been classified as such in the West; see chapter 13). For example, Sharpston (1975, p. 100) suggests that, while there are differences between countries, sub-contracted work

> tends to be intensive in [the] use of unskilled or semi-skilled labour, but not intensive in [the] use of skilled labour or professional manpower [sic]. Manual dexterity of a high order may be required but the typical international sub-contracting job is one which can be learned in roughly six weeks, perhaps from the base of traditional skills. Thus in Morocco, in six weeks, girls (who may not be literate) are taught the assembly of memory planes for computers – this is virtually darning with copper wire, and sewing is a traditional Moroccan skill.

3 They are *carried out by women workers*. Elson (1982, p. 11), drawing on work by UNIDO (1980b), has pointed out that in EPZs over 70 per cent of the employees are women and suggests that 'The intensity of female employment in an industry in a developed country is usually a strong predictor of this industry's propensity to relocate'.

But how much of this industrial production is the result of the relocation of production formerly carried out in the First World? Although it is impossible to quantify exactly the extent of relocation, we can say that, particularly where labour costs form a high percentage of the costs of component production, manufacture is prone to relocation to low-wage areas. In other production systems, it is possible to separate stages of the production process. For example, silicon chips have mainly been manufactured in the USA and Japan, but much of their subsequent assembly to semi-conductors and integration on circuit boards, and final assembly in calculators and other products, is located in the Third World (see figure 31). Frobel et al. (1980) found similar examples in the textile and garment industry of weaving and cutting in West Germany followed by sewing-up in Morocco, Tunisia and other southern Mediterranean countries.

Frobel has summarized these developments in characterizing the new international division of labour thus:

> (i) the development of a world wide reservoir of potential labour power;
> (ii) the development of the labour process in manufacturing which has led to the decomposition of production processes into elementary units and the deskilling of the labour force; and
> (iii) the development of the forces of production in the fields of transport and communications which has made industry less tied to specific locations. (Jenkins, 1984, p. 29)

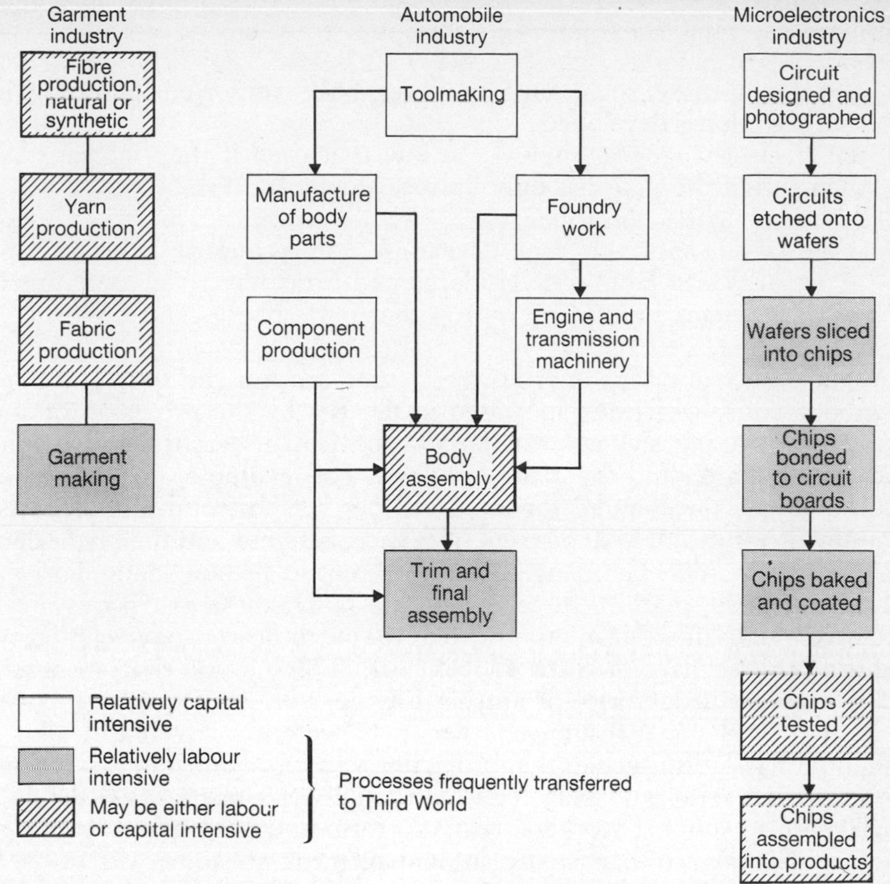


FIGURE 31 Production processes in three industries

It is these preconditions, then, that are held to account for a new kind of comparative advantage in some industrial sectors in certain Third World countries, based on the fragmentation of production processes.

Let us look in a little more detail at some of the factors associated with the new international division of labour, particularly those of cheap labour supplies and the nature of women's work.

*Labour costs, wages, and salaries* Although relocation cannot be explained only by cheap labour (the importance of financial incentives offered by Third World countries was noted earlier), cheap labour costs are, nevertheless, very significant. Surveys of comparative wage levels in industrialized countries (ICs) and NICs show wages in NICs to be much lower, often between 10 and 15 per cent of those for comparable work in the ICs with higher wages, such as West Germany, the USA and France. There is always a possibility that labour shortages may, in turn, develop in the Third World but it is argued that four factors limited any danger of this:

1 some countries, such as Singapore, have imported labour where shortages have developed;
2 the level of wages is, anyway, so low that even if they increase faster than in ICs the gap will only narrow slowly;
3 labour is tightly controlled;
4 while labour shortages may develop in some countries, the total pool of Third World labour is very large and firms have overcome this and other problems by moving on to other parts of the Third World.

While wages are very low, however, they are not the only component in labour costs, which are increased in the ICs by the provision of social insurance covering sickness, maternity, accident and retirement incomes, and health care, and by paid holidays. For example, in 1977, these additional costs accounted for about 47 per cent of total labour costs in manufacturing in Italy, 40 per cent in France, Belgium and the Netherlands, 37 per cent in West Germany and 20 per cent in Britain (de la Torre and Bacchetta, 1980, p. 102). In general in the NICs, these provisions are less extensive and, of course, are related to much lower pay, significantly reducing this element of costs. Frobel et al. (1980) found that, in practice, many workers in factories producing for the world market were covered only by limited social insurance schemes or were not covered at all.

Labour legislation such as that protecting workers against unfair dismissal also increases costs and may reduce an employer's operational flexibility. Legislation to support workers' rights to form and join unions, to bargain and, in Europe, to participate in management to some extent is less extensive, not enforced or non-existent in some NICs, providing a further element in competition between countries.

Possibly of even greater importance for labour costs and operational flexibility is safety and health legislation, the coverage and effectiveness of which have also been progressively extended. For example, such legislation may limit maximum working hours, impose limits on the weight of items to be lifted by hand, prohibit night working by women, prohibit the employment of children, limit noise levels and control the use of toxic or other dangerous materials. While this establishes some protection for workers, it has corresponding adverse implications for employers in terms of labour costs and operational flexibility. Some products or processes may be threatened: asbestos is perhaps the best current example.

Conventions and recommendations of the International Labour Office (ILO) attempt to establish international minimum standards, but compliance with them is not mandatory and standards are often below ILO levels, even in Britain. Standards may not be enforced but, even where they are, there are often provisions for exemptions, which are particularly relevant to world market factories competing for employers' interest. In South Korea, for example:

> Working hours for women are set at seven per day, but, if approved by the Ministry of Health and Social Affairs, even young workers, aged 13–18, are allowed to work up to nine hours per day. Overtime work for men is unregulated; for women to work the night shift is contrary to international standards but it is made possible by allowing for 'exceptions' to the laws. While giving the external appearance of protecting the life, welfare and rights of workers, this sort of Labour Standards Law, in practice, provides a legalistic basis for gross exploitation. (Kei, 1977, pp. 69–70)

There are implications for the jobs of workers in ICs and for those in NICs. The British TUC, for example, has expressed concern about:

> The growing tendency for trade in dangerous substances or in products produced by dangerous methods. As standards of occupational health and safety are improved in some countries, there is evidence that production and thus employment has shifted to countries without adequate safety standards. For instance, following new standards for the US asbestos industry, imports from Mexico and Taiwan where asbestos is manufactured in conditions known to be lethal, have virtually eliminated the US industry. Unless trade regulations are altered, preferably under the GATT [General Agreement on Tariffs and Trade], there is a danger that a new form of international competition in inferior health and safety standards will develop. (Trades Union Congress, 1978, p. 35)

*Labour availability and flexibility* Apart from lower cost, one of the advantages for employers is the greater mobility and flexibility of Third World work-forces, which come close to meeting 'ideal' requirements. Labour is not only easy to recruit but can more readily be laid-off or discarded; there are fewer pressures to retain workers arbitrarily categorized as 'less efficient' such as those over, say, twenty-five or thirty or whose health has deteriorated from arduous working conditions. Workers are more easily controlled and can more easily be switched between jobs. They are likely to be available for more hours per day, more days per week and more weeks per year than workers in the ICs with their longer holidays, sick pay, etc. They may be more ready to undertake tasks regarded as hazardous or undesirable in the ICs.

*Political security and stability* Keeping labour costs down has often been regarded by investing companies as associated with political stability. The stability of the controlling regime and its apparent ability to ensure that the question of social ownership (or 'appropriation') does not become an actively contested issue, is fundamental. What sort of factors – such as types of political system and government policies – are likely to convince potential investing firms of this? Is one type of governmental and political system likely to be more amenable than others to investing firms? One of the criticisms of the way in which much relocation is accomplished is that it contributes to strong pressures for certain types of economic and social policy: if Third World governments do not follow 'appropriate' policies, then inward investment is less likely. One manifestation of this is said to be the concentration of export oriented investment in countries such as Singapore, Hong Kong, Taiwan, South Korea, the Philippines and Thailand, which remain highly dependent upon Western countries for military and other forms of support.

*Control over unions* The inherent pressure to adopt certain types of economic and social policies may also be reflected in policies towards worker organization. The package offered to potential investors in export processing can include restrictions that aim to prevent worker organization completely or permit trade union organization only on lines that support rather than challenge state and managerial authority; that limit the legitimate areas of bargaining; and that control or prevent industrial action. Thus '(a) Singapore offers a strike holiday to multinational corporations for a number of years; (b) countries such as Singapore, Malaysia and Indonesia advertise their repressive labour legislation [Barnet and Muller, 1974, pp. 30, 312]; (c) in South Korea a special labour law rules out industrial disputes with foreign firms. [See Yang, 1972, p. 264]' (Nayyar, 1978, p. 77).

Clearly, then, the comparative advantage gained has developed partially from cheap wages, but also from a range of other related factors.

*Women's work* The implications for labour seem clear-cut but no more so than relocated work aimed at women. There is no obvious reason why so much relocated work is undertaken by women workers. Since it is not only women's wages that are very low in Third World countries, and since there is an abundance of male workers available as well as women, why is there not a more even balance of male and female workers, or even the predominance of male workers found in manufacturing in the ICs?

One answer might be that in the industries or parts of industries most affected by relocation, women workers tend to form a large part, sometimes a predominant part, of the work-force in the ICs: for example, in clothing and much electrical assembly. But there is no inherent reason why jobs in these industries should not be carried out by men, so why when these jobs are moved to the Third World are they still undertaken by women, possibly to a greater extent than in the ICs?

To what extent are gender roles 'relocated' together with jobs? Does this explain the predominance of women's employment in export production? To answer this, it is worth looking at the possible reasons for segregation of work by gender in the ICs, at what employers are seeking in recruiting workers in relocated industries and at the influence of cultural and other factors within the Third World.

There is no single or generally acceptable explanation. At one level, there is an emphasis on the 'family role' of women, particularly in child-bearing and child-rearing, as 'requiring' work involvement that is essentially short-term and interruptable, thus 'explaining' why women are concentrated in lower status and lower skilled occupations. But this is hardly a satisfactory explanation on any level. It does not explain women's concentration within only some low-status occupations. Nor does it explain the experience of women without children or other family 'responsibilities'. It raises other questions, since the extent to which child-bearing and rearing affect work experience is not a 'given' unalterable factor but a reflection of social organization and choice. Why are societies organized in ways that create 'problems' of child-rearing when these are avoidable through day care and other provisions? In a different way, patterns of family organization and the role of women within these may contribute to the supposed characteristics of women workers that employers claim to prefer. From Elson and Pearson (1981), these can be seen as important in four ways.

1 There may be family pressure on daughters in Third World countries to work to improve levels of family income, thus increasing the available work-force.

2 Within the family, daughters may be taught skills such as sewing and needlework that can be readily extended into similar industrial work because they 'already have the manual dexterity and capacity for spatial assessment required' (Elson and Pearson, 1981, p. 93). These skills can also be adapted with limited training or 'on the job' learning to other types of work.

3 The subordination of women within the patriarchal family also contributes to a 'docility' and acceptance of (male) authority, which is desirable for employers and is apparently in contrast to the attitudes of many male Third World workers. (However, Elson and Pearson, 1981, suggest that this docility is more apparent than real.)

4 Finally, in both ICs and Third World countries, marriage and child-bearing within the prevailing patterns of family organization do affect women's presence in the labour force in a number of ways that are beneficial to employers. For example, women are more likely to have to accept work outside the regular patterns of employment, such as temporary work, part-time work, or 'out-work' undertaken in the home at very low rates of reward. Women are more likely to have to leave jobs, 'voluntarily' or otherwise, providing a further element of flexibility for employers. The presence of women in marginal jobs, and the pressures on them to leave and to re-enter, illustrate their reserve army role as low-paid labour to be discarded or drawn into new jobs as economic or market conditions require. This reserve army role can be seen as partly explaining the disadvantaged status of women in work.

Other explanations of women's occupational concentration emphasize supposedly innate 'feminine characteristics', which make them more suited to endure some of the adverse consequences of the development of technology, its application in production and consequent impact on the social extending division of labur. For example, during the 'restructuring' of industry in North America and Western Europe in the 1930s depression, many women were employed in new consumer goods industries:

> A report to the ILO in 1936 went so far as to argue that the employment of women in these jobs was a 'technical necessity ... 'their delicacy of touch is indispensable for a large number of tasks in which most men would be completely incapable or deplorably inferior'. Women's manual dexterity and quickness of eye, their delicacy and lightness of touch, made them cleaner, neater and quicker at noticing defects, sewing up bags, assembling and packaging goods and mending machines ... Feminity is apparently a special qualification for repetitive, sedentary, monotonous occupations'. (Alexander, 1980, p. 23)

Similarly, in the 'restructuring' of the 1980s, Elson and Pearson (1981) note (as quoted in chapter 12) that the answers that companies give when asked why they employ women, as well as the statements made by governments trying to attract world market factories, show that there is a widespread belief that it is a 'natural' differentiation, produced by innate capacities and personality traits of women and men. A good example is the following passage in a Malaysian investment brochure, designed to attract foreign firms: 'The manual dexterity of the oriental female is famous the world over. Her hands are small and she works fast with extreme care. Who, therefore, could be better qualified *by nature and inheritance* to contribute to the efficiency of a bench-assembly production line than the oriental girl' (Elson and Pearson, 1981, p. 93).

There often appears to be an acceptance of such characteristics almost as biological 'givens', the consequence of physical inheritance. Yet differences in categorizations of men's and women's work vary, both between societies, as we have seen, and within societies over time, as economic and other contingencies require the shifting of gender-based divisions of work, most notably in wartime. The artificiality of such distinctions should, thus, be emphasized, without denying differences in both the attitudes and skills that are brought to work. However, these can be seen as socially derived, the consequence of very powerful pressures evident within the family, within educational systems, in religious beliefs, and so on, that push children into very different roles and attitudes according to gender.

Where relocation to the Third World is concerned, work is moved from societies in which it has been given classification and status by gender to countries in which there are parallel patterns of male domination, so that factors within both the sending and receiving societies perpetuate the segregation. The advantages for employers of an even lower-cost and more compliant segment of the work-force remain as strong as in industrialized countries, and patterns of male domination in Third World societies do not easily allow any questioning of it. As was argued in chapter 13, such gender differences allow women's work to be characterized as unskilled or semi-skilled even when women are trained and experienced as in sewing: 'skilled work is work that women don't do' (Phillips and Taylor, 1980, p. 86).

To summarize, the fragmentation argument is based on the availability of cheap docile labour in the Third World and the increasing possibilities for

FIGURE 32 Female clothing workers in Taiwan

segmentation of production allowing relocation of jobs classified as semi-skilled or unskilled. There is a new international division of labour where 'commodity production is being increasingly sub-divided into fragments which can be assigned to whichever part of the world can provide the most profitable combination of labour and capital' (Frobel et al., 1980, p. 14).

### *Internationalization of capital*

It is true that cheap labour and associated costs are central causative factors in the competition between firms that has led to relocation. But they cannot account completely for such changes. For one thing, low wages can only be turned to advantage if output is sufficiently high to keep *unit labour costs* relatively lower in the Third World country than in other countries. (Unit labour cost means the labour cost per unit of output.) If output per unit of labour can be made higher in any Third World firm, then relocation becomes a profitable possibility. Low wages can extend the viability of earlier generations of labour intensive technology, say by exporting second-hand plant to new locations. Third World labour, if less experienced, might produce less per hour with less sophisticated equipment but, the combination of lower labour costs and longer working hours can still result in more output for a given labour cost.

However, it seems that, in many instances, output of comparable products takes place in similar conditions. Evidence (Frobel et al., 1980 and Sharpston, 1975) indicates that productivity in NICs is comparable in industries where it is possible to compare types of work. Sharpston suggests that labour productivity in NICs is increasing rapidly as work experience grows and that it may sometimes be better than in industrialized countries, partly because of less absenteeism and labour turnover. For firms located in ICs in sectors where profitability or production is declining – often in labour intensive areas such as textiles – the attractions of moving to areas of low-cost labour are obvious.

However, productivity can be increased *both* by intensifying work (for example requiring people to work faster) *and* by investment in improving the means of production (for example buying more efficient and faster machinery). Although the contribution of intensified effort has been significant, recent changes in NICs have at least partially involved the use of newer industrial technologies.

Jenkins (1984) argues that a more complex analysis of the new international division of labour is needed than that based on mono-causal cheap labour explanations. If cheap labour was the sole explanation, then more relocation would have taken place. Imports of manufactures from the Third World still account for less than 2 per cent of total consumption in North America, Europe and Japan. In the sectors where this is higher (e.g. 11 per cent in clothing), he argues that this arises not from any 'natural' need for relocation but from specific conditions of capitalist development through 'the production of relative surplus value' (see Elson, chapter 13, p. 408), given major obstacles to increasing mechanization with existing technologies in the First World countries. Specifically in clothing, technical change has been extremely slow until very recently, and is now becoming much more significant.

In these circumstances where relative surplus value rather than absolute surplus value is the basis of capital accumulation: 'Relocation can be seen as a specific response which arises in circumstances when there are major obstacles to increasing relative surplus value. Thus it occurs primarily in industries such as electronics and clothing where economic and technological considerations make increased mechanization difficult with existing technologies' (Jenkins, 1984, p. 43).

In some of the sectors referred to by Jenkins, technological improvement has been hard to achieve, making improved profitability and improved living standards increasingly difficult in countries with relatively high wages, even when measures are taken to keep wages down by using women and ethnic minority workers, in 'sweated labour' conditions.

But relocation for cheap labour production is just one alternative to falling profitability. TNCs can make other choices. Instead of relocating production, they can invest in existing production processes by buying factories in cheaper cost NICs, or elsewhere. Indeed, most foreign direct investment has been, and is increasingly, to other industrialized countries rather than to the Third World. A TNC can also enter into marketing arrangements with firms in cheaper locations avoiding relocation of its own production. TNCs can also, of course, attempt a mix of these strategies.

Many firms do none of these things. They do not attempt to internationalize their operations. They can call for state protection and they can invest in new technologies. Many have been at the centre of attempts to protect domestic industry in industrialized countries from Third World imports. Some of the bigger companies have increased investment in new technologies to remain profitable in higher-wage locations.

Thus, TNCs have alternatives. Certainly, they can relocate to low-labour-cost zones. But they can also take over existing companies in profitable zones, in NICs or anywhere else. They can concentrate on marketing and avoid direct ownership of manufacturing processes. Finally, they can sit tight and shout for protection from imports, or stay in Britain but invest in new technologies to upgrade productivity and remain profitable without relocation.

So, explanations of relocation based solely on cheap labour are misleading, particularly when we turn to the issue of whether relocation will continue, or whether First World countries can turn back Third World competition. Use of Jenkins' approach based on tendencies in the internationalization of capital avoids various analytical shortcomings with the cheap labour explanation.

1 One shortcoming, for example, is in its analysis of industrialized countries. The estimate of 200,000 jobs lost in Britain as a direct result of cheap imports from the Third World pales into insignificance in comparison with the total loss of over 1.8 million manufacturing jobs between 1977 and 1984. A large number of firms in Britain, moreover, remain sufficiently internationally competitive to produce for world markets, including Third World markets.

2 This explanation may also be an over-simplification of the nature of changes in industrialization in the Third World. It concentrates too much on certain export oriented sectors in export free zones with transnational ownership. As we saw in chapters 10 and 13 this is just one of several

TABLE 28 Share of foreign-owned firms in manufacturing output and exports of selected Third World countries

| | *Year*[a] | *Manufacturing output (%)* | *Manufactured exports (%)* |
|---|---|---|---|
| Argentina | 1972/73 | 31 | 42 |
| Brazil | 1969/74 | 42[b] | 40 |
| Colombia | 1974 | 43 | 50 |
| Mexico | 1970/74 | 35 | 50 |
| Hong Kong | 1971/72 | 11 | 10 |
| India | 1973/70 | 13 | 5 |
| Malaysia | 1971 | 50 | > 70 |
| Singapore | 1968/75 | 30 | 92 |
| South Korea | 1974 | 11 | 31 |
| Taiwan | 1971 | na | > 20 |

*Notes*: [a] Where two dates are given, the first refers to output, the second to exports. [b] Share of assets. [c] Share of employment. na = not available.
*Source*: Jenkins (1984).

tendencies. Table 28 shows that foreign ownership in manufacturing is more varied than this, in most more industrialized Third World countries. The most general tendency is production for the domestic market, by both local firms and TNCs, as in Brazil (chapter 11), rather than export oriented production.

3 There is an implied inevitability that investment will only take place where the cheapest labour is, and will relocate if wages increase. Chapter 13 deals with this issue in some detail concluding that the NICs are moving beyond the stage where cheap unskilled labour working longer and harder than anywhere else is the main basis for their growth. It is clear that wages have risen in some NICs without massive re-relocation or loss of profitability.

This is an important conclusion for those who believe that low wages are not an inevitable consequence of capitalist development. The inevitability argument leads to a 'vicious circle' trap: the logic of which is that low wages are crucial for the survival of companies; so if wages go up, then firms will relocate; therefore attempts to improve conditions of work are counter-productive since they lead to loss of employment through relocation. Fortunately for the workers of the Third World (and the First) there is no such inevitability.

I say fortunately for two reasons. Firstly, because there are instances of successful organization for improved working conditions even in the most authoritarian military-ruled NICs. In every NIC there are large and small groups of workers struggling to improve their situations, sometimes being repressed, but sometimes gaining significant improvements to strengthen their organization. Secondly, as Jenkins points out (1984, p. 50–1), the cheap labour argument can be used to argue against Third World industrialization on the grounds that such industrialization will be based on the extreme exploitation of Third World workers. It can, therefore, be used as a prop for protectionist measures and for arguments that the interests of workers in First and Third Worlds are in conflict. This can be particularly divisive if argued by First World trade unionists. Although new divisions of labour do potentially lead to differences of interest within labour, such differences of interest can occur between different groups of workers to a significant degree wherever they are located. Arguments in favour of protecting First World jobs by emphasizing the need to protect Third World workers from exploitation are, in this sense, disingenuous and run counter to those that stress that successful struggles involve the unity of labour.

Finally, in summary, an approach that allows for other options than an inevitable progression to extreme exploitation not only holds out the hope and possibility of improvement of life through organization and links between the Third and First Worlds, but also allows us to keep open more options for development in the future than would otherwise be possible.

## Is the New International Division of Labour Permanent?

Kaplinsky (1984) reports an increase in the number of free trade zones between 1978 and 1980 from 220 to over 350, indicating a continuation of export oriented industrialization strategies and an expansion of efforts by non-NIC Third World countries to jump on the export bandwagon. This suggests that relocation will continue and export oriented industrialization will expand.

An associated hypothesis is that capital will become increasingly mobile, moving from NICs where wages and regulations increase to other cheaper NICs. Chapter 13 cited evidence that large electronics TNCs have sought out new and cheaper locations, though so far this is for the expansion of capacity rather than the relocation of existing plants. South Korea is now rated as the least desirable site for new investment among the nine fastest growing Asian sites. Thus, the fragmentation of production and cheap labour approach would suggest a series of re-relocations of branch plants unlinked to the rest of the national economy concerned.

We have seen, however, that most industrial production in the NICs has been for domestic markets. In chapters 10 and 13 it was argued that the level of industrialization in the top ten or so leading industrializers in the Third World was on an entirely different scale than for the rest of the Third World. The infrastructural changes in many of the NICs (in the broadest sense of infrastructure – air, sea and road transport, containerization, computerized stock control and planning, high levels of education, technical capacity, and so on), together with the growth of domestically based, strong, sometimes transnational firms, makes it difficult to argue that these NICs will not hold and even expand their share of world industry, whatever happens to the rest of the Third World.

But some are pessimistic even about the NICs chances of consolidating their industrial development. They argue that the present trend in First World protectionism, coupled with technological innovation, will improve the possibilities for reindustrialization in the First World. It is argued that depressed and saturated markets in the First World are producing more specialized product segmentation, some markets requiring more rapid product changes. In these circumstances, it is more difficult to supply from standardized production facilities remote from market locations, since the products may go out of fashion 'on the boat'. Related to this is the argument advanced by Kaplinsky (1985), that there is *an increasing* adoption of Japanese-type production techniques as a response to economic crisis, which may shift comparative advantage in some sectors back to the First World. For example, Kaplinsky (1984) thinks that computer-aided design systems are likely to diffuse first to sectors in which NICs manufacturing exports grew fastest in the 1970s. He also believes that Third World countries may find these new techniques more difficult to assimilate.

Kaplinsky points to the possibility of restructuring of traditional industries using the French policy approach of 'there are no obsolete industries, only obsolete technologies'. Innovation allows all sectors to be competitive. Technological innovation together with Japanese-style management control that rests not just on technical change but on diligent control of the whole production process (including 'just-in-time' delivery of inputs and strong marketing production links) will bode ill for fragmented suppliers far from headquarters plants.

Kaplinsky quotes a UNIDO document that there may be a polarization of industrial production with 'standardized lines of production – located in developing countries precisely because of their standardization – [being] shifted again: this time back to the developed market economies' (UNIDO, 1983, p. 245). He believes that a few NICs may be able to make the necessary investment in automation technologies to undermine this reversal but, overall, he is pessimistic of the chances for the vast majority of Third World countries.

If it is difficult to make generalizations about industrial location between the First and Third Worlds, it is perhaps easier to draw conclusions about capitalist development more generally. Both Elson and Humphrey have argued that the internationalization of capital would not be reversed during this economic crisis (Open University, 1983). Elson suggested an increasing interlinking between companies in the industrialized and newly industrializing countries, citing the plans of Hong Kong businessmen to set up denim factories in the North of England, and the Taiwanese investment in Wales. Humphrey suggested

> that the major similarity between the developed countries and Third World countries in the 1980s is that both face an extremely difficult international situation which will lead probably to much slower growth in the 1980s than in the 1960s and 1970s. I see developed and Third World countries sharing the same misery rather than the same happiness of rapid growth. (Open University, 1983)

Elson and Humphrey both relegate the relocation and fragmentation issue as a subset of more general issues about the possibilities for internationalization of capital and the implications for producers of strategies by companies to remain profitable in the difficult conditions of economic crisis.

Nevertheless, one conclusion on relocation is that the economic crisis makes industrialization a very different matter for most other Third World countries now than it did for the NICs in the 1950s–1970s. It would be misguided to take the model of a South Asian newly industrializing country, or Brazil or India, and apply it to the situation of the remaining 130 or so countries of the Third World in the latter half of the 1980s. The same conditions that allowed the rapid growth of the NICs *do not now exist* for other Third World countries and changes in strategy are required as we approach the twenty-first century.

CHAPTER FIFTEEN

# The IMF and Mechanisms of Integration

This chapter is about the International Monetary Fund or, to be more precise, about the IMF in the Third World. Its subject matter turns to a great degree on the impact of credit given to Third World countries by the officials of the IMF in Washington, but let us begin with an occasion when the IMF itself was meeting in the Third World.

In October 1985, the IMF and the World Bank, its twin institution born at Bretton Woods at the end of the Second World War, were holding their annual joint meetings in Seoul, South Korea. In their own right these meetings were more important than usual, but a short disturbance experienced by some of the participants highlights some illuminating paradoxes. This report of it appeared in the *Guardian*:

> *IMF Outing Ends in Tears*
>
> Delegates to the IMF meeting had their first taste of pepper gas as security forces broke up a demonstration in Seoul's famous It' Aewon cut price shopping and red light district yesterday.
>
> The bankers, finance officials and IMF and World Bank staff, had descended in droves for cut-price shopping on what for most of them was their last day in Seoul. Official cars jostled for kerb-side space as bankers clad in Savile Row suits emerged from Mr C. S. Kim, and his competitors, clutching local versions at one fifth the price.
>
> The Merrill Lynch chauffeur-driven car was parked outside Mr. Yung's brass shop, next door to Dr. Lee's 'Skin and VD Clinic' and hard by the seedy Hamilton Hotel, well-frequented by successive generations of GIs.
>
> Suddenly, the delegates were startled as a group of stylish students, carrying flaming torches and streaming banners carrying anti-government slogans, jogged up It' Aewon's main thoroughfare shouting in time to their march. Local youths and girls ran across to join the throng.
>
> Bankers emerged into the street, still clutching the fake Cartier watches, Samsonite cases, Gucci bags asnd Cabbage Patch dolls and other examples of Korea's extraordinary enthusiasm for mass-producing copies of the baubles of the rich . . .
>
> But the moment the demo reached It' Aewon's main intersection, the riot squad struck. Pepper gas grenades burst on the tarmac. The flares were scattered and dozens of plain clothes guards emerged from the crowd to grab and lead away as many of the fleeing demonstrators as they could catch.
>
> The clouds of pepper gas drove the sneezing delegates with their eyes streaming back into the shops . . .

> Ten minutes later It' Aewon was back to its usual bustle. A shopkeeper made a quick sale of a 'Samsonite' holdall for $7. The prostitutes had returned to their pitches.
>
> And the bankers' limousines swept the financiers and their fake purchases back to the Seoul Hilton where they picked up buses to take them to a party with 'a taste of Korean culture' as its theme.
>
> One other taste lingered. As the gassed delegates found, the rasp of pepper gas, which attacks the nasal passages and eyes, lasts about an hour, giving them a modest personal experience of the way South Korea conducts its political affairs. Come back for the Olympics in '88. (*The Guardian*, 11 October 1985)

There are three points in this report that are indirectly relevant to understanding the position of the IMF in the Third World.

1 The conference participants caught up in the episode appear to be bankers and financiers, to a large extent. This is indicative of the fact that, in the 1970s and 1980s, private banks and finance houses became closely involved with the IMF and the World Bank. But at one level it is surprising, for these are official, intergovernmental institutions. Their close involvement with private bankers is almost as surprising as the presence of bankers at policy making meetings of the British Treasury would be. At least, it would have been surprising to the two individuals credited with founding the IMF – John Maynard Keynes and Harry Dexter White – for they saw it as an official body to take the international financial system out of the banks' hands.

2 The meetings came face to face with political action on the streets (albeit minor) and police reaction. Although this demonstration was not aimed at the IMF, it must have raised echoes of the protest riots and political violence that have occurred in one Third World country after another, directed at IMF policies.

3 The meeting's venue, Seoul, was highly symbolic of the IMF's position in the world. As the capital of South Korea, a country which was divided from North Korea in the first major East–West confrontation after the Second World War, Seoul faces the border with the North, and symbolizes the frontline of the capitalist world. A client state of the USA, South Korea is a showcase of capitalism's highest promise and worst costs, an exhibit facing North Korea and the Soviet Union beyond. Seoul's geopolitical position meshes with the IMF's. The Soviet Union is not a member of the IMF; for most of the IMF's life, and until quite recently, virtually no socialist countries have been members; it has been dominated by the USA, with the Western European powers and some other US allies playing secondary roles. A related but distinct element in these parallels is directly economic: South Korea is one of the prime examples of the newly industrialized countries that, in the 1970s, experienced remarkable growth and prominence in the world market; the principle responsibility of the IMF has been, in effect, the construction of that world market and the integration of individual countries into it.

The construction of the new international division of labour in the 1970s was the context for South Korea's economic growth which, as in countries such as Singapore, Hong Kong and Taiwan, was characterized by export oriented and manufacturing industries. It is also the key to understanding the IMF's policies. The IMF's importance in the post-war world lies in its construction of a world order where individual economies are integrated into a world market and their production is oriented toward the dictates of that market. Politicians and academic critics have pejoratively described the IMF as a capitalist institution because of these policies but, to be more precise, the world order it has sought to reinforce and to regulate is capitalist. In helping construct the modern international market, the IMF has consistently attempted to reduce governments' role in trade, and so has strengthened both a capitalist mechanism – market forces of price determined by demand and supply – and a capitalist agency – the TNCs that dominate those market forces, trade and production for the market. In working to increase the integration of national economies into the world market, the IMF's policies shift the character of those national economies themselves, reducing the state sector and increasing scope for TNCs to operate.

The main theme of this chapter is an elaboration of this perspective of the IMF. Our main question is, How does the IMF integrate Third World producers and production into the global system for which it has (a shared) responsibility?

This is a rather unusual perspective from which to view the IMF. A more common concern is with its purely monetary or financial operations (in contrast to its impact on the production and trading system) and most modern commentators examine its role principally from the point of view of the individual countries, or groups of countries with which it deals, rather than as its systemic role. But although this chapter's perspective is unusual, each aspect is interrelated; financial operations are key to the whole IMF project and individual countries' problems are where policies have their impact, so these are examined in the course of analysing the IMF's overall role.

In this chapter, the IMF's global and integrative role is discussed by, first, examining the origins of the Fund and considering its role in creating and controlling today's Third World. That involves an outline of the way in which the conditions on IMF loans to member countries have developed. We then consider the character of the 'stabilization programmes' attached to stand-by loans and the view that they are best seen as programmes for economic transformation rather than stabilization. Finally, we outline the role of banks in the world order the IMF is constructing.

## Origins and Transformation of the IMF

In 1944, the small town of Bretton Woods (New Hampshire, USA) hosted the conference at which the International Monetary Fund and the World Bank (International Bank for Reconstruction and Development) were born, with great hopes for their ability to create the conditions for post-war prosperity. Thirty six years later, in 1980, the small Tanzanian town of Arusha hosted a conference of politicians, economists and officials concerned about the IMF's impact on the Third World. The contrast was stark. Whereas the founders saw the IMF's purpose as obtaining the objectives of world-wide sustained prosperity through increasing national autonomy over economic policy, the Arusha conference concluded that it was 'fundamentally incompatible with an equitable conception of structural change, self-reliance and endogenous development' (Abdalla et al., 1980, pp. 13–14). In this section, we discuss the original conceptions of the IMF and the manner in which its mode of operating was changed. This historical examination has a direct relevance for our understanding of today's Third World, for the position of the Third World in the international order is not unchanging and there is nothing 'natural' about it. It is not simply that the position of the Third World in the world economic system has been directly and indirectly determined by definite policies and actions, it is also that the international economic system itself has been constructed and substantially changed over the years. The way this system was constructed at the end of the Second World War and the way it has changed in subsequent decades, has proved to be crucial for the situation of developing countries.

At the end of the Second World War, and during the early post-war period, the IMF was central to the direct actions and policies the victorious powers took to construct a new international economic order. It is the order under which we have lived for nearly half a century and it has been quite different from the arrangements that existed before the war. The Fund was created through a series of conscious policies and negotiations as part of this order and it, in turn, has had a central role in shaping them.

If we examine the ways in which the post-war international monetary system was constructed, there are two points that stand out. Each is directly relevant to the position of the Third World countries in the international system.

1 The construction of the new system was strongly conditioned by competition between the USA and Britain for the leadership and economic domination of the non-socialist world.
2 It was also strongly conditioned by a struggle between liberal and conservative economists and politicians. The prize was post-war institutions that would guarantee the adoption of their respective policies, and this struggle centred in part on the question of whether the IMF should operate its lending policies like a bank or more like a cooperative fund.

These points are the key to understanding the IMF's position today.

### *Conservatives in the ascendancy*

The IMF was created at a conference of forty-four nations at Bretton Woods in July 1944. Hence the particular system at the centre of which it stood until 1973 was called the Bretton Woods system. The presence of forty-four participants however, is misleading. In truth, the IMF was created by the governments of the USA and Britain. At the time, an American banker noted: 'We are told that forty-four nations agreed to this. I think a more exact statement would be that three or four groups of very expert chaps got together and wrote a plan, and then took it up with forty-four other technicians stating that "this is what the United States and Great Britain are willing to stand for with you"' (Leon Fraser, First National City Bank, quoted in Harris, 1983, p. 51).

Fraser's reference to 'three or four groups of very expert chaps' within the two main countries was, moreover, quite accurate. Not only were the British and Americans pursuing interests that were partly in conflict with each other but also, within each country's government, there were divisions between groups of politicians and civil servants holding rival perspectives. The chief US negotiator was Harry Dexter White and Britain's was John Maynard Keynes. Their views had much in common although, reflecting the difference in their countries' situation, they were in opposition in certain significant respects. Their views were, however, opposed by important political groupings in their own countries. The IMF that emerged was a compromise between the views of the different groups.

Harry White argued for the establishment of the IMF as a central institution in the new economic system. In so doing, he was pursuing two principles:

1 that when countries run balance of payments deficits, credit should be available to them to ensure that their governments could pursue Keynesian policies and increase their spending without outside pressure, thereby maintaining full employment and effecting social reforms;
2 that channelling funds through an institution such as the IMF, controlled by member governments, was preferable to having flows of international capital under the control of private banks and private investors.

The stance of the US State Department, however, rested on two rather different principles, which reflected the interest of major business sectors in America. These two principles, which won the day at Bretton Woods, were multilateralism and conservative macro-economic policies.

Broadly, multilateralism meant that all countries should open their frontiers to trade with all others. There should, as far as possible, be no discriminatory import duties and no direct controls such as import quotas. Ultimately, all currencies should be freely convertible so that finance and capital could switch freely from one currency and one country to another. The direct attraction of multilateralism was that it would open up the British spheres of influence to US business; the countries in which British capital's operations were protected by the Empire-based system of import duties (Imperial Preference) and foreign exchange controls (Sterling Area) would be increasingly opened to US activity. Less directly but, in the long term, more significantly, multilateralism meant the construction of a new world order of markets. multinational corporations and banks, in which the IMF would be central.

Conservative macro-economic policies meant that when the IMF loaned currency to a member country to cover a deficit, it would require that country to adopt firm policies to cure the deficit; full-employment and expansion would have to be sacrificed or given a lower priority than austerity action, to ensure the loan could be repaid quickly.

### *The principle of conditionality*

The principle of tying loans to 'conditionality' contrasted with Keynes' idea that the IMF should be more of a cooperative society in which member countries had an automatic right to borrow, since all contributed to its pool of currencies. But US power made 'conditionality' inescapable. After all, if American capital was dominant internationally its representatives could surely adopt the view that 'their' money was not to be handed out too easily (although, of course, the funds of the IMF were provided by all its members, not just the USA).

Edward Bernstein, one of the US economy's midwives at the IMF's birth (and genetic engineer at an earlier stage), has recalled the influences at work: 'We wanted the United States to have a dominant role primarily because we believed the contribution of the United States in money would be the first to be used and we felt we had to be able to tell our congress that this institution would be operated conservatively and that our subscription would be safe.' (Open University/BBC, 1983)

The Fund's conditionality developed over the years but at the beginning it combined with the idea of dismantling the barriers around British markets to ensure that the conditions the US State Department wanted imposed on borrowers should include the removal of government controls over trade and over the movements of international money. Moreover, adopting the principles of bankers meant adopting conservative policies regarding conditionality on government spending and a rejection of a Keynesian commitment to full employment. The victory of this bankers' principle was evident even at Bretton Woods when a proposal by Australia was defeated. The Australian proposal was that the members of the IMF: 'should be invited to accept concurrently an international agreement in which the signatories will pledge themselves to their own people and to one another to maintain high levels of employment' (quoted in Scammell, 1961, p. 151). This rejection was also evident when the US representatives prevented the US Treasury man, Harry White, with his commitment to Keynesianism and full employment, from becoming Managing Director of the IMF.

These policies of conditionality were not explicitly oriented toward the Third World, but their development has had a major impact on the IMF's relations with Third World countries. The immediate post-war conflict between British and US business interests in the IMF has been displaced by several other conflicts, the main one being between the interests of Third World countries (which themselves differ) and the policies of the US and European states that dominate the IMF.

That conflict within the IMF and official bodies has turned, above all, on the conditions the IMF attaches to credit. The principle Keynes tried to promote is not on the agenda now. Since there can be no harmony of interest, the cooperative principle where each member has automatic, unconditional rights to as much credit as they might wish to draw, is irrelevant; the issue is the *type* of conditions that should be attached to loans. It is an issue that arose in the early days of the Fund but which has grown, since the 1970s, to become a flashpoint for conflict at one international gathering after another.

The impact of the IMF's conditions has also become a flashpoint for conflict on the streets, with 'IMF riots' sparked by price rises in many countries whose governments have withdrawn food subsidies in order to obtain IMF loans. Two were reported in one issue of the *Financial Times*, but they were typical of many: 'Several hundred people died during food riots in Morocco [which signed an IMF agreement in March 1981] last June [1981], while protestors took to the streets in Sudan in January [1982] after price rises for basic commodities followed agreement on a [IMF loan] programme in October [1981]. Both governments were attempting to meet targets agreed with the fund' (*Financial Times*, 1 April 1982, p. 4).

## The IMF and Control of the Third World

The concept of the Third World did not exist at the time of Bretton Woods and it was only in advanced circles that Western economic and political planners had any conception of a world of politically independent, economically less developed states, that would strongly affect world developments in subsequent decades. The reason for this is evident. Apart from the independent states of Central and South America, which were largely clients of the USA, the majority of poor Asian, African and Pacific countries were colonies whose independence was hardly foreseen by the industrialized capitalist countries. This pattern was strongly reflected in the attendance at the Bretton Woods conference.

Of the forty-four countries attending, twenty-six countries were from the Third World. These included China, nineteen Latin American countries (all, that is, except Argentina), three African (Egypt, Ethiopia, Liberia), and four Asian (India, Iran, Iraq, the Philippines). None of the other colonized countries of Africa, Asia and the Caribbean had any part. Even those that were there were far from independent: Egypt and Iraq were effectively under British control; Iran was occupied by British and Soviet troops; India was not yet independent; the Philippines were under US control; and Liberia, like the Latin American countries, had close ties with the USA. Despite their presence in some numbers, the Third World countries found themselves embroiled in an institution largely constructed by Britain and, especially, the USA.

The effective absence of Third World strength at the IMF's foundation has been compounded by the fact that the IMF has since helped to create the particular problems of the Third World. What does this mean? The

Third World is defined by its particular position in a world system. The economic and social structure, and cultural character, of Third World countries have been shaped and determined by their relations with the advanced capitalist and socialist nations. From the last quarter of the nineteenth century until the middle of the twentieth, the vast majority of the countries that were to become identified as 'underdeveloped' or 'Third World' were related to advanced capitalist countries as colonies, subordinate parts of the Empires of Britain, Holland, France, Portugal or with other countries at their centre. It was through the colonial systems that these countries were related to the industrialized capitalist nations. Government of them was directly controlled, although to varying degrees, and with that went control of their financial arrangements. Their development programmes, to the extent that they existed, were oriented toward the needs of the metropolitan countries and were financed from there. Their currencies were either the same as the metropolitan country's or directly linked to it, and the net receipts of gold or foreign currency received for exports went to build up the treasure of the metropolitan country. These financial arrangements benefitted the metropolitan countries and emanated from their political domination of the colonies. After the Second World War, the position changed. The independence of India and Pakistan was followed by that of a succession of other colonies. But with formal political independence there developed a financial system that severely curtailed the real political power that could be exercised by the independent governments. A central institution in this system was the IMF. As one country after another gained political independence, they were admitted as members of the IMF, so that Third World membership of the Fund had grown to 114 countries by 1980.

The future development of a non-colonial, politically independent, Third World was part of the (unwritten) agenda at Bretton Woods in 1944, in the sense that US policy towards the IMF was directed towards undermining the economic integration of the British Empire. The 1944 conference and the 1946 founding meeting of the IMF were US–British affairs but the Third World countries present spoke out against the ties of the British Empire. India, in particular, argued that the IMF should solve on an international basis a particular problem that had been inherited from her subordination within the British Empire during the war. This was the problem of the blocked 'Sterling Balances'. Britain had financed its war effort partly by borrowing from the Empire and other members of the Sterling Area (like Egypt). Britain imported materials from them but instead of paying for them with real money such as dollars or gold, with which they could buy manufactured goods or food from the USA, Britain issued IOUs. These were debts denominated in Sterling and issued by the British government, they were called the Sterling Balances and they were frozen: the Third World holders could not convert them to dollars or gold. The Indian delegate, with Egyptian support, pressed at Bretton Woods for the IMF to solve the problem on the grounds that: 'India, as a relatively poor, underdeveloped and over-populated country had great need of capital goods and that multilateral convertibility of at least a part of India's blocked balances was necessary if she was to procure them' (quoted in Scammell, 1961, p. 148).

The plea failed, with the US supporting Britain (rather against its own principle of multilateralism), but this was a harbinger of the fact that the post-war world was going to witness the rise of Third World countries, free of imperial tutelage, and with interests, policies and demands of their own.

The IMF has had an increasing role in the Third World, through its power to provide loans to cover balance of payments deficits. IMF loans were originally designed to cover 'temporary disequilibria'. But the balance of payments problems of the Third World countries that eventually joined the IMF were not temporary. They are structural and long-term, and result from their position within the world economic system. Indeed, the 'structuralist' view that dominates the perspectives of many Third World economists argues that persistent balance of payments deficits are a necessary concomitant of development. Drawn into the affairs of Third World countries by the existence of these deficits, the IMF has become an overseer of their development efforts. The existence of financial needs and financing mechanisms gives the institutions that control finance a greater or lesser measure of control over what the borrower does: money is power. The IMF is not the only institution to wield such power, but it has become the most significant.

In the following section, we shall examine the nature of IMF control. In particular, we discuss how it has *developed*, for control over the internal affairs of its members was not explicitly written into the IMF at its inception.

## The Development of Conditionality

The development of the IMF's credit policy has seen it move from an emphasis on automatic access for member countries to one of 'conditionality', where specific conditions are laid down for the borrower to follow and their observance of the conditions is monitored. Below is a calendar of specific events and policy declarations from 1947, leading to the comprehensive formulation of the policy of conditionality in 1968. The word 'tranche' which appears in it refers to different amounts of borrowing. As conditionality has developed, IMF policy has been that the conditions applied to borrowers are more stringent, the greater the amount of borrowing. The relevant amounts are divided into predetermined bands or 'tranches', such that if the amount borrowed is within the gold 'tranche' there are no conditions attached, but amounts in subsequent tranches (called 'first' credit tranche, 'second', 'third' tranche, etc.) attract increasingly tough conditions.

*1947* IMF opened its doors for business as a lender.
IMF Executive Board resolved to interpret the *Articles of Agreement*, Article

V [Section 3 (A) (i)], so that the Fund may postpone or reject a request for credit or accept it subject to conditions.

*1948* Through the Marshall Plan (George Marshall was then the US Secretary of State), the USA concluded an independent agreement quite separately from the IMF, to give financial aid to several West European states for post-war reconstruction from 1948 to 1952. The IMF then agreed to a US request to restrict its loans so that European countries in receipt of this Marshall Aid did not simultaneously receive IMF loans. This was one of the first IMF conditions put into practice.

*1948* The *IMF Annual Report* made clear the Fund's interest in persuading members to adopt measures to correct their balance of payments deficits: 'The Fund has emphasized to members that the purpose of the use of its resources is to give members time to make necessary adjustment and not to avoid the necessity of such readjustments.'

*1952* Through the *Rooth Plan* (Rooth was Managing Director of the IMF), the IMF Executive Board agreed on principles of lending after extensive discussion over how to reconcile assurance of access to Fund resources with corresponding assurance that drawings would be repaid on time. The principles established were:

1 credit should be only for short periods: 'within an outside range of three to five years';
2 the borrowing country should agree with the IMF on policies to ensure that it could repay as soon as possible (maximum five years);
3 a country requesting credit would 'be expected to include in its authenticated request a statement that it will comply' with the principles agreed;
4 the Fund would monitor the use of the credit to determine whether the borrower used it in accordance with the agreed principles;
5 requests for finance within the gold tranche (i.e. relatively small amounts) would be treated liberally.

The Rooth Plan made provision for the Fund to enter into stand-by arrangements to provide an assured line of credit. Over the years these arrangements became the principal mechanism for the Fund to lend in large amounts and for ensuring that the credit was available only if the borrower observed certain conditions.

*1959* The *IMF Annual Report* summarized the principle adopted in preceding years that more stringent conditions would be required the greater the amount of credit (i.e. the higher the tranche).

*1968* The IMF codified the application of conditions to *stand-by* arrangements. The two principal considerations were:

1 for all borrowing above the gold tranche the country had to keep in regular consultation with the IMF;
2 drawings on credit at levels above the gold and first tranches could only take place if the country had at each stage satisfactorily met performance criteria laid down in the stand-by agreement.

These were the steps involved in transforming the IMF from an institution organized on the principles of cooperation between sovereign governments that had pooled their resources for common use, to one that acted as a banker carefully monitoring the policies and performance of customers. It was a movement from 'automaticity' to 'conditionality'. Because stand-by arrangements have come to be the principal type of loan agreement through which the IMF imposes conditions on borrowers, let us consider them in more detail. We begin by quoting the words of the IMF's council-general on the 'complete metamorphosis' of the stand-by arrangement since it was first devised:

> Originally it was considered as something in the nature of a confirmed line of credit that gave a member an absolute right to make purchases subject only to those provisions of the Articles on ineligibility and the general suspension of operations that were *lex cogens* and therefore necessarily applicable. At the present time it has become the main instrument for conditionality, and, in particular, for making the Fund's resources available beyond the first credit tranche only if the member observes certain policies. Annexed to each stand-by arrangement is a letter of intent from the member's authorities in which they set forth the program they will pursue. The stand-by arrangements that permit purchases beyond the first credit tranche include performance clauses establishing criteria on the non-observance of which the member's right to make purchases under the stand-by arrangement will be interrupted without the need for a decision by, or even notice to, the Executive Directors. Performance criteria are invariably objective in character, in the sense that a subjective judgement is not necessary in order to ascertain whether they are being observed, with the result that a member will know at all times whether it is able to make purchases [i.e. borrow from the Fund]. The movement, therefore, has been from the assurance of use without the review of request to the definition of the circumstances in which there is assured use without review. [IMF, 1969, p. 533)

For the country involved, the negotiation of a stand-by arrangement involves a flurry of activity. The IMF's inscrutable officials descend on the country to 'examine the books', so to speak. They negotiate with the would-be borrower and then a letter of intent is signed by an official of the borrowing country, although not written independently by him or her. Here is a description of the process by Cheryl Payer, one of the IMF's critics.

> *The IMF standby arrangement and stabilization programme: a model*
>
> A standby arrangement with the IMF is negotiated by the affected country's top financial officials (usually the Minister of Finance and the Governor of

the Central Bank) and a team of IMF staff members visiting that country. These negotiations are often hard-fought and bitter – a far cry from the image which the IMF would like to project of its highly competent staff dispensing impartial expert advice to grateful country officials. The IMF mission members have consulted before leaving Washington with all the Executive Directors most concerned with that particular country, including always the US director. They are *de facto* empowered to negotiate on behalf of the Fund, and their decisions are seldom if ever overruled in Washington. Once negotiations are concluded, they assist the borrowing country's officials to draft a 'Letter of intent' which sets forth the promises which have been made in order to qualify for the Fund's assistance. Items covered by the Letter of Intent include exchange rate practices, import regulations, control of the domestic budget deficit, bank credit controls and policies towards foreign investment. It often contains very specific quantitative commitments for many of these times; it is understood that if the government fails to keep the commitments in its Letter of Intent, its right to borrow under the standby arrangement will be suspended.

Although the details of each programme will vary, the IMF standard of a desirable economic policy is uniform and predictable enough to allow us to sketch a model of it here. The basic components of any such programme are the following:

(1) Abolition or liberalization of foreign exchange and import controls.
(2) Devaluation of the exchange rate.
(3) Domestic anti-inflationary programmes, including:
  (a) control of bank credit; higher interest rates and perhaps higher reserve requirements;
  (b) control of the government deficit: curbs on spending increases in taxes and in prices charged by public enterprises; abolition of consumer subsidies;
  (c) control of wage rises, so far as within the government's power;
  (d) dismanting of price controls.
(4) Greater hospitality to foreign investment. (Payer, 1974, pp. 32–3)

Although Cheryl Payer's description of stand-by arrangements was one of the first and based on experience of the early years of IMF lending to the Third World, the expansion of those operations in the 1970s and the first half of the 1980s was based on similar conditions. Later studies, such as those of UNDP/UNCTAD (1979) and Killick et al. (1984a, 1984b) surveyed the conditions attached to the loans made to a number of Third World countries and, although there are some differences, the nature of the conditions remains the same.

Those conditions relate both to external and internal relations. Directly oriented to the country's foreign trade and international finance, is the condition that import controls and foreign exchange controls must be relaxed and the currency devalued. The majority of Third World countries have at times attempted to conserve foreign exchange by using licences and restrictions to control the volume of imports and the availability of foreign currencies to businesses and individuals. Prescriptions from the IMF to relax them are accompanied by a requirement that the currency be devalued. Devaluation discourages imports by making them more expensive (and encourages exports by reducing their price to foreigners). The direction of these policies is to 'liberalize' the country's foreign trade and exchanges, in the sense of reducing its government's direct intervention. On the domestic front, the conditions are a prescription for austerity. Controls over the government deficit and bank credit restrict demand and reduce inflationary pressures. Control over wages (incomes policies) works in the same direction, although the dismantling of price controls can never be presented as an anti-inflationary policy.

The package of conditions attached to stand-by loan agreements is called a 'stabilization programme' by the IMF. But what is being stabilized? Are the programmes better seen as aimed at transformation and *de*stabilization, in some respects? These questions, to which we now turn, have yielded some highly contentious answers.

## Stabilization or Transformation?

The IMF describes its loan conditions as stabilization programmes, on the grounds that their purpose is to stabilize the balance of payments. To be more precise, the balance of payments deficit is seen as the result of a disequilibrium in the economy, in which demand outstrips supply and the excess demand is reflected in excessive imports compared with exports. In that sense, stabilization is intended to mean the restoration of 'equilibrium'. This is a version of the original Bretton Woods perspective of the IMF: at the outset, loans were to be made to cover temporary disequilibria and today's loan conditions are presented as remedies to ensure that disequilibria are temporary. Firstly, we examine this interpretation of IMF policies, which is one shared by the IMF and many of its critics. Secondly, we consider the alternative view, that IMF loan conditions are one element in a programme to transform Third World economies root and branch, rather than stabilize their balance of payments.

The stabilization view presents cuts in government deficit spending, restrictions on bank credit, and wage controls, as means to reduce overall demand and, therefore, to reduce the amount of net imports sucked in by excess demand. It presents devaluation as a means to change the relative price of imports and home-produced goods to discourage imports and stimulate exports. If the country's currency is devalued it makes dollars, pounds, marks and other foreign currencies more expensive to residents, so imports that have to be paid for in such currencies become more expensive (and exports become cheaper to foreigners). The abolition of food subsidies is presented as complementing devaluation's discouragement of imports by, similarly, raising the local price of food imports (as well as that of home-produced food), and it also contributes to the reduction in overall demand by reducing the real value of people's incomes.

Many economists accept this view of the role IMF conditions are intended to have but argue, on the basis of empirical studies, that these have not been achieved. A classic statement of such criticisms is that of the Dell Report, 1979:

> The problems arising during the period of adjustment covered by the present study were not merely problems of demand management in the short term. Major structural changes were required, while the time horizon of the Fund's operations was much too short to provide adequate support for longer-term measures of adjustment. In many cases the restoration of equilibrium in the balance of payments in any meaningful sense calls for structural shifts that can be achieved only over a considerable period of time. An obvious example is the adjustment to higher fuel prices, involving a process of long-term industrial change that may require investment in alternative sources of energy, as well as in industrial technologies that economize on fuel. The oil facility of the Fund was designed to take some account of this kind of problem since the facility was intended to permit medium-term financing of oil deficits that would give some time for the structural adjustments to be made that would realize economies in the use of energy. But this was only one example of a whole series of cases in which essentially similar problems of long-term adjustment arise.
>
> Consequently adjustment, if it is to be effective for more than a brief period cannot be limited to reducing the level of aggregate demand to the extent required to minimize pressures on the balance of payments or on domestic prices. Where such pressures are of domestic origin they usually reflect the existence of some obstacle to non-inflationary growth that the authorities were unable to overcome. A particularly important obstacle of this type is rigidity in the supply of key wage goods or of certain special skills or material inputs. Another obstacle often encountered is the difficulty of introducing and implementing an equitable system of taxation. A mere reduction in demand may return the economy to its previous position but the obstacles will probably persist unless dealt with explicitly and directly, and the pressures will emerge once more as soon as the development process is resumed. There is therefore a need for measures to tackle the basic causes of disequilibrium and the long-run obstacles to growth along with the proximate phenomena of inflation and balance of payments pressure that accompany them. (UNDP/UNCTAD, 1979, p. 11)

Such critics see the IMF's role as directed to curing balance of payments deficits but argue that its policies are ill-designed because they are short-term, requiring rapid internal changes in response to problems that are often externally generated and require difficult long-term adjustments. In fact, in the 1980s, IMF stabilization programmes have allowed longer periods of adjustment and liaison has developed between the IMF and the World Bank to link stabilization programmes with more structural economic reforms. These changes are presented as improvements to the means of stabilizing the balance of payments, but their effectiveness in that respect is yet to be tested.

The alternative view is that the IMF is not in the business of stabilization or achieving balance of payments equilibrium as such. Instead, its role is to transform Third World economies in such a way as to integrate them more strongly into the capitalist world market: the international system as such is its prime concern. A related task is their internal transformation to strengthen capitalist enterprises within the country. The IMF's power to influence a country's economy arises from the control it has over the finance Third World countries in deficit need in order to pay for imports, but although its policies are framed in terms of the balance of payments, their significance is more fundamental.

Devaluation, for example, is not an objectively necessary or neutral policy for curing balance of payments deficits, even if the IMF argument that imports and exports are highly responsive to price were valid. Import controls and export subsidies are alternative methods but the IMF firmly opposes them, partly in order to ensure that Third World markets are open without restriction to world trade dominated by the TNCS. If the international division of labour dictated by the world market is one whereby a particular country must expand production of cash crops for export and import manufactured goods, the abolition of import controls originally imposed to foster internal industrialization is a necessity. Moreover, devaluation acts in conjunction with other policies to decrease real wages and increase profit potential: it pushes up the price of imports; abolition of food subsidies directs much of the price increase toward food prices; and wage controls prevent wages rising to compensate. Although these policies have sparked off food riots in one country after another, the IMF persists with them because of their underlying strategic significance.

Similar considerations apply to the policy of restricting government deficits. This condition is complemented by the restriction on the expansion of bank credit, since that limits the extent to which banks can finance government deficits. If a Third World government finds that it is failing to meet the set of conditions imposed by the IMF before further instalments of credit are paid, it is frequently these particular conditions that act as the trip-wire. From the perspective that sees the IMF as instrumental in transforming economies to construct and strengthen a capitalist world order, restrictions on government deficit spending have a straightforward rationale (although one that Keynesians would not accept). They increase the proportion of a country's resources for the private sector by reducing the public sector's claim on them. In practice this has generally meant cuts in welfare spending and government subsidies, and increases in taxation on consumer goods. With respect to international integration, reductions in the government deficit by these means are seen as relieving the pressure to tax the profits of TNCs and, hence, as encouraging foreign investment. The construction of a world economic system in which the freedom of such international capital and trade is ensured, is the IMF's principal role.

The IMF's role in constructing an international economic system and transforming and integrating Third World economies into it puts the concept of stabilization programmes into a new light. In one sense they are clearly destabilizing, since they are designed to overturn the existing way of running the economy in many borrowing countries. They directly destabilize the social order, insofar as the sharp cuts they induce in the living standards of the poor lead to disaffection and, frequently, to riots. Moreover, they are often seen as a form of political destabilization designed to undermine socialist governments. For example, the supporters of Michael Manley's government in Jamaica saw the difficulties created by the IMF's conditions in the 1978–80 period as much an act of political destabilization

FIGURE 33 Writing on the wall: anti-Manley graffiti (Peter Stalker, *New Internationalist*)

as the 'dirty-tricks' campaign of the CIA had been in Allende's Chile (1970–3).

## The IMF and Private Banks

The conditions the IMF attaches to its credit to Third World countries can be seen as aspects of its role in creating a global order, rather than being directed specifically toward a particular country's economic difficulties. This is a global order in which the elements of a changing international division of labour are connected through and conditioned by international trade. And the international market is one where the IMF tries to ensure there are no state barriers to trade and, hence, a high degree of freedom for the TNCs that dominate it.

This role of the IMF relates to the aims that were uppermost in the earliest days of the Fund – the principle of 'multilateralism'. However, another element in the world order created by the IMF runs counter to the themes favoured by White, Keynes and others at its birth. A prominent view among the IMF's founders was that it would be a public body administering the world's financial system and curtailing the influence banks had over it but, by the 1980s, the IMF had become, in practice, largely a bankers' organization. Formally, it remains an intergovernmental body, but the major states that control it have, to a great extent, facilitated the growth of transnational private banking and the world order the IMF seeks to create is one where those banks have a strong, influential position. The presence of the bankers in that embarrassing incident in Seoul quoted at the beginning of this chapter was highly symbolic of the modern unity between the IMF and the banks.

What is the role of the banks in the international economic order that has been constructed between 1960 and 1985? How is it assisted by the IMF?

Since the end of the 1950s, transnational private commercial banks controlling billions upon billions of dollars have come to dominate the international financial system, regaining and surpassing the position they held in the 1920s and 1930s by using banking techniques considerably more advanced than those employed previously. One aspect of this domination that greatly affects the position of the Third World is that the banks have vastly expanded the volume of international money that they themselves create, i.e. international bank deposits generically known as Eurocurrency (especially Eurodollar) deposits. The second aspect affecting the Third World is that the banks have dominated the flows of credit to Third World countries.

The expansion of the volume of international bank money has had a significant, if indirect, effect on the Third World. In some of the original plans for the IMF, it was proposed that the Fund should create its own money to supplement or replace the dollars, pounds and other national currencies in the international sphere. This was not adopted and, in the 1950s and early 1960s, several economists claimed that there was a shortage of international money to sustain growing world trade. In 1967, agreement was reached on a scheme to enable the IMF to create its own international money for use by member states. This currency is called the Special Drawing Rights (SDR) and some saw it as a potential replacement for the dollar as the main international currency.

Third World countries subsequently came to see the SDR as a means through which money could be transferred from the rich to the poor nations and argued for a 'link' between SDR creation and aid. The idea of the link is that when the IMF creates new quantities of SDRs, it should not distribute them equally to all member states but, instead, should issue higher proportions to poor countries and lower to the rich.

The 'link' could only have a really significant impact on redistributing resources if the SDR were to be a major component of the world's total stock of international money. In fact, although there have been several new issues of SDRs since their inception, they have remained a minute proportion of the total stock. At the end of 1981, there were SDR21.3 billion in existence, but the volume of international money in the form of Eurodollar deposits in major banks was estimated in 1984 at US$2,100 billion, or about one hundred times the volume of SDRs. After the birth of SDRs at the end of the 1960s, the potential for a 'link' became dwarfed by the rapid expansion of Eurocurrency banking in the 1970s, by which the banks created that vast quantity of bank deposits. (In any case, issues of SDRs were hindered and the idea of a 'link' was blocked by the governments of the major Western industrial powers unwilling to see dollar bank deposits replaced by such an autonomous form of money.)

The second element in the private banks' domination of the financial system – their credit to Third World countries – is more prominent than their creation of new forms of international money, although the two are related. Credit and finance flows to Third World countries from several sources: other governments (as export credits, for example); multilateral state bodies (such as the World Bank); savings institutions (such as pension funds buying bonds); or private banks lending to Third World borrowers. Developments in the 1960s and 1970s led to private banks taking the most prominent role. A simplistic view of this bank lending has seen it as recycling funds from some countries in surplus to help other Third World countries finance their deficits. In this 'recycling' view, the loans are seen as the counterparts to oil payments. When OPEC prices for oil quadrupled between 1973 and 1974, several oil exporters achieved historically unprecedented surpluses on their balance of payments, and deposited these surplus funds with the international banks. In this view, these banks used the surplus funds to expand their loans to assist Third World countries (and others) to pay for their more expensive oil imports. This view is inaccurate; a more detailed picture of the banks' role is necessary in order to understand their relation to the IMF.

Instead of lending generally to Third World countries to cover their deficits related to the oil price rise in the 1970s, the expanded lending went predominantly to a small group of newly industrializing countries. Some twelve countries accounted for almost all the Third World's bank debt by the beginning of the 1980s, and the seven largest of these dominated the total. Estimates of their total bank debt vary, but the seven largest debtors in March 1985 were Brazil, Mexico, South Korea, Argentina, Venezuela, Indonesia and the Philippines. Three of these (Mexico, Indonesia and Venezuela) were themselves oil exporters; all the seven are countries that expanded their industrial sectors significantly. The growth in industrial profits was achieved with a high degree of internationalization; as well as being financed by foreign bank loans, their production growth was export-led to a large extent, and depended on high imports. In many cases, this industrial growth was under the aegis of restructuring by the TNCs of their international production, although some countries, especially South Korea, had very little direct involvement of TNCs in production.

From this perspective, the expansion of bank lending has been seen as the foundation for a major restructuring of world capitalism, a 'new international division of labour' (see chapter 14). It has been a key element in one of those periods in world history when a major economic shift is on the agenda; it has financed new growth centres of capitalist production, while poverty-stricken countries such as those of sub-Saharan Africa have had almost no access to bank finance for their balance of payments deficits. If this period has been one where a major restructuring of the world economy has occurred, there had to be some overarching power or agencies to pursue it and support it in the way that the US had done through Marshall Aid and the Organisation for European Economic Cooperation (now the OECD) in restructuring post-war European capitalism. The IMF has been crucial in that respect and this is reflected in its relation to bank lending.

The IMF has had a two-sided relation with the banks. The largest bank loans of the 1970s went to Brazil, Mexico and other countries that explicitly used bank loans to avoid IMF regulation and discipline, for the banks were

*'. . . So you see, the entire future of the international financial system hinges on your capacity for quick recovery and vast economic growth.'*

FIGURE 34 (*Guardian*, 8 February 1983)

willing to lend funds to them for general use without attaching any conditions like the IMF's 'stabilization programme' prescriptions. On the other hand, less commercially attractive, weaker, borrowers had to obtain IMF Loans and agree to an IMF stabilization programme as a precondition for the banks to consider further loans. That concept of IMF agreement as a 'seal of approval' became universal in the 1980s, as countries that had previously borrowed from the banks without it ran into difficulties. When Mexico effectively defaulted on its loans in 1982, it was only able to reschedule its bank debt as part of packages of measures that included acceptance of IMF stabilization. Brazil met the same problem.

The expansion of bank lending in the 1970s was facilitated by two techniques, invented in 1969, that helped banks to reduce risk. One was the use of variable interest rates on bank loans, which enabled banks to match the interest rate received with the variable rate they have to pay for deposits. Another was the syndicated loan, under which the risk of a loan to a particular country is shared among a large number of participating banks. These techniques, however, worsened risks in other respects: syndication encouraged banks to lend without considering whether the country was borrowing too much; while variable interest rates meant that borrowers were immediately hard hit when real interest rates rose sharply in 1980. Moreover, they did nothing to overcome the underlying risk that the borrowing country might fail to generate enough foreign exchange to service the debt. That was a risk that became real in the debt crisis of the 1980s when one country after another had to negotiate a rescheduling of debts with their bankers. The IMF's stabilization programmes, thus, acquired significance partly by appearing to reduce those risks borne by the banks. When the debt crisis broke, the IMF's early response was that, if countries pursued the austerity measures embodied in their stabilization programmes, they would be able soon to meet their obligations to the banks and the banks would return to lending to the third World.

As the authority with responsibility for giving a 'seal of approval', the IMF thus combined its function of shaping individual country's positions in the world economy with a role as 'semi-guarantor' of the banking system.

Outside the IMF, this policy was increasingly seen as unconvincing. Stabilization programmes that reduce wage-earners' living standards can achieve temporary improvements in the balance of payments (whatever the injustice to the poor in having to suffer for debts they did not incur) but they have not been able to overcome structural balance of payments problems. In some countries, these have been magnified by the local elite exporting large personal fortunes of their own to the US and Switzerland, and by large arms imports. More generally, it is now accepted wisdom that since IMF loans are short-term and not oriented toward a country's long-term development, they are irrelevant to overcoming structural deficits. As a result, at the 1985 meetings of the IMF, World Bank, governments and bankers in Seoul (with which this chapter opened), the USA put forward a proposal – the Baker Plan – for changing the relative roles of these institutions in ways that could appear to meet some of the most common criticisms.

The plan associated with US Treasury Secretary James Baker confirmed, and was designed to strengthen, the links between the private banks, the IMF, and the World Bank. The existing system had been proved inadequate for, although the debt crisis had not led to major bank failures, the rescheduling of debts and IMF programmes had left the banks highly exposed while also intensifying the stagnation of borrowing countries' growth prospects. Baker proposed that the banks commit themselves to an expansion of credit by 2.5 per cent for each of the subsequent three years, lending US$20 billion to the most heavily indebted countries. The IMF would be strengthened in its role overseeing such credit, but its conditionality would adopt a new, but unspecified emphasis. The increased bank loans would be matched and supported by $20 billion of new loans from the World Bank and similar bodies. The plan partly reflected changes already occurring. For example, in preceding years, the IMF, World Bank and private banks had begun to cooperate in lending to support countries adopting stabilization programmes together with longer-term structural adjustment programmes, and the World Bank had begun to play an increased role in promoting the macro-economic policies that the IMF had previously had to promulgate alone. But the Baker Plan rested on the readiness of private banks to expand lending and, given their already high degree of risk exposure, even the IMF's overseer role is unlikely to lead to a resumption of lending of the old type.

## Conclusion

The IMF is primarily a financial institution but its role is wider than finance; its concern ultimately is with the conditions under which trade and production occur. It deals with each Third World state as an individual member but in fact its role is global; its concern is with the international division of labour and its market and financial arrangements. In all these roles, the relationship between the IMF and the international banks has come to be central. Contrary to the hopes of its founders, the world order the IMF has been constructing is one in which international finance and the impact it has on individual countries is dominated by immensely powerful private banks. The fact that their power also involves considerable risks and the danger of a bank crash through default has not displaced the banks; it has only served to strengthen the ties between them and the IMF.

CHAPTER SIXTEEN

# Conclusion

## The Invidious Dilemmas of Capitalist Development

This chapter was written on a day when the BBC World Service reported

1 the first nationwide strike in Brazil for more than twenty years, a strike demanding that the Brazilian government negotiate with international private financiers terms that impose less austere living conditions on Brazilian workers;
2 the first Soviet industrial fair in Beijing since China rejected Soviet industrial aid thirty years ago;
3 that riots in Zambia forced the government to rescind a 30 per cent rise in staple food prices – President Kaunda, in a televised address to the nation, said that this was a great setback for the country's economic development (subsequently it was reported that the price increase was more than 100 per cent, and had been prompted by the IMF).

This book has been about the background to these issues: about the achievements and contradictions of economic development in a world dominated by capitalism; the cruel dilemmas of development that inflict privation upon millions. It has touched upon difficult choices, with historical constraints and far-reaching consequences, between agriculture and industry, the national and the international, consumption and accumulation, the state and the people. It has, in other words, been about survival and change in Third World economies.

One of the central questions of the book has been, What is the relationship between capitalism and development? This concluding chapter uses some of the analytical ideas and examples introduced earlier to take up these issues and examine the question, Can capitalism develop Third World economies? (And, if not capitalism, what?) The question has been given new prominence recently, in part because several writers on development (Warren, 1980; Kitching, 1982 and 1983; Sender and Smith, 1985 and 1986) have suggested that the 'progressive' aspects of capitalism have been forgotten. These writers decide that capitalism *can* develop Third World countries.

The simple formulation of the question almost invites answers at a glib or over-generalized level. One intention of this book has been, nevertheless, to discourage such answers by suggesting ways of approaching the major issues of development, and ways of understanding the real life struggles they express.

The three active ingredients in the question – capitalism, development and the Third World – are each large categorizations. One function of this chapter will be to summarize some of the range of meanings for each ingredient introduced in the preceding chapters.

The search for a simple answer to the question is likely to be fruitless. There are, nevertheless, three general groups of answers to the question: 'Yes', 'No', and 'It all depends what you mean by ... '

## Meanings of Development

Setting aside, for a moment, the diversity of interpretations that can be put on 'successful development', *complete* success is unknown: few would argue that either the first or the most recent countries to industrialize have achieved unqualified success. Britain, the USA, West Germany, and Japan all have both economic and social characteristics that would make at least some of their citizens hesitate before pronouncing unqualified success in their development strategies. The question of success is always a relative judgement and one to be asked of history. There are periods in the history of each of those countries that their citizens would, in retrospect, judge successful in some particular or another. Few would be willing to extend that commendation to the whole of their nation's history, and to all aspects of their contemporary society ... to say, in other words, that capitalism had successfully developed their economies. It is also misleading to suggest that there is an end state for development, a point at which the process will have been concluded. The question can, therefore, only be usefully asked about specific periods and in relation to particular aspects of social change (or meanings of development).

There is a second caveat to be noted in relation to the meaning of success. By its nature, capitalism is subject to cycles of boom and slump. The injunction to relate the question to specific periods of development, therefore, takes on a particular emphasis – capitalism is periodic in its processes (of accumulation and growth).

The question is also about what development means, or what constitutes progress. Two meanings of development have been distinguished (initially in chapter 4). The first is economic growth, the development of productive forces through the accumulation of capital. Development in this sense can be measured by examining changes in labour productivity. The second meaning of development is the achievement of the wider objective of meeting basic needs, abolishing poverty, creating a reasonable standard of living for the whole population. The expression of this meaning quoted in chapter 4, that of Dudley Seers, extended the idea of meeting basic needs to include the creation of conditions in which human potential can be realized: adequate education, political participation and belonging to an independent nation, were amongst Seers' criteria.

A broader understanding of basic needs, and a third meaning of development – socialist construction – was sketched out in chapter 5. This meaning of development presumed a collective transformation of the economy, encompassing economic growth and the achievement of people's material needs, through decentralized, popular institutions, in other words, neither market nor state.

Our initial questions can, thus, be reformulated:

1 Does capitalist development in Third World countries imply economic growth?
2 Can capitalist development meet basic needs in Third World countries?
3 What are the alternatives within and without capitalism?

These are difficult questions to tackle head on. In what follows, they will be tackled from four different angles suggested by earlier chapters. Does successful development require:

1 More or less capitalism?
2 More or less industry?
3 More or less state?
4 More or less national control?

## Does Successful Development Require More or Less Capitalism?

Capitalism is neither homogeneous nor simple. It would be naive to expect that the social arrangements that were midwife to modern history could be either. In addition, capitalism does not stand still. Capitalist development is not, therefore, a single 'road'.

One of the intentions of this book was to describe some of the diversity and unevenness of capitalist development. The question of what constitutes more or less capitalism has, nevertheless, not been explored directly. This is because, in one sense, described in chapter 6, everything is capitalism. There is now virtually nowhere in the Third World that is unaffected by the world economy, which is essentially capitalist. Talk of feudal, precapitalist and traditional economies, or economic sectors, is misleading. There are dramatically different forms of production, highly diverse ways of making a living, but they are almost all integrated, to lesser or greater extents and in varying ways, into the capitalist world economy. It is possible to distinguish more and less developed (in terms of productive forces and accumulation) forms of capitalist production but, since they are interdependent, it is unwise to call one capitalism and the other not capitalism.

Capitalist production in its more developed form requires three sets of social arrangements: a class of labourers dispossessed of means of production, the concentration of means of production in private hands, and the generalized exchange of land, labour, tools and products as commodities. These social arrangements are widespread in the advanced capitalist economies of Western Europe and North America, but less so in the Third World. The form of production based on wage labour, private ownership of means of production and generalized commodity exchange can be seen as a more developed form of capitalism.

More capitalism in the Third World has two faces. It may mean *both* more of these social relations, that is, proletarianization, commercialization and the concentration of accumulation, *and* less of them. The example given in chapter 6 of the latter is the creation of 'subsistence' sectors in economies supplying migrant labour. Households in these economies do produce the food they need for their own consumption but they are not just subsistence producers. They also reproduce and sell labour power – the ability of family members to work as migrant labourers. This too is more capitalism. This face of more capitalism is often termed 'underdevelopment'. For the households supplying migrant labour, it results in the intense use of labour with primitive tools in generally harsh conditions. It is a face of capitalism that can be interpreted as development only with a stretch of the imagination. It may conceivably be associated with economic growth somewhere (for example in increased rates of profit and accumulation by certain types of capital) but it is also, generally, a denial of basic needs.

The first face of capitalism, the emergence of the social relations necessary for the more developed form of capitalist production, is known as primitive accumulation (chapter 1). This face of development has almost everywhere been associated with prolonged material deprivation caused by social disruption, but it is also more clearly associated with economic growth. Those peasant households whose hold on the land becomes more tenuous, and those craft plough and hoe makers who are displaced by factory production, cannot immediately transform themselves into factory workers, nor is there work available. The more developed form of capitalist production which emerges in some places and some times does, nevertheless, hold out the prospect of increased production and a different world.

The cases of India and Brazil (chapters 9 and 11) provide illustration of the spread of more developed forms of capitalist production. In both cases 'success' has been achieved in some aspects of development. There are, nevertheless, important differences that can be indicated along the dimensions of scale of production and concentration of accumulation.

Capitalist development in Indian agriculture has brought increases in the scale of wheat production but the scale of production remains small. The size of farm is small by the standards of North American or even European wheat farms – a few rather than hundreds of hectares – the capital invested per worker is also much smaller, and the technical division of labour, less.

The adoption of new technologies in Indian agriculture has led to the extension and intensification of commodity relations but the concentration of capital remains relatively low: it is a development process based on diffused accumulation. The number of workers and the capital invested in each production unit are small.

Capitalist production in Brazilian industry has been on a much larger scale and based on a greater concentration of accumulation. The motor vehicle factories established during the period of the economic miracle employ large numbers of workers and a complex division of labour. The

Brazilian state's decision to invite foreign investors to establish the engine and body production units was, in part, a recognition of the high concentration of capital required. The amount of capital required to enter the production process was beyond the levels of accumulation reached by Brazilian capital.

In both cases, capitalism has achieved rapid growth in at least some sectors of the economy and, in both cases, the spread of more developed forms of production has led to increases in output and in labour productivity, to more diversified production and to greater economic integration. However, that growth has not necessarily met basic needs. Brazilian industrialization has brought increased living standards, but the increases for large sections of the population have been only slight and have been associated with widening inequality. The *Economist* (22 November 1986) recently noted that Brazil has 'one of the most unequal distributions of income in the world', with the top 1 per cent of Brazilians earning in total more than the bottom 50 per cent earn altogether. The effects were not, however, uniformly deleterious to basic needs. A Brazilian economist summarized the effect of the economic miracle on workers' wages in these words: 'The real wages of the unskilled positions definitely went down; the story for the skilled positions is a mixed one; on the average these workers managed to get some moderate increases in real wages; those on top however reaped most of the gains with an 8.1 per cent real salary growth per year in the period' (Bacha, 1977, quoted in Humphrey and Wield, 1983, p. 25).

In India, the growth of cereal production has been accompanied by increasing malnutrition and poverty. Deprivation is so widespread in India that, in the words of an Indian economist, India is 'probably the largest single contributor to the pool of the world's poor' (Bardhan, 1984, p. 1).

We thus arrive at a first tension of capitalist development, between growth and basic needs. Whilst in these cases capitalist development has brought growth, its contribution to the living standards of large parts of the population has been small or even negative. This tension was summarized in chapter 3 (in a précis of Marx): the development of productive capacities under capitalism represents an enormous potential force for human emancipation and freedom from want and necessity, at the same time as the class relations through which the productive forces have developed deny their promise to the majority of people.

Analysis that aggregates everything happening in the economy, however, encourages a focus on broad, generalized, categorizations of producers and production units. In analysing a particular instance of development, it is necessary to ask, as earlier chapters have done, how capitalism changes different existing forms of production. Can capitalism develop production in agriculture (chapter 7)? How does it change the different forms of small-scale production in agriculture (chapter 8)? These sorts of questions lead on to questions such as: Does the development of small-scale production in agriculture sustain generalized economic growth? Does it lead to industrialization?

## More or Less Industry?

Does capitalism mean more industry? If so, what sorts of industry and what are the implications of the development of capitalist industry for people's livelihoods? Populist opposition to industrial development (chapter 8) has been influential and persistent (particularly amongst peasants and those concerned for their livelihoods), mainly because the development of industry required the material deprivation associated with primitive accumulation. Is this unavoidable?

Three alternative ways of thinking about industry have been identified and used in this book: (i) not agriculture; (ii) a range of products and the sectors in which they are used; and (iii) a way of organizing production with the ability to increase the quantity of goods in an economy (chapter 10). These ways of thinking about industry have been used to investigate the industrialization process. But it should be re-emphasized here that, although industrialization has been central to both capitalist and socialist development, the British and Soviet models (chapters 5 and 10) do not exhaust the potential roads to industrialization.

The first definition of industry, as 'not agriculture', raises questions about the balance between agriculture and industry, the source of capital accumulation, and the kinds of agriculture and industry associated with the industrialization process (chapter 10). The second definition, based on the sectoral distribution of production, prompts questions about the sorts of products and who they are produced for. The third definition, a way of organizing production, introduces the five characteristic changes embodied in industrial production that enable more goods to be produced – enlargement of scale, diversification of linkages, increased division of labour and coordination, replacement of human energy by machine power, and increasing skills.

Brazil, South Korea, Japan, Taiwan, are some of the newly industrializing and recently industrialized economies that suggest that capitalism can mean more industry. In some cases, capitalist development does bring industrialization. That benefit is, however, by no means universal; it is an uneven process, both within and between economies, and a halting one.

The unevenness of capitalist industrialization needs little emphasis when the whole world is in the midst of a recession causing deindustrialization even in the countries first to industrialize – Britain and the USA. Important historical precedents should, nevertheless, be recalled. When a British Governor of India graphically described how the 'bones of the weavers' were 'bleaching the plains' of India, he was noting the obverse of the coin of British industrialization. Many subsequent phases of industrialization and primitive accumulation have exacted similar costs in human misery. Capitalist development in one economy, one sector, one industry, may be matched by the destruction of skills, capital and livelihoods elsewhere.

For a significant number of generally small, strategically placed, and legislatively specific economies, more capitalism means more tourism, more banking or more commerce. For these beauty spots, offshore tax havens and *entrepôt* economies, more capitalism means less industry.

The cases of Brazil and India illustrate the uneven development of industry. Despite the fact that India is already, in some senses, an industrial giant (it is, for example, amongst the largest steel producers in the world, and has its own TNCs), the development of wheat production in India has not been associated with a significant growth of industry. During the Green Revolution, there was a deceleration of industrial growth. It has been argued that the capital accumulated in agriculture was not invested in industry on an adequate scale (Byres, 1974). Another element of the explanation for India's nearly stagnant industrial growth is related to the immiseration of the population. Industry cannot grow because the majority of the population cannot afford to buy those things an expanded industry would produce (Bardhan, 1984, p. 22).

To a certain extent, in India, and more successfully in Brazil, this constraint on the growth of industry has been surmounted by producing 'luxury' goods for the wealthiest in society. This is an aspect of a concentrated capitalist accumulation strategy, as opposed to one that is more diffuse. Both productive wealth and consumption are concentrated in a small section of society. But, as was noted in chapter 11, this aspect of uneven industrial development may, to a certain extent, be balanced by the growing power of industrial workers to organize collectively for better wages and conditions. Industrial production creates the conditions for effective collective bargaining as well as the conditions for increased productivity. In the Brazilian case, during the economic miracle and since, industrial workers have been able to achieve better material standards, and ownership of what were initially 'luxury' goods has begun to broaden (table 18). The 1987 Brazilian strike, noted at the start of this chapter, is an expression of the new-found strength (as well as much else) of Brazilian workers. That collective strength is, in part, an unintended outcome of capitalist industrialization. This 'side-effect' is one reason why Marx said that capitalism contained the seeds of its own destruction.

There can be little doubt, then, that capitalism can bring economic growth and industrialization to some economies. There is a question as to how far that coincides with basic needs. There is also a substantial area for investigation, relating to the nature of the economic growth that occurs. We have seen that there is substantial variation in the forms of industrial production, their integration and the characteristics of the development they are associated with.

Whilst populists in the nineteenth century opposed industrialization because of its impact on livelihoods, contemporary neo-populist theorists, like Schumacher and the International Labour Office, have argued that the costs of industrialization can be avoided or minimized if small-scale industry and appropriate technology have a central role in the industrialization process. Kitching's vigorous defence of the 'old orthodoxy' of industrialization (chapter 8) was based on theoretical imperatives (economies of scale and of concentration) and the failure of neo-populist experiments (notably in Tanzania). This brings us back to the question of whether the material deprivations associated with all previous experiences of rapid industrialization are avoidable. Kitching says not – that all development is 'nasty'. He goes on to say that the attempt to pursue 'nice' development may lead to greater costs than would otherwise have been incurred. Small, in other words, is ugly.

Chapter 12 looked at this debate and concluded that there is no generalizable positive or negative answer to the question of whether small enterprises have growth and employment potential. If they have that potential, then the neo-pouplist road may not be totally blocked. There is a strong tendency in capitalist development toward increased scale, argued chapter 12, but specific combinations of technical and social conditions determine production processes and condition change, not technology on its own. The important question, then, is not whether small industrial production units have growth and employment potential, but under what specific conditions of capitalism (chapters 6 and 12). The possibility that 'nicer' development is attainable through some combination of small and large industry is not, therefore, totally ruled out.

One central issue in these debates about (socialist and capitalist) industrialization – debates about luxury versus wage goods production, about the inegalitarian nature of capitalist industrialization and about small and large industry – is the tension between accumulation and consumption. Some models of development put accumulation before all else. The Brazilian ambassador in London described how the regime he represented had chosen such a strategy: 'there appears to be, at least in the short run, a trade off between fast capital accumulation and the creation of a welfare state ... we had to make an option in favour of the productivist state as against the distributivist state' (quoted in Humphrey and Wield, 1983, pp. 12–13).

The choice may not be as stark as a straight 'trade off'. In the case of socialist industrialization, the path followed by China is perceived to have avoided some gross impoverishment by combining small and large industry, by ensuring national food stocks were high before each major social transformation (between the stages of collectivization of agriculture, for example), and by maintaining a complex and interactive system of national, regional and local planning. Nevertheless, evidence has emerged in recent years of a catastrophic famine during the Great Leap Forward phase of rapid industrialization. Too little is known about the causes of the famine to determine whether it contradicts the perception that Chinese development went further towards resolving the contradiction between consumption and accumulation.

Some crucial differences between capitalist and socialist industrialization cluster around the planning of production, consumption and accumulation. It is not the case that capitalist development is completely unplanned. The different units involved in production engage in economic regulation of greater or lesser sophistication. More developed, and larger-scale forms of capitalist production from the more advanced industrial economies (transnational corporations, for example) make plans that have significant effects on the economies within which they operate. Nevertheless, *the cyclical and uneven nature of capitalist development, combined with the overriding criterion of profitability, suggest that balanced development is unlikely to be achieved, and the tension between consumption and accumulation will rarely be resolved.* Economic regulation is, however, also undertaken by all modern capitalist states.

One of the important elements of our topic which, as we warned in our introduction, we would not be able to deal with adequately in this book, was the question of the state in the Third World. The discussion in earlier chapters does nevertheless, provide leads for the examination of this question and the discussion here begins to indicate a second tension related to capitalist development. These pointers can be summarized under three headings: (i) the social nature of the state; (ii) state capacities; and (iii) forms of state control.

## More or Less State Direction?

A common understanding of capitalist development is free enterprise: producers and consumers interacting in an unfettered market (chapter 4). According to this understanding, more capitalism means allowing more to be decided in the market-place and less by the state. This view of capitalist development has been given particular impetus during the 1980s by two international agencies – the International Monetary Fund (IMF) and the World Bank. These agencies have argued in a number of different contexts that many Third World economies, and particularly those of Africa, have not developed because they have too much state intervention and not enough competition. If Third World states reduce their influence on commodity prices, and stop trying to protect their indigenous industries, these agencies argue, then competition will increase the efficiency of their producers and assist economic growth.

Historically, the state has been required to play an increasing role in development. In all modern examples of rapid industrialization, the state has played a central role. The IMF and World Bank view, therefore, has to be understood in the context of their views of capitalist development.

The reasons why states coming 'late' to industrialization have to play a greater role, relate to the increasing scale and concentration of industrial production. As the scale of production in an industry has increased, the capital required to establish production in the industry has also risen. In many industries, the size of capital required puts them beyond the resources of all but TNCs and states or state-backed capitalists. In addition, recently industrializing states have fostered capital accumulation and the acquisition of skills by protecting infant industries from international competition. Tariff-barriers have been used to reserve national markets for national industry (chapter 10). In general, these imperatives of worldwide production, and the corresponding needs for state intervention, continue to increase.

In these circumstances, the advice of the IMF and World Bank is an advocacy of defeatism: rapid, state-backed industrialization is unattainable for most countries in Africa. They must accept whatever capitalism has in store, and in most cases that will be agricultural export production.

There are, nevertheless, important variations in the social nature of the state, state capacities and forms of state control. These variations have implications both for the form of capitalist development that occurs within a national economy and for the nature of the economy's integration with the world economy.

The state is not an impartial executor of some homogeneous national will. Third World nations, in particular, have been constructed, frequently by colonial rulers, from heterogeneous cultural traditions and social groups with divergent interests. In addition, states represent the interests of the different groups within a nation unevenly. The state is, thus, rarely the uncontradictory proponent of a single group within society. The social nature of the state, in other words, is generally complex and contradictory.

The social nature of the state cannot be 'read off' from the structure of an economy but there are significant differences between the interests of social groups associated with different forms of production, and differences in the way that those interests are expressed. The analytical categories introduced in these chapters provide starting points for understanding the social nature of the state.

In the case of Brazil, during the period of the economic miracle, the state provided strategic planning, a demarcation of the economy – laying down the sectors for foreign investment, Brazilian private investment and state investment – and the legal and economic framework required to ensure that capital and labour would conform to the strategy.

This form of state-led capitalism brought development, in the sense of growth, to Brazil. In the motor vehicle industry, assembly plants were replaced by manufacturing plants, and a set of industries were established both 'backwards' and 'forwards' of the motor vehicle factories. The demarcation of the economy allocated the largest-scale production units, and hence the heaviest investment, to foreign companies, keeping the smaller-scale components manufacture for Brazilian capital.

As chapter 11 described, capitalist development in Brazil depended on a strong state with clear objectives, the technical capacity to undertake economic planning, the forms of state control required to ensure that its plans were implemented. In Brazil, as frequently elsewhere, the combination of technical capacity and determinate objectives originated with a section of the military, and their perception that security and strength required rapid industrialization.

The case of Indian agricultural development provides a contrasting example, though still within capitalism. There are important differences between the two governments, most obviously in respect of their electoral participation. During the period of the economic miracle, the Brazilian government was a military one. Most Indian governments since independence have been elected. Both states, nevertheless, oversee economies in which the primary dynamic is capitalism. The success of capitalist development requires a level of tacit agreement (amongst those in control of production, notably the capitalists) on the accumulation strategy to be followed, and a state capacity to ensure that that unity is translated into a disciplined process of accumulation. In recent decades, such unity and discipline have most frequently been achieved in capitalist economies with military or, at least, highly authoritarian states. The full reasons for this coincidence of authoritarianism and successful capitalist development need to be examined in their particular historical circumstances. In general, they are related to the ability to achieve compliance from the labour force. In addition, they seem to be associated with the conditions of unity amongst capitalists. In certain historical periods and during certain phases of the development of capitalism, successful development seems to be less compatible with a measure of popular participation than with military or authoritarian rule.

The description of Indian state action given in chapter 9 certainly gives the impression of a much less decisive government, one that is uncertain of its objectives, and with more limited capacities to plan and implement its intentions. One of the state's first ventures in agricultural development was a land reform including abolition of the landlord class and an intention to establish independent peasant farming. The conditions for rich peasant farming were established but fair and secure tenancies were not achieved for poor peasants.

When it came to the 'new strategy' of agricultural development, based on Green Revolution technologies, the state's commitments and its achievements diverged to a greater extent. This strategy provides an example of a less-state-directed capitalism. Although the state made commitments – to ensure adequate seeds, fertilizer, credit and irrigation – it left their implementation to private agencies and, in contrast to the Brazilian case, was unable to ensure that these traders, banks, and manufacturers met the commitments of the plan. What emerged, instead, as the coordinating element in the strategy was the collective expression of rich peasant (and other kinds of capitalist) interests. This class was rapidly becoming the dominant force in the Indian countryside and was able to hold both state and private agencies to the commitments that were essential to its version of the plan. These commitments included ensuring that cereal prices remained high. This brings us back to a point made earlier, which reinforces the overall impression of less single-minded state direction, that the relative stagnation of industrial growth can be partially attributed to the failure to direct capital accumulated in agriculture to industry. In this case, the relative absence of state direction has been blamed on the heterogeneity of the dominant coalition influencing the state and the diversity of interests it represents (Bardhan, 1984). More specifically, the Indian state seems to have been unable to resolve the contradictions between agricultural capital and industrial capital. Less state direction left agricultural policy in rich peasant hands, and deprived industry of the resources required for rapid industrialization.

A third case, that of Taiwan, provides an important contrast to the other two, suggesting the complexity of factors influencing the extent and character of state direction of capitalist development. Taiwan is a newly industrializing country that achieved an agricultural transformation as part of a successful phase of rapid economic growth. In this case, the thoroughness and speed of the agricultural change can be attributed to the particular historical origins of the state.

Taiwan is the final redoubt of the nationalist forces defeated by the

Chinese revolution. Its state is dominated by a military with ambitions, at least in the early years after 1949, to reconquer mainland China, and with a sharp consciousness of the power of an organized socialist peasantry. These particular features of the state's historical formation had important consequences. Firstly, the state was conscious of the potential power of egalitarian demands from the mass of poor peasants. Secondly, the dominant military element in the state, who came from China, had no links and historical obligations to the more powerful elements in the countryside of Taiwan. Thirdly, the state was seized with the need to industrialize rapidly in order to build its military strength (Amsden, 1985).

This example of state-directed agricultural transformation was much more thorough and effective than the Indian one. Land was redistributed to establish the basis for individual peasant agriculture, state agents effectively disseminated the skills required for new forms of agriculture and the extension of state agencies supplanted the 'traditional' providers of usurious credit and beneficiaries of unequal exchange. Then, a significant proportion of the increased surplus from this small-scale capitalist agriculture was extracted to finance capitalist development. That was the basis, initially, for Taiwan's industrial development.

These three examples suggest some of the ways in which the social nature of the state and its capacities may influence the character of state direction of capitalist development. These suggestions lead us toward a second tension of capitalist development. The state embodies in its social character, history and capacities a more or less inchoate conception of development. Progress for the military in Taiwan would have been victory on the mainland. That required industrialization, and the particular formation of the state enabled economic growth to take place. In Brazil, internal security and national independence require economic growth and the state had the capacity to ensure the conditions for its achievement. *The tension, then, is between the need for the state to establish the conditions required for capitalist development, and the objectives 'built in' to the character of the state. This is where the first two meanings of development, growth and basic needs, divide. A state with the clarity of purpose, unity of structure, and the technical capacity to ensure the conditions required for economic growth will rarely also be concerned to secure the basic needs of the population.* As the Brazilian ambassador viewed it, the provision of welfare would have detracted from the ability to achieve growth. The conclusion is wider than the division between these two meanings of development. The social character of the state is more complicated than has been portrayed here. The influences of history, the strengths of different social groups, and the ways that the political and economic interests gain expression, generate a range of meanings for development which could be the subject of another book.

## More or Less National Control?

It is not surprising that countries that were formerly subjected to colonial rule should place a high value on national independence, and that high value has implications for development. 'Nation building' is seen as a priority and, within that task, the construction of adequate national defence is generally perceived essential. At the same time, the initial experiences of many newly independent nations created widespread dissatisfaction with the achievements of political independence. What was the use of independence if the dictates of the world market and its powerful agents, the advanced countries and their TNCs, severely constrained the economic opportunities of the nation and kept its level of development low? These priorities and dissatisfactions placed economic development and, specifically, industrialization high on the agendas of most Third World states.

These concerns explain why growth and industrialization are central priorities of Third World states and provide a part of the explanation for the charge on the issue of national control of economic development. These concerns also make it necessary to ask, Does capitalist development require more or less national control? The 'success' of the newly industrializing countries has brought extra attention to this question because their growth appears to have been fostered by non-national capitalism.

There has been a tendency, because of the charge on the issue of the nationality of development, to blame developmental 'failures' on the machinations of the international economy and, by contrast, to see an indigenous bourgeoisie as national saviour. It is not as simple as that. To see why there is no simple dichotomy between national capital (= good) and international capital (= bad), let us examine some alternative definitions of more or less national capitalism.

One definition of more national capitalism would be less involvement with the world economy: less foreign investment and less international trade. This is the definition which led many development theorists and some Third World states, during the 1960s and 1970s, to favour autarkic development. If, as the dependency school argued (chapters 10 and 13), the causes of underdevelopment were to be found in an economy's links to the world economy, then those links should be minimized or cut altogether.

There are two sorts of difficulties with this definition of national capitalism and the policies it encouraged. Essentially, the definition is neither uncontroversial nor workable. The first difficulty has already been noted. Almost all production and consumption in Third World economies is already integrated, directly or indirectly, with the world economy (chapter 6). The integration may not be equitable (chapters 13 and 15), but it cannot be wished away. Attempts to decrease foreign trade and foreign investment cannot be conceptualized as the cutting of links to a small 'modern' sector of the economy. The 'modern sector' has organic links with the 'traditional sector', and the 'traditional sector' is also integrated with the world economy. Autarky would have extensive consequences. The definition, thus, suggests too simple a distinction between the national and the foreign: much that is national already depends on the world economy. Then, secondly, as we have made clear in earlier chapters, it is not the case that the backwardness of Third World economies can be simply attributed to their integration with the world economy. However problematic that integration, it is still not the sole cause of underdevelopment.

A second definition of more or less national capitalism could be: import substitution industrialization (ISI) = less, export oriented industrialization (EOI) = more (chapter 10). ISI is commonly seen as an organized attempt by the state to implant a national industrial base. EOI, on the other hand, may be interpreted as conceding planning to international forces, the vagaries of world trade and the accumulation strategies of TNCs. When particular examples have been investigated we have found that they do not fit those preconceptions.

Countries popularly portrayed as following EOI strategies, such as South Korea, have developed major sectors of production for their national markets. Countries portrayed as following ISI strategies, such as Brazil, have depended upon foreign capital for significant sectors of investment. In both of these cases, EOI has followed periods of ISI, rather than one strategy being pursued consistently over time. For different sectors and during different periods of time, capitalist industrialization has occurred with combinations of more and less national capitalism.

A third definition of more or less national capitalism might be associated with differences of scale and/or concentration. Large-scale capitalism might be less national and small-scale capitalism more national. Some of the industries associated with recent Third World industrialization are amongst the largest in scale and require the greatest concentrations of capital. Competition and innovation in the car industry have driven all but the largest manufacturers out of business. Those that remain require plants in several countries and a multinational, frequently worldwide market. These are the manufacturers the Brazilian state invited to assist their industrialization plan. A second internationally integrated industry particularly associated with the development of the newly industrializing countries (NICs) is the electronics industry. This is another very large-scale industry requiring large concentrations of capital to establish certain parts of the production process. A third industry that has been strategic in the development of the NICs is the textile and clothing industry. The scale of production and the capital required to establish a foothold in the clothing industry are much less than in the motor industry or in electronics. It is difficult to determine in the abstract the extent to which these industries, the large and the small, will choose between the dictates of the national and the international economy. It is a question requiring investigation.

In general, the nationality of capitalism is ambiguous. As chapters 13, 14 and 15 have indicated, there is a ubiquitous and longstanding tendency toward the internationalization of capital. The implications of this trend for capitalist development in one economy are ambiguous, and they place individual Third World economies in an invidious dilemma. *The imperatives of independence may require both a measure of freedom from the world economy* and *economic growth. For most economies, most of the time, economic growth requires increasing integration with the world economy. This is the third tension of capitalist development*. Nevertheless, as the cases of the NICs indicate in different ways, the diversity of forms of integration, and innovation in the forms of state control, have allowed some routes out of the dilemma.

Another aspect of the question of whether capitalist development is more or less national is the issue of the size of an economy. The imperatives of the increasing scale of production bear down more heavily upon small economies. An economy with a small labour force and a small 'home market' has less prospect of developing industry for its national market. In these cases, industrial development requires a particularly strong integration with the world economy.

It is instructive that some of the most prominent of the recently industrializing economies are also amongst the largest in the world: Brazil, China, India. Even these countries, most recently China with its 'opening', have chosen to establish important links with the world economy. The case of the Chinese economy is notable because of the thoroughness of its preceding autarky but its integration is still relatively small and confined primarily to trade. The economy is still largely, though not completely, cut-off from international investment and finance. What is significant to note, however, and this may be true to a greater extent for the smaller NICs, is that the extent and character of integration with the world economy has been an important site for political and economic negotiations. This is where the role of the IMF is so central. How, then, does the IMF relate to the issue of whether capitalist development is more or less national? The IMF does promote capitalism, but of a particular kind. As was noted earlier, it propagates the simplistic definition of more capitalism: less state. That, however, is not all it propagates. Through its trusteeship of one of the largest funds of capital available to Third World states, the IMF is able to promote, and generally have accepted, a specific form of integration with the world economy and a particular school of economic management. The IMF's consistent measures to reduce state control over trade and thereby strengthen the role of private capital, particularly the TNCs, have been described in chapter 15. The power and the ubiquity of the IMF has allowed it to choose the terrain for a range of important discussions, disagreements and struggles.

It is, first of all, important not to lose sight of the historical origins of the IMF: the struggle over alternative conceptions of the Fund (cooperative fund or commercial bank), the consequences of the outcome for the forms of integration the IMF is now promoting, and the role of the then world-contending powers in the determination of the struggle. Then, to note the different levels of struggle entailed by the operation of the IMF:

1 'national' discussion – between mission and state representatives over the conditions for a particular credit facility or line. This tussle between 'experts' has its counterpart in
2 the demonstrations that frequently erupt once the implications of a stabilization package become clear to wider sections of the population, those who are directly affected by the 'austerity' of the package. Then there are
3 struggles that take place within the work-places and households over wages, income from production and opportunities to make a living, as a result of the implementation of the new relationships with the world economy ushered in by the IMF.

The significance of the connection between these different levels of struggle goes beyond the immediate question of analysing the role of the IMF. Once the connections between the different levels of struggle are identified, and the different forces involved in these struggles are perceived, then the constraint of conceiving development only in one economy can be overcome.

This is where we return again to the news of the national strike in Brazil. According to the BBC World Service, the strikers specifically identified prime movers in the international economy (private banks, and no doubt the IMF too) and made demands for the Brazilian state to negotiate a different deal with them, a deal requiring less accumulation in the international economy to allow less austere conditions of consumption within Brazil. These Brazilian workers do not, apparently, have national boundaries to their conception of a better life. They are not affected by the myopia that can only perceive development within one country. The realities of international integration are clearly understood in this case.

Much discussion of development fails to go beyond the assumption that developmental objectives relate to the national economy, but to what extent can development be realized within a national economy? What is involved when an attempt is made to construct development in one village (as Gandhi proposed), one town, or one nation (as the dependency school has proposed)? There are severe implications for everyday life as well as for more exalted spheres of national economic growth and state policy. Isolation tends to be reflected both in very simple and low levels of consumption, and in an inability to defend an economy from the implications of changes taking place in the world around. Not only is control over the natural world (developing productive capacity) likely to stagnate, contacts with other counties may be characteristically powerless.

The constraints that autarky places upon the scale of production, consumption and accumulation, may not only halt economic growth, but may foreclose any potential for wider social change. Again, the question of size is central. The Chinese economy presented the greatest opportunity for successful autarkic development. The size of the labour force and of the national market provided a potential for development available to no other economy. Fundamental social transformation presented both the capacity and reasons for cutting links with the world economy. The opportunity was seized. Even in this case, however, the imperatives of scale have become significant. In recent years China has sought international finance, advanced technology, and markets for its products. The scale of accumulation and consumption, and the rate of innovation, generated by the capitalist world economy, have drawn even China to begin to negotiate a level of integration. Some of the same considerations no doubt play a part in the Sino–Soviet rapprochement noted at the beginning of this chapter. The potential for integration between socialist economies is the subject for another book, not one which can be examined here. It is important to note, however, that Soviet aid to the industrialization of China was a key aspect of the initial links between these two huge socialist economies. Its cessation in 1956 was both a blow to the Chinese revolution and an indication of the ability of the revolution to enter uncharted territory. The tentative moves toward the re-establishment of the link suggests, nevertheless, the importance of economic integration.

## Dilemmas and Opportunities of Economic Integration

The case of China re-emphasizes the inexorable pressures for integration with the world economy. Earlier chapters have also outlined some of the diversity of forms of integration. This final section briefly rehearses some of the constraints imposed and the spaces left open by the diversity and unevenness of capitalist development.

Thus far, three 'tensions' of capitalist development have been identified:

1 between growth (requiring resources for accumulation) and basic needs (requiring the allocation of resources to consumption and an equitable distribution of consumption);
2 between the need for the state to establish the conditions required for capitalist development and the objectives which states, with particular origins and social representation, bring to the capitalist development they foster;
3 between economic independence (requiring and imposing constraints on growth) and economic integration (with the potential for growth but imposing constraints on sovereignty).

These three tensions, and much more fully, the book as a whole, begin to provide an answer to one of the questions this conclusion set out to answer: Can capitalism develop Third World countries? The answers to the question given in this chapter qualify and transcend the simple view that capitalism is a progressive force bringing development. It has been suggested that capitalism brings economic growth and opportunities for 'progress' only sometimes, in some places, for some social groups and under some conditions. Elsewhere it brings misery. Answering the question for a particular economy requires an examination of existing production forms, their integration, how they relate to the world economy, and the nature of the state (to indicate a very abbreviated list) and of how all these factors interact to enable the emergence or submergence of different social groups.

A particular conception of capitalist development has been emphasized in this concluding chapter – that (most) Third World economies are capitalist, and they contain within them production forms that are more or less developed examples of capitalist production. By implication this idea provides a way into the questions: If capitalism won't develop Third World economies, what will? What are the alternatives within and without capitalism?

The unevenness of capitalist development and the variety of forms of production it can integrate gives rise to spaces for alternative constructions of development. The prevalence of petty commodity production, the persistence of household production, the diversity of urban 'informal sector' production, testify to the varity of economic 'logics' that capitalism can encompass. Different livelihoods form specific ways of thinking about the world (and those ideas in turn influence how people seek their livelihood) and give rise to different modes of political expression. The diversity of capitalist development can create the conditions that foster criticism and alternatives.

The way that integration in world production has forced Brazilian workers to develop ideas about the world economy, and has also fostered the strength to act collectively to begin to influence it, have already been noted. This is an example of how livelihoods are associated with ideas about the world. As production and producers in Third World economies are integrated into the world economy in new and unexpected ways, we can anticipate that new ideas, and new ways of organizing to make things happen, will also arise.

It has been argued (Kitching, 1983) that poverty in the Third World forecloses any option other than capitalism. The imperatives of immediate survival, according to this argument, impose a politics of unenlightened individualism – corruption, cruelty and authoritarian rule. The prospect for both socialism and democracy await capitalism's progressive dawn – economic growth and the liberty of wage labour. Both the ideas about development contained here, and the examples of recent history, rebut this line of argument.

All recent attempts at socialist transformation have occurred in Third World economies – China, Cuba, Vietnam, Mozambique, Kampuchea, Angola, Grenada, Nicaragua. That they occurred in the Third World is testimony to the strength of the idea of national liberation, to the ability of 'the empire' to strike back, and to the spaces for opposition generated by the uneven development of capitalism. The picture is, nevertheless, hardly rosy. Some of these states have collapsed as a consequence of their internal contradictions and the weight of external opposition, several are fighting for their survival. For these states, the imperatives of size have an added dimension: not only are the smaller economies forced toward greater levels of economic integration with the world economy, they also risk becoming embroiled in the global military and political struggle – a small socialist state risks being identified, by larger, advanced capitalist states, as the weakest link in an alternative conception of development.

We have taken the opportunity in this final section to suggest some implications of economic integration for politics and struggle. One consequence of the view that capitalism is an encompassing and integrating social system is that different political and economic struggles are interconnected. What has been described as the 'global reach' of an internationalizing capitalism has its counterpart in the growing interconnection of opposition. The resolution of the tensions of capitalist development depend on this opposition as well as upon the dynamics of capitalism.

# References

Abdalla, I-S. et al. (1980) 'The Arusha Initiative', *Development Dialogue*, 2 July 1980, The Dag Hammarskjold Centre, Uppsala, Sweden.

Agarwal, B. (ed.) (1981) 'Agricultural mechanization and labour use: a disaggregated approach' *International Labour Office Review* 120 (1) (Jan.–Feb.).

Alexander, S. (1980) 'Introduction', to M. Herzog, *From Hand to Mouth* Penguin, Harmondsworth.

Amin, S. (1976) *Unequal Development* Harvester Press, Hassocks.

Amsden, A. H. (1985) 'The state and Taiwan's economic development', in P. Evans et al. *Bringing the State Back In*, Cambridge University Press, Cambridge.

Asian Productivity Organization (1975) *Survey on Duty Free Export Processing Zones in APO Member Countries* Sup 11/75, APO, p. 86.

Attwood, N. (1967) *The Reds and the Blacks: a personal adventure* Harper and Row, New York.

Bacha, E. (1977) 'Issues and evidence in recent Brazilian economic growth', *World Development* 5 (1/2) (Jan./Feb.).

Bardhan, P. (1984) *The Political Economy of Development in India* Basil Blackwell, Oxford.

Barnet, R. J. and Muller, R. E. (1974) *Global Reach: The Power of the Multinational Corporation* Simon and Schuster, New York.

Barone, C. A. (1983) 'Dependency, Marxist theory and salvaging the idea of capitalism in South Korea', *Review of Radical Political Economics* XV (1).

Barratt Brown, M. (1963) *After Imperialism* Heinemann, London.

Benachenhou, A. (1980) 'For autonomous development in the Third World', *Monthly Review* Jul./Aug., pp. 43–52.

Bernstein, H. (1977) 'Notes on capital and peasantry', *Review of African Political Economy* 10.

—— (1981) 'Notes on state and peasantry: the case of Tanzania', *Review of African Political Economy* 21, pp. 44–62.

—— (1982a) 'Contradictions of the Tanzanian Experience', in S. Jones, P. C. Joshi, and M. Murmis (eds) *Rural Poverty and Agrarian Reform* Allied, New Delhi.

—— (1982b) 'Industrialisation, Development and Dependence', in H. Alavi and T. Shanin (eds) *Introduction to the Sociology of 'Developing Societies'* Macmillan, London.

—— (1986) 'Capitalism and Petty Commodity Production', in *Rethinking Petty Commodity Production* special issue of *Social Analysis*, ed. A. M. Scott.

Bhalla, S. (1977) 'Agricultural growth: role of institutional and infrastructural factors', *Economic and Political Weekly*, 12 (45–6).

Bharadwaj, K. (1982) 'Regional differentiation in India: a note', *Economic and Political Weekly* April.

Binswanger (1978) *The Economics of Tractors in South Asia: An Analytical Review*. Agricultural Development Council, New York and Hyderabad.

Brandt, W. (1980) *North–South: A Programme for Survival* (the Brandt Report), Pan Books, London.

Brass, T. (1986) 'Unfree labour and capitalist restructuring in the agrarian sector', *Journal of Peasant Studies* 14 (1).

Brett, E. A. (1973) *Colonialism and Underdevelopment in East Africa* Heinemann, London.

Browett, J. (1985) 'The newly industrializing countries and radical theories of development', *World Development* 13 (7).

Bujra, J. (1983) *Cultural and Social Diversity: a Third World in the making* Part A of Block 2 of *Third World Studies*, The Open University, Milton Keynes.

Bundy, C. (1979) *The Rise and Fall of the South African Peasantry* Heinemann, London.

Byres, T. J. (1972) 'The dialectic of India's Green Revolution', *South Asian Review* 5 (2), pp. 99–116.

—— (1974) 'Land reform, industrialization and the marketed surplus in India: an essay on the power of rural bias', in D. Lehmann (ed.) *Agrarian Reform and Agrarian Reformism* Faber, London.

Cable, V. (1983) 'Cheap imports and jobs', in P. Mauner (ed.) *Case Studies and Economics* Heinemann Educational, London.

Cardoso, F. H. (1977) 'The consumption of dependency theory in the United States', *Latin American Research Review* XII (3).

Chomsky, N. (1969) *American Power and the New Mandarins* Penguin, Harmondsworth.

Chonchol, J. (1970) 'Eight fundamental conditions of agrarian reform in Latin America', in R. Stavenhagen (ed.) *Agrarian Problems and Peasant Movements in Latin America* Doubleday, New York.

Clairmonte, F. and Cavanagh, J. (1985) 'Transnational corporations and services', *Economic and Political Weekly XX* (8 and 9).

Cliffe, L. and Cunningham, G. L. (1973) 'Ideology, organization and the settlement experience in Tanzania', in L. Cliffe and J. S. Saul (eds) *Socialism in Tanzania* East African Publishing House, Nairobi, vol. 2.

Cline, W. (1982) 'Can the East Asian model of development be generalised?', *World Development* 10 (2).

Cole, K., Cameron, J. and Edwards, C. (1983) *Why Economists Disagree: the political economy of economics* Longman, London.

Colman, D. and Nixson, F. (1978) *Economics of Change in Less Developed Countries* Phillip Allan, Oxford.

Cook, M. (1965) 'Introduction' to L. S. Senghor, *African Socialism* Praeger, New York.

Corrigan, P., Ramsey, H. and Sayer, D. (1978) *Socialist Construction and Marxist Theory: Bolshevism and its critique* Macmillan, London.

Crow, B. and Thomas, A. (1983) *Third World Atlas* Open University Press, Milton Keynes.

Crowder, M. (1968) *West Africa under Colonial Rule* Hutchinson, London.

Cummings, J. R., Cummings, R. W. and Ray, S. K. (1969) 'The new agricultural strategy: its contribution to 1967–68 production', *Economic and Political Weekly*, 4 (13).

Curtin, P. D. (1969) *The Atlantic Slave Trade* University of Wisconsin Press, Wisconsin.

—— (1984) *Cross-Cultural Trade in World History* Cambridge University Press, London.

de La Torre, J. and Bacchetta, M. (1980) 'The uncommon market: European policies towards the clothing industry in the 1970s', *Journal of Common Market Studies* XIX (2).

de Oliveira, F. and Travolo, M. A. (1979) *El Complejo Automotor en Brasil* ILET/ Nueva Imagen, Mexico City.

Diaz, Bernal (1963) *The Conquest of New Spain* Penguin, Harmondsworth.

Dowd, D. F. (1967) 'Some issues of economic development and of development economics', *Journal of Economic Issues* 1 (3), pp. 149–60.

Eisenstadt, S. (1966) *Modernization: protest and change* Prentice Hall, Englewood Cliffs, N.J.

Ellis, F. (forthcoming) *Peasant Economies* Cambridge University Press, Cambridge.

Elson, D. (1982) 'Export oriented industrialization and the internationalization of capital', unpublished.

—— (1984) 'Imperialism', in G. McLennan, D. Held and S. Hall (eds) *The Idea of the Modern State* Open University Press, Milton Keynes.

—— (1986) 'The new international division of labour in the textile and garment industry: how far does the "Babbage principle" explain it?', *International Journal of Sociology and Social Policy*.

Elson, D. and Pearson, R. (1981) 'Nimble fingers make cheap workers: an analysis of women's employment in third World manufacturing' *Feminist Review* 7, pp. 87–107.

Ernst, D. (1985) 'Automation and the worldwide restructuring of the electronics industry: strategic implications for developing countries', *World Development* 13 (3).

Food and Agriculture Organisation (1978) *The State of Food and Agriculture* FAO Agriculture Series, No. 9, Rome.

—— (1981) *Production Yearbook*, FAO, Rome.

—— (1983) *Production Yearbook*, FAO, Rome.

Frank, A. G. (1981) *Crisis in the Third World* Heinemann, London.

Frankel, F. R. (1968) 'India's new strategy of agricultural development: Political costs of agrarian modernization', *Journal of Asian Studies* 28 (24).

—— (1971) *India's Green Revolution: economic gains and political costs* Princeton University Press, Princeton.

Fransman, M. and King, K. (eds) (1984) *Technological Capacity in the Third World*, Macmillan, London.

Friedmann, H. (1978) 'Simple commodity production and wage labour in the American Plains', *Journal of Peasant Studies* 6 (1).

Frobel, F., Heinrichs, J. and Kreye, O. (1980) *The New International Division of Labour* Cambridge University Press, Cambridge.

Furtado, C. (1970) *Economic Development of Latin America* Cambridge University Press, Cambridge.

Gerschenkron, A. (1962) *Economic Backwardness in Historical Perspective*, Belknap Press, Cambridge, Mass.

Ghosh, M. P. (1980) 'Small engineering workshops in Howrah', *Economic and Political Weekly* 13 December. Reprinted in H. Johnson and H. Bernstein (eds) (1982) *Third World Lives of Struggle*, Heinemann, London.

Gibbon, P. and Neocosmos, M. (1985) 'Some problems in the political economy of "African Socialism"', in H. Bernstein and B. K. Campbell (eds) *Contradictions of Accumulation in Africa: studies in economy and state* Sage, Beverly Hills.

Goldstein, N. (forthcoming) 'Women's employment and semi-conductor multinationals in Scotland', in D. Elson and R. Pearson (eds) *Women's Employment and Multinational Companies in Europe* Macmillan, London.

Government of India, Ministry of Home Affairs, Research and Policy Division, (1969) *The Causes and Nature of Current Agrarian Tensions* Delhi.

—— Planning Commission (1966) *Fourth Five Year Plan: A Draft Outline*, Delhi.

—— Planning Commission (1970) *Fourth Five-Year Plan, 1969–74* Delhi.

—— (1978) *Draft Five-Year Plan, 1978–83* Delhi.

—— Irrigation Commission (1972) *Report, vol. 1* New Delhi.

Hamilton, C. (1983) 'Capitalist industrialisation in the four little tigers of East Asia', in P. Limqueco and B. McFarlane (eds) *NeoMarxist Theories of Development* Croom Helm, London.

Harriss, J. (ed.) (1982) *Rural development: theories of peasant economy and agrarian change* Hutchinson, London.

Harris, L. (1983) *Banking on the Fund – the IMF*, Open University Press, Milton Keynes.

Hayter, T. (1981) *The Creation of World Poverty* Pluto Press, London.

Helleiner, G. K. (1979) 'Structural aspects of Third World trade: some trends and some prospects', *Journal of Development Studies* 15 (3).

—— (1981) *Intra Firm Trade and the Developing Countries* Macmillan, London.

Hobsbawm, E. J. (1954) 'The general crisis of the European economy in the seventeenth century', *Past and Present* 5.

—— (1969) *Industry and Empire* Pelican, Harmondsworth.

Hoffman, K. (1985) 'Clothing, chips and competitive advantage: the impact of micro-electronics on trade and production in the garment industry', *World Development* 13 (3).

Humphrey, J. (1979) 'Auto workers and the working class in Brazil', *Latin American Perspectives* 6 (4).

—— (1982) *Capitalist Control and Workers' Struggle in the Brazilian Auto Industry*, Princeton University Press, Princeton.

Humphrey, J. and Wield, D. V. (1983) *Industrialization and Energy in Brazil*, Open University Press, Milton Keynes.

Iliffe, J. (1979) *A Modern History of Tanganyika* Cambridge University Press, London.

IMF (1969) *The International Monetary Fund 1945–65*, vol. 2, Washington, D.C.

Indian Council of Agricultural Research (1980) *Handbook of Agriculture.*

International Labour Office (1972) *Employment, Incomes and Equality: a strategy for increasing productive employment in Kenya* ILO, Geneva.

—— (1973) *Mechanization and Employment in Agriculture* ILO, Geneva.

Johnson, H. and Bernstein, H. (eds) (1982) *Third World Lives of Struggle* Heinemann, London.

Jenkins, R. (1984) 'Divisions over the international division of labour' *Capital and Class* 22, pp. 28–57.

Kaplinsky, R. (1979) 'Export oriented growth: a large international firm in a small developing country', *World Development* 7 (8/9).

—— (1982) *Computer Aided Design: electronics, comparative advantage and development* Frances Pinter, London.

—— (1984) *Automation* Longman, London.

—— (1985) 'Does de-internationalization beget industrialization which begets re-industrialization?', *Journal of Development Studies* October, 22 (1) pp. 227–42.

Kedourie, E. (1960) *Nationalism* Hutchinson, London.

Keesing, D. B. and Wolf, M. (1981) 'Questions on international trade in textiles and clothing', *The World Economy*4 (1).

Kei, M. (1977) 'South Korea: the working class in the Masan free export zone', in *Free Trade Zones and Industrialization of Asia*, Special Issue AMPO, Tokyo, Pacific–Asia Resources Center, pp. 67–78.

Killick, T. et al. (1984a) *The IMF and Stabilisation: Developing Country Experiences*, Heinemann, london.

—— (1984b) *The Quest for Economic Stabilisation*, Heinemann, London.

Kirkpatrick, C. (1985) 'Export Oriented growth: industrialisation and labour market regulation', mimeo, Department of Economics, University of Manchester.

Kitching, G. (1980) *Class and Economic Change in Kenya* Yale University Press, New Haven.

—— (1982) *Development and Underdevelopment in Historical Perspective: populism, nationalism and industrialization* Methuen, London.

—— (1983) *Rethinking Socialism* Methuen, London.

Kloosterboer, W. (1960) *Involuntary Labour Since the Abolition of Slavery* E. J. Brill, Leiden.

Landes, D. (1969) *The Unbound Prometheus* Cambridge University Press, London.

Lall, S. (1981) *Developing Countries in the International Economy* Macmillan, London.

Lehman, D. (1979) *Development Theory: Four Critical Studies* Frank Cass, London.

Lenin, V. I. (1916) *Imperialism: the highest stage of capitalism. A popular outline* (English version, New York, International Publishers, 1939).

Lerner, D. (1967) 'Comparative analysis of the process of modernization', in H. Miner (ed.) *The City in Modern Africa* Pall Mall Press, London.

—— (1968) 'Social aspects of modernization', in D. Sills (ed.) *International Encyclopaedia of the Social Sciences* Macmillan and Free Press, New York, vol. 10.
Lever, H. and Hulme, C. (1985) *Debt and Danger: The World Financial Crisis*, Penguin, Harmondsworth.
List, F. (1841) *The National System of Political Economy* (English edition, Longman, London, 1904).
Low, D. A. (1973) *Lion Rampant* Frank Cass, London.
Lugard, Frederick, Baron (1922) *The Dual Mandate in British Tropical Africa.*

Maizels, A. (1963) *Industrial Growth and World Trade* Cambridge University Press for NIESR, London.
Mamdani, M. (1986) 'Extreme but not exceptional: towards an analysis of the agrarian question in Uganda', Development Policy and Practice Working Paper, The Open University, Milton Keynes. Also forthcoming in *Journal of Peasant Studies* 14 (2).
Mapolu, H. (1973) 'Tradition and the quest for socialism', *Taamuli* 4 (1), pp. 3–15.
Martinez-Alier, J. (1984) *L'Ecologisme i L'Economica. Historia d'unes relacions amagades* Edicions 62, Barcelona (in Catalan; English version in preparation).
—— (1985) 'Agricultural energetics: its early history and its present use for ecological neo-populism', paper presented at Congreso de Americanistas, Bogota.
Marx, K. (1973) *Grundrisse* ed. M. Nicolaus, Penguin, Harmondsworth.
—— (1974) 'The civil war in France', in K. Marx, *The First International and After* Penguin, Harmondsworth.
—— (1976) *Capital* Penguin, Harmondsworth, vol. 1, first published 1867.
McClelland, D. (1963) 'The achievement motive in economic growth', in B. F. Hoselitz and W. E. Moore (eds) *Industrialization and Society* UNESCO and Mouton, The Hague.
—— (1964) 'Business drive and national achievement', in A. and E. Etzioni (eds) *Social Change* Basic Books, New York.
McMichael, P., Petras, J. and Rhodes, R. (1974) 'Imperialism and the contradictions of development', *New Left Review* 85 (May/Jun.), pp. 83–104.
Mellor, J. W. (1968) 'The evolution of rural development policy', in Mellor, J. W., Weaver, T. F., Lele, U. and Simon, S. R. (eds) *Developing Rural India: plan and practice* Cornell University Press, New York.
Murphy, Y. and Murphy, R. F. (1974) *Women of the Forest* Columbia University Press, New York.

Nayyar, D. (1978) 'Transnational corporations and manufactured exports from poor countries', *Economic Journal* 88 (349).
Nyerere, J. K. (1966) *Freedom and Unity* Oxford University Press, Dar es Salaam.
—— (1968) *Freedom and Socialism* Oxford University Press, Dar es Salaam.
—— (1973) *Freedom and Development* Oxford University Press, Dar es Salaam.
Nzula, A. T., Potekhin, I. I. and Zusmanovich, A. Z. (1979) *Forced Labour in Colonial Africa* Zed Press, London (first published in Moscow, 1933).

Open University (1983) *U204 Third World Studies Course* Cassette 4, Band 24, 'National and International Economies'.

Open University/BBC (1983) *Perceptions of the IMF*, TV programme for Third World Studies Course.

Palma, G. (1978) 'Dependency: a formal theory of underdevelopment or a methodology for the analysis of concrete situations', *World Development*.

Payer, C. (1974) *The Debt Trap: the IMF and the Third World*, Penguin, London.

Phillips, A. and Taylor, B. (1980) 'Sex and skill: notes towards a feminist economics', *Feminist Review* 6, pp. 79–88.

Radice, H. (ed.) (1975) *International Firms and Modern Imperialism*, Penguin, Harmondsworth.

Raj, K. N. (1973) 'Mechanization of agriculture in India and Sri Lanka (Ceylon)', in International Labour Office, *Mechanization and Employment in Agriculture* ILO, Geneva.

Ranger, T. (1985) *Peasant Consciousness and Guerilla War in Zimbabwe* James Currey, London.

Rao, C. H. H. (1975) *Technological Change and Distribution of Grains in Indian Agriculture* Macmillan, Delhi.

Ruisque-Alcaino, J. and Bromley, R. (1979) 'The bottle buyer: an occupational biography', in R. Bromley and C. Gerry (eds) *Casual Work and Poverty in Third World Cities* John Wiley, Chichester. Also extracted in H. Johnson and H. Bernstein (eds) *Third World Lives in Struggle*, Heinemann, London.

Sahlins, M. (1972) *Stone Age Economics* Tavistock, London.

Said, E. (1985) *Orientalism* Penguin, Harmondsworth.

Scammell, W. H. (1961) *International Monetary Policy*, Macmillan, London.

Schmitz, H. (1979) *Factory and Domestic Employment in Brazil: a study of the hammock industry and its implications for employment theory and policy* Institute of Development Studies Discussion Paper No. 146, Sussex University.

—— (1982) 'Growth constraints on small scale manufacturing in developing countries: a critical review', *World Development* 10 (6) pp. 429–50.

Schmukler, B. (1977) 'Relacions actuales de produccion en industrias tradicionales Argentinas', Centra de estudios de Estado y Sociedad, Buenos Aires.

Schumacher, E. F. (1973) *Small is Beautiful: economics as if people mattered* Harper and Row, New York.

Seers, D. (1979) 'The meaning of development', in D. Lehmann (ed.) *Development Theory: four critical studies* Frank Cass, London.

Sen, A. K. (1972) *Choice of Techniques: an aspect of the theory of planned economic development* Basil Blackwell, Oxford.

Sender, J. and Smith, J. (1985) 'What's right with the Berg Report and what's left of its critics?' *IDS Discussion Paper* University of Sussex.

—— (1986) *The Development of Capitalism in Africa* Methuen, London.

Shanin, T. (ed.) (1983) *Late Marx and the Russian Road* Routledge and Kegan Paul, London.

Sharma, U. (1980) *Women, Work and Property in North West India* Tavistock, London.

Sharpston, M. (1975) 'International sub-contracting', *Oxford Economic Papers*

March, pp. 94–135.
Shenton, R. W. (1986) *The Development of Capitalism in Northern Nigeria*, University of Toronto Press, Toronto.
Shivji, I. G. (1976) *Class Struggles in Tanzania* Tanzania Publishing House, Dar es Salaam.
Singer, P. (1976) 'Evolucao da Economia Brasileira, 1955–1975', *Estudos CEBRAP*, 17, pp. 66–83.
Skillen, A. (1977) *Ruling Illusions: philosophy and the social order*, Harvester, Hassocks.
Smelser, N. J. (1968) 'Toward a theory of modernization', in N. J. Smelser *Essays in Sociological Explanation* Prentice-Hall, Englewood Cliffs, N.J.
Srinivisan, T. N. (1979) 'Trends in agriculture in India, 1949–50 to 1977–8', *Economic and Political Weekly*, 14 (30–2) (special number).
Stein, B. (1977) 'Privileged land-holding', in R. E. Frykenberg (ed.) *Land Tenure and Peasant in South Asia* Orient Longman, New Delhi.
Subramaniam, C. (1979) *The New Strategy in Indian Agriculture* Vikas, New Delhi.
Singh, K. Suresh (1975) *The Indian Famine, 1967: a study in crisis and change* People's Publishing House, New Delhi.
Sutcliffe, R. B. (1971) *Industry and Underdevelopment* Addison-Wesley, London.

Takeo, T. (1977) 'Introduction' to *Free Trade Zones and Industrialization of Asia* Special Issue, AMPO, Tokyo, Pacific–Asia Resources Center, pp. 139–48.
Tinker, H. (1974) *A New System of Slavery* Oxford University Press, London.
Tinker, I. (1979) *New Technologies for Food Chain Activities: the imperative for women* Office of Women in Development, US Agency for International Development, Washington.
Tolipan, R. and Tinelli, A. C. (eds) (1975) *A Controversia sobre a Distribuicao de Renda e Desenvolvimento* Zahar, Rio de Janeiro.
Trades Union Congress (1978) *Economic Review* London.

United Nations (1981) *Statistical Yearbook*, New York.
United Nations Centre for Transnational Corporations (1973) *Multinational Corporations in World Development*, New York.
—— (1978) *Transnational Corporations in World Development: a re-examination.*
United Nations Development Program (UNDP)/United Nations Conference on Trade and Development (UNCTAD) (1979) *The Balance of Payments Adjustment Process in Developing Countries. Report to the Group of Twenty Four*, New York.
United Nations Industrial Development Organization (UNIDO) (1980a) *World Industry since 1960* UNIDO, Vienna.
—— (1980b) 'Export processing zones in developing countries', *UNIDO Working Papers on Structural Change* 18 (July).
—— (1983) *Industry in a Changing World: special issue of the industrial development survey for the fourth general conference of UNIDO* New York.
United States Senate, Committee on Finance (1973) *Implications of Multinational Firms for World Trade and Investment and for U.S. Trade and Labour*, Washington DC.

Vaitsos, C. (1973) 'Bargaining and the distribution of returns in the purchase of technology by developing countries' in H. Bernstein (ed.) *Underdevelopment and Development* Penguin, Harmondsworth.

—— (1974) *Inter-Country Income Distribution and Transnational Enterprises* Oxford University Press, Oxford.

—— (1975) 'The process of commercialization of technology in the Andean Pact', in H. Radice (ed.) *International Firms and Modern Imperialism* Penguin, Harmondsworth.

—— (1979) 'World industrial development and the transnational corporations', *Industry and Development* 3.

von Freyhold, M. (1977) 'The post-colonial state and its Tanzanian version', *Review of African Political Economy* 8, pp. 75–89.

—— (1979) *Ujamaa Villages in Tanzania: analysis of a social experiment* Heinemann, London.

Warren, B. (1980) *Imperialism: pioneer of capitalism* Verso, London.

Weiner, M. (ed.) (1966) *Modernization* Basic Books, New York.

Wells, J. R. (1977) 'Growth and fluctuations in the Brazilian manufacturing sector during the 1960s and early 1970s', unpublished Ph.D. thesis, University of Cambridge.

Wolf, E. (1966) *Peasants*, Prentice-Hall, New York.

—— (1982) *Europe and the People without History* University of California Press, Berkeley.

World Bank (1981a) *Accelerated Development in Sub-Saharan Africa: an agenda for action* World Bank, Washington.

—— (1981b) *Agricultural Research: sector policy paper* World Bank, Washington.

—— (1982) *World Development Report 1982*, Oxford University Press, London.

—— (1985) *World Development Report 1985* Oxford University Press, London.

Worsley, P. (1964) *The Third World*, Weidenfeld and Nicolson, London.

—— (1979) 'How many worlds?', *Third World Quarterly* 1 (2), pp. 100–7.

Yang, Y. (1972) 'Foreign investment in developing countries: Korea', in Drysdale, P. (ed.), *Direct Foreign Investment in Asia and the Pacific*, ANU Press, Canberra.

# Index